BEETHOVEN
SCHUBERT
MENDELSSOHN

BEETHOVEN
SCHUBERT
MENDELSSOHN

BY

SIR GEORGE GROVE

With an Introduction by
ERIC BLOM

LONDON
MACMILLAN & CO. LTD
1951

PRINTED IN GREAT BRITAIN

CONTENTS

INTRODUCTION

SIR GEORGE GROVE's three famous long articles on Beethoven, Schubert and Mendelssohn hardly need to be introduced to the musical world at this time of day; but their appearance in the form of a separate book after more than seventy years may call for a little explanation. They originally formed part of the first edition of *Grove's Dictionary of Music and Musicians*, published in 1878–89. The next three editions, one edited by J. A. Fuller-Maitland and two by Dr. H. C. Colles, retained these articles substantially as they stood, with some slight revisions and occasional new footnotes. Both these editors felt, very properly, that Grove could not decently be evicted from the building so painstakingly erected by himself.

When I was first invited to undertake the fifth edition I took the same view as a matter of course, or rather, to put it more precisely, as a matter both of expediency and fairness. But as soon as I had begun planning details for that new edition, which it was decided to reset entirely and thus to lay open to any amount of revision and replacement, I saw that these three articles had grown out of date in many respects, not to mention the fact that they had always been out of scale with the rest of the Dictionary. They deal with three subjects on which Grove had turned himself, with infinite labour coupled with great insight, into a very fine specialist, and it was only natural that he should yield to the temptation of expanding on them to an extent that left comparable or (as we now see the case of Mendelssohn) greater masters too far behind.

On making comparisons I discovered, for example, that in the first edition Bach was given 12 pages against Beethoven's 46, Schubert 63 against Mozart's 27, and that Mendelssohn was allotted 57 while Handel had 10 and Haydn 22. I could not doubt that my two predecessors had recognised these discrepancies, for they had in fact done something to enlarge the articles on those great composers whom Grove had given comparatively cursory treatment. Still, the sheer bulk of his own three major articles remained an embarrassment, and I could not help coming to the conclusion that they had been left standing from sheer piety as ancient monuments.

Yet I remained keenly aware that they are very noble monuments and that the respect paid them was no more than deserved. I could not bring myself to the decision of allowing them to share the fate of Holbein's Gate in Whitehall, which was demolished and buried. What I felt to be indicated, if they really had to be taken down as obstructions to traffic or to make way for new buildings, was that they should be re-erected elsewhere, like Temple Bar and the gate of Devonshire House — preferably like the latter, for in the present book Grove's monuments have, as it were, been taken only just across the road. Speaking without metaphor, they remain with the same publishers, who, when I discussed the matter fully with them, generously agreed that the course I suggested was the proper one to take. What is more, we all felt that Grove himself, could he have been consulted, would have been the first to say that the claims of his Dictionary as a whole — for it does remain his Dictionary — must come before those of any individual contributor, not excepting himself.

It is with the certainty that this book will serve Grove as an author and at the same time solve one of the major problems of his Dictionary that his three great articles are sent forth in this new form. They are thus made safe for the future, as they should be, for they remain a magnificent contribution to musical biography and criticism, though they may not always represent modern views and unite what may now seem rather an odd trinity to choose from the divinities of music.

The idea of re-publication is not a new one. In *The Life and Letters of Sir George Grove*, by Charles Graves, published in 1903, p. 230, we read the following from a paper of reminiscences by the late George A. Macmillan :

We used often to urge him to put together his reminiscences or at any rate to set down some of his inexhaustible fund of good stories. He seemed to shrink from the task, but fortunately his biographer found that he had acted upon the suggestion so far as to dictate in 1897 the contents of several note-books of which effective use has been made in the present volume. I am only sorry that another favourite project, the expansion and separate publication of his brilliant lives of Beethoven, Schubert and Mendelssohn from the *Dictionary of Music,* was never realised.

In one respect at least greater justice is done to Sir George Grove in this book than it was in the Dictionary after the first edition. There a certain amount of revision had gradually crept in, justified by the requirements of reference, but running counter to the author's original text; here that text is reproduced exactly as it appeared in its first form, except for some minor matters of typography and for a few corrections of actual mistakes, which are, however, clearly shown by the use of square brackets. There are no other editorial interferences whatever, so that Grove's articles may stand or fall by their own qualities and defects. And they will assuredly stand. This book will preserve them unaltered while the Dictionary will continue undergoing changes in subsequent editions.

ERIC BLOM

LONDON, *January* 1950

BEETHOVEN

LUDWIG VAN BEETHOVEN[1]

B ORN at Bonn, probably December 16, 1770.[2] The earliest form of the name is that with which we are familiar, but it takes many other shapes in the uncertain spelling of the time, such as Biethoffen, Biethofen, Biethoven, Bethoven, Betthoven, and Bethof. He himself appears to have always spelt it as we know it.[3] The family belonged originally to a village near Louvain; thence in 1650 they moved to Antwerp, where in 1685 [1680] the name appears in the registers. His father Johann or Jean, and his grandfather Ludwig, were both musicians in the court band of the Elector of Cologne, at Bonn — the latter a bass singer, and afterwards Capellmeister, appointed March 1733, the former a tenor singer, March 27, 1756. The grand-father lived till December 24, 1773, when the little Ludwig had just completed his third year. He was a small lively person with extraordinarily bright eyes, much respected and esteemed as a musician, and made an indelible impression on his grand-son. His portrait was the only one which Beethoven took from Bonn to Vienna, and he often spoke of it to the end of his life. Beethoven's mother — daughter of the chief cook at Ehren-breitstein — was married to Johann on November 12, 1767. She was twelve years younger than her husband; her original name had been Keverich, but at the time of the marriage she was a widow — Maria Magdalena Leym or Laym. She died after a long illness on July 17, 1787, a woman of soft heart and easy ways, much beloved by her son. The father, on the other hand, was a severe hard man of irregular habits, who evidently saw his son's ability, gave him the best instruction that his poverty would allow, and kept him to his music with a stern,

---

[1] *Van* in Dutch is not, like *von* or *de*, a sign of nobility.
[2] The baptism is registered on the 17th, and it was the custom to baptise on the day following birth. Beethoven's own belief was that he was born in 1772, which accounts for an occasional mistake in his estimate of the age at which he wrote his early works.
[3] In his letters; but in an advertisement of his, March 31, 1804, it is Bethofen (Nottebohm, *Beethoveniana*, p. 4).

3

strict, perhaps cruel, hand.   It is perhaps fortunate he did so.
The first house they occupied in Bonn, that in which the great
composer was born, was 515 in the Bonngasse, now designated
by a tablet erected in 1870.   Besides their eldest, Ludwig Maria,
who was born April 1, 1769, and lived but six days [and Ludwig
the second], the Beethovens had three other sons — Caspar
Anton Carl, April 7, 1774; Nikolaus Johann, October 1,
1776;   and August Franz Georg, January 16, 1781, died
August 16, 1783;   a daughter, February 23, 1779, who lived
only four days, and a second girl, Maria Margaretha Josepha,
May 4, 1786.   The first of these was the father of the ill-fated
youth who gave his uncle so much distress, and was probably
the ultimate cause of his death.   He died at Vienna, November
5, 1815.   The second, Johann, was an apothecary, at Linz and
Vienna, the ' Gutsbesitzer ' of the well-known anecdote, his
brother's *bête noire*, and the subject of many a complaint and
many a nickname.   He died at Vienna, January 12, 1848.
From the Bonngasse the family migrated to 7 or 8 on the
Dreieck, and thence to the Rheingasse, No. 934.   To the latter
they came in 1775 or 76, and there they remained for a few
years.   Johann Beethoven's income from the chapel was 300
florins a year (£25) — a miserable pittance, but that of most
musicians of the chapel ; and this appears to have been his sole
means of subsistence, for his voice was nearly gone, and there
is no sign of his having had other employment.[1]

According to Beethoven's own statement in the dedication
to his earliest publication — the 3 Sonatas for Pianoforte (1781
or 82) [1783] — he began music in his fourth year.   The few
traits preserved of that early period show that, like other
children, he did not acquire it without tears.   His father was
his first teacher, and from him he learned both violin and
clavier ; reading, writing, arithmetic, and a little Latin he
obtained in one of the common public schools, and even this
ceased when he was thirteen.   At school he was shy and un-
communicative, and cared for none of the ordinary games of
boys.   Before he was nine his music had advanced so far that
his father had no longer anything to teach him, and in 1779 he
was handed over to Pfeiffer, a tenor singer who had recently
joined the opera in Bonn, and seems to have lodged with the
Beethovens, and by whom he was taught, irregularly enough,

[1] See the register in Thayer, *Ludwig van Beethovens Leben*, i. 147.

but apparently with good and lasting effect, for a year. At the same time he fell in with a certain Zambona, who taught him Latin, French, and Italian, and otherwise assisted his neglected education. The organ he learned from Van den Eeden, organist to the court chapel, and an old friend of his grandfather. About this time, 1780, 81, there is reason to believe that the Beethovens found a friend in Mr. Cressener, the English *chargé d'affaires*, long time resident at Bonn, and that he assisted them with a sum of 400 florins. He died on January 17, 1781, and Beethoven (then just past ten) is said to have written a funeral cantata to his memory,[1] which was performed. The cantata, if it ever existed, has hitherto been lost sight of. One composition of this year we have in 9 Variations on Dressler's March in C minor,[2] which though published in 1783, are stated on the title to be ' composées .... par un jeune amateur L. v. B. agé de dix ans. 1780.' In February 1781 Neefe succeeded Van den Eeden as organist at the court, and Beethoven became his scholar. This was a great step for the boy, since Neefe, though somewhat over-conservative as a musician, was a sensible man, and became a real friend to his pupil.

There is ground for supposing [3] that during the winter of 1781 Ludwig and his mother made a journey in Holland, during which he played at private houses, and that the tour was a pecuniary success. On June 29 [19], 1782, old Van den Eeden was buried, and on the next day the Elector's band followed him to Münster, where as Bishop he had a palace, Neefe leaving Ludwig, then $11\frac{1}{2}$ years old, behind him as his regularly appointed deputy at the chapel organ, a post which, though unpaid, was no sinecure, and required both skill and judgment. This shows Neefe's confidence in his pupil, and agrees with his account of him, written a few months later, as ' playing with force and finish, reading well at sight, and, to sum up all, playing the greater part of Bach's Well-tempered Clavier, a feat which will be understood by the initiated. This young genius,' continues he, ' deserves some assistance that he may travel. If he goes on as he has begun, he will certainly become a second Mozart.'

On the 26th April 1783, Neefe was promoted to the direction

[1] Thayer, i. 115.
[2] Breitkopf & Härtel, Complete Edition, No. 166.
[3] Thayer, i. 116.

of both sacred and secular music, and at the same time Beethoven (then 12 years and 4 months old), was appointed ' Cembalist im Orchester,' with the duty of accompanying the rehearsals in the theatre; in other words, of conducting the opera-band, with all the responsibilities and advantages of practice and experience which belong to such a position. No pay accompanied the appointment at first, but the duties ceased when the Elector was absent, so that there was leisure for composition. The pieces published in this year are a song, ' Schilderung eines Mädchens,' [1] and 3 Sonatas for piano solo,[2] composed, according to the statement of the dedication, in 1781. On August 16, 1783, the youngest boy, August Franz, died, the father's voice began still further to fail, and things generally to go from bad to worse.

The work at the theatre was now rather on the increase. From October 1783 to October 1785, two operas of Gluck, four of Salieri, two of Sarti, five of Paisiello, with a dozen others, were studied and performed; but Ludwig had no pay. In February 1784 he made an application for a salary, but the consideration was postponed, and it was probably as a set-off that he was shortly afterwards appointed second court-organist. Meantime, however, on April 15, 1784, the Elector Max Friedrich died, and this postponed still further the prospect of emolument. The theatrical company was dismissed, and Neefe, having only his organ to attend to, no longer required a deputy. The Beethovens were now living at No. 476 in the Wenzelgasse, whither they appear to have moved in 1783, and Ludwig played the organ in the Minorite church at the six o'clock mass every morning.

The music of 1784 consists of a Rondo for the piano in A,[3] published early in the year, and a song ' An einen Säugling ' [4]: a concerto for piano and a piece in three-part harmony, both in MS., are mentioned as probably belonging to this year.[5]

One of the first acts of the new Elector Max Franz, was to examine his establishment, and on June 27, 1784, he issued a list of names and salaries of his band,[6] among which Beethoven's father appears with a salary of 300 florins, and Beethoven himself, as second organist, with 150 florins, equivalent to £25 and £13 respectively. A memorandum of the same date [7] shows that an idea was entertained of dismissing Neefe and

[1] B. & H. No. 228.   [2] Ibid. 156-158.   [3] Ibid. 196.   [4] Ibid. 229.
[5] Thayer, i. 128.   [6] Ibid. i. 154.   [7] Ibid. i. 152.

putting Beethoven into his place as chief organist. In fact
Neefe's pay was reduced from 400 to 200 florins, so that 50
florins a year was saved by the appointment of Beethoven. An
economical Elector! In the Holy Week of 1785 the incident
occurred (made too much of in the books) of Beethoven's
throwing out the solo singer in chapel by a modulation in the
accompaniment, which is chiefly interesting as showing how
early his love of a joke showed itself.[1] During this year he
studied the violin with Franz Ries — father of Ferdinand. The
music of 1785 is 3 quartets for piano and strings,[2] a minuet
for piano in Eb,[3] and a song ' Wenn jemand eine Reise thut '
(op. 52, No. 1).

In 1786 nothing appears to have been either composed or
published, and the only incident of this year that has survived
is the birth of a second girl to the Beethovens — Maria Margaretha Josepha, May 4.

In 1787 occurred the first real event in Beethoven's life —
his first journey to Vienna. Concerning this there is an absolute
want of dates and details. Someone must have been found to
supply the means for so expensive a journey, but no name is
preserved. As to date, his duties as organist would probably
prevent his leaving Bonn before the work of Holy Week and
Easter was over. The two persons who were indelibly impressed
on his recollection by the visit [4] were Mozart and the Emperor
Joseph. From the former he had a few lessons, and carried
away a distinct — and not very appreciative [5] — recollection
of his playing; but Mozart must have been so much occupied
by the death of his father (May 28) and the approaching production of ' Don Giovanni ' (October 29) that it is probable
they had not much intercourse. The well-known story of
Beethoven's introduction to him, when divested of the ornaments [6] of Seyfried and others, stands as follows : — Mozart
asked him to play, but thinking that his performance was a
prepared piece, paid little attention to it. Beethoven seeing
this entreated Mozart to give him a subject, which he did;
and the boy, getting excited with the occasion, played so finely
that Mozart, stepping softly into the next room, said to his
friends there, ' Pay attention to him; he will make a noise in
the world some day or other.' His visit seems not to have

---

[1] Schindler, *Biographie*, i. 7; Thayer, i. 161.   [2] B. & H. 75-77.   [3] Ibid. 193.
[4] Schindler, i. 15.   [5] Thayer, ii. 363.   [6] See Jahn, in Thayer, i. 164.

lasted more than three months, but, as we have said, all certain information is wanting. He returned by Augsburg, where he had to borrow three Carolins (£3) from Dr. von Schaden. His return was hastened by the illness of his mother, who died of consumption July 17, 1787, and his account of himself in a letter [1] to von Schaden, written seven weeks after that date, is not encouraging. A short time more and the little Margaretha followed her mother, on November 25, so that 1787 must have closed in very darkly. The only compositions known to belong to that year are a trio in E♭,[2] and a prelude in F minor for piano solo.[3] However, matters began to mend; he made the acquaintance of the von Breuning family — his first permanent friends — a mother, three boys, and a girl. He gave lessons to the girl and the youngest boy, and soon became an inmate of the house, a far better one than he had before frequented, and on terms of close intimacy with them all. The family was a cultivated and intellectual one, the mother — the widow of a man of some distinction — a woman of remarkable sense and refinement; the children, more or less of his own age. Here he seems to have been first initiated into the literature of his country, and to have acquired the love of English authors which remained with him through life. The intimacy rapidly became strong. He often passed whole days and nights with his friends, and accompanied them on excursions of several weeks duration to their uncle's house at Kerpen, and elsewhere. At the same time he made the acquaintance of Count Waldstein, a young nobleman eight years his senior, an amateur musician, whose acquaintance was peculiarly useful in encouraging and developing Beethoven's talent at a time when it naturally wanted support. On Waldstein Beethoven exercised the same charm that he did later on the proud aristocracy of Vienna. The Count used to visit him in his poor room, gave him a piano, got him pecuniary help under the guise of allowances from the Elector, and in other ways sympathised with him. Either now or shortly afterwards, Beethoven composed a set of variations for four hands on a theme of the Count's,[4] and in 1805 made him immortal by dedicating to him the grand sonata (op. 53), which is usually known by his name. Another acquaintance was the Countess of Hatzfeld, to whom he dedicated a set of variations, which were for long his show-piece.

[1] Nohl, *Briefe*, No. 2.   [2] B. & H. 86.   [3] Ibid. 195.   [4] Ibid. 122.

In the summer of 1788, when Beethoven was 17½ years old, the Elector altered the plan [1] of his music, and formed a national theatre on the model of that of his brother the Emperor Joseph. Reicha was made director, and Neefe pianist and stage-manager. The band was 31 strong, and contains names such as Ries, the two Rombergs, Simrock, Stumpff — which often recur in Beethoven's life. He himself played second viola, both in the opera and the chapel, and was still assistant Hof-organist. In this position he remained for four years; the opera *répertoire* was large, good, and various, the singers were of the best, and the experience must have been of great practical use to him. Among the operas played in 1789 and 1790 were Mozart's ' Entführung,' ' Figaro,' and ' Don Giovanni ' — the two first apparently often. Meantime Johann Beethoven was going from bad to worse. Stephen Breuning once saw Ludwig take his drunken father out of the hands of the police, and this could hardly have been the only occasion. At length, on November 20, 1789, a decree was issued ordering a portion of the father's salary to be paid over to the son, who thus, before he was nineteen, became the head of the family.

The compositions of 1789 and 90 are 2 Preludes for the piano (op. 39), 24 Variations on Righini's ' Venni [Vieni] Amore,' [2] a song ' Der freie Mann,' [3] and probably a Cantata on the death of the Emperor Joseph II, still in MS. [4] The only extra musical event of this year was the visit of Haydn and Salomon on their road to London. They arrived on Christmas Day. One of Haydn's Masses was performed; he was complimented by the Elector, and entertained the chief musicians at dinner at his lodgings. 1791 opened well for Beethoven with a ' Ritter Ballet,' a kind of masked ball, in antique style. Count Waldstein appears to have arranged the plan, and Beethoven composed the music; but his name does not seem to have been connected with it at the time, and it remained unpublished till 1872, when it appeared arranged for piano. In the autumn the *troupe* accompanied the Elector to Mergentheim, near Aschaffenburg, to a conclave of the *Deutschen Orden*; the journey was by water along the Rhine and Main, the weather was splendid, — there was ample

---

[1] Thayer, i. 182.   [2] B. & H. 178.   [3] Ibid. 232.
[4] Thayer, i. 232. He died Feb. 20, 1790. [The Cantata is now published in B. & H. Suppl. i.]

leisure, and the time long remained in Beethoven's recollection 'a fruitful source of charming images.' At Aschaffenburg he heard a fine player — the Abbé Sterkel, and showed his instant appreciation of the Abbé's graceful finished style by imitating it in extemporising. In Mergentheim the company remained for a month (18 September–20 October). An interesting account of the daily musical proceedings is given by Junker, the Chaplain at Kirchberg,[1] including an account of Beethoven's extempore playing. He compares it with that of Vogler, whom he knew well, and pronounces it to have displayed all Vogler's execution, with much more force, feeling, and expression, and to have been in the highest degree original.

The Beethovens were still living in the Wenzelgasse, Carl learning music, and Johann under the Court Apothecary. Ludwig took his meals at the Zehrgarten [2] — a great resort of the University professors, artists, and literary men of Bonn, and where the lovely Babette Koch, daughter of the pro-prietress, was doubtless an attraction to him.[3] His intimacy with the Breunings continued and increased ; Madame von Breuning was one of the very few people who could manage him, and even she could not always make him go to his lessons in time : when he proved too obstinate she would give up the endeavour with the remark ' he is again in his *raptus*,' an ex-pression which Beethoven never forgot. Music was their great bond, and Beethoven's improvisations were the delight of the family. His duties at the organ and in the orchestra at this time were not very great ; the Elector's absences were frequent, and gave him much time to himself, which he spent partly in lessons, partly in the open air, of which he was already very fond, and partly in assiduous practice and composition. The sketch-books of that time are crammed with ideas, and confirm his statement, made many years later,[4] that he began thus early the method of working which so emphatically distinguishes him.

In July 1792 Haydn again passed through Bonn on his return from London. The Elector's band gave him a dinner at Godesberg, and Beethoven submitted a cantata to him, ' which Haydn greatly praised, warmly encouraging the com-

[1] Thayer, i. 200-215.   [2] Ibid. i. 218.

[3] He wrote twice to her within a year after he left Bonn. See his letter to Eleonore Breuning, Nov. 2, 1793.

[4] Letter to Archd. Rodolph, July 23, 1815. Sketches of the Bonn date are in the British Museum.

poser to proceed with his studies.' What the cantata was is not known, though it is conjectured to have been on the death of the Emperor Leopold II.[1]

The compositions which can be fixed to the years 1791 and 92 consist of songs (portions of op. 52), a Rondino[2] for wind instruments, the Trio for strings, op. 3, an Allegro and Minuet for 2 flutes (August 23, MS.), and perhaps a set of 14 Variations[3] for pianoforte, violin, and cello, in E♭, published in 1804 as op. 44; 12 Variations[4] for piano and violin on ' Se vuol ballare '; 13 ditto for piano[5] on ' Es war einmal '; and 12 ditto[6] for piano, four hands, on an air of Count Waldstein's.

Hitherto the Elector seems to have taken no notice of the most remarkable member of his orchestra. But in the course of this year — whether prompted by Neefe or Waldstein or by his own observation, or possibly by Haydn's approbation — he determined that Beethoven should visit Vienna in a more permanent manner than before, for the purpose of studying at his expense. Haydn was communicated with, and in the very beginning of November Beethoven left Bonn, as it proved, never to return to it again. His parting words to Neefe are preserved :[7] — ' Thank you for the counsel you have so often given me on my progress in my divine art. Should I ever become a great man you will certainly have assisted in it, which will be all the more gratifying to you, since you may be convinced that ' etc. The album in which his friends — Waldstein, the Breunings, the Kochs, Degenhart, and others — inscribed their farewells is still existing,[8] and the latest date is November 1. E. Breuning's lines contain allusions to ' Albion,' as if Beethoven were preparing to visit England — possibly with Haydn ? Waldstein's entry is as follows : — ' Dear Beethoven, you are travelling to Vienna in fulfilment of your long-cherished wish. The genius of Mozart is still weeping and bewailing the death of her favourite. With the inexhaustible Haydn she found a refuge, but no occupation, and is now waiting to leave him and join herself to some one else. Labour assiduously, and receive Mozart's spirit from the hands of Haydn. Your true friend Waldstein. Bonn, October 29, 1792.'

What provision the Elector made for him beyond his

[1] Thayer, i. 232. He died Mar. 1, 1792.   [2] B. & H. No. 60.
[3] Nottebohm, *Beethoveniana*, III.   [4] B. & H. No. 103.   [5] Ibid. No. 175.
[6] Ibid. No. 122.   [7] Thayer, i. 227.   [8] Nottebohm, *Beethoveniana*, XXVII.

modest pay of 150 florins is not known. An entry of 25 ducats
(£12 : 10s.) is found in his notebook shortly after he reached
Vienna, but there is nothing to show what length of time that
moderate sum represented, or even that it came from the
Elector at all.

Thus ended the first period of Beethoven's life. He was
now virtually twenty-two. The list of his known compositions
to this time has been given year by year. If we add the Bagatelles (op. 33), the 2 easy Sonatas (op. 49), the 2 Violin
Rondos (op. 51), the Serenade Trio (op. 8), and a lost Trio
for piano, flute, and bassoon,[1] — all probably composed at
Bonn — and compare them with those of other composers of
the first rank, such as Mozart, Schubert, or Mendelssohn, it
must be admitted that they are singularly few and unimportant.
For the orchestra the Ritter-ballet already referred to is the
single composition known, while Mozart — to mention him
only — had in the same period written 36 symphonies, including so mature a masterpiece as the ' Parisian ' in D. Against
Mozart's 28 operas, cantatas, and masses, for voices and full
orchestra, composed before he was 23, Beethoven has absolutely nothing to show. And the same in other departments.
That he meditated great works, though they did not come to
paper, is evident in at least one case. A resident in Bonn,
writing to Schiller's sister [wife] Charlotte, on January 26,
1793,[2] says : — ' I enclose a setting of the *Feuer-farbe* on which
I should like your opinion. It is by a young man of this place
whose talent is widely esteemed, and whom the Elector has
now sent to Vienna to Haydn. He intends to compose Schiller's
Freude, and that verse by verse. I expect something perfect ;
for, as far as I know him, he is all for the grand and sublime.
Haydn informs us that he shall set him to great operas, as he
himself will shortly leave off composing. He does not usually
occupy himself with such trifles as the enclosed, which indeed
he composed only at the request of a lady.' This letter, which
shows how early Schiller's ' Hymn to Joy ' had taken possession
of Beethoven — there to remain till it formed the finale to the
Ninth Symphony thirty years later — is equally interesting for
the light it throws on the impression which Beethoven had
already made on those who knew him, and who credited him
with the intention and the ability to produce great works,

---

[1] Thayer, *Verzeichniss*, No. 22.   [2] Thayer, *Leben*, i. 237.

although he had not yet produced even small ones. This impression was doubtless due mainly to the force and originality of his extempore playing, which even at this early age was prodigious, and justified his friends in speaking of him [1] as one of the finest pianoforte-players of the day.

By the middle of November Beethoven was settled at Vienna. His first lodging was a garret at a printer's in the 'Alservorstadt' [2] outside the walls, in the direction of the present Votive-Church; but this was soon exchanged for one 'on the ground floor,' [3] of which we have no nearer description. On the journey from Bonn we find him for the first time making notes of little occurrences and expenses — a habit which never left him. In the entries made during his first few weeks in Vienna we can trace the purchase of a wig, silk stockings, boots, shoes, overcoat, writing-desk, seal, and hire of piano. From the same source we can infer the beginning of his lessons. The first payment to Haydn is 8 groschen (say $9\frac{1}{2}d.$, we may surely presume for one hour) on December 12. The lessons took place in Haydn's house [4] (Hamberger Haus, No. 992) now destroyed. They were lessons in 'strict counterpoint,' and the text-book was Fux's 'Gradus ad Parnassum.' Of Beethoven's exercises 245 have been preserved,[5] of which Haydn has corrected 42. Haydn was naturally much occupied, and it is not surprising that Beethoven should have been dissatisfied with his slow progress, and with the cursory way in which his exercises were corrected, and have secretly accepted the offer of additional instruction from Schenk, a well-known Vienna composer. But no open rupture as yet took place. Beethoven accompanied Haydn to Eisenstadt some time in 1793, and it was not until Haydn's departure for England on January 19, 1794, that he openly transferred himself to another master. He then took lessons from Albrechtsberger in counterpoint, and from Schuppanzigh on the violin, three times a week each. In the former the text-book was Albrechtsberger's own 'Anweisung zur Composition,' and the subject was taken up where Haydn had left it, and pursued much farther. No less than 263 exercises are in existence under the following heads — Simple strict counterpoint; Free composition in simple counterpoint;

[1] Ibid. i. 227 and 213. [2] Ibid. ii. 103.
[3] Ibid. i. 255, ' auf der Erd.' [4] Ibid. i. 259.
[5] For all the exercises here mentioned and an able faithful commentary, see Nottebohm's invaluable edition of *Beethoven's Studien*, vol. i. 1873.

Imitation; Simple fugue; Fugued chorale; Double fugue; Double counterpoint in the 8th, 10th, and 12th; Triple counterpoint and Triple fugue; Canon. Nottebohm has pointed out the accuracy and pains which Albrechtsberger bestowed on his pupil, as well as [1] the care with which Beethoven wrote his exercises, and the characteristic way in which he neglected them in practice. He also gives his reasons for believing that the lessons did not last longer than March 1795. The impression they left on Albrechtsberger was not flattering: ' Have nothing to do with him,' said the old contrapuntist to an enquiring lad, ' he has learnt nothing, and will never do anything in decent style.' [2] In fact what was a contrapuntist to do with a pupil who regarded everything in music — even consecutive fifths [3] — as an open question, and also thought it a good thing to ' learn occasionally what is according to rule, that one may hereafter come to what is contrary to rule' ? [4] Besides the lessons with Haydn and Albrechtsberger, some exercises exist in Italian vocal composition, dating from 1793 to 1802, and showing that Beethoven availed himself of Salieri's well-known kindness to needy musicians, to submit his pieces to him. Salieri's corrections are chiefly in the division of the Italian syllables. Another musician whom he consulted, especially in his early attempts at quartet writing, was Aloys Förster, to whom he remained long and greatly attached.[5]

Meantime Beethoven kept up communication with Bonn. On December 18, 1792, his poor father died, and the 100 thalers applied to the support of his brothers naturally stopped. On Beethoven's application, however, the grant was allowed to go on, in addition to his own pay. Ries drew and transmitted the money for him.[6] The Breunings still held their place in his heart; two letters to Eleonore, full of affection, are preserved, and he mentions having also written twice to one resident of Bonn, and three times to another, in the course of the first twelvemonth. In January 1794 the Elector visited Vienna, and with the March quarter-day Beethoven's allowance ceased. In the following October the Emperor declared war with

[1] Nottebohm, *Beethoven's Studien*, p. 196.
[2] Dolezalek, in Thayer, ii. 117.
[3] Ries, *Biographische Notizen*, p. 87.
[4] Czerny, quoted in note to Lady Wallace's edition of the *Letters*, ii. 12.
[5] Thayer, i. 281.　　　　　　[6] Ibid. 225, 257.

France, Bonn was taken possession of by the republican army, and the Elector fled.

Now that Beethoven is landed in Vienna — as it turns out, never again to leave it — and is left to his own resources, it may be convenient to pause in the narrative of his life, and sketch his character and person as briefly as possible. He had already a large acquaintance among the aristocracy of Vienna. Among his kindest friends and most devoted admirers were the Prince and Princess Karl Lichnowsky. They devoured his music, gave him a quartet of valuable instruments [1] for the performance of it, put up with his caprices and eccentricities, gave him an annuity of £60, and made him an inmate of their house for years. He was also frequently at the houses of Baron van Swieten, Prince Lobkowitz, Count Fries, and other noblemen, at once leaders of fashion and devoted amateurs. At these houses he was in the constant habit of playing, and in many of them no doubt he taught, but as to the solid results of this no record remains — nor do we know the prices which he obtained for his published works, or the value of the dedications, at this period of his career. Musical public, like that which supported the numerous concerts flourishing in London at this date,[2] and enabled Salomon to risk the expense of bringing Haydn to England, there was none; musicians were almost directly dependent on the appreciation of the wealthy.

That Beethoven should have been so much treasured by the aristocracy of Vienna notwithstanding his personal drawbacks, and notwithstanding the gap which separated the nobleman from the *roturier*, shows what an immense power there must have been in his genius, and in the absolute simplicity of his mind, to overcome the abruptness of his manners. If we are to believe the anecdotes of his contemporaries his sensitiveness was extreme, his temper ungovernable, and his mode of expression often quite unjustifiable. At the house of Count Browne, when playing a duet with Ries, a young nobleman at the other end of the room persisted in talking to a lady: several attempts to quiet him having failed, Beethoven suddenly lifted Ries's hands from the keys, saying in a loud voice ' I play no longer for such hogs '; nor would he touch another

---

[1] These were in his possession for more than 20 years, and are now in the Bibliothek at Berlin. Pohl, *Jahresbericht des Conservatoriums* &c. p. 16.
[2] See Pohl, *Haydn in London*, 7—53.

note nor allow Ries to do so, though entreated by all.[1] On
another occasion, when living in the house and on the bounty
of the Lichnowskys, the prince, knowing how sensitive Beethoven was to neglect, ordered his servants whenever they
heard Beethoven's bell and his at the same time to attend to
Beethoven's first. No sooner however did Beethoven discover
that such an order had been given than he engaged a servant
of his own to answer his bell.[2] During one of the rehearsals of
' Leonora,' the third bassoon was absent, at which Beethoven
was furious. Prince Lobkowitz, one of his best friends, tried to
laugh off the matter, saying that as the first and second were
there the absence of the third could not be of any great consequence. But so implacable was Beethoven that in crossing
the Platz after the rehearsal he could not resist running to the
great gate of the Lobkowitz Palace and shouting up the
entrance,[3] ' Lobkowitzscher Esel ' — ' ass of a Lobkowitz.'
Any attempt to deceive him, even in the most obvious pleas-
antry, he could never forgive. When he composed the well-
known ' Andante in F ' he played it to Ries and Krumpholz.
It delighted them, and with difficulty they induced him to
repeat it. From Beethoven's house Ries went to that of Prince
Lichnowsky, and not being able to contain himself played what
he could recollect of the new piece, and the Prince being equally
delighted, it was repeated and repeated till he too could play
a portion of it. The next day the Prince by way of a joke asked
Beethoven to hear something which he had been composing,
and thereupon played a large portion of his own ' Andante.'
Beethoven was furious ; and the result was that Ries was never
again allowed to hear him play in private. In fact it led in
the end to Beethoven's ceasing to play to the Prince's circle
of friends.[4] And on the other hand, no length of friendship
or depth of tried devotion prevented him from treating those
whom he suspected, however unjustly, and on however in-
sufficient grounds, in the most scornful manner. Ries has[5]
described one such painful occurrence in his own case à propos
to the Westphalian negotiations ; but all his friends suffered
in turn. Even poor Schindler, whose devotion in spite of every
drawback was so constant, and who has been taunted with

[1] Ries, p. 92.
[2] See also the letter to Zmeskall on the Countess Erdödy's influence over her
servant; Nohl, *Briefe Beethovens*, No. 54.
[3] Thayer, ii. 288.   [4] Ries, p. 102.   [5] Ibid. p. 95.

having 'delivered himself body and soul to Beethoven,' had
to suffer the most shameful reproaches behind his back, the
injustice of which is most surely proved by the fact that they
are dropped as suddenly as they were adopted.[1] When Moritz
Lichnowsky, Schuppanzigh, and Schindler were doing their
utmost to get over the difficulties of arranging a concert for
the performance of the Choral Symphony and the Mass in D,
he suddenly suspected them of some ulterior purpose, and dismissed them with the three following notes;[2] — 'To Count
Lichnowsky. Falsehoods I despise. Visit me no more. There
will be no concert. Beethoven.' 'To Herr Schindler. Visit
me no more till I send for you. No concert. Beethoven.' 'To
Herr Schuppanzigh. Visit me (*besuche er mich*) no more. I
give no concert. Beethoven.'

The style of the last of these three precious productions —
the third person singular — in which the very lowest rank only
is addressed, seems to open us a little door into Beethoven's
feeling towards musicians. When Hummel died, two notes
from Beethoven[3] were found among his papers, which tell
the story of some sudden violent outbreak on Beethoven's part.
'Komme er (the same scornful style as before) nicht mehr zu
mir! er ist ein falscher Hund, und falsche Hunde hole der
Schinder. Beethoven.' And though this was followed by an
apology couched in the most ultra-affectionate and coaxing
terms — 'Herzens Natzerl,' 'Dich küsst dein Beethoven,' and
so on — yet the impression must have remained on Hummel's
mind. There can be no doubt that he was on bad terms with
most of the musicians of Vienna. With Haydn he seems never
to have been really cordial. The old man's neglect of his
lessons embittered him, and when after hearing his first three
trios, Haydn, no doubt in sincerity, advised him not to publish
the third, which Beethoven knew to be the best, it was difficult
to take the advice in any other light than as prompted by
jealousy. True he dedicated his three Pianoforte Sonatas (op. 2)
to Haydn, and they met in the concert-room, but there are
no signs of cordial intercourse between them after Beethoven's
first twelve months in Vienna. In fact they were thoroughly
antagonistic. Haydn, though at the head of living composers,
and as original a genius as Beethoven himself, had always been

[1] Schindler, ii. 68.   [2] See *Briefe*, Nos. 278, 280, 284 [289, 290, 291].
[3] Thayer, ii. 54.

punctilious, submissive, subservient to etiquette.   Beethoven was eminently independent and impatient of restraint.   It was the old world and the new — De Brézé and Mirabeau [1] — and it was impossible for them to agree.   They probably had no open quarrel, Haydn's tact would prevent that, but Haydn nicknamed him ' the Great Mogul,' and Beethoven retorted by refusing to announce himself as ' Haydn's scholar,' [2] and when they met in the street their remarks were unfortunate, and the antagonism was but too evident.

For Salieri, Eybler, Gyrowetz, and Weigl, able men and respectable contrapuntists, he had a sincere esteem, though little more intimate feeling.   Though he would not allow the term as regarded Haydn, he himself left his characteristic visiting card on Salieri's table as his ' scholar ' — ' Der Schüler Beethoven war da.' [3]   But with the other musicians of Vienna, and the players of his own standing, Beethoven felt no restraint on open war.[4]   They laughed at his eccentricities, his looks and his Bonn dialect,[5] made game of his music, and even trampled [6] on it, and he retorted both with speech and hands.   The pianoforte-players were Hummel, Woelffl [Woelfl], Lipawsky, Gelinek, Steibelt.   Steibelt had distinctly challenged him,[7] had been as thoroughly beaten as a man could wish, and from that day forward would never again meet him.   Gelinek, though equally vanquished, compensated himself by listening to Beethoven on all occasions, and stealing his phrases [8] and harmonies, while Beethoven retorted by engaging his next lodging where Gelinek could not possibly come within the sound of his piano.   Woelffl and Hummel were openly pitted against him, and no doubt there were people to be found in Vienna in 1795, as there are in London in 1876, to stimulate such rivalry and thus divide artists whom a little care might have united. Hummel is said to have excelled him in clearness, elegance, and purity, and Woelffl's proficiency in counterpoint was great, and his huge hands gave him extraordinary command of the

---

[1] Carlyle's *French Revolution*, bk. v. ch. 2.   [2] Ries, p. 86.
[3] *Aus Moscheles' Leben.* i. 10.
[4] He calls them his ' deadly enemies.'   Letter to Eleonore von Breuning, Nov. 2, 93.
[5] Thayer, ii. 55.
[6] Kozeluch, see Thayer, ii. 108.   Romberg did the same thing some years later ;   and see Spohr's curious story of him, *Selbstbiog.* i. 85.
[7] See the story in Ries, p. 81.
[8] Letter to Eleonore v. Breuning, Nov. 2, 1793, with Wegeler's remarks, *B. Notizen*, p. 59.

keys; but for fire, and imagination, and feeling, and wealth
of ideas in extempore playing, none of them can have approached Beethoven. ' His improvisation,' says Czerny,[1] ' was
most brilliant and striking; in whatever company he might
chance to be, he knew how to produce such an effect upon every
hearer, that frequently not an eye remained dry, while many
would break out into loud sobs; for there was something
wonderful in his expression, in addition to the beauty and
originality of his ideas, and his spirited style of rendering them.'
He extemporised in regular ' form,' and his variations — when
he treated a theme in that way — were not mere alterations
of figure, but real developments and elaborations of the subject.[2] ' No artist,' says Ries,[3] ' that I ever heard came at all
near the height which Beethoven attained in this branch of
playing. The wealth of ideas which forced themselves on him,
the caprices to which he surrendered himself, the variety of
treatment, the difficulties, were inexhaustible.' Even the Abbé
Vogler's admirers were compelled to admit as much.[4] He
required much pressing, often actual force, to get him to the
piano, and he would make a grimace or strike the keys with
the back of his hand [5] as he sat down; but when there he
would extemporise for two hours and even more at a time,
and after ending one of his great improvisations, he would burst
into a roar of laughter, and banter his hearers on their emotions. ' We artists,' he would say, ' don't want tears, we want
applause.' [6] At other times he would behave as if insulted
by such indications of sympathy, and call his admirers fools,
and spoiled children.

And yet no outbursts of this kind seem to have made any
breach in the regard with which he was treated by the nobility
— the only unprofessional musical society of Vienna. Certainly Beethoven was the first musician who had ever ventured
on such independence, and there was possibly something
piquant in the mere novelty; but the real secret of his lasting
influence must have been the charm of his personality — his
entire simplicity, joined to his prodigious genius. And he enjoyed good society. ' It is good,' said he, ' to be with the
aristocracy; but one must be able to impress them.' [7]

[1] Thayer, ii. 10.
[2] Czerny gives the various forms of his improvisations. Thayer. ii. 347.
[3] *Notizen*, p. 100.   [4] Thayer, ii. 236.   [5] Ibid. ii. 349, 312.
[6] Conversation with Bettina [Brentano]. Thayer, ii. 13.   [7] Ibid. ii. 313.

This personal fascination acted most strongly on his immediate friends — on Krumpholz (who seems to have played
the part of Coleridge's humble follower John Chester [1]), on
the somewhat cold and self-possessed Breuning, as well as on
Ries, Zmeskall, Schindler, Holz, and others, who had not, like
Haslinger or Streicher, anything to gain from him, but who
suffered his roughest words and most scurvy treatment, and
returned again and again to their worship with astonishing
constancy.   Excepting Breuning none of these seem really to
have had his confidence, or to have known anything of the
inner man which lay behind the rough husk of his exterior, and
yet they all clung to him as if they had.

Of his *tours de force* in performance too much is perhaps
made in the books. His transposing the Concerto in C into C♯
at rehearsal was exactly repeated by Woelffl; [2] while his playing the piano parts of his Horn Sonata, his Kreutzer Sonata,
or his C minor Concerto without book, or difficult pieces of
Bach at first sight, is no more than has been done by Mozart,
Mendelssohn, Sterndale Bennett, and many inferior artists.
No, it was no quality of this kind that got him the name of the
' giant among players ' ; but the loftiness and elevation of his
style, and his great power of expression in slow movements,
which when exercised on his own noble music fixed his hearers
and made them insensible to any faults of polish or mere
mechanism.

It was not men alone who were attracted by him, he was
an equal favourite with the ladies of the Court.   The Princess
Lichnowsky watched over him — as Madame von Breuning
had done — like a mother.[3]   The Countesses Gallenberg and
Erdödy, the Princess Odescalchi, the Baroness Ertmann, the
sisters of the Count of Brunswick, and many more of the reign-
ing beauties of Vienna adored him, and would bear any rude-
ness from him.   These young ladies went to his lodgings or
received him at their palaces as it suited him.   He would storm
at the least inattention during their lessons, and would tear
up the music and throw it about.[4]   He may have used the
snuffers as a toothpick in Madame Ertmann's drawing-room ;

[1] ' One of those who were attracted to Coleridge as flies to honey, or bees
to the sound of a brass pan.' Hazlitt, in *The Liberal.*
[2] Thayer, ii. 26.
[3] ' She would have put me under a glass case if she could,' said Beethoven.
[4] Countess Gallenberg, in Thayer, ii. 172.

but when she lost her child he was admitted to console her;
and when Mendelssohn saw her [1] fifteen years later she doted
on his memory and recalled the smallest traits of his character
and behaviour. He was constantly in love, and though his
taste was very promiscuous,[2] yet it is probably quite true that
the majority of his attachments was for women of rank, and
that they were returned or suffered. Unlike poor Schubert,
whose love for the Countess Marie [Caroline] Esterhazy was
so carefully concealed, Beethoven made no secret of his attachments. Many of them are perpetuated in the dedications of
his sonatas. That in E♭ (op. 7), dedicated to the Countess
Babette de Keglevics, was called in allusion to him and to her,
' die verliebte.' To other ladies he writes in the most intimate,
nay affectionate style. He addresses the Baroness Ertmann by
her Christian name as ' Liebe, werthe, Dorothea Cäcilia,' and
the Countess Erdödy — whom he called his confessor — as
' Liebe, liebe, liebe, liebe, liebe, Gräfin.' [3] Thayer's investiga-
tions [4] have destroyed the romance of his impending marriage
with Giulietta Guicciardi (afterwards Countess Gallenberg);
yet the fact that the story has been so long believed shows its
abstract probability. One thing is certain, that his attachments
were all honourable, and that he had no taste for immorality.
' Oh God! let me at last find her who is destined to be mine,
and who shall strengthen me in virtue.' Those were his sentiments
as to wedded love.

His dedications have been mentioned. The practice seems
virtually to have begun with him,[5] to have sprung from the
equal and intimate relation in which he — earliest among
musicians — stood to his distinguished friends; and when one
looks down the list,[6] from op. 1 to op. 135 — unsurpassed even
by any later composer — and remembers that the majority
were inspired by private friendship,[7] and that only a minority
speak of remuneration, it is impossible not to be astonished.

Formal religion he apparently had none; his religious

[1] Letter of July 14, 1831.
[2] See the anecdote in Thayer, ii. 104: and Ries's remark about the tailor's
daughters, *Notizen*, p. 119.
[3] Nohl, *Neue Briefe*, No. 150.   [4] See vol. ii. 166, etc.
[5] Mozart's six quartets are dedicated to Haydn, but this is quite an exception.
Haydn dedicated a sonata or two in London, but it was not his practice.
[6] As given in Nottebohm's *Thematisches Verzeichniss*, Anhang lv. c.
[7] In dedicating opus 90 to Prince Moritz Lichnowsky he says that ' anything
approaching a gift in return would only distress him, and that he should decidedly
refuse it.' See also the letter to Zmeskall (Dec. 16, 1816) dedicating op. 95.

observances were on a par with his manners. It is strange that
the Bible does not appear to have been one of his favourite
books. He once says to a friend,[1] ' It happens to be Sunday,
and I will quote you something out of the Gospel — Love one
another ' ; but such references are very rare. But that he was
really and deeply religious, ' striving sacredly to fulfil all the
duties imposed on him by humanity, God, and nature,' [2] and
full of trust in God, love to man, and real humility, is shown
by many and many a sentence in his letters. And that in
moments of emotion his thoughts turned upwards is touchingly
shewn by a fragment of a hymn — ' Gott allein ist unser Herr '
— which Mr. Nottebohm [3] has unearthed from a sketch-book
of the year 1818, and which Beethoven has himself noted to
have been written, ' Auf dem Wege Abends zwischen den und
auf den Bergen.' The following passages, which he copied out
himself and kept constantly before him, served him as a kind
of Creed, and sum up his theology : —

I am that which is.

I am all that is, that was, and that shall be. No mortal man
hath lifted my veil.

He is alone by Himself, and to Him alone do all things
owe their being.

How he turned his theology into practice is well exemplified
in his alteration of Moscheles' pious inscription. At the end
of his arrangement of ' Fidelio ' Moscheles had written ' Fine.
With God's help.' To this Beethoven added, ' O man, help
thyself.' [4]

In his early Vienna days he attempted to dress in the fashion,
wore silk stockings, perruque, long boots, and sword, carried a
double eye-glass and a seal-ring. But dress must have been as
unbearable to him [5] as etiquette, and it did not last ; ' he was
meanly dressed,' says one of his adorers, ' and very ugly to
look at, but full of nobility and fine feeling, and highly cultivated.' [6] Czerny first saw him in his own room, and there his
beard was nearly half an inch long, his black hair stood up in
a thick shock, his ears were filled with wool which had apparently been soaked in some yellow substance, and his clothes

[1] Frau Streicher, *Briefe*, No. 200.
[2] Letter to Archd. Rodolph, July 18, 1821.
[3] *Neue Beethoveniana*, No. VII.   [4] Moscheles, *Leben*, i. 18.
[5] It is no object to me to have my hair dressed,' says he, à propos to a servant
who possessed that accomplishment, Feb. 25, 1813.
[6] Countess Gallenberg, in Thayer, ii. 172.

were made of a loose hairy stuff, which gave him the look of
Robinson Crusoe. But we know that he never wore his good
clothes at home; [1] at any rate the impression he usually made
was not so questionable as this. Those who saw him for the
first time were often charmed by the eager cordiality of his
address, and by the absence of the bearishness and gloom [2]
which even then were attributed to him. His face may have
been ugly, but all admit that it was remarkably expressive.
When lost in thought and abstracted his look would naturally
be gloomy, and at such times it was useless to expect attention
from him; but on recognising a friend his smile was peculiarly
genial and winning.[3] He had the breadth of jaw which distinguishes so many men of great intellect; the mouth firm and
determined, the lips protruded with a look almost of fierceness :
but his eyes were the special feature of the face, and it was in
them that the earnestness and sincerity of his character beamed
forth. They were black, not large but bright, and when under
the influence of inspiration — the *raptus* of Madame von
Breuning — they dilated in a peculiar way. His head was
large, the forehead both high and broad, and the hair abundant.
It was originally black, but in the last years of his life, though
as thick as ever, became quite white, and formed a strong
contrast to the red colour [4] of his complexion. Beard or
moustache he never wore. His teeth were very white and
regular, and good up to his death; [5] in laughing he shewed
them much. The portraits and busts of Beethoven are with
few exceptions more or less to blame; they either idealise him
into a sort of Jupiter Olympus, or they rob him of all expression.
It must have been a difficult face to take, because of the constant variety in its expression, as well as the impatience of the
sitter. The most trustworthy likenesses [6] are (1) the miniature
by Hornemann, taken in 1802, and photographed in Breuning's
' Schwarzspanierhaus ' (Vienna, 1874) ; (2) the head by La-
tronne [Letronne], engraved by Höfel, and (badly) by Riedel

---

[1] Letter of June 15, 1825.
[2] Spohr, *Selbstbiog.* 198. E. B., in Thayer ii. 297.
[3] Rochlitz, *Für Freunde d. Tonkunst*, iv. 350; and the charming account (by a
niece of Dr. Burney) in the *Harmonicon*, Dec. 1825.
[4] Sir Julius Benedict's recollection.
[5] Breuning, *Aus dem Schwarzspanierhaus*, p. 67.
[6] I heartily wish it were in my power to give these two portraits, so full of
character and so unlike the ordinary engravings. The first of the two has a
special interest as having been sent by Beethoven to Breuning as a pledge of
reconciliation. See the letter, p. 81.

C

for the A.M.Z., 1817; (3) the little full length sketch by Lyser, to the accuracy of which Breuning expressly testifies, except that the hat should be straight on the head, not at all on one side. He was below the middle height — not more than 5 feet 5 inches; but broad across the shoulders and very firmly built — 'the image of strength.' [1] His hands were much covered with hair, the fingers strong and short (he could barely span a tenth), and the tips broad, as if pressed out with long practising from early youth. He was very particular as to the mode of holding the hands and placing the fingers, in which he was a follower of Emanuel Bach, whose *Method* he employed in his earlier days. In extempore playing he used the pedal far more than one would expect from his published sonatas, and this made his quick playing confused, but in adagios he played with divine clearness and expression.[2] His attitude at the piano was perfectly quiet and dignified, with no approach to grimace, except to bend down a little towards the keys as his deafness increased.[3] This is remarkable, because as a conductor his motions were most extravagant.[4] At a *pianissimo* he would crouch down so as to be hidden by the desk, and then as the *crescendo* increased, would gradually rise, beating all the time, until at the *fortissimo* he would spring into the air with his arms extended as if wishing to float on the clouds. When, as was sometimes the case after he became deaf, he lost his place, and these motions did not coincide with the music, the effect was very unfortunate, though not so unfortunate as it would have been had he himself been aware of the mistake. In the orchestra, as at the piano, he was urgent in demanding expression, exact attention to *piano* and *forte*, and the slightest

[1] Seyfried, *Biogr. Notizen*, 13.—' In that limited space was concentrated the pluck of twenty battalions.'—*Eothen*, ch. xviii.
[2] Czerny, in Thayer, ii. 348.   [3] Thayer, ii. 236.
[4] Seyfried, p. 17, confirmed by Spohr, *Selbstbiog.* i. 201.

shades of *nuance*, and to *tempo rubato*. Generally speaking he was extremely courteous to the band, though to this rule there were now and then exceptions. Though so easily made angry his pains as a teacher must have been great. ' Unnaturally patient,' says one pupil,[1] ' he would have a passage repeated a dozen times till it was to his mind ' ; ' infinitely strict in the smallest detail,' says another,[2] ' until the right rendering was obtained.' ' Comparatively careless [3] as to the right notes being played, but angry at once at any failure in expression or *nuance*, or in apprehension of the character of the piece ; saying that the first might be an accident, but that the other showed want of knowledge, or feeling, or attention.' What his practice was as to remuneration does not appear, but it is certain that in some cases he would accept no pay from his pupils.

His simplicity and absence of mind were now and then oddly shown. He could not be brought to understand why his standing in his nightshirt at the open window should attract notice, and asked with perfect simplicity ' what those d——d boys were hooting at.' [4] At Penzing in 1823 he shaved at his window in full view, and when the people collected to see him, changed his lodging rather than forsake the practice.[5] Like Newton he was unconscious that he had not dined, and urged on the waiter payment for a meal which he had neither ordered nor eaten. He forgot that he was the owner of a horse until recalled to the fact by a long bill for its keep. In fact he was not made for practical life ; never could play at cards or dance, dropped everything that he took into his hands, and overthrew the ink into the piano. He cut himself horribly in shaving. ' A disorderly creature ' (ein unordentlicher Mensch) was his own description, and ' ein konfuser Kerl ' that of his doctor,[6] who wisely added the saving clause ' though he may still be the greatest genius in the world.' His ordinary handwriting was terrible, and supplied him with many a joke. ' Yesterday I took a letter myself to the post-office, and was asked where it was meant to go to. From which I see that my writing is as often misunderstood as I am myself.' [7] It was the same twenty years before — ' this cursed writing that I cannot alter.' [8] Much of his difficulty probably arose from want of pens, which he often begs from Zmeskall and Breuning ; for some of his

[1] Ries, p. 94.   [2] Countess Gallenberg, in Thayer, ii. 172.   [3] Ries, p. 94.
[4] Moscheles, *Leben*, i. 17.   [5] Breuning, p. 44.   [6] Thayer, ii. 340.
[7] Letter to Zmeskall, Oct. 9, 1813.   [8] Letter to Simrock, Aug. 2, 1794.

MSS.[1] are as clear and flowing as those of Mozart, and there is a truly noble character in the writing of some of his letters, e.g. that to Mr. Broadwood (see p. 85, of which we give the signature.

Louis Van Beethoven

Notwithstanding his illegible hand Beethoven was a considerable letter writer. The two collections published by Nohl contain 721, and these are probably not more than half of those he wrote.[2] Not a large number when compared with those of Mendelssohn or even Mozart — both of whom died so early, —but large under all the circumstances. ' Good letters ' they cannot be called. They contain no descriptions or graces of style ; they are often clumsy and incorrect. But they are also often eminently interesting from being so brimfull of the writer's personality. They are all concerned with himself, his wants and wishes, his joys and sorrows ; sometimes when they speak of his deafness or his ill health, or confess his faults and appeal to the affection of his correspondent, they overflow with feeling and rise into an affecting eloquence, but always to the point. Of these, the letters to Wegeler and Eleonore von Breuning, and that to his brothers (called his ' Will '), are fine specimens. Many of those addressed to his nephew are inexpressibly touching. But his letters are often very short. Partly perhaps from his deafness, and partly from some idiosyncrasy, he would often write a note where a verbal question would seem to have been more convenient. One constant characteristic is the fun they contain. Swift himself never made worse puns with more pleasure, or devised queerer spelling[3] or more miserable rhymes, or bestowed more nicknames on his friends. Krumpholz is ' my fool ' ; he himself is ' the Generalissimus,' Haslinger ' the Adjutant,' Schindler ' the Samothracian ' and ' Papageno ' ; Schuppanzigh is ' Falstaff '; Bernard, ' Ber-

---

[1] For instance a MS. of the B flat Concerto, formerly in possession of Mr. Powell.
[2] Thayer's two vols. contain many not before published.
[3] See Nos. 298, 302 of Nohl's *Briefe*.

nardus non Sanctus'; Leidesdorf is 'Dorf des Leides';
Hoffmánn is adjured to be 'kein Hófmann,' Kuhlau is 'Kühl
nicht lau,' and so on. Nor are they always *comme il faut,* as
when he addresses Holz as 'lieber Holz vom Kreuze Christi,'
or apostrophises 'Monsieur Friederich, nommé Liederlich.'
Sometimes such names bite deeply: — his brother Johann is
the 'Braineater,' 'Pseudo-brother,' or 'Asinus,' and Caspar's
widow the 'Queen of Night.' No one is spared. A canon to
Count Moritz Lichnowsky runs 'Bester Herr Graf, du bist ein
Schaf.' The anecdote about his brother already alluded to is
a case in point.[1] Johann, who lived on his own property, called
on him on some *jour de fête,* and left his card 'Johann van
Beethoven, Gutsbesitzer' (land proprietor), which Beethoven
immediately returned after writing on the back 'L. van Beethoven, Hirnbesitzer' (brain proprietor). This fondness for
joking pervaded his talk also; he liked a home-thrust, and
delivered it with a loud roar of laughter. To tell the truth he
was fond of horse-play, and that not always in good taste. The
stories — some of them told by himself — of his throwing
books, plates, eggs, at the servants; of his pouring the dish of
stew over the head of the waiter who had served him wrongly;
of the wisp of goat's beard sent to the lady who asked him for
a lock of his hair — are all instances of it. No one had a
sharper eye or ear for a joke when it told on another. He
was never tired of retailing the delicious story of Simon the
Bohemian tenor who in singing the sentence 'Auf was Art
Elende' transformed it into 'Au! fwa! Sartellen Thee!'[2]
But it must be confessed that his ear and his enjoyment were
less keen when the joke was against himself. When at Berlin
in 1796 he interrupted Himmel in the middle of an improvisation to ask when he was going to begin in earnest. But when
Himmel, months afterwards, wrote to him that the latest
invention in Berlin was a lantern for the blind, Beethoven not
only with characteristic simplicity did not see the joke, but
when it was pointed out to him was furious, and would have
nothing more to do with his correspondent.

The simplicity which lay at the root of so many of his
characteristic traits, while it gave an extraordinary force and
freshness to much that he did and said, must often have been
very inconvenient to those who had intercourse with him.

[1] Schindler (1st ed.) 121.   [2] Thayer, ii. 227.

One of his most serious quarrels arose from his divulging the name of a very old and intimate friend who had cautioned him privately against one of his brothers. He could see no reason for secrecy; but it is easy to imagine the embarrassment which such disregard of the ordinary rules of life must have caused. Rochlitz describes the impression he received from him as that of a very able man reared on a desert island, and suddenly brought fresh into the world. One little trait from Breuning's recollections exemplifies this — that after walking in the rain he would enter the living room of the house and at once shake the water from his hat all over the furniture, regardless, or rather quite unaware, of the damage he was doing. His ways of eating in his later years became quite unbearable.

One fruitful source of difficulty in practical life was his lodgings. His changes of residence were innumerable during the first year or two of his life in Vienna; it is impossible to disentangle them. Shortly after his arrival the Lichnowskys took him into their house, and there for some years he had nominally a *pied à terre*; but with all the indulgence of the Prince and Princess the restraint of being forced to dress for dinner, of attending to definite hours and definite rules, was too much for him, and he appears very soon to have taken a lodging of his own in the town, which lodging he was constantly changing. In 1803, when an opera was contemplated, he had free quarters at the theatre, which came to an end when the house changed hands early in 1804. A few months later and he was again lodged in the theatre free. At Baron Pasqualati's house on the ramparts he had rooms — with a beautiful lookout [1] — which were usually kept for him, where he would take refuge when composing, and be denied to every one. But even with this he had a separate and fresh quarter nearly every winter.[2] In summer he hated the city, and usually followed the Vienna custom of leaving the hot streets for the delicious wooded environs of Hetzendorf, Heiligenstadt, or Döbling, at that time little villages absolutely in the country, or for Mödling or Baden, further off. To this he 'looked forward with the delight of a child. . . . No man on earth loves the country more. Woods, trees, and rocks give the response which man requires.' 'Every tree seems to say Holy,

---

[1] Thayer, ii. 258.   [2] See the list for 1822, 3, and 4, in Breuning, 43-45.

Holy.'[1]   Here, as already remarked, he was out of doors for hours together, wandering in the woods, or sitting in the fork of a favourite lime-tree in the Schönbrunn gardens[2] sketch-book in hand; here his inspiration flowed, and in such circumstances the 'Mount of Olives,' 'Fidelio,' the 'Eroica' Symphony, and the majority of his great works were sketched and re-sketched, and erased and rewritten, and by slow degrees brought far on to perfection.

His difficulties with his lodgings are not hard to understand; sometimes he quarrelled with them because the sun did not shine into the rooms, and he loved the light; sometimes the landlord interfered.   Like other men of genius whose appearance would seem to belie the fact, Beethoven was extremely fond of washing.[3]   He would pour water backwards and forwards over his hands for a long time together, and if at such times a musical thought struck him and he became absorbed, he would go on until the whole floor was swimming, and the water had found its way through the ceiling into the room beneath.   On one occasion he abandoned a lodging for which he had paid heavily in advance, because his landlord, Baron Pronay, insisted on taking off his hat to him whenever they met.   One of the most momentous of his changes was in 1804.   After he was turned out of his lodgings at the theatre Beethoven and Stephen Breuning inhabited two sets of rooms in a building called the *Rothes Haus*.   As each set was large enough for two, Beethoven soon moved into Breuning's rooms, but neglected to give the necessary notice to the landlord, and thus after a time found that he had both lodgings on his hands at once.   The result was a violent quarrel, which drove Beethoven off to Baden, and estranged the two friends for a time. We have Beethoven's version of the affair in two letters to Ries — July, and July 24, 1804 — angry implacable letters, but throwing a strong light on his character and circumstances, showing that it was not the loss of the money that provoked him, but an imputation of meanness; showing further that here, as so often elsewhere, his brother was his evil genius; and containing other highly interesting personal traits.

[1] Letter to Mme. von Drossdick, *Briefe*, No. 61; also to Archd. Rodolph, May 27, 1813, and to Hauschka, No. 210. Nohl, *Leben*, ii. 573.
[2] Thayer, ii. 278.
[3] In a letter to Countess Erdödy accepting an invitation he stipulates for ' a little bath room.'

Besides the difficulties of the apartments there were those with servants. A man whose principles were so severe as to make him say of a servant who had told a falsehood that she was not pure at heart, and therefore could not make good soup; [1] who punished his cook for the staleness of the eggs by throwing the whole batch at her one by one, and who distrusted the expenditure of every halfpenny — must have had much to contend with in his kitchen. The books give full details on this subject, which need not be repeated, and indeed are more unpleasant to contemplate than many other drawbacks and distresses of the life of this great man.

In the earlier part of his career money was no object to him, and he speaks as if his purse were always open to his friends. [2] But after the charge of his nephew was thrust upon his hands a great change in this, as in other respects, came over him. After 1813 complaints of want of money abound in his letters, and he resorted to all possible means of obtaining it. The sum which he had been enabled to invest after the congress he considered as put by for his nephew, and therefore not to be touched, and he succeeded in maintaining it till his death.

It is hard to arrive at any certain conclusion on the nature and progress of Beethoven's deafness, owing to the vagueness of the information. Difficulty of hearing appears first to have shown itself about 1798 in singing and buzzing in his ears, loss of power to distinguish words, though he could hear the tones of voice, and great dislike to sudden loud noise. It was even then a subject of the greatest pain to his sensitive nature; [3] like Byron with his club-foot he lived in morbid dread of his infirmity being observed, a temper which naturally often kept him silent; and when a few years later [2] he found himself unable to hear the pipe of a peasant playing at a short distance in the open air, it threw him into the deepest melancholy, and evoked the well-known letter to his brothers in 1802, which goes by the name of his Will. Still many of the anecdotes of his behaviour in society show that during the early years of the century his deafness was but partial; and Ries, intimate as he was with his master, admits that he did not know it till told by S. Breuning. [4] It is obvious from Schindler's statement that

---

[1] See Nohl, *Leben*, iii. 841.   [2] Letter to Wegeler, June 29, 1800.
[3] *Letter to Amenda* (1800); Wegeler, June 29, Nov. 16 (1801). Ries, p. 98.
[4] Ries, p. 98.

he must have been able to hear the yellowhammers in the
trees above him when he was composing the Pastoral Symphony in 1807 and 1808. A few facts may be mentioned
bearing on the progress of the malady. In 1805 he was able
to judge severely of the *nuances* in the rehearsal of his opera.
In 1807, 1809, 1813 he conducted performances of his own
works. In 1814 he played his B flat trio — his last appearance
in public in concerted music. From 1816 to 1818 he used an
ear trumpet.[1] At the opening of the Josephstadt Theatre in
1822, he conducted the performance — nearly to ruin it is true,
but at the same time he was able to detect that the soprano
was not singing in time, and to give her the necessary advice.
A subsequent attempt (in November 1822) to conduct ' Fidelio '
led to his having to quit the orchestra, when his mortification
was so great that Schindler treats the occurrence as an epoch
in his life.[2] At this time the hearing of the right ear was almost
completely gone; what he did hear — amongst other things a
musical box[3] playing the trio in ' Fidelio,' and Cherubini's
overture to ' Medea ' — was with the left ear only. After this
he conducted no more, though he stood in the orchestra at
the performance of the Choral Symphony, and had to be
turned round that he might see the applause which his music
was evoking. From this to the end all communication with
him was carried on by writing, for which purpose he always
had a book of rough paper, with a stout pencil, at hand.

The connexion between this cruel malady and the low tone
of his general health was closer than is generally supposed.
The *post mortem* examination showed that the liver was shrunk
to half its proper size, and was hard and tough like leather,
with numerous nodules the size of a bean woven into its texture
and appearing on its surface. There were also marks of
ulceration of the pharynx, about the tonsils and Eustachian
tubes. The arteries of the ears were athrumatous [athero-
matous], and the auditory nerves — especially that of the right
ear — were degenerated and to all appearance paralysed. The
whole of these appearances are most probably the result of
syphilitic affections at an early period of his life.[4] The pains

[1] Schindler, ii. 170.   [2] Ibid. 11.   [3] Ibid. 9.
[4] This diagnosis, which I owe to the kindness of my friend Dr. Lauder Brunton,
is confirmed by the existence of two prescriptions, of which, since the passage in
the text was written, I have been told by Mr. Thayer, who heard of them from
Dr. Bartolini.

in the head, indigestion, colic, and jaundice, of which he
frequently complains, and the deep depression which gives
the key to so many of his letters, would all follow naturally
from the chronic inflammation and atrophy implied by the
state of the liver, and the digestive derangements to which
it would give rise, aggravated by the careless way in which
he lived, and by the bad food, hastily devoured, at irregular
intervals, in which he too often indulged. His splendid
constitution and his extreme fondness for the open air must
have been of great assistance to him. How thoroughly he
enjoyed the country we have already seen, for, like Mendelssohn, he was a great walker, and in Vienna no day, however
busy or however wet, passed without its ' constitutional ' — a
walk, or rather run, twice round the ramparts, a part of the
city long since obliterated ; or farther into the environs.

Beethoven was an early riser, and from the time he left his
bed till dinner — which in those days was taken at, or shortly
after, noon — the day was devoted to completing at the piano
and writing down the compositions which he had previously
conceived and elaborated in his sketch-books, or in his head.
At such times the noise which he made playing and roaring
was something tremendous. He hated interruption while thus
engaged, and would do and say the most horribly rude things
if disturbed. Dinner — when he remembered it — he took
sometimes in his own room, sometimes at an eating-house,
latterly at the house of his friends the Breunings ; and no
sooner was this over than he started on his walk. He was
fond of making appointments to meet on the glacis. The
evening was spent at the theatre or in society. He went nowhere without his sketch-books, and indeed these seem to
distinguish him from other composers almost as much as his
music does. They are perhaps the most remarkable relic that
any artist or literary man has left behind him. They afford
us the most precious insight into Beethoven's method of composition. They not only show — what we know from his own
admission — that he was in the habit of working at three, and
even four, things at once,[1] but without them we should never
realise how extremely slow and tentative he was in composing.
Audacious and impassioned beyond every one in extemporising, the moment he takes his pen in hand he becomes the

[1] Letter to Wegeler, June, 1800.

most cautious and hesitating of men.   It would almost seem
as if this great genius never saw his work as a whole until it
actually approached completion.   It grew like a plant or tree,
and one thing produced another.[1]   There was nothing sudden
or electric about it, all was gradual and organic, as slow as a
work of nature and as permanent.   One is prompted to believe,
not that he had the idea first and then expressed it, but that
it often came in the process of finding the expression.   There
is hardly a bar in his music of which it may not be said with
confidence that it has been rewritten a dozen times.   Of the
air 'O Hoffnung' in 'Fidelio' the sketch-books show 18 attempts,
and of the concluding chorus 10.   Of many of the brightest
gems of the opera, says Thayer, the first ideas are so trivial that
it would be impossible to admit that they were Beethoven's if
they were not in his own handwriting.   And so it is with all
his works.   It is quite astonishing to find the length of time
during which some of his best-known instrumental melodies
remained in his thoughts till they were finally used, or the
crude vague commonplace shape in which they were first
written down.   The more they are elaborated the more fresh
and spontaneous do they become.

To quote but two instances out of many.   The theme of
the Andante in the C minor Symphony, completed in 1808, is
first found in a sketch-book of the year 1800, mixed with
memoranda for the 6 Quartets, and in the following form : [2] —

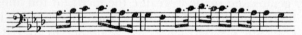

Another is the first subject of the Allegro in the Sonata op. 106.
It first appears [3] thus —

then, with a slight advance,

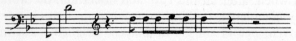

---

[1] Thus the 3-bar rhythm of the Scherzo of the 9th Symphony gradually came
as he wrote and re-wrote a fugue subject apparently destined for a very different
work. Nottebohm, *N. B.* XXIII.
[2] First given by Thayer, *Chron. Verzeichniss*, No. 140. For further information
on this interesting subject see Nottebohm's *Ein Skizzenbuch Beethoven's*.
[3] Nottebohm, *N. B.* VII.

next

then

and finally, after several pages more of writing and rewriting, it assumes its present incisive and spontaneous shape.

In those books every thought that occurred to him was written down at the moment; he even kept one by his bedside for use in the night.[1] Abroad or at home it was all the same, only out of doors he made his notes in pencil, and inked them over on his return to the house. It is as if he had no reliance whatever on his memory. He began the practice as a boy [2] and maintained it to the last. In the sale catalogue of his effects more than 50 of such books are included. Many of them have been parted and dispersed, but some remain intact. They are usually of large coarse music paper, oblong, 200 or even more pages, 16 staves to the page, and are covered from beginning to end, often over the margin as well, with close crowded writing. There is something very affecting in the sight of these books,[3] and in being thus brought so close to this mighty genius and made to realise the incessant toil and pains which he bestowed on all his works, small and great. In this he agreed with Goethe, who says, à propos to his 'Ballad,' 'Whole years of reflection are comprised in it, and I made three or four trials before I could bring it to its present shape.' [4] The sketch-books also show how immense was the quantity of his ideas. 'Had he,' says Nottebohm,[5] 'carried out all the symphonies which are begun in these books we should have at least fifty.'

But when, after all this care and hesitation, the works were actually completed, nothing external made him change them. No convenience of singers or players weighed for a moment against the integrity of his finished composition. When

[1] Breuning, 98.   [2] Letter, July 23, 1815.
[3] There is one in the MS. department of the British Museum.
[4] *Conversations with Eckermann*, Oxenford's translation, ii. 112.
[5] *Neue Beethoveniana*, XIII.

Sonntag [Sontag] and Ungher [Unger] protested against the
unsingable passages in the Ninth Symphony, and besought
him to bring them within the compass of their voices, ' Nein
und immer nein,' was the dry answer.[1] When Kraft, the cellist
in the Schuppanzigh Quartet, complained that a passage ' did
not lie within his hand,' the answer was ' it must lie ' — ' muss
liegen.' [2]

A man to whom his art was so emphatically the business
of his life, and who was so insatiable in his standard of perfection, must have been always advancing.   To him more
than to any other musician may be applied Goethe's words
on Schiller : — ' Every week he altered and grew more complete, and every time I saw him he appeared to me to have
advanced since the last in knowledge, learning, and judgment.' [3]
It is no wonder then that he did not care for his early works,
and would sometimes even have destroyed ' Adelaide,' [4] the
Septet, and others of his youthful pieces, if he could.   Towards
the end of his life he heard a friend practising his 32 Variations in C minor.[5]   After listening for some time he said
' Whose is that? '   ' Yours,' was the answer.   ' Mine?   That
piece of folly mine? ' was his retort ; ' Oh, Beethoven, what an
ass you were in those days ! '   A good deal of this may have
been momentary caprice ; but making all allowance, one can
imagine his feelings at the close of his life on receiving a commission from an English amateur for a ' Symphony in the
style of his Second or of his Septet,' or on reading the contemporary effusions on the ' Eroica ' and C minor Symphonies, in
which his honest and well-meaning critics [6] entreated him to
return to the clearness and conciseness of his early works.

Hardly less characteristic than the sketch-books are his
diaries or journals, in which the most passionate and personal
reflections, resolutions, prayers, aspirations, complaints, are
mixed up with memorandums of expenses and household
matters, notes about his music, rules for his conduct, quotations
from books, and every other conceivable kind of entry.   These
books have been torn up and dispersed as autographs ; but a
copy of one extending from 1812 to 1818 fortunately exists,
and has been edited with copious notes and elucidations by

[1] Schindler, p. 154.   [2] Thayer, ii. 53.   [3] Eckermann, Jan. 18, 1825.
[4] Letter to Matthison [Matthisson], Aug. 4, 1800.   Czerny, in Thayer, ii. 99 ;
also 186.
[5] Thayer, ii. 324.   [6] See the quotations in Thayer, ii. 275.

Herr Nohl, the whole throwing great light on that unfortunate period of his life. A ray of light is also occasionally to be gained from the conversation-books already mentioned, some of which have been preserved, though as Beethoven's answers were usually spoken this source is necessarily imperfect.

If now we ask what correspondence there is between the traits and characteristics thus imperfectly sketched and Beethoven's music, it must be confessed that the question is a difficult one to answer. In one point alone the parallel is obvious — namely, the humour, which is equally salient in both. In the finale of the 7th and 8th Symphonies there are passages which are the exact counterparts of the rough jokes and horse-play of which we have already seen some instances. In these we almost hear his loud laugh. The Scherzo of Symphony No. 2, where the F♯ chord is so suddenly taken and so forcibly held, might almost be a picture of the unfortunate *Kellner* forced to stand still while the dish of stew was poured over his head. The bassoons in the opening and closing movements of No. 8 are inimitably humorous ; and so on in many other instances which will occur to every one. But when we leave humour and go to other points, where in the life shall we look for the grandeur and beauty which distinguish the music? Neither in letters nor anecdotes do we find anything answering to the serene beauty of the slow movements (No. 2, No. 4, No. 9), or the mystic tone of such passages as those of the horns at the end of the Trio of the ' Eroica ' or of certain phrases in the finale of the Choral Fantasia and of the Choral Symphony, which lift one so strangely out of time into eternity. These must represent a state of mental absorption when all heaven was before his eyes, and in which he retired within himself far beyond the reach of outward things, save his own divine power of expression.

Equally difficult is it to see anything in Beethoven's life answering to the sustained nobility and dignity of his first movements, or of such a piece as the ' Overture to Leonora, No. 3.' And then if we come to the most individual and characteristic part of all Beethoven's artistic self, the process by which his music was built up — the extraordinary caution which actuated him throughout, the hesitation, the delays, the incessant modification of his thoughts, the rejection of the first impressions — of the second — of the third — in favour of something only gradually attained to, the entire subordination of his own peculiarities to the constant thought of his audience, and of what would endure rather than what pleased him at first — to all this there is surely nothing at all corresponding in his life, where his habit was emphatically a word and a blow. The fact is that, like all musicians, only in a greater degree than any other, in speech Beethoven was dumb, and often had no words for his deepest and most characteristic feelings. The musician has less connexion with the outside world than any other artist, and has to turn inward and seek his art in the deepest recesses of his being only.[1] This must naturally make him less disposed to communicate with others by the ordinary channels of speech and action, and will account for much of the irritability and uncertainty which often characterise his dealings with his fellow men. But the feelings are there, and if we look closely enough into the life we shall be able to detect their existence often where we least expect it. In Beethoven, for example, what was his treatment of his nephew — the strong devotion which seized him directly after his brother's death, and drove him to sacrifice the habits of a lifetime ; his inexhaustible forgiveness, his yearning tenderness — what are these, if properly interpreted, but a dumb way of expressing that noble temper which, when uttered in his own natural musical language, helps to make the first movement of the ' Eroica ' so lofty, so dignified, and so impressive?

We must now return to the chronicle of the events of Beethoven's life.

His position at Bonn as organist and pianist to the Emperor's uncle [brother], his friendship with Count Waldstein, who was closely related to some of the best families in Vienna, and his connexion with Haydn, were all circumstances sure to secure him good introductions. The moment was a favourable one, as since Mozart's death, a twelvemonth before, there had been no player to take his place ; and it was as a player that Beethoven was first known. It is pleasant to know that his show piece, with which he took the Vienna connoisseurs by storm, was his Variations on ' Venni [Vieni] amore,' which we have already mentioned as composed before he left Bonn. Public concerts in our sense of the word there were few, but a player had every opportunity at the musical parties of the

[1] Goethe, *Wilhelm Meisters Wanderjahre*, Bk. ii. chap. 9.

nobility, who maintained large orchestras of the best quality, and whose music meetings differed from public concerts chiefly in the fact that the audience were better educated, and were all invited guests. Prince Lichnowsky and Baron van Swieten appear to have been the first to secure Beethoven, the former for his regular Friday morning chamber performances, the latter for soirées, when he had either ' to bring his night-cap in his pocket ' or else to stay after the other guests had gone, and send his host to bed with half-a-dozen of Bach's fugues as an *Abendsegen*. The acquaintance probably began shortly after Beethoven's arrival; and after a twelvemonth of unpleasant experience in the Vienna lodgings, the Prince induced him to accept apartments in his house. His wife was a Princess of Thun, famous for her beauty and her goodness; he himself had been a pupil of Mozart; and both were known as the best amateur musicians of Vienna. Beethoven was poor enough to be tempted by such hospitality, but it was an absurd arrangement, and he very soon infringed it by disregarding the Prince's hours, often dining at the *Gasthof*, having a lodging of his own elsewhere, and other acts of independence. Here however he was frequently heard, and thus became rapidly known in the most musical circles, and Ries's anecdotes show (after making allowance for the inaccuracy of a man who writes 30 years after the events) how widely he was invited, how completely at his ease he was, and how entirely his eccentricities were condoned for the sake of his playing and his great qualities. Not that we are to suppose that Beethoven gave undue time to society. He was too hard a worker for that. His lessons with Haydn and Albrechtsberger (from the latter he had three a week) were alone enough to occupy a great deal of time, and his own studies in counterpoint exist to show that he did not confine himself to the mere tasks that were set him. Moreover his lessons with Albrechtsberger contain sketches for various compositions, such as ' Adelaide,' a part of one of the Trios (op. 1), and the Symphony in C,[1] all showing how eager he was to be something more than a mere player or even a splendid improviser. These sketches afford an early instance of his habit of working at several compositions at one and the same time. The date of one of them, about February 1795, seems to imply either that the story — grounded on Ries's statement — that

---

[1] See Nottebohm's *Beethoven's Studien*, i. 202.

the Trios were in MS. for many months [1] before they were
printed is inaccurate, or, more probably, that Beethoven rewrote one of the movements very shortly before delivering the
work to the publisher, which he did on May 19. In this case
it would show the wisdom of the plan which he adopted with
most of his early works,[2] of keeping them in MS. for some time
and playing them frequently, so as to test their quality and
their effect on the hearers, a practice very consistent with his
habitual caution and fastidiousness in relation to his music.
At any rate the Trios were published first to the subscribers,
by July 1795, and then, on October 21, to the public. They
were shortly followed by a work of equal importance, the first
three Pianoforte Sonatas,[3] which were first played by their
author at one of the Prince's Fridays in presence of Haydn,
and published on the 9th of the following March as op. 2,
dedicated to him. He had not then written a string quartet,
and at this concert Count Appony [4] proposed to Beethoven to
compose one, offering him his own terms, and refusing to make
any conditions beyond the single one that the quartet should
be written — a pleasant testimony to the enthusiasm excited
by the new sonatas, and to the generosity of an Austrian
[Hungarian] nobleman. In addition to the Trios, the publications of his three first years in Vienna include the 12 Variations
on ' Se vuol ballare ' (July 1793) ; the 13 on ' Es war einmal '
(early in 1794) ; the 8 for four hands on Count Waldstein's theme
(1794); and 9 for piano solo on 'Quant' è più bello'[5] (December
30, 1795). The compositions are more numerous, and besides
the Trios and Sonatas (op. 1 and 2) include a Trio for oboes
and corno inglese (op. 87), which remained unpublished till
1806 ; a Rondo in G for pianoforte and violin,[6] which he sent
to Eleonore von Breuning, and which remained unpublished
till 1808 ; the two Concertos for piano and orchestra, of which
' No. 2 ' is the earlier, and ' No. 1 ' was composed before March
29, 1795 ; songs, ' Adelaide,' and ' Opferlied,'[7] both to Matthi-

---

[1] Haydn left Vienna for London on Jan. 19, 1794, and did not return till Sept.
1795, when the Trios had been printed and in the suscribers' hands for some weeks.
If he therefore advised Beethoven not to publish the third it must have been
before he left Vienna. Ries's statement is so explicit that the alternative suggested in the text seems the only escape from the difficulty.

[2] He maintained this plan till 1812, when he informs Varenna that he never
publishes until a year after composition. Letter Feb. 8, 1812.

[3] In the Adagio of No. 1 the corresponding movement in No. 3 of the early
Piano Quartets is partially adopted—a rare thing with Beethoven.

[4] Wegeler, p. 29.   [5] B. & H. 167.   [6] Ibid. 102.   [7] Ibid. 233.

son's [Matthisson's] words, and ' Seufzer eines Ungeliebten,' [1] all probably composed in 1795; canon ' Im Arm der Liebe,' [2] an exercise with Albrechtsberger; 12 Minuets and 12 ' Deutsche Tänze ' for orchestra,[3] composed November 1795.

On March 29, 1795, Beethoven made his first appearance before the outside public at the annual concert in the Burg Theatre, for the widows' fund of the Artists' Society. He played his Concerto in C major.[4] The piece had probably been suggested by Salieri, and with it Beethoven began a practice which he more than once followed when the work was bespoken — of only just finishing the composition in time; the Rondo was written on the afternoon of the last day but one, during a fit of colic. At the rehearsal, the piano being half a note too flat, Beethoven played in C♯.[5] Two days after he appeared again at the same theatre at a performance for the benefit of Mozart's widow, playing a concerto of Mozart's between the acts of the ' Clemenza di Tito.' [6] Later in the year he assisted another benevolent object by writing [the above-mentioned] 12 minuets and 12 waltzes for orchestra for the ball of the ' Gesellschaft der bildenden Künstler ' on the 22nd November. He was evidently a favourite with the Artists, who advertise ' the master-hand of Herr Ludwig van Beethoven,' while they mention Süssmayer [Süssmayr] — who also contributed music — without an extra word. These dances, after publication, remained in favour for two more seasons, which is mentioned as a great exception to rule. On December 18 he again appeared in public at a concert of Haydn's in the ' little Redoutensaal,' playing a concerto of his own — but whether the same as before is not stated. The dedication of the Sonatas and his co-operation at Haydn's concert allow us to hope that the ill-feeling already alluded to had vanished. So closed the year 1795. Bonn was at this time in the hands of the Republican army, and Beethoven's brother the Apotheker was serving as a ' pharmacien de 3ème classe.'

1796 was a year of wandering. Haydn and he appeared together at a second concert on January 10.[7] In the interval Beethoven went perhaps to Prague, certainly to Nuremberg. On February 19 he was in Prague again, where he composed

---

[1] B. & H. 253.   [2] Ibid. 256.   [3] Ibid. 16, 17.   [4] Thayer, i. 294.
[5] Wegeler, p. 36.   [6] Wlassack, *Chronik des Hofburgtheaters*, p. 98.
[7] Hanslick, *Concertwesen in Wien*, p. 105.

the Scena [1] 'Ah! perfido' for Madame Duschek [Dušek], the friend of Mozart. From thence he travelled to Berlin, played at court, amongst other things the two cello sonatas op. 5, probably composed for the occasion, and received from the King a box of louis d'or, which he was proud of showing as 'no ordinary box, but one of the kind usually presented to ambassadors.' At Berlin his time was passed pleasantly enough with Himmel the composer and Prince Louis Ferdinand. He went two or three times to the Singakademie,[2] heard the choir sing Fasch's psalms, and extemporised to them on themes from those now forgotten compositions. In July the Court left Berlin, and Beethoven probably departed also; but we lose sight of him till November 15, the date of a 'farewell-song' [3] addressed to the volunteers on their leaving Vienna to take part in the universal military movement provoked by Napoleon's campaigns in Italy. The war was driving all Germans home, and amongst others Beethoven's old colleagues the two Rombergs passed through Vienna from Italy, and he played for them at a concert.

The publications of 1796 consist of the 3 Piano Sonatas, op. 2 (March 9); 12 Variations on a minuet *à la Vigano* [4] [*Viganò*] (February), and 6 on 'Nel cor più [non mi] sento' [5] (March 23); 6 Minuets (also in March) for piano, originally written for orchestra — perhaps the result of his success with the 'Bildende Künstler.' [6] Of the compositions of the year, besides those already named, may be mentioned as probable the Piano Sonata in G,[7] the second of the two small ones (op. 49); and another of the same rank in C [8] for Eleonore von Breuning; we may also ascribe to the latter part of this year the Duet Sonata (op. 6); 12 Variations on a Russian dance; [9] the String Quintet (op. 4), arranged from an octet for wind instruments, very probably of his pre-Vienna time. The Russian Variations were written for the Countess Browne, wife of an officer in the Russian service, and were acknowledged by the gift of the horse which we have already mentioned as affording an instance of Beethoven's absence of mind. But the

[1] 'Une grande Scène mise en musique, par L. v. Beethoven, à Prague, 1796,' is Beethoven's own title (Nottebohm, *Beethoveniana*, p. 1, note).

[2] Fasch's Journal, Thayer ii. 13. Strange that Zelter (*Corr. with Goethe*) should not refer to this visit. Mme. von Voss's Journal, too, is blank during these very months.

[3] B. & H. 230. [4] Ibid. 169. [5] Ibid. 168. [6] Ibid. 194.

[7] Nottebohm, *Catalogue*, p. 205. [8] B. & H. 159. [9] Ibid. 170.

winter months must have been occupied by a more serious work
than variations — the Quintet for piano and wind (op. 16),[1]
which Beethoven produced at a concert of Schuppanzigh's on
April 6, 1797, and which is almost like a challenge to Mozart
on his own ground, and the not less important and far more
original Pianoforte Sonata in E♭ (op. 7). This great work,
' quite novel, and wholly peculiar to its author, the origin of
which can be traced to no previous creation, and which proclaimed his originality so that it could never afterwards be
disputed,' was published on October 7, 1797, but must have
been often played before that date. The sketches for the 3
Sonatas, op. 10, are placed by Nottebohm in this period, with
the Variations on the ' Une fièvre brûlante.' The three String
Trios, op. 9, also probably occupied him during some part of
the year. The Serenade Trio, op. 8, though published in 1797,
more probably belongs with op. 3 to the Bonn date. The
Variations on ' See the conquering hero ' for pianoforte and
cello, dedicated to the Princess Lichnowsky,[2] were published
during this year, and were probably written at the time.

Vienna was full of patriotism in the spring of 1797. Haydn's
' Emperor's Hymn ' had been sung in the theatre for the first
time on February 12,[3] and Beethoven wrote a second military
Lied, ' Ein grosses deutsches Volk sind wir,' [4] to Friedelberg's
words, which is dated April 14, but did not prove more successful than his former one. In May he writes to Wegeler in terms
which show that with publications or lessons his pecuniary
position is improving ; but from that time till Oct. 1 — the
date of an affectionate entry in Lenz von Breuning's album —
we hear nothing whatever of him. A severe illness has to
be accounted for,[5] and this is probably the time at which it
happened. In November occurred the annual ball of the
' Bildende Künstler,' and his dances were again played for
the third time ; the seven Ländler,[6] ascribed to this year,
were not improbably written for the same ball. His only other
publications of 1797 not yet mentioned are the Pianoforte
Rondo in C major, which many years afterwards received the
opus number 51, and last, but not least, ' Adelaide.' Some

---

[1] An unusual combination, which may explain why so fine a work remained
in MS. till 1801.
[2] B. & H. 110.
[3] Schmid, *Joseph Haydn und N. Zingarelli*, etc. (Vienna, 1847), p. 8.
[4] B. & H. 231.   [5] Thayer, ii. 18.   [6] B. & H. 198.

variations [1] for 2 oboes and corno inglese on ' La [Là] ci
darem ' were played on December 23 at a concert for the
Widows and Orphans Fund, but are still in MS.

The chief event of 1798 is one which was to bear fruit later
— Beethoven's introduction to Bernadotte the French ambassador, by whom the idea of the ' Eroica ' Symphony is said [2]
to have been first suggested to him.   Bernadotte was a person
of culture, and having R. Kreutzer, the violin-player, as a
member of his establishment may be presumed to have cared
for music.   Beethoven, who professed himself an admirer of
Bonaparte, frequented the ambassador's levees ; and there is
ground for believing that they were to a certain extent intimate.
On April 2 Beethoven played his Piano Quintet (op. 16) at the
concert for the Widows and Orphans Fund.   The publications
of this year show that the connexion with the von Brownes
indicated by the dedication of the Russian Variations was
kept up and even strengthened ; the 3 String Trios, op. 9
(published July 21), are dedicated to the Count, and the 3
Sonatas, op. 10 (subscribed July 7, published Sept. 26), to the
Countess.   The 3rd of these sonatas forms a landmark in
Beethoven's progress of equal significance with op. 7.   The
letter [3] which he appended to the Trios speaks of ' munificence
at once delicate and liberal ' ; and it is obvious that some
extraordinary liberality must have occurred to draw forth such
an expression as ' the first Mæcenas of his muse ' in reference
to any one but Prince Lichnowsky.   In other respects the letter
is interesting.   It makes music depend less on ' the inspiration
of genius ' than on ' the desire to do one's utmost,' and implies
that the Trios were the best music he had yet composed.   The
Trio for piano, clarinet, and cello (op. 11), dedicated to the
mother of Princess Lichnowsky, was published on October 3.
This is the composition which brought Steibelt and Beethoven
into collision, to the sad discomfiture of the former.[4]   Steibelt
had shown him studied neglect till they met at Count Fries's,
at the first performance of this Trio, and he then treated him
quite *de haut en bas*.   A week later they met again, when Steibelt
produced a new quintet and extemporised on the theme of

---

[1] Not the Trio, op. 87 (Nottebohm, *Neue Beethoveniana*).
[2] By Schindler, on the statement of Beethoven himself and others.
[3] See Thayer, ii. 33, and Nottebohm's Catalogue, op. 9.   Why are not such
interesting matters as this Letter or the Dedications reprinted in all cases with
Beethoven's works ?   [4] Ries, p. 81.

Beethoven's Finale — an air from Weigl's ' Amor marinaro.'
Beethoven's blood was now fairly up ; taking the cello part of
Steibelt's quintet he placed it upside down before him, and
making a theme out of it played with such effect as to drive
Steibelt from the room. Possibly this fracas may account for
Beethoven's known dissatisfaction with the Finale.[1] The other
publications of 1798 are variations : 12 for piano and cello on
an air in the ' Zauberflöte,' afterwards numbered as op. 66 ;
6, easy,[2] for piano or harp, possibly written for some lady
friend, and published by his old ally Simrock at Bonn ; and
8 on ' Une fièvre brûlante.'[3]

This year he again visited Prague, and performed at two
public concerts, making an immense impression.[4] After his
return, on October 27, he played one of his two concertos at
the Theatre *auf den [der] Wieden*. Wölfl [Woelfl] was in Vienna
during this year, and in him Beethoven encountered for the first
time a rival worthy of his steel. They seem to have met often
at Count Wetzlar's (Wölfl's friend), and to have made a great
deal of music together, and always in a pleasant way.[5] It must
have been wonderful to hear them, each excited by the other,
playing their finest, extemporising alternately and together
(like Mendelssohn and Moscheles), and making all the fun
that two such men at such an age and in capital company
would be sure to make. Wölfl commemorated their meeting
by dedicating three sonatas to Beethoven, but met with no
response.

But Beethoven did not allow pleasure to interfere with
business, as the publications of the following year fully show.
The 3 Sonatas for piano and violin, dedicated to Salieri (op.
12), published on January 12, 1799, though possibly composed
earlier, must at any rate have occupied him in correction during
the winter. The little Sonata in G minor (op. 49, No. 1) is a
child of this time, and is immediately followed in the sketch-
books by the ' Grande Sonate pathétique ' — Beethoven's own
title — (op. 13), dedicated to Prince Lichnowsky, as if to make
up for the little slight contained in the reference to Count
Browne as his ' first Mæcenas.' The well-known Rondo to
the Sonata appears to have been originally intended for the
third of the String Trios.[6] Of the origin of the 2 Sonatas,

[1] Thayer, ii. 32, note.   [2] B. & H. 176.   [3] Ibid. 171.
[4] See Tomaschek's interesting account in Thayer, ii. 29.
[5] See Seyfried, *Notizen*, 6.   [6] Nottebohm, *N. B.* No. XX.

op. 14 (published December 21), little is known. The sketches for the first of the two are coincident in time with those for the Concerto in B♭, which was completed in 1794 [1795],[1] and there is ground for believing that it was originally conceived as a string quartet, into which indeed Beethoven converted it a few years after. The second is probably much later, and is specially interesting from the fact that Beethoven explained it [2] to be a dialogue between two lovers, he entreating and she resisting. The Sonatas are dedicated to the Baroness Braun.

The other publications of 1799 are variations: 10 on Salieri's ' La Stessa '; 7 on Winter's ' Kind, willst du '; and 8 on Süssmayer's ' Tändeln.' [3] A comparison of the dates of publication with those of the appearance of the operas from which the themes are taken, shows that two of these were written shortly before publication.

Beethoven was now about to attack music of larger dimensions than before. His six String Quartets, the Septet, the 1st Symphony, and the ' Mount of Olives,' are fast approaching, and must all have occupied him more or less during the last year of the century. In fact the sketches for the three first of the Quartets (first in date of composition), Nos. 5, 1, 6, are positively assigned to this year, though there is evidence that the earliest of the three had been begun as far back as 1794 or 1795.[4] And though sketches of the Septet have not yet been made public, yet it is contrary to all Beethoven's habits in the case of so important a piece, and apparently quite spontaneously undertaken, that he should not have been at work at it for a long while before its production. The same with regard to the 1st Symphony. Both were produced on April 2, 1800. Traces of the Symphony, or of a previous one in the same key,[5] are found as early as the beginning of 1795, and there is no doubt that two such experiments in a new field must have occupied much time and labour. Besides these he was working on a very important new sonata in B♭ (op. 22).

The few recorded events of 1800 are all closely connected with music. On Wednesday, April 2, Beethoven gave the first concert which he had attempted in Vienna for his own benefit. It took place at the Burg Theatre, which was given him for

---

[1] Ibid. *N. B.* No. II.
[2] Schindler, on Beethoven's authority, *Biographie* (1840), p. 224, Moscheles' ed. ii. 124.   [3] B. & H. 172, 173, 174.
[4] Nottebohm, *N. B.* No. XVI.   [5] Ibid. No. XIX.

the occasion, at 7 [6.30] p.m., and the programme was as
follows : — 1. Symphony, Mozart. 2. Air from The Creation.
3. A grand Pianoforte Concerto, ' played and composed ' by
Beethoven. 4. The Septet. 5. Duet from The Creation. 6.
Improvisation by Beethoven on Haydn's Emperor's Hymn.
7. Symphony, No. 1. The Concerto was doubtless one of the
two already known — the Septet had been previously performed at Prince Schwarzenberg's,[1] had pleased immensely,
and Beethoven was evidently proud of it. ' It is my Creation,'
said he — let us hope not in Haydn's presence. He had not
forgotten Bonn, and the theme of the variations is said by
Czerny[2] to be a Rhine *Volkslied*. The work was dedicated in
advance to the Empress, and though not published for some
time, became rapidly popular. So much for the compositions,
but the performance appears from the report in the Leipzig
paper[3] to have been shameful ; the band disliked Wranitzky
the conductor, and vented their dislike on the music. In
addition to this it appears that the rehearsal, if it took place
at all, was a very imperfect one. A reference in one of Beethoven's letters (April 22, 1801) shows that it was his custom
not to write in the piano part into his concertos, and therefore
to play them from memory.

On the 18th of the same month Beethoven appeared again
at the concert of Punto the horn-player, with a sonata for horn
and piano, composed for the occasion. This he had naturally
not been able to touch while preparing for his own concert,
and in fact it was written down on the day before the performance.[4] Here again there cannot have been much chance
of rehearsal. But with two such players it was hardly needed ;
and so much did the sonata delight the hearers, that in defiance of a rule forbidding applause in the Court Theatre the
whole work was unanimously encored. On the 27th, the anniversary of the day on which he first entered Bonn, Beethoven's
old master, the Elector, returned to the capital. In May
Steibelt made his appearance in Vienna from Prague, where
his *charlatanerie* and his real ability had gained him prodigious
financial success. We have already alluded to his conflict with
Beethoven. In Vienna he does not appear to have succeeded,
and in August he was again in Paris.

The announcement of Beethoven's benefit concert names

No. 241 'im tiefen Graben,' 3rd storey, as his residence. He had now left Prince Lichnowsky's, and he maintained this lodging for two years. In this year we hear for the first time of his going to the country for the autumn. He selected Unter-Döbling, a village two miles north of Vienna, and his lodging was part of the house occupied by the Grillparzer family. Madame Grillparzer long recollected his fury on discovering her listening to his playing outside the door, and the stern revenge he took.[1]

As regards publications 1800 is a blank, but composition went on with immense energy. If we throw back the Symphony and the Septet into 1797, we have still the Horn Sonata and the Piano Sonata in B♭ (op. 22) — a work of great moment — the six Quartets, the String Quintet in C, the Piano Concerto in C minor. Of all these very important works we have Beethoven's own mention in a letter of December 15, 1800, in addition to the evidence as to date afforded by the sketch-books.[2] And besides these we are bound to believe that the Ballet of Prometheus, performed March 28, 1801, occupied him at least during the latter portion of the year. An incident of this summer was Beethoven's letter to Matthison (Aug. 4) sending him his 'Adelaide,' a letter interesting for its courteous and genial tone, for its request for another poem, and for its confession that his early works had already begun to dissatisfy him. After his return to town occurred Czerny's introduction to him. Czerny, then a lad of just upon 10, became Beethoven's pupil in pianoforte playing, and has left a delightful account of his first interview, and of much which occurred after it.[3] Among the letters of this winter and the spring of 1801 are some to Hoffmeister, formerly a composer, and then a music-publisher in Leipzig, which ended in his publishing the Septet, the Symphony in C, the Piano Concerto in B♭, and the Sonata (op. 22) in the same key. The price given for these works was 20 ducats each, except the Concerto, which was 10. The ducat was equal to 10s. English. The Concerto is priced so low because 'it is by no means one of my best, any more than that I am about to publish in C major, because I reserve the

[1] Thayer, ii. 104.   [2] Ibid. ii. 115.
[3] Published by C. F. Pohl, *Jahres-Bericht des Conservatoriums der Gesellschaft der Musikfreunde in Wien*, 1870. Also Thayer, ii, 106. The drawback to this, and to so much of the information regarding Beethoven, is that it was not written till many years after the events it describes.

best for myself, for my journey ' [1] — a confession which proves that the Concerto in C minor was already in existence. The letters show keen sympathy with projects for the publication of Bach's works, and of Mozart's sonatas arranged as quartets.[2] They speak of his having been ill during the winter, but the vigorous tone of the expression shows that the illness had not affected his spirits. On January 30, 1801, he played his Horn Sonata a second time, with Punto, at a concert for the benefit of the soldiers wounded at Hohenlinden.

He was now immersed in all the worry of preparing for the production of his Ballet of Prometheus, which came out on March 28 at the Court (Burg) Theatre. Its great success is evident from the fact that it was immediately published in a popular form — Pianoforte Solo,[3] dedicated to Princess Lichnowsky — and that it had a run of 16 nights during 1801, and 13 during the following year. Apart from its individual merits the Prometheus music is historically interesting as containing a partial anticipation of the Storm in the Pastoral Symphony, and (in the Finale) an air which afterwards served for a Contretanz, for the theme of elaborate variations, and for the subject of the last movement of the ' Eroica ' Symphony. The Ballet gave occasion for an unfortunate little encounter between Beethoven and Haydn, evidently unintentional on Beethoven's part, but showing how naturally antagonistic the two men were. They met in the street the day after the first performance, ' I heard your new Ballet last night,' said Haydn, ' and it pleased me much.' ' *O lieber Papa*,' was the reply, ' you are too good : but it is no *Creation* by a long way.' This unnecessary allusion seems to have startled the old man, and after an instant's pause he said ' You are right : it is no *Creation*, and I hardly think it ever will be ! '

The success of ' Prometheus ' gave him time to breathe, and possibly also cash to spare : he changed his lodgings from the low-lying ' tiefen-Graben ' to the Sailer-stätte, a higher situation, with an extensive prospect over the ramparts.[4] For the summer of 1801 he took a lodging at Hetzendorf, on the

---

[1] Letter of Dec. 15, 1800.

[2] In curious contradiction to the strong expressions on the subject of arrangements in a subsequent letter, quoted by Thayer, ii. 183.

[3] Originally numbered op. 24, but when the Overture was issued in Parts it was numbered op. 43, and op. 24 was given to the Violin Sonata in F.

[4] Thayer, ii. 131.

south-west side of the city, attracted by the glades and shrub-
beries of Schönbrunn, outside which the village lies, and
perhaps by the fact that his old master the Elector was living
in retirement there. It was his practice during these country
visits to live as nearly as possible in entire seclusion, and to
elaborate and reduce into ultimate form and completeness the
ideas which had occurred to him during the early part of the
year, and with which his sketch-books were crowded. His
main occupation during this summer was ' The Mount of
Olives,' which Ries found far advanced when he arrived in
Vienna in 1800.[1] The words were by Huber,[2] and we have
Beethoven's own testimony [3] that they were written, with his
assistance, in 14 days. He was doubtless engaged at the same
time, after his manner, with other works, not inferior to that
oratorio in their several classes, which are known on various
grounds to have been composed during this year. These are
2 Violin Sonatas in A minor and F, dedicated to Count von
Fries — originally published together (October 28) as op. 23,
but now separated under independent nos. ; the String Quintet
in C (op. 29) ; and not less than four masterpieces for the piano
— the Grand Sonatas in A♭ (op. 26) and D (op. 28) ; the two
Sonatas entitled ' Quasi [una] Fantasia ' in E♭ and in C♯ minor
(op. 27) ; which, though not published till 1802, were all four
completed during this year. To each of them a word or two
is due. The Sonata in A♭ — dedicated, like those of op. 1
and 13, to his prime friend Prince Carl Lichnowsky — is
said [4] to owe its noble Funeral March to pique at the praises
on a march by no means worthy of them in Paer's ' Achille.'
That opera — produced at Vienna on the 6th June of this
year — is the same about which Paer used to tell a good story
of Beethoven, illustrating at once his sincerity and his terrible
want of manners. He was listening to the opera with its
composer, and after saying over and over again, ' O ! que
c'est beau,' ' O ! que c'est intéressant,' at last could contain
himself no longer, but burst out ' il faut que je compose cela.' [5]
The Grand Sonata in D received its title of ' Pastorale ' (more

[1] Thayer (ii. 160) has shown that Ries has mistaken the year, and did not
come to Vienna till 1801.
[2] Author of Winter's ' Unterbrochene Opferfest,' and other pieces.
[3] His letter of Jan. 23, 1824, printed by Pohl in *Die Gesellschaft der Musikfreunde* (Vienna, 1871), p. 57.
[4] Ries, p. 80.   [5] F. Hiller, in Thayer, ii. 134.

appropriate than such titles often are) from Cranz the publisher, of Hamburg. The Andante, by some thought inferior
to the rest of the Sonata, was Beethoven's peculiar favourite,
and very frequently played by him.[1] The flyleaf of the autograph of the work contains a humorous duet and chorus —
' the praise of the fat [one],' making fun of Schuppanzigh [2]
— ' Schuppanzigh ist ein Lump, ein Lump,' etc. The remaining two, qualified as ' Fantasia ' by their author, have had
very different fates. One, that in E♭, has always lived in the
shadow of its sister, and is comparatively little known. The
other, the so-called ' Moonlight Sonata,' [3] is as widely played
and as passionately loved as any of Beethoven's pianoforte
works. It is one of his most original productions. The dedication to the Countess Guicciardi, upon which so much romance
has been built, has had a colder light thrown on it by the lady
herself. ' Beethoven,' said she, ' gave me the Rondo in G, but
wanting to dedicate something to the Princess Lichnowsky
he took the Rondo away, and gave me the Sonata in C♯
minor instead.' [4]

Meantime his deafness, which began with violent noise in
his ears, had gradually merged into something more serious.
He consulted doctor after doctor, Frank, his friend Wegeler,
and Wering [Vering], but the malady constantly increased.
It gave him the keenest distress ; but so great were his resolution and confidence that not even the prospect of this tremendous affliction could subdue him. ' I will as far as possible
defy my fate, though there must be moments when I shall be
the most miserable of God's creatures.' . . . . ' Not unhappy :
no, that I never could endure ! I will grapple with fate ; it
shall never drag me down.' The letters to Wegeler of June 29 [5]
and November 16, 1801, from which these words are taken,
give an extraordinary picture of the mingled independence and
sensibility which characterised this remarkable man, and of
the entire mastery which music had in him over friendship,
love, pain, deafness, or any other external circumstance.
' Every day I come nearer to the object which I can feel, though
I cannot describe it, and on which alone your Beethoven can

[1] Czerny, in Thayer, ii. 134.   [2] Thayer, *Verzeichniss*, No. 91.
[3] This foolish sobriquet is derived from a criticism on the work by Rellstab
mentioning moonlight on the Lake of Lucerne.   [4] Thayer, ii. 172.
[5] No year is given in the date of the letter. Wegeler places it in 1800, but
Thayer (ii. 155, 6) has proved it to belong to 1801.

exist. No more rest for him!' 'I live only in my music, and
no sooner is one thing done than the next is begun. As I am
now writing, I often work at three and four things at once.'
How truly this describes the incessant manner in which his
ideas flowed may be seen from the sketch-book published by
Nottebohm,[1] and which is the offspring of this very period —
October 1801 to May 1802. It contains sketches for the Finale
of the Second Symphony, for the 3 Violin Sonatas (op. 30);
for Piano Sonatas in G and D minor (op. 31); for the Variations in F (op. 34), and in E♭ (op. 35); and a large number of
less important works, the themes of which are so mixed up and
repeated as to show that they were all in his mind and his
intention at once.

The spring of 1802 saw the publication of several very
important pieces, the correction of which must have added to
his occupations — the Serenade (op. 25); the Sonatas in B♭ [2]
(op. 22), A♭ (op. 26), E♭ and C♯ minor (op. 27); the Variations for piano and cello on Mozart's air ' Bei Männern,' and
6 Contretänze. It is curious to notice that up to op. 22 all
the solo Sonatas, as well as the Duet (op. 6) and the 3 with
Violin (op. 12) are published ' for Clavecin or Pianoforte.'
The Sonata in B♭ is the first to break the rule, which comes
to an end with the two quasi-fantasias, op. 27. One would
like to know if this is a mere publisher's freak — which, knowing Beethoven's care of details, it is hard to believe — or
whether great works like op. 7; op. 10, No. 3; and op. 26
were intended for instruments so unlike the piano as the
whispering clavichord or the prancing harpsichord — for
' Clavecin ' may mean either. All the works just enumerated
were out by April, and were followed in the later months by
the Septet, issued in two portions; the Sonata in D (op. 28);
6 Ländler;[3] the Rondo in G (op. 51, No. 2); and in December by the Quintet in C (op. 29).

Beethoven had recently again changed his doctor. Vering
did not satisfy him, and he consulted Schmidt, a person apparently of some eminence, and it was possibly on his recommendation that he selected the village of Heiligenstadt, at that time
a most retired spot, lying beyond Unter-Döbling, among the
lovely wooded valleys in the direction of the Kahlenberg and

---

[1] *Ein Skizzenbuch von Beethoven*, etc., Leipzig, B. & H.
[2] ' Well engraved,' says Beethoven to Hoffmeister, ' but you have been a
fine time about it!'   [3] B. & H. 197.

Leopoldsberg.   Here he remained till October, labouring at
the completion of the works mentioned above, which he had
sketched early in the year, and which he probably completed
before returning to Vienna.   Here too he wrote the very
affecting letter usually known as ' Beethoven's will,' dated
October 6, and addressed to his brothers, to be opened after
his death,[1] a letter full of depression and distress, but perhaps
not more so than that written by many a man of sensibility
under adverse temporary circumstances, and which does not
give us a high idea of Dr. Schmidt's wisdom in condemning
a dyspeptic patient to so long a course of solitude.   At any rate,
if we compare it with the genial, cheerful strains of the music
which he was writing at the time — take the Symphony in D
as one example only — and remember his own words : ' I live
only in my music,......letter-writing was never my *forte* ' — it
loses a good deal of its significance.[2]   Once back in town his
spirits returned ;   and some of his most facetious letters to
Zmeskall are dated from this time.   On returning he changed
his residence from the Sailer-Stätte, where we last left him,
to the Peters-Platz, in the very heart of the city, and at the
top of the house.   In the storey above Beethoven lived his old
friend Förster, who had won his affection by giving him hints
on quartet writing on his first arrival in Vienna.   Förster had
a little son whom Beethoven undertook to instruct, and the
boy, then just 6, long [3] remembered having to get up in the
dark in the winter mornings and descend the stairs for his
lessons.   This winter again there were many proofs to correct
— the 2 Piano Sonatas (op. 31, 1 & 2), the 3 Violin ditto, 2
sets of Variations (op. 34, 35), all which appeared early in
1803.   The Piano Sonatas he regarded as a change in his
style [4]— which they certainly are, the D minor especially.
The Variations he mentions [5] as distinct in kind from his earlier
ones, and therefore to be included in the series of his large
works, and numbered accordingly.   In addition there were
published 2 Preludes (op. 39), dating from 1789 ; 7 Bagatelles,
some of them as old as 1782, but one at least (No. 6) written
within the last twelve months.   Also the Romance in G for
violin and orchestra (op. 40), which was published this year,

[1] The autograph is in possession of Madame Lind-Goldschmidt, to whom
was given by Ernst.   [2] See the sensible remarks of Thayer, ii. 196.
[3] Thayer, ii. 199, 200.   [4] Ibid. 186.
[5] See his letter (Dec. 26, 1802) in Thayer, ii. 213.

and 6 Sacred Songs (op. 48), dedicated to his Russian friend Count von Browne. And proofs at that date appear to have been formidable things, and to have required an extraordinary amount of vigilance and labour. Not only had the engravers' mistakes to be guarded against, and the obscurities of Beethoven's writing, but the publishers were occasionally composers and took on themselves to correct his heresies and soften his abruptnesses as they passed through their hands. Thus in the Sonata in G (op. 31, No. 1), Nägeli of Zurich interpolated four bars.[1] Of course Beethoven discovered the addition on hearing Ries play from the proof, and his rage was naturally unbounded. The mistakes were corrected, and an amended proof was transmitted at once to Simrock of Bonn, who soon got out an ' Edition très correcte '; — but Nägeli adhered to his own version of Beethoven's music, and editions are still issued [2] containing the four redundant bars. It is needless to say that after opus 31 he published no more for Beethoven. But even without such intentional errors, correcting in those days was hard work. ' My Quartets,' he complains,[3] ' are again published full of mistakes and *errata* great and small; they swarm like fish in the sea — innumerable.' The Quintet in C (op. 29), published by Breitkopf, was pirated by Artaria of Vienna, and being engraved from a very hasty copy was extraordinarily full of blunders.[4] Beethoven adopted a very characteristic mode of revenge; fifty copies had been struck off, which he offered Artaria to correct, but in doing so caused Ries to make the alterations with so strong a hand that the copies were quite unsaleable.[5] It was an evil that never abated. In sending off the copies of the A minor Quartet twenty years later, he says, ' I have passed the whole forenoon to-day and yesterday afternoon in correcting these two pieces, and am quite hoarse with stamping and swearing ' — and no wonder when the provocation was so great. The noble Sonatas, op. 31, to the first of which one of the above anecdotes refers, were unfortunate in more ways than one. They were promised to Nägeli, but Caspar Beethoven [6] by some blunder — whether for his own profit or his brother's does not appear — had sold

---

[1] Between the 28th and 27th bars from the end of the first movement.
[2] *E.g.* that of Holle of Wolfenbüttel. An equally gratuitous alteration has been made in the Sonata op. 81 *a*. See Thayer, *Verzeichniss*, p. 192.
[3] Letter to Hoffmeister, April 8, 1802.   [4] Ries, 120.
[5] Ries, 120. He issued a notice to the public, cautioning them against this incorrect edition.   [6] Ries, 87.

them to a Leipzig house.[1]   The discovery enraged Beethoven,
who hated any appearance of deceit in his dealings; he
challenged his brother with the fact, and the quarrel actually
proceeded to blows.   Knowing how much Beethoven disliked
his early works, it is difficult not to imagine that the appearance
of the two boyish Preludes, op. 39, and of the Variations, op. 44
(1792 or 3), both published at Leipzig — was due to the
interference of Caspar.

A great event in 1803 was the production of 'The Mount
of Olives,' his first vocal composition on a larger scale than a
scena.   The concert took place in the Theatre 'an der Wien'
on April 5, and the programme included three new works —
the Oratorio, the Symphony in D, and the Pianoforte Concerto
in C minor, played by himself.   Interesting accounts of the
rehearsal (in which Prince Lichnowsky showed himself as
friendly as ever) and of the performance will be found in Ries
and Seyfried.[2]   Difficult as it is to conceive of such a thing,
the Symphony appears to have been found too laboured by
the critics, and not equal to the former one.[3]   The success of
the Oratorio is shown by the fact that it was repeated three
times (making four performances) by independent parties in
the course of the next twelve months.   The Sonata for piano
and violin, now so well known as the 'Kreutzer Sonata,' was
first played on May 17, at the Augarten, at 8 a.m.   There was
a curious bombastic half-caste English violin-player in Vienna
at that time named Bridgetower.   He had engaged Beethoven
to write a sonata for their joint performance at his concert.
Knowing Beethoven's reluctance to complete bespoke works,
it is not surprising to find him behind time and Bridgetower
clamouring loudly for his music.   The Finale was easily attain-
able, having been written the year before for the Sonata in A
(op. 30, No. 1), and the violin part of the first movement
seems to have been ready a few days before the concert, though
at the performance the pianoforte copy still remained almost
a blank, with only an indication here and there.   But the
Variations were literally finished only at the last moment, and
Bridgetower had to play them at sight from the blurred and
blotted autograph of the composer.   Beethoven's rendering of

[1] Caspar had already offered them to Andre of Offenbach.   See Thayer,
ii. 202.
[2] Ries, 76; Seyfried, *Notizen*, 19; and see Thayer, ii. 223, 224.
[3] See the report in Thayer, ii. 225.

the Andante was so noble, pure, and chaste, as to cause a universal demand for an encore. A quarrel with Bridgetower caused the alteration of the dedication.

Before Beethoven left town this year he made an arrangement to write an opera for Schikaneder, Mozart's old comrade, the manager of the Theatre ' an der Wien.' [1] Beyond the bare fact nothing is known on the subject. It is possible that a MS. trio [2] preserved in the library of the ' Gesellschaft der Musikfreunde ' at Vienna, and afterwards worked up into the duet in ' Fidelio,' is a portion of the proposed work, but this is mere conjecture. The arrangement was announced on June 29, and Beethoven had before that date, perhaps as early as April, taken up his quarters at the theatre with his brother Caspar, who, with all his faults, was necessary to a person so inapt at business as Ludwig. His summer and autumn were again spent — after a few weeks *Kur* at Baden [3] — at Ober-Döbling, and were occupied principally with his third Symphony on ' Napoleon Bonaparte,' the idea of which, since its suggestion in 1798, appears to have ripened with the contemplation of the splendid career of the First Consul as soldier, lawgiver, statesman, and hero, until it became an actual fact.

Of the order in which the movements of this mighty work were composed we have not yet any information, but there is no doubt that when Beethoven returned to his lodgings in the theatre in the autumn of 1803 the Finale was complete enough, at least in its general outlines,[4] to be played through by its author. There are traces of Beethoven being a great deal in society this winter. Two young Rhinelanders — Gleichenstein, a friend and fellow official of Breuning in the War Office, and Mähler, also a government official and an amateur portrait painter, were now added to his circle.[5] With another painter, Macco, he appears to have been on terms of great intimacy.[6] The Abbé Vogler was in Vienna this season with his pupil Carl Maria von Weber, and a record [7] survives of a soirée given by Sonnleithner, at which Vogler and Beethoven met, and each gave the other a subject to extemporise upon. The subject given by Beethoven to Vogler we merely know to have been 4½ bars long, while that on which he himself held forth

---

[1] See Thayer, ii. 221, 242. [2] Nottebohm, *Beethoveniana*, p. 82.
[3] Not Baden-Baden, but a mineral-water bath 16 or 18 miles south of Vienna.
[4] Thayer, ii. 236. [5] Ibid. 234. [6] Ibid. 241.
[7] By Gänsbacher, ibid. 236.

E

was ' the scale of C major, three bars, *alla breve.*' Vogler was
evidently the more expert contrapuntist, but Beethoven astonished even his rival's adherents by his extraordinary playing,
and by a prodigious flow of the finest ideas. *Noctes coenaeque
deorum.*—Clementi too was in Vienna about this time, or a
little later, with his pupil Klengel. He and Beethoven often
dined at the same restaurant, but neither would speak first,
and there was no intercourse.[1] Not for want of respect on
Beethoven's side, for he had a very high opinion of Clementi,
and thought his *Method* one of the best. This winter saw the
beginning of a correspondence[2] which was not destined to bear
fruit till some years later — with Thomson the music-publisher
of Edinburgh. Thomson had already published arrangements
of Scotch airs by Pleyel and Kozeluch, and, with the true eye
of a man of business, was now anxious to obtain from a greater
and more famous musician than either, six sonatas on Scotch
themes. Beethoven replies on October 5, offering to compose
six sonatas for 300 ducats (£150). Thomson responded by
offering half the sum named, and there for the present the
correspondence dropped. The prospect of an opera from
Beethoven was put an end to at the beginning of 1804 by the
theatre passing out of Schikaneder's hands into those of Baron
von Braun, and with this his lodging in the theatre naturally
ceased.[3] He moved into the same house with Stephen Breuning
— the ' Rothes Haus,' near the present Votive Church, and
there the rupture already spoken of took place.

The early part of 1804 was taken up in passing through the
press the Symphony No. 2 (dedicated to Prince Carl Lichnowsky), and the three 4-hand Marches, which were published
in March — but the real absorbing occupation of the whole
winter must have been the completion of the Bonaparte Symphony. At length the work was done, a fair copy was made,
the outside page of which contained the words ' Napoleon
Bonaparte......Louis van Beethoven,'[4] and it lay on the
composer's table for the proper opportunity of official trans-
mission to Paris. On May 3 the motion for making Napoleon
emperor passed the Assembly, and on the 18th, after his
election by *plébiscite*, he assumed the title. The news must
have quickly reached Vienna, and was at once communicated

---

[1] Thayer, ii. 246.   [2] See the letters and replies in Thayer, ii. 239.
[3] Thayer, ii. 246.
[4] These words can still be made out on the cover of the MS. score at Vienna.

to Beethoven by Ries. The story need not be given here in
detail. In a fury of disappointment and with a torrent of
reproaches he tore off the title page and dashed it on the
ground. At some future time it received the new name by
which we know it, and under which it was published —
' Sinfonia eroica per festeggiare il sovvenire d' un gran uomo '
— but this was probably an afterthought, and the cover of the
MS. now in the Bibliothek at Vienna,—

Sinfonia grande

Napoleon Bonaparte

804 im August

del Sigr.

Louis Van Beethoven

Sinfonie 3   Op. 55

an intermediate title. The right to use the Symphony was
purchased by Prince Lobkowitz, to whom it is dedicated. It
was played at his house during the winter, and remained in
MS. till October 1806.

The *fracas* at Breuning's rooms ended by Beethoven's dashing off to Baden, and then returning to his old quarters at
Döbling. There he composed the Grand Sonata in C, which
he afterwards dedicated to Count Waldstein, and that in F,
op. 54, which, though only in two movements and dedicated
to no one, is not inferior in originality to its longer companion.
It is to the Finale of this work, and not that of the ' Appassionata ' as usually believed, that Ries's story applies. Ries appears
to have often gone out, as he often did, to Döbling — within
an easy walk of Vienna — and to have remained with his
master all the after part of the day. They went for an immense
walk, and did not get home till eight in the evening. During
the whole time Beethoven had been humming and growling
to himself, but without anything like a tune. On Ries asking
him what it was, he replied that it was a theme for the finale
of the Sonata. The instant they reached the house he sat
down to the piano without taking off his hat, and for more
than an hour pounded away at his new idea. Ries sat in a
corner listening. — The Sonata in C, just mentioned, contained

when completed a long Andante in F — the subject of a very characteristic story, already alluded to (p. 16). This, however, at the advice of some judicious critic, he was induced to take out and replace by the present short introductory Adagio, after which it was published separately, and became the well-known 'Andante favori.' [1]   During this summer, on July 19 or 26, there was a concert at the Augarten, at which Beethoven conducted; the Symphony in D was performed, and Ries made his first public appearance as Beethoven's scholar in the C minor Concerto. Ries's story of his cadence is too long for these pages, but should be read.[2]   The pianoforte part having to be written out for Ries, the Concerto was at last ready for publication, and in fact made its appearance in November, dedicated to Prince Louis Ferdinand of Prussia, an amateur of remarkable musical gifts, whose acquaintance Beethoven made when he visited his father's court in 1796, and who while in Vienna at this very time was one of the first to hear and appreciate the new Symphony. When Beethoven came back it was to a new lodging, in a house of Baron Pasqualati, on the Mölker-Bastion near Prince Lichnowsky's, and in some sense this was his last; for though he left it more than once yet the Baron always forbid the rooms to be let, saying that Beethoven was sure to come back to them again. Breuning and he soon met, and a reconciliation took place which was not interrupted for many years — but they never again put their friendship so far to the proof as to live together.

Breuning's attitude through the whole affair is in keeping with his solid sensible character, and does him infinite credit. His letter to Wegeler of November 13 gives no hint of a quarrel, but is full of the deepest sympathy with Beethoven under the affliction of his deafness. In addition to the works already mentioned as published during 1804 must be named the great Sonata in E♭, which ultimately became the 3rd of opus 31; 7 Variations on 'God save the King,' [3] and 5 on 'Rule Britannia'; a song, 'Der Wachtelschlag,' [4] and 'Ah! perfido.' Why he selected these two English airs does not appear. At a later date he said, à propos to its use in his Battle Symphony, 'I must show the English a little what a blessing they have in God save the King.' [5]   It is satisfactory to find him

[1] B. & H. 192.   [2] *Notizen*, p. 114.
[3] B. & H. 179, 180.   [4] Ibid. 234.
[5] In his journal 1812-1818. Nohl, *Die Beethoven-Feier* (1871), p. 55.

so fond of it.—The first trial of the 'Eroica' took place in December [1] at Prince Lobkowitz's. The opinions expressed concerning it are collected by Thayer, and should be read and digested by all who are tempted to regard music from the 'finality' point of view.

Beethoven's connection with the Theatre an der Wien, though interrupted, was not at an end. Baron von Braun took Schikaneder into his service, and one of their first acts was to renew the offer. Bouilly's opera [libretto], which had been already set by Gaveaux [2] and Paer,[3] was chosen, and Sonnleithner was employed to make the German translation. Beethoven went back to his rooms at the theatre, and set to work with energy. But, remembering his habit of doing several things at once, we need not suppose that, though at work on an opera, he dropped other compositions. A letter to Artaria shows that on June 1, 1805, he was engaged on a new quintet, the suggestion of Count Fries.[4] Though he had even proceeded so far as to mention it to the publisher, its ultimate fate must be left to the discovery of Herr Nottebohm ; it certainly never arrived at publication. He also completed the Sonata in F (op. 54), and probably entirely composed the Triple Concerto (op. 56). But the opera was his main and absorbing business. During the whole of the spring he was hard at work, and in June he betook himself to Hetzendorf, there to put his sketches into shape, and to get inspiration from his favourite woods and fields. To give an idea of the extraordinary amount of labour and pains which he bestowed on his work, and of the strangely tentative manner in which so great a genius proceeded, we may mention [5] that in the sketch-book which contains the materials for the opera — a thick oblong volume of 300 [346] pages, 16 staves to the page — there are no less than 18 distinct and different beginnings to Florestan's air ' In des Lebens Frühlingstagen,' and 10 to the chorus ' Wer ein holdes Weib.' To reduce these chaotic materials to order, and to score the work, was the entire occupation of these summer months. Closely as he was occupied he could occasionally visit Vienna, and on one occasion in July [6] we find him at Sonnleithner's

---

[1] Thayer, ii. 261 ; and Ries, p. 79.
[2] 'Léonore ou l'amour conjugale, opéra comique,' Feb. 19, 1798.
[3] ' Leonora ossia l' amore conjugale,' Dresden, Oct. 3, 1804.
[4] Letter to Artaria, June 1, 1805.
[5] Thayer, ii. 281.   [6] Ibid. 282.

rooms with Cherubini and Vogler. Cherubini arrived in
Vienna with his wife early in the month, and remained till the
following April. His operas had long been favourites on the
Vienna stage. The ' Deux Journées ' was performed under
his direction shortly after his arrival, and ' Faniska ' was produced for the first time on Feb. 25, 1806. Beethoven knew
them well, and has left on record [1] that he esteemed their
author above all then living writers for the stage. He also
thought so highly of Cherubini's Requiem as to say that he
should borrow largely from it in the event of his writing one.
But the influence of Cherubini on Beethoven's vocal music is
now [2] acknowledged. The two artists were much together,
and agreed as well as two men of such strong character and
open speech were likely to agree. Cherubini presented the
composer of ' Fidelio ' with a copy of the *Méthode* of the Conservatoire, and the scores of ' Médée ' and ' Faniska ' are conspicuous in the sale catalogue of Beethoven's scanty library.[3]

One proof that ' Fidelio ' was complete before his return to
town is afforded by the fact that he allowed others to hear it.
On one occasion he played it to a select set of friends,[4] when
Ries (as already mentioned) was excluded ; and thus — as he
was shortly afterwards called to Bonn by the conscription — lost
his chance of hearing the opera at all in its first shape. That
Beethoven's voice in singing was ' detestable ' [5] will not have
diminished the interest of the trial. The work of rehearsing
the music now began, and was evidently attended with
enormous difficulties, especially in regard to the singers. They
complained that their passages were unsingable, while Beethoven on his part was determined to make no alterations
— and apparently none were made.[6] With the band he fared
little better. He even invokes his deafness as an assistance.
Writing only two days before the first performance, he says,[7]
' Pray try to persuade Seyfried to conduct my opera to-day,
as I wish to see and hear it from a distance ; in this way my
patience will at least not be so severely tried by the rehearsal

[1] Seyfried, p. 22 ; also Czerny in *Cäcilia*. See Thayer, ii. 353.
[2] See Hiller, in *Macmillan's Magazine*, July 1875 ; also the report of a conversation with Mendelssohn in Marx's *Music of the 19th Century*. A fragment
of a sketch-book of Beethoven in Mr. Joachim's possession contains the Trio
in the ' Deux Journées ' and a piece from the ' Zauberflöte,' mixed up with
bits of ' Fidelio ' and of the Finale of the B flat Symphony.
[3] Thayer, *Chron. Verzeichniss*, 180, 181.   [4] Ries, 102.
[5] *Abscheulich* ; Czerny, in Thayer, ii. 202.
[6] Schindler (1860), i. 135, 136.   [7] Letter to Meyer.

as when I am close enough to hear my music so bungled. I really do believe it is done on purpose. Of the wind I will say nothing, but——. All *pp. cresc.*, all *decresc.*, and all *f. ff.* may as well be struck out of my music, since not one of them is attended to. I lose all desire to write anything more if my music is to be so played.' And again,[1] ' the whole business of the opera is the most distressing thing in the world.'

The performance was fixed for Wednesday, November 20. External events could hardly have been more unpropitious. The occupation of Ulm and Salzburg had been followed on November 13 by the entry of the French army into Vienna. Bonaparte took up his quarters at Schönbrunn; the Emperor of Austria, the chief nobility and other wealthy persons and patrons of music had deserted the town, and it was a conquered city tenanted by Frenchmen. It was in such circumstances that ' Fidelio, oder die eheliche Liebe ' was produced. The opera was originally in 3 acts. It was performed on the 20th, 21st, and 22nd, and was then withdrawn by the composer.[2] The overture on these occasions appears to have been that known as ' Leonora No. 2.' It was felt by Beethoven's friends that, in addition to the drawbacks of the French occupation and of the advanced character of the music, the opera was too long; and a meeting was held at Prince Lichnowsky's house, when the whole work was gone through at the piano, and after a battle lasting from 7 till 1 in the morning, Beethoven was induced to sacrifice three entire numbers. It is character-istic of Beethoven that though furious and unpleasant to the very greatest degree while the struggle was going on, yet when once the decision was made he was in his most genial temper.[3] The libretto was at once put into the hands of Stephen Breuning, by whom it was reduced to two acts and generally improved, and in this shortened form, and with the revised overture known as ' Leonora No. 3,' it was again performed on March 29, 1806, but, owing to Beethoven's delays over the alterations, with only one band rehearsal. It was repeated on April 10, each time to fuller and more appreciative houses [April 10 only, to a fuller and more appreciative house] than before, and then, owing to a quarrel between Beethoven and Baron Braun, the intendant of the theatre, suddenly and finally with-

[1] To Treitschke, in Schindler, i. 136.
[2] Breuning's letter of June 2, 1806.
[3] See Roeckel's account of the whole transaction in Thayer, ii. 295.

drawn. Attempts were made to bring it out at Berlin, but they came to nothing, and this great work was then practically shelved for seven or eight years.

It is an astonishing proof of the vigour and fertility of the mind of this extraordinary man that in the midst of all this work and worry he should have planned and partly carried out three of his greatest instrumental compositions. We have the assurance of Mr. Nottebohm [1] that the Piano Concerto in G and the Symphony in C minor were both begun, and the two first movements of the latter composed, in 1805. The two last of the String Quartets, op. 59, appear to have been written during this winter — before that in F,[2] which now stands first. There are many indications in his letters that his health was at this time anything but good, and the demands of society on him must have been great. Against them he could arm himself by such reflections as the following pencil note [3] in the margin of a sketch-book of this very date. ' Struggling as you are in the vortex of society, it is yet possible, notwithstanding all social hindrances, to write operas. Let your deafness be no longer a secret — even in your Art ! '

On April 10, 1806, ' Fidelio ' was performed for the [second and] last time ; on May 25 [4] the marriage contract of Caspar Carl Beethoven with Johanna Reis was signed — harbinger of unexpected suffering for Ludwig — and on May 26 he began the scoring of the first of the three Quartets which were afterwards dedicated to the Russian Ambassador, Count Rasoumoffsky [Rasumovsky], as op. 59. So says his own writing at the head of the autograph.[5] These Quartets, the Russian airs in which it is natural to suppose were suggested by the Ambassador (a brother-in-law of Prince Lichnowsky), are another link in the chain of connection between the republican composer and the great Imperial court of Petersburg, which originated some of his noblest works.

His favourite summer villages had been defiled by the French, and perhaps for this reason Beethoven did not pass the summer of 1806 at the usual spots, but went to the country-house of his friend Count Brunswick — whose sisters [6] were also his great allies — [at Martonvásár] in Hungary. Here he

---

[1] Nottebohm, *Catalogue*, op. 67 and 58.   [2] Letter to Brunswick, May 11.
[3] Thayer, ii. 311.   [4] Ibid. ii. 311.   [5] *Catalogue*, op. 59.
[6] ' Lieber, lieber Brunswick.....küsse deine Schwester Therese.' Letter, May 11. His favourite Sonata, op. 78, was dedicated to this lady.

wrote the magnificent Sonata in F minor, than which nothing more impetuous, more poetical, or more enduring ever came from his pen. His letters may have been full of depression [1] — but it vanished when he spoke in music, and all is force, elevation, and romance. In October he left Count Brunswick for the seat of Prince Lichnowsky, near Troppau, in Silesia, 40 miles N.E. of Olmütz. The war was in full progress (Jena was fought on October 16), and the Prince had several French officers quartered upon him. They were naturally anxious to hear Beethoven, but he refused to play to them ; and on being pressed by his host and playfully threatened with confinement to the house, a terrible scene took place — he made his escape, went off by night post to Vienna, and on his arrival at home was still so angry as to demolish a bust of the Prince in his possession. He brought back with him not only the Sonata just named, but the Pianoforte Concerto in G, the Symphony in B flat (No. 4), the Rasoumoffsky Quartets, and the 32 Variations in C minor. The Quartets were played frequently in MS. during the winter at private concerts, but the larger orchestral works were not heard till later. The Violin Concerto (op. 61) was first played by Clement — a well-known virtuoso, and at that time principal violin of the Theatre an der Wien — at his concert on December 23, and there is evidence to show, what might have been assumed from Beethoven's habit of postponing bespoken works to the last, that it was written in a hurry, and Clement played his part without rehearsal, at sight. What chance can such great and difficult works, new in spirit and teeming with difficulties, have had of influencing the public when thus brought forward? No wonder that the Concerto was seldom heard till revived by Joachim in our own time. The MS. shows that the solo part was the object of much thought and alteration by the composer — evidently after the performance.

The publications of 1806 consist of the Sonata in F, op. 54 (April 9) ; a trio for two violins and viola (April 12), adapted from a trio [2] for two oboes and cor anglais, and afterwards numbered op. 87 ; the Andante in F (May [10]) already mentioned as having been originally intended for the Waldstein Sonata ; and lastly, on October 29, in time for the winter

---

[1] Breuning's letter of October, in Thayer, ii. 312.
[2] Composed in or about 1794. Nottebohm, *Catalogue*, op. 87.

season, the ' Eroica ' Symphony, dedicated to Prince Lobkowitz. In addition to these an arrangement of the 2nd Symphony as a pianoforte trio,[1] by Beethoven's own hand, was published at Vienna.

The first external musical event of 1807 was the performance of the new Symphony, No. 4, which took place before a very select audience in the middle or end of March.[2] The concert was organised for Beethoven's benefit, no doubt to compensate him for his disappointment with the opera, and was largely subscribed to. No programme of equal length was probably ever put together ; it contained the 1st and 2nd Symphonies, the ' Eroica ' — hardly known as yet, and in itself a programme — and the new work — 2½ hours of solid orchestral music without relief ! A second performance of the Symphony was given at a public concert on November 15. The overture to ' Coriolan ' — a tragedy by Collin — must have occupied him during the opening of the year, since it is included with the new Symphony, the new Concertos for violin and piano, and the 3 String Quartets in a sale of copyrights for England,[3] which Beethoven effected on April 20 to Clementi, who had for some years been at the head of a musical business in London. For these and an arrangement of the Violin Concerto for piano (dedicated to the wife of Stephen von Breuning), Clementi paid £200 down, Beethoven binding himself to compose three new sonatas for the sum of £60 more — a part of the bargain which was not carried out. Beethoven's finances were thus for the time flourishing, and he writes in high spirits on his prospects.[4]

Another overture belonging to this period is that in C, known as op. 138, and erroneously styled ' Leonora No. 1,' the fact being that it was written as ' a new overture ' for the production of ' Fidelio ' in Prague in the spring of this year.[5] Another great work approaching completion during the summer was the Mass in C, which was written for Prince Esterhazy, Haydn's patron, and after considerable delay was first sung in the chapel at Eisenstadt on September 13, the name-day of the Princess Marie of Esterhazy [September 8]. Beethoven and his old rival Hummel — then the Prince's

---

[1] B. & H. 90.   [2] *Allgemeine musikalische Zeitung*, ix. 400.
[3] Schindler, i. 142.
[4] To Brunswick, ' an einem Maytage.' Nohl, *Neue Briefe*, No. 7.
[5] Nottebohm, *Beethoveniana*, p. 70, etc.

Chapelmaster — were both present. After the mass the Prince, perhaps puzzled at the style of the music, so different from that to which he was accustomed in his chapel — hinted as much to Beethoven, in the strange question 'What have you been doing now?' Hummel overheard the remark, and probably amused at the *naïveté* of the question (for Hummel can have found nothing to question in the music) unfortunately smiled. Beethoven saw the smile, misinterpreted it, and left the palace in a fury. This occurrence possibly explains why the name of Esterhazy, to whom the Mass is dedicated in Beethoven's autograph, is replaced by that of Prince Kinsky in the published copy (1812).

The date of the C minor Symphony has not yet been conclusively ascertained, but there is good ground for believing that it and the Pastoral Symphony were completed, or at any rate much advanced, during this year, at Heiligenstadt and in the country between that and the Kahlenberg, as Beethoven pointed out to Schindler in 1823 [1] — the visit to Eisenstadt being probably undertaken for the sake of the Mass only. Of his activity in town during the winter there are more certain traces. A musical society of amateurs was formed, who held their concerts in the Hall of the Mehlgrube. At one of these, in December, the 'Eroica' Symphony was performed, and the overture to 'Coriolan' played for the first time. At another the B flat Symphony was performed for the second time, with immense appreciation. Beethoven himself conducted both of these concerts. December is also the date of a memorial to the directors of the Court Theatre, praying that he might be engaged at an annual salary of 2400 florins, with benefit performances, to compose one grand opera and an operetta yearly — a memorial evidently not favourably received.

The publications of 1807 are not numerous, they consist of the Sonata in F minor (op. 57), dedicated to Count Brunswick (February 18), and since designated 'Appassionata' by Cranz of Hamburg; the 32 Variations for piano [2] (April); and the Triple Concerto (op. 56), dedicated to Count Lobkowitz (July 1).

1808 opened with the publication of the overture to 'Coriolan' (op. 62), dedicated to the author of the tragedy, and the 3 new String Quartets (op. 59). There is reason to

[1] Schindler, i. 153.   [2] B. & H. 181.

believe [1] that Beethoven again passed the summer at Heiligenstadt, whence he returned to Vienna, bringing with him ready for performance the two Symphonies, C minor and Pastoral, the two Pianoforte Trios in D and E flat, and the Choral Fantasia, a work new not only in ideas and effects but also in form, and doubly important as the precursor of the Choral Symphony. It and the Symphonies were produced at a concert given by Beethoven in the Theatre an der Wien on December 22. It was announced to consist of pieces of his own composition only, all performed in public for the first time. In addition to the three already mentioned the programme contained the Piano Concerto in G, played by himself; two extracts from the Eisenstadt Mass; ' Ah! perfido '; and an extempore fantasia on the pianoforte.[2] The result was unfortunate. In addition to the enormous length of the programme and the difficult character of the music the cold was intense and the theatre unwarmed. The performance appears to have been infamous, and in the Choral Fantasia there was actually a breakdown.[3]

The Concerto had been published in August, and was dedicated to Beethoven's new pupil and friend the Archduke Rodolph [Rudolph]. It commemorates the acquisition of the most powerful and one of the best friends Beethoven ever possessed, for whom he showed to the end an unusual degree of regard and consideration, and is the first of a long series of great works which bear the Archduke's name. The Sonatina in G, the fine Sonata for piano and cello in A, and the Piano Fantasia in G minor — the last of less interest than usual — complete the compositions of 1808, and the pianoforte adaptation of the Violin Concerto,[4] dedicated to Madame Breuning, closes the publications.*

Hitherto Beethoven had no settled income beyond that produced by actual labour, except the small annuity granted him since 1800 by Prince Lichnowsky. His works were all the

---

[1] Schindler.

[2] Reichardt in Schindler, i. 150 note; and see Beethoven's note to Zmeskall of ' Dec. 1808.'

[3] On this occasion the Introduction to the Choral Fantasia was extemporised; it was not written down for 8 or 9 months later. Nottebohm, *N. B.* No. V.

[4] B. & H. No. 73.

* [Actually the publications of the year 1808 were: the pianoforte concerto in G (op. 58), the 3 quartets (op. 59), the PF. arrangement of the violin concerto (op. 61), the ' Coriolan ' overture (op. 62), and No. 1 of the four settings of Goethe's ' Sehnsucht.']

property of the publishers, and it is natural that, as his life advanced (he was now 39) and his aims in art grew vaster, the necessity of writing music for sale should have become more and more irksome. Just at this time, however, he received an invitation from Jerome Bonaparte, King of Westphalia, to fill the post of Maître de Chapelle at Cassel, with a salary of 600 gold ducats (£300) per annum, and 150 ducats for travelling expenses, and with very easy duties. The first trace of this offer is found in a letter of his own, dated November 1, 1808; but he never seems seriously to have entertained it except as a lever for obtaining an appointment under the Court of Austria. In fact the time was hardly one in which a German could accept service under a French prince. Napoleon was at the height of his career of ambition and conquest, and Austria was at this very time making immense exertions for the increase of her army with a view to the war which broke out when the Austrians crossed the Inn on April 9. With this state of things imminent it is difficult to imagine that King Jerome's offer can have been seriously made or entertained. But it is easy to understand the consternation into which the possibility of Beethoven's removal from Vienna must have thrown his friends and the lovers of music in general, and the immediate result appears to have been an undertaking on the part of the Arch-duke Rodolph, Prince Lobkowitz, and Prince Kinsky, dated March 1, 1809, guaranteeing him an annual income of 4000 (paper) florins, payable half-yearly, until he should obtain a post of equal value in the Austrian dominions.[1] He himself, however, naturally preferred the post of Imperial Kapellmeister under the Austrian Government, and with that view drew up a memorial,[2] which, however, appears to have met with no success, even if it were ever presented. At this time, owing to the excessive issue of bank notes, the cash value of the paper florin had sunk from 2s. to a little over 1s., so that the income secured to Beethoven, though nominally £400, did not really amount to more than £210, with the probability of still further rapid depreciation.

Meantime the work of publication went on apace, and in that respect 1809 is the most brilliant and astonishing year of Beethoven's life. He now, for the first time, entered into relations with the great firm of Breitkopf & Härtel. Simrock

---

[1] Schindler, i. 167.   [2] See Nohl, *Briefe*, No. 48, 49, and *Neue Briefe*, 41.

published (in March) the 4th Symphony, dedicated to Count Oppersdorf as op. 60, and Breitkopf & Härtel head their splendid list with the Violin Concerto, dedicated to Breuning as op. 60, and also issued in March. This they followed in April by the C minor and Pastoral Symphonies (op. 67 and 68), dedicated jointly to Prince Lobkowitz and Count Rasoumoffsky, and by the Cello Sonata in A (op. 69), dedicated to the Baron von Gleichenstein, who with Zmeskall shared Beethoven's intimate friendship at this date; and these again in October,[1] by the two Pianoforte Trios (op. 70), dedicated to the Countess Erdödy, in whose house Beethoven had been living since his rupture with Lichnowsky;[2] and lastly on November 22 by a song, 'Als die Geliebte sich trennen wollte.'[3]

On May 12 the French again entered Vienna; on the 21st Aspern was fought, and Napoleon took possession of the island of Lobau, close to the city. Wagram took place on July 6, and the whole summer, till the peace was concluded on October 14, must have been a very disturbed season for the inhabitants of Vienna. Beethoven's lodging, being on the wall, was much exposed to the firing. The noise disturbed him[4] greatly, and at least on one occasion he took refuge in the cellar of his brother's house in order to escape it. He had his eyes open, however, to the proceedings of the French, and astonished a visitor many years afterwards with his recollections of the time.[5] It is remarkable how little external events interfered with his powers of production. As far as quality goes the Piano Concerto in E flat and the String Quartet in the same key — both of which bear the date 1809 — are equal to any in the whole range of his works. The 6 Variations in D (op. 76) — the theme afterwards used for the March in the 'Ruins of Athens' — are not remarkable, but the Piano Sonata in F♯ written in October is very so. Though not so serious as some, it is not surpassed for beauty and charm by any of the immortal 33 [32]. It seems to have been a special favourite of the author's. 'People are always talking of the C♯ minor Sonata,' said he once, 'but I have written better

[1] See the A. M. Z. for Oct. 18.
[2] See the letter to Oppersdorf just cited, and Reichardt in Nohl, Leben.
[3] B. & H. 235.
[4] Since the above was written Mr. Nottebohm has published an account of a sketch-book of 1809, which shows a good deal of agitation. N. B. No. XXV.
[5] Rochlitz, Für Freunde der Tonkunst, iv. 353.

things than that. The F♯ Sonata is something very different.' [1]
A more important (though not more delightful) sonata had
been begun on May 4 to commemorate the departure of
the Archduke from Vienna on that day. It is dated and inscribed by Beethoven himself, and forms the first movement
of that known as ' Les Adieux, l'Absence et le Retour.' Among
the sketches for the Adieux is found a note [2] ' Der Abschied
am 4ten Mai — gewidmet und aus dem Herzen geschrieben
S. K. H.' — words which show that the parting really inspired
Beethoven, and was not a mere accident for his genius to
transmute, like the four knocks in the Violin Concerto, or the
cook's question in the last Quartet. A March for a military
band in F, composed for the Bohemian Landwehr under Archduke Anton, and 3 Songs — ' L' amante impaziente ' (op. 82,
No. 4), ' Lied aus der Ferne,' [3] and [probably] ' Die laute
Klage ' [4] — complete the compositions of 1809. Haydn had
gone to his rest on May 31, in the middle of the Austrian
[French] occupation, but we find no allusion to him in any of
Beethoven's journals or letters.

The correspondence with Thomson of Edinburgh, opened
in 1806, was renewed this autumn. It began with a letter from
Thomson, sending 43 airs, which was promptly answered by
Beethoven, and it lasted until February 21, 1818 [May 25,
1819], during which time Beethoven harmonised no less than
164 national melodies. For these he received in all a sum of
some £200.[5]

1810 began with the return of the Archduke on January 30,
and the completion of the Sonata. The sketch-books [6] show
that the next few months were occupied with the composition
of the music to ' Egmont,' the String Quartet in F minor,
songs of Goethe's (including the Erl King,[7] which, though
well advanced, was never completed), and with the preliminary
ideas of the B flat Trio. The music to ' Egmont ' was first performed on May 24, probably at some private house, as no
record of it survives in the theatrical chronicles. It was in
May [8] that Beethoven had his first interview with Bettina
Brentano, then twenty-five years old, which gave rise to the

[1] Thayer, ii. 172.   [2] Nottebohm, N. B. No. V.
[3] B. & H. 236.   [4] Ibid. 254.
[5] See the ample details in Thayer, Chron. Verzeichniss, No. 174-177.
[6] Nottebohm, N. B. XXI.   [7] Ibid. Beethoveniana, XXIII.
[8] See Letter of Aug. 15, 1812.

three well-known letters, the authenticity of which has been so
hotly disputed.   Knowing Beethoven's extreme susceptibility,
it is not difficult to believe that the letters are in the main
genuine, though some of the expressions have probably been
tampered with.   Beethoven's relation to the Archduke, and his
increasing reputation, were beginning to produce their natural
result.   He complains [1] that his retirement is at an end, and
that he is forced to go too much into society.   He has taken
up his summer quarter at Hetzendorf as before, but the old
seclusion is no longer possible, he has to be in and out of
Vienna at the season which he detested, and which hitherto
he had always devoted entirely to composition.   That he was
also at Baden in August is evident from some MS. pieces of
military music, all dated Baden, 1810, and one of them August.[2]
He seems to have had some prospect of marriage at this time,
though the only allusion to it is that it has been broken
off.[3]   Meantime this winter was a busy one for the publishers
of his music.   The pianoforte arrangement of ' Fidelio,' as
revised for 1806 (without Overture or Finales), was published
by Breitkopf in October, and is dedicated to the Archduke
Rodolph.   In December the same firm issued the Quartet
in E♭ (op. 74), inscribed to Prince Lobkowitz, the Variations
in D (op. 76), the Fantasia in G minor, the Sonata in F♯ —
dedicated respectively to Count Brunswick, and his sister
Therese — and the Sonatina in G ; [4] also earlier in the year
the Sestet for wind instruments (op. 71), and the song ' Andenken ' (No. 248).   Another Sestet (op. 81 b) — probably,
like that just mentioned, an early work — was issued by Simrock, and four settings of Goethe's ' Sehnsucht,' with a few
more songs by other publishers.   The frequent appearance of
Goethe's name in the music of this year is remarkable, and
coupled with the allusion in his letter to Bettina of August 11,
implies that the great poet was beginning to exercise that
influence on him which Beethoven described in his interview
with Rochlitz in 1823.

The Trio in B flat was completed during the winter, and
was written down in its finished form between March 3 and 26,
as the autograph informs us with a particularity wanting in

¹ Letter to Wegeler, May 2, and to Zmeskall, July 10.
² Thayer, *Verzeichniss*, No. 153, 157.
³ Letter of Breuning, in Wegeler, *Nachtrag*, 14.
⁴ First sketched in C, as ' Sonate facile,' *N. B.* XXV.

Beethoven's earlier works, but becoming more frequent in future. The Archduke (to whom it was ultimately inscribed) lost no time in making its acquaintance, and as no copyist was obtainable, seems to have played it first from the autograph.[1] The principal compositions of 1811 were the music to two dramatic pieces written by Kotzebue, for the opening of a new theatre at Pesth, and entitled ' Hungary's first hero, or King Stephen,' and the ' Ruins of Athens.' The Introduction to the Choral Fantasia, which may be taken as a representation of Beethoven's improvisation, inasmuch as it was actually extemporised at the performance — was written down à propos to the publication of the work in July, and a song ' An die Geliebte '[2] is dated December in the composer's own hand.

The publications of the year are all by Breitkopf, and include the Overture to ' Egmont ' in February; the Piano Concerto in E♭, and the Sonata in the same key (op. 81 *a*), in May and July respectively, both dedicated to the Archduke; — the Choral Fantasia (op. 80), dedicated to the King of Bavaria (July), and the ' Mount of Olives ' (November [October]). The preparation of the last-named work for the press so long after its composition must have involved much time and consideration. There is evidence that an additional chorus was proposed;[3] and it is known that he was dissatisfied with the treatment of the principal character. A note to Treitschke (June 6) seems to show that Beethoven was contemplating an opera. The first mention of a metronome[4] occurs in a letter of this autumn.

The depreciation in the value of paper money had gone on with fearful rapidity, and by the end of 1810 the bank notes had fallen to less than 1-10th of their nominal value — i.e. a 5-florin note was only worth half a florin in silver. The *Finanz Patent* of February 20, 1811, attempted to remedy this by a truly disastrous measure — the abolition of the bank notes (*Banco-zettel*) as a legal tender, and the creation of a new paper currency called *Einlösungsscheine*, into which the bank notes were to be forcibly converted at 1-5th of their ostensible value, i.e. a 100-florin note was exchangeable for a 20-florin *Einlösungsschein*. Beethoven's income might possibly have been

---

[1] *Briefe*, No. 70.   [2] B. & H. 243.
[3] To follow the air; Nottebohm, *N. B.* XXV. This was as far back as 1809.
[4] Letter to Zmeskall, Sept. 10—under the name not of ' Metronome ' but of ' Zeitmesser.'

F

thus reduced to 800 florins, or £80, had not the Archduke and Prince Lobkowitz agreed to pay their share of the pension (1500 + 700 = 2200 florins) in *Einlösungsscheine* instead of bank notes. Prince Kinsky would have done the same as to his 1800 florins, if his residence at Prague and his sudden death (November 13 [3], 1812) had not prevented his giving the proper instructions. Beethoven sued the Kinsky estate for his claim, and succeeded after several years, many letters and much heart-burning, in obtaining (January 18, 1815) a decree for 1200 florins *Einlösungsscheine* per annum [with arrears]; and the final result of the whole, according to Beethoven's own statement (in his letter to Ries of March 8, 1816), is that his pension up to his death was 3400 florins in *Einlösungsscheine*, which at that time were worth 1360 in silver, = £136, the *Einlösungsscheine* themselves having fallen to between ½ and ⅓rd of their nominal value.*

1812 opens with a correspondence with Varenna, an official

---

* [This paragraph on the effect of the Austrian finance patent of 1811 upon Beethoven's annuity, and his suit against the Kinsky estate, accords perfectly with all the authorities known at the time it was written. But these authorities, from Schindler down, are in error. It is true that from and after Mar. 1811, the bank-notes (*Bancozettel*) then in circulation were reduced in value to the rate of five for one in silver; and notes of redemption (*Einlösungsscheine*), equal to silver, were issued in their place at that rate; but the payment of contracts previously made, Beethoven's annuity included, was regulated by the depreciation at the date of the contract. The date of the document conferring the annuity is Mar. 1, 1809, when the depreciation (decimally) was 2·48 for one, and it follows that his income under the finance patent was reduced—not to one-fifth or 800 florins, as Schindler and his copyists unanimously state, but to 1612·90 florins. That is to say,

> Kinsky, instead of 1800, paid 725·80 fl.
> Rudolph,   ,,   1500,   ,,   604·84 ,,
> Lobkowitz, ,,   700,   ,,   <u>282·26</u> ,,
>   1612·90

When the subscribers continued to pay the annuity in full, regardless of the patent, Kinsky unfortunately neglected to do this, and thus, upon his untimely death, unwittingly deprived Beethoven of all *legal* claim to more than the above-named 725·80 florins; for the trustees of the estates had no power to add to that sum, being responsible to the Landrecht or high tribunal at Prague for their action. Beethoven, trusting to the equity of his claim, seems to have been so foolish as to instruct his advocate in Prague, Dr. Wolf, to enter a suit—which could have had no favourable issue. It was fortunate for him that the legal agent of the Kinsky estates (*Verlassenschaftscurator*), Dr. Johann Kanka, was a musician of considerable attainments, a great admirer of his music and on intimate terms with him during his first years in Vienna. On a visit to the capital, Kanka discussed the matter with him; the suit was abandoned, and a compromise at last effected—confirmed by the Landrecht, Jan. 18, 1815—by which 1200 florins a year were secured to him, and arrears to the amount of 2479 florins, paid in cash, on Mar. 26, to his representative, Baron Joseph von Pasqualati.

Beethoven's letters to Kanka (Thayer's *Beethoven*, iii. App. viii.) and his dedication of op. 94, 'An die Hoffnung,' to the widowed Princess Kinsky, prove how well satisfied he was with the result.]

in Gratz [Graz], as to a concert for the poor, which puts
Beethoven's benevolence in a strong light.   He sends the
' Mount of Olives,' the Choral Fantasia, and an overture
as a gift to the Institution for future use — promises other (MS.)
compositions, and absolutely declines all offer of remuneration.
The theatre at Pesth was opened on February 9 with the music
to the ' Ruins of Athens ' and ' King Stephen,' but there is
no record of Beethoven himself having been present.   This
again was to be a great year in composition, and he was destined
to repeat the feat of 1808 by the production of a second pair
of symphonies.   In fact from memoranda among the sketches
for the new pair, it appears that he contemplated [1] writing
three at the same time, and that the key of the third was already
settled in his mind — ' Sinfonia in D moll — 9te Sinf.'   However, this was postponed, and the other two occupied him the
greater part of the year.   The autograph score of the first of
the two, that in A (No. 7), is dated May 13 ; so that it may
be assumed that it was finished before he left Vienna.   The
second — in F, No. 8 — was not completed till October.   His
journey this year was of unusual extent.   His health was bad,
and Malfatti [Staudenheim], his physician,[2] ordered him to
try the baths of Bohemia — possibly after Baden or some other
of his usual resorts had failed to recruit him, as we find him
in Vienna on July 4, an unusually late date.   Before his departure there was a farewell meal, at which Count Brunswick,
Stephen Breuning, Maelzel, and others were present.[3]   Maelzel's metronome was approaching perfection, and Beethoven
said goodbye to the inventor in a droll canon, which was sung
at the table — he himself singing soprano [4] — and afterwards
worked up into the lovely Allegretto of the 8th Symphony.
He went by Prague to Töplitz, and Carlsbad — where he
notes the postilion's horn [5] among the sketches for the 8th
Symphony — Franzensbrunn, and then Töplitz again ; [6] and
lastly to his brother Johann's at Linz, where he remained
through October and into November, as the inscriptions on the
autographs of the 8th Symphony and of three Trombone pieces
[' Equali '] written for All Souls Day demonstrate.   The Trom-

[1] Nottebohm, N. B. VI.   [2] Letter to Schweiger, Köchel, No. 1.
[3] Schindler, i. 195. For the canon see B. & H. 233, No. 2.   There is some
great error in the dates of this period—possibly there were two journeys.   The
whole will be settled in Mr. Thayer's new volume.
[4] Conversation-book, Nohl, Leben, iii. 841.
[5] Nottebohm, N. B. VI.   [6] Letter to the Archduke, Aug. 12.

bone pieces became his own requiem. At Töplitz he met Goethe, and the strange scene occurred in which he so unnecessarily showed his contempt for his friend the Archduke Rudolph and the other members of the Imperial family.[1] At Töplitz he met Amalie Sebald, and a series of letters [2] to her shows that the Symphony did not prevent him from making love with much ardour. While in Carlsbad he [3] gave a concert for the benefit of the sufferers in a fire at Baden.[4] The fact of his extemporising at the concert, and hearing the postilion's call, as well as an entry among the sketches for the 8th Symphony, to the effect that ' cotton in his ears when playing took off the unpleasant noise ' [5] — perhaps imply that his deafness at this time was still only partial.

One of his first works after returning to Vienna was the fine Sonata for piano and violin, published as op. 96. It was completed by the close of the year, and was first played by the Archduke and Rode — whose style Beethoven kept in view in the violin part [6] — at the house of Prince Lobkowitz, on December 29. A comparative trifle is the ' Lied an die Geliebte,' [7] written during this winter in the album of Regina Lang. The only work published in 1812 is [were the ' Egmont ' entr'actes and] the Mass in C, [the latter] dedicated — possibly as an acknowledgment of his share in the guarantee — to Prince Kinsky, and issued in November as op. 86 by Breitkopf & Härtel. The state of his finances about this time compelled him to borrow 2300 florins from the Brentanos of Frankfort, old friends who had known and loved him from the first. A trace of the transaction is perhaps discernible in the Trio in Bb in one movement,[8] written on June 2, 1812, ' for his little friend Maximiliana Brentano, to encourage her in playing.' The effect of the Bohemian baths soon passed away, the old ailments and depression returned, the disputes and worries with the servants increased, and his spirits became worse than they had been since the year 1803.

The only composition which can be attributed to the spring

[1] Letter to Bettina, Aug. 15, 1812.
[2] Nohl, *Neue Briefe*, No. 79-85. The lock of hair which she cut from his head is still preserved by her family.
[3] Letter to Zmeskall, *Briefe*, No. 95. Letter to Archduke, Aug. 12, *A. M. Z.* xiv. 596.   [4] Notes to Letter of July 4.   [5] Nottebohm, *N. B.* VI.
[6] Letter to Archduke, Köchel No. 4.
[7] Nottebohm, in the *Catalogue*. B. & H. 243 *a*.
[8] B. & H. No. 85.

of 1813 is a Triumphal March, written for Kuffner's tragedy [1] of 'Tarpeia,' which was produced — with the March advertised as 'newly composed' — on March 26. On April 20 the two new symphonies appear to have been played through for the first time at the Archduke's.[2] On the advice of his medical men he went at the end of May to Baden, where [3] he was received with open arms by the Archduke. Hither he was followed by his friend Madame Streicher, who remained at Baden for the summer, and took charge of his lodgings and clothes, which appear to have been in a deplorable state. On his return to town he reoccupied his old rooms in the house of Pasqualati, on the Mölk Bastion. The Streichers continued their friendly services; after some time procured him two good servants, and otherwise looked after his interests. These servants remained with him for a year or two, and this was probably the most comfortable time of the last half of Beethoven's life.[4]

As early as April we find him endeavouring to arrange a concert for the production of his two symphonies; but without success.[5] The opportunity arrived in another way. The news of the great defeat of the French at Vittoria (fought June 21) reached Vienna on July 13, following on that of the disaster of Moscow and the battles of Lützen and Bautzen (May 2 and 21), and culminating in Leipzig October 19. It is easy to understand how great the sensation was throughout the whole of Germany, and how keenly Beethoven must have felt such events,[6] though we may wonder that he expressed his emotion in the form of the Orchestral programme-music, entitled 'Wellington's Victory, or the Battle of Vittoria,' a work conceived on almost as vulgar a plan as the 'Battle of Prague,' and containing few traces of his genius. This, however, is accounted for by the fact that the piece was suggested by Maelzel [7] the mechanician, a man of undoubted ability, who knew the public taste far better than Beethoven did. An occasion for its performance soon suggested itself in a concert for the benefit of the soldiers wounded at Hanau (October 30),

---

[1] Published in Kuffner's complete works as 'Hersilia.'
[2] Letter to Zmeskall, April 19.   [3] Letter to Archduke.
[4] Schindler, i. 187.   [5] Letters to Zmeskall, April 19, 26.
[6] See the note to Thayer, ii. 313. The idea noted in his diary is a far nobler one—a National Hymn, each nation engaged to be represented by a march, and the whole to close with a Te Deum. Nohl, *Beethovenfeier*, pp. 71, 72.
[7] See Moscheles' note to his edition of Schindler, i. 153.

where the Austrians endeavoured to cut off the retreat of the
French after Leipzig. The concert took place on December 8,
in the large Hall of the University, and was organised by
Maelzel. The programme, like the Battle Symphony itself,
speaks of a man who knew his audience. It was of reasonable
length and contained the 7th Symphony — in MS. and produced for the first time — two Marches performed by Maelzel's
mechanical trumpet, and the Battle Symphony. The orchestra
was filled by the best professors of the day — Salieri, Spohr,
Mayseder, Hummel,[1] Romberg, Moscheles, etc. Beethoven
himself conducted, and we have Spohr's testimony that the
performance of the Symphony was really a good one. The
[programme was repeated on the 12th and the] success of both
concerts was immense, and Beethoven addressed a letter of
thanks to the performers, which may be read at length in
Schindler and elsewhere.

It was probably about this time that Beethoven forwarded
a copy of the Battle Symphony to the Prince Regent. The
letter which accompanied it has not been preserved, but it
was never acknowledged by the Prince, and Beethoven felt the
neglect keenly. The work was produced at Drury Lane a year
afterwards — February 10, 1815, and had a great run, but
this was through the exertions of Sir George Smart, who
himself procured the copy from Vienna.

Early in January 1814 a third concert was given in the
great Redoutensaal with the same programme and nearly the
same performers as before, except that some numbers from
the ' Ruins of Athens ' were substituted for Maelzel's march
[marches] ; and on the 27th February a fourth, with similar
programme and with the important addition of the Symphony
in F — placed last but one in the list. The huge programme
speaks of Beethoven himself as clearly as the two first did of the
more practical Maelzel. The 7th Symphony was throughout
a success, its Allegretto being repeated three times out of the
four. But the 8th Symphony did not please, a fact which
greatly discomposed Beethoven. On April 11 Beethoven
played the B♭ Trio at Schuppanzigh's benefit concert, and in
the evening a chorus of his to the words ' Germania, Germania,' was sung as the finale to an operetta of Treitschke's,

---

[1] Beethoven's droll note to Hummel (Nohl, *Neue Briefe*, No. 96) shows that
there was no quarrel between them.

à propos to the fall of Paris (March 31). Moscheles was present at the concert, and gives [1] an interesting account of the style of Beethoven's playing. Spohr heard [2] the same trio, but under less favourable circumstances. A month later Beethoven again played the B♭ Trio — his last public appearance in chamber music. The spring of 1814 was remarkable for the revival of ' Fidelio.' Treitschke had been employed to revise the libretto, and in March we find Beethoven writing to him — ' I have read your revision of the opera with great satisfaction. It has decided me once more to rebuild the desolate ruins of an ancient fortress.' This decision involved the entire rewriting and rearrangement of considerable portions; others were slightly altered, and some pieces were reintroduced from the first score of all. The first performance took place at the Kärnthnerthor Theatre on May 23. On the 26th the new Overture in E was first played, and other alterations were subsequently introduced. On July 18 the opera was played for Beethoven's benefit. A pianoforte score, made by Moscheles under Beethoven's own direction,[3] carefully revised by him, and dedicated to the Archduke, was published by Artaria in August. One friendly face must have been missed on all these occasions — that of the Prince Lichnowsky, who died on April 15.

During the winter of 1814–15 an unfortunate misunderstanding arose between Beethoven and Maelzel. The Battle Symphony was originally written at the latter's suggestion for a mechanical instrument of his called the Panharmonicon, and was afterwards orchestrated by its author for the concert, with the view to a projected tour of Maelzel in England.[4] Beethoven was at the time greatly in want of funds, and Maelzel advanced him £25, which he professed to regard as a mere loan, while the other alleged it was for the purchase of the work. Maelzel had also engaged to make ear-trumpets for Beethoven, which were delayed, and in the end proved failures. The misunderstanding was aggravated by various statements of Maelzel, and by the interference of outsiders, and finally by Maelzel's departure through Germany to England, with an imperfect copy of the Battle Symphony clandestinely obtained. Such a

[1] Moscheles, *Leben*, i. 15.
[2] Spohr, *Selbstbiog.* i. 203. He says it was a new Trio in D, but the Trio in D had been out for five years.
[3] See Moscheles, *Leben*, i. 17, 18. [4] *A. M. Z.* 1814, p. 71.

complication was quite sufficient to worry and harass a sensitive, obstinate, and unbusinesslike man like Beethoven. He entered an action against Maelzel, and his deposition on the subject, and the letter [1] which he afterwards addressed to the artists of England, show how serious was his view of the harm done him, and the motives of the doer. Maelzel's case, on the other hand, is stated with evident *animus* by Beethoven's adherents,[2] and it should not be overlooked that he and Beethoven appear to have continued friends after the immediate quarrel blew over. If to the opera and the Maelzel scandal we add the Kinsky lawsuit now in progress, and which Beethoven watched intently and wrote much about, we shall hardly wonder that he was not able to get out of town till long past his usual time. When at length he writes from Baden it is to announce the completion of the Sonata in E minor, which he dedicates to Count Moritz Lichnowsky. The letter [3] gives a charming statement of his ideas of the relation of a musician to his patron.

The triumphant success of the Symphony in A, and of the Battle-piece, and the equally successful revival of 'Fidelio,' render 1814 the culminating period of Beethoven's life. His activity during the autumn and winter was very great; no bad health or worries or anything else external could hinder the astonishing flow of his inward energy. The [E minor] Sonata is dated 'Vienna, 16th August,' and was therefore probably completed — as far as any music of his was ever completed till it was actually printed — before he left town. On August 23 he commemorated the death of the wife of his kind friend Pasqualati in an 'Elegischer Gesang' (op. 118). On October 4 he completed the Overture in C ('Namensfeier,' op. 115), a work on which he had been employed more or less for two [six] years, and which has a double interest from the fact that its themes seem to have been originally intended [4] to form part of that composition of Schiller's 'Hymn to Joy' which he first contemplated when a boy at Bonn, and which keeps coming to the surface in different forms, until finally embodied in the 9th Symphony in 1823. Earlier in the year he had made some progress with a sixth piano concerto — in D — of which not only are extensive sketches in existence, but sixty pages in

[1] *Briefe*, Nos. 113, 114.
[2] The whole evidence will be given by Mr. Thayer in his forthcoming volume. He assures me that Maelzel has been much sinned against.
[3] Sept. 21, 1814.   [4] Nottebohm, *Beethoveniana*, XIV.

complete score. It was composed at the same time with the
Cello Sonatas (op. 102) ; and finally gave way to them.[1] But
there was a less congenial work to do — Vienna had been
selected as the scene of the Congress, and Beethoven was bound
to seize the opportunity not only of performing his latest
symphonies but of composing some new music appropriate to
so great an occasion.[2] He selected in September a cantata
by Weissenbach, entitled ' Die glorreiche Augenblick '[3] — an
unhappy choice, as it turned out — composed it more quickly
than was his wont,[4] and included it with the Symphony in A, and
the Battle of Vittoria, in a concert for his benefit on November 29.
The manner in which this concert was carried out gives a
striking idea of the extraordinary position that Beethoven held
in Vienna. The two Halls of the Redoutensaal were placed
at his disposal for two evenings by the government, and he
himself sent personal invitations in his own name to the various
sovereigns and other notabilities collected in Vienna. The
room was crowded with an audience of 6000 persons, and
Beethoven describes himself as ' quite exhausted with fatigue,
worry, pleasure, and delight.'[5] At a second performance on
December 2 the hall was less crowded. One of the fêtes provided during the Congress was a tournament in the Riding
School on November 23, and for this Beethoven would appear [6]
to have composed music, though no trace of it has yet been
found. During the continuance of the Congress he seems to
have been much visited and noticed, and many droll scenes
doubtless occurred between him and his exalted worshippers.
The Archduke and Prince Rasoumoffsky as Russian Ambassador, were conspicuous among the givers of fêtes, and it
was at the house of the latter that Beethoven was presented to
the Empress of Russia.

In addition to the profit of the concerts Schindler implies
that Beethoven received presents from the various foreign
sovereigns in Vienna. The pecuniary result of the winter was
therefore good. He was able for the first time to lay by money,
which he invested in shares in the Bank of Austria.[7]

The news of Bonaparte's escape from Elba broke up the

---

[1] See Nottebohm, *N. B.* X; and *Crystal Palace Programme*, Nov. 6, 1875.
[2] Schindler, i. 198.
[3] The glorious Moment. See Nottebohm, *Catalogue*, op. 136.
[4] Nottebohm, *N. B.* No. XII.   [5] Letter to Archduke, Köchel, p. 31.
[6] His note to the Archduke, Köchel, p. 29.   [7] Schindler, i. 202.

Congress, and threw Europe again into a state of perturbation. In Vienna the reaction after the recent extra gaiety must have been great. Beethoven was himself occupied during the year by the Kinsky lawsuit; his letters upon the subject to his advocate Kanka are many and long, and it is plain from such expressions as the following that it seriously interrupted his music. ' I am again very tired, having been forced to discuss many things with P — [Kx]. Such things exhaust me more than the greatest efforts in composition. It is a new field, the soil of which I ought not to be required to till, and which has cost me many tears and much sorrow.' . . . . [And in another letter], ' Do not forget me, poor tormented creature that I am.' [1]

Under the circumstances it is not surprising that he composed little during 1815. The two Sonatas for piano and cello (op. 102), dated ' July ' and ' August '; the chorus ' Es ist vollbracht,' as finale to a piece of Treitschke's, produced to celebrate the entry into Paris (July 15); the ' Meeresstille und glückliche Fahrt,' and a couple of songs, ' Sehnsucht ' and ' Das Geheimniss ' [2] — are all the original works that can with certainty be traced to this year. But the beautiful and passionate Sonata in A (op. 101), which was inspired by and dedicated to his dear friend Madame [Baroness] Ertmann — ' Liebe werthe Dorothea Cäcilia ' — was probably composed at the end of this year, since it was played in public on February 18, 1816, though not published for a year after. The national airs which he had in hand since 1810 for Thomson of Edinburgh were valuable at such a time, since he could turn to these when his thoughts were too much disturbed for original composition — a parcel of Scotch songs is dated May 1815.

The publications of 1815 are still fewer than the compositions. The Polonaise in C (op. 89) — dedicated to the Empress of Russia,[3] who had greatly distinguished Beethoven at one of Prince Rasoumoffsky's receptions — appeared in March; the Sonata op. 90, and a song, ' Kriegers Abschied,' in June. These are all. On June 1 he wrote to Salomon, then resident in London, offering his works from op. 92 to 97 inclusive for sale, with ' Fidelio,' the Vienna Cantata, and the Battle Symphony. And this is followed in November by letters to Birchall, sending

---

[1] To Kanka, Feb. 24, 1815.   [2] B. & H. 239 and 245.
[3] The pianoforte arrangement of the Symphony in A is also dedicated to her.

various pieces. Salomon died on November 25.

The second quarrel with Stephen Breuning must have occurred in 1815.[1] Someone had urged him to warn Beethoven against pecuniary relations with his brother Caspar, whose character in money matters was not satisfactory. Breuning conveyed the hint to Beethoven, and he, with characteristic earnestness and simplicity, and with that strange fondness for his unworthy brothers which amounted almost to a passion, at once divulged to his brother not only the warning but the name of his informant. A serious quarrel naturally ensued between Breuning and Caspar, which soon spread to Beethoven himself, and the result was that he and Breuning were again separated — this time for several years. The letter in which Beethoven at last asks pardon of his old friend can hardly be omitted from this sketch. Though undated it was written in 1826.[2] It contained his miniature painted by Hornemann in 1802, and ran as follows (the original has *Du* and *dein* throughout) :—

' Beneath this portrait, dear Stephen, may all that has for so long gone on between us be for ever hidden. I know how I have torn your heart. For this the emotion that you must certainly have noticed in me has been sufficient punishment. My feeling towards you was not malice. No — I should no longer be worthy of your friendship ; it was passionate love for you and myself ; but I doubted you dreadfully, for people came between us who were unworthy of us both. My portrait has long been intended for you. I need not tell you that I never meant it for any one else. Who could I give it to with my warmest love so well as to you, true, good, noble Stephen? Forgive me for distressing you ; I have suffered myself as much as you have. It was only when I had you no longer with me that I first really felt how dear you are and always will be to my heart. Come to my arms once more as you used to do.'

October was passed in Baden, chiefly in bed.

On November 15 of this year Caspar Carl Beethoven died — a truly unfortunate event for Ludwig. Caspar had for long received pecuniary assistance from his brother, and at his death he charged him with the maintenance of his son Carl, a lad between 8 and 9. This boy, whose charge Beethoven under-

---

[1] Schindler (i. 228) says 1817; but it is obvious that it happened before Caspar's death (Breuning, 46).   [2] Schindler, i. 228; ii. 128.

took with all the simplicity and fervour of his nature, though
no doubt often with much want of judgment, was quite unworthy of his great uncle. The charge altered Beethoven's
nature, weaned him from his music, embroiled him with his
friends, embittered his existence with the worry of continued
contentions and reiterated disappointments, and at last,
directly or indirectly, brought the life of the great composer to
an end long before its natural term.

On Christmas Day, at a concert in the Redoutensaal for
the benefit of the Bürger Hospital, Beethoven produced his
new Overture and Meeresstille, and performed the 'Mount
of Olives.' As an acknowledgment for many similar services
the municipal council had recently [(November 16)] conferred
upon him the freedom of the city — *Ehrenbürgerthum*. It was
the first public title that the great *roturier* had received. He
was not even a Capellmeister, as both Mozart [1] and Haydn
had been, and his advocate was actually forced to invent that
title for him, to procure the necessary respect for his memorials
in the lawsuit which occupied so many of his years after this
date.[2] It is a curious evidence of the singular position he held
among musicians. He was afterwards made a member of the
Philharmonic Societies of Stockholm and Amsterdam, and
received Orders from some of the Courts in exchange for his
Mass, but the one title he valued was that of *Ton-dichter* —
'Poet in music.' [3]

The resuscitation of his oratorio is perhaps connected with
a desire in Beethoven's mind to compose a fresh one. At any
rate he was at this time in communication both with the Tonkünstler Societät and the Gesellschaft der Musik-Freunde of
Vienna on the subject. By the latter body the matter was taken
up in earnest. Subject and poet were left to himself, and a
payment of 300 gold ducats was voted to him for the use of the
oratorio for one year. The negotiation dragged on till 1824
and came to nothing, for the same ostensible reason that his
second opera did, that no good libretto was forthcoming.[4]

1816 was a great year for publication. The Battle Sym-

---

[1] 'Was haben Sie da?' was the enquiry of the 'privilegirte Bettlerin' when
the hearse drew up with Mozart's body at the gate of the cemetery, 'Ein Capellmeister' was the answer.   [2] Schindler, i. 262.

[3] See Breuning, 101; and compare letter to Mlle. Streicher, *Briefe*, No. 200;
and the use of the word 'gedichtet' in the title of the Overture op. 115.

[4] See the very curious letter from Beethoven of Jan. 23, 1824, in Pohl's
pamphlet, *Gesellschaft*, etc., 1871.

phony in March; the Violin Sonata and the B♭ Trio (op. 96, 97) — both dedicated to the Archduke — in July; the 7th Symphony — dedicated to Count Fries, with a pianoforte arrangement to the Empress of Russia; the String Quartet in F minor (op. 95) — to Zmeskall; and the beautiful Liederkreis (op. 98) to Prince Lobkowitz; all three in December. These, with the 8th Symphony and three detached songs, form a list rivalling, if not surpassing, that of 1809. The only compositions of this year are the Liederkreis (April), a Military March in D, ' for the Grand Parade ' (Wachtparade), June 4, 1816; [1] a couple of songs; and a trifle in the style of a birthday cantata for Prince Lobkowitz.[2] This is the date of a strange temporary fancy for German [directions] in preference to Italian which took possession of him. Some of his earlier pieces contain German terms, as the Six Songs, op. 75, and the Sonata 81*a*. They reappear in the Liederkreis (op. 98) and Merkenstein (op. 100) and come to a head in the Sonata op. 101, in which all the indications are given in German, and the word ' Hammerklavier ' appears for ' Pianoforte ' in the title. The change is the subject of two letters to Steiner.[3] He continued to use the name ' Hammerklavier ' in the Sonatas op. 106, 109, and 110; and there apparently this vernacular fit ceased.[4]

Beethoven had a violent dislike to his brother's widow, whom he called the ' Queen of Night,' and believed, rightly or wrongly, to be a person of bad conduct. He therefore lost no time in obtaining legal authority for taking his ward out of her hands and placing him with Giannatasio del Rio, the head of an educational institution in Vienna; allowing his mother to see him only once a month. This was done in February 1816, and the arrangement existed till towards the end of the year, when the widow appears to have appealed with success against the first decree. The cause had been before the *Landrecht* court, on the assumption that the *van* in Beethoven's name indicated nobility. This the widow disputed, and on Beethoven's being examined on the point he confirmed her argument by pointing successively to his head and his heart

---

[1] B. & H. 15.   [2] See Thayer's Catalogue, No. 208.
[3] *Briefe*, Nos. 167, 168.
[4] The German comes out, however, when he is deeply moved, as in the ' Bitte für innern and äussern Frieden,' and the ' Aengstlich ' in the ' Dona ' of the Mass, the ' beklemmt ' in the Cavatina of the B flat Quartet, etc.

saying — ' My nobility is *here* and *here*.' The case was then
sent down to a lower court, where the magistrate was notoriously inefficient, and the result was to take the child from his
uncle on the ground that his deafness unfitted him for the
duties of a guardian.   Carl's affairs were then put into the
hands of an official, and all that Beethoven had to do was to
pay for his education.   Against this decree he entered an appeal
which was finally decided in his favour, but not till January 7,
1820.   Meantime his energies were taken up with the contest
and the various worries and quarrels which arose out of it,
involving the writing of a large number of long and serious
letters.   How he struggled and suffered the following entry in
his diary of the early part of 1818 will show : — ' Gott, Gott,
mein Hort, mein Fels, o mein Alles, du siehst mein Inneres
und weisst wie wehe mir es thut Jemanden leiden machen
müssen bei meinem guten Werke für meinen theuren Karl ! ! !
O höre stets Unaussprechlicher, höre mich — deinen unglück-
lichen unglücklichsten aller Sterblichen.'   Between the dates
just mentioned, of the beginning and ending of the lawsuits,
he completed no orchestral music at all.   Apart from sympathy
for a great composer in distress, and annoyance at the painful
and undignified figure which he so often presented, we have
indeed no reason to complain of a period which produced the
three gigantic Pianoforte Sonatas, op. 106,[1] op. 109,[2] and op.
110 [3] — which were the net product of the period ; but such
works produce no adequate remuneration, and it is not difficult
to understand that during the lawsuit he must have been in
very straitened circumstances, cheap as education and living
were in Vienna at that date.   His frequent letters to Ries and
Birchall in London at this time urging his works on them for the
English market are enough to prove the truth of this.   One
result of these negotiations was the purchase by the Philharmonic Society, through Mr. Neate, under minute of July 11,
1815, of the MS. overtures to the ' Ruins of Athens,' ' King
Stephen ' and op. 115, for 75 guineas.   To make matters worse
Prince Lobkowitz died on December 16, 1816, and with him —
notwithstanding that here too Beethoven appealed to the law —
all benefit from that quarter ceased.   His pension was therefore

---

[1] Composed 1818-19, and published Sept. 1819.
[2] Composed 1819-20, published Nov. 1821.
[3] Dated Dec. 25, 1821, and published Aug. 1822.

from that date diminished to about £110. The few compositions attributable to this period are an arrangement of his early
C minor Trio (op. 1) as a String Quintet (op. 104); two sets of
national airs with variations for piano and flute (op. 105 and
107), a few songs — ' So oder so,' ' Abendlied,' and the Hymn
of the Monks in ' William Tell ' [1] in memory of his old friend
Krumpholz, who died May 2 — and others. None of these
can have been remunerative; in fact some of them were certainly presented to the publishers.

An incident of this date which gratified him much was the
arrival of a piano from Broadwoods. Mr. Thomas Broadwood,
the then head of the house, had recently made his acquaintance
in Vienna, and the piano seems to have been the result of the
impression produced on him by Beethoven. The Philharmonic
Society are sometimes credited with the gift, but no resolution
or minute to that effect exists in their records. The books of
the firm, however, show that on December 27, 1817, the grand
piano No. 7362 [2] was forwarded to Beethoven's address. A
letter appears to have been written to him at the same time
by Mr. Broadwood, which was answered by Beethoven immediately on its receipt. His letter has never been printed, and
is here given exactly in his own strange French.[3]

' A Monsieur Monsieur Thomas Broadvood a Londres (en
Angleterre).

Mon très cher Ami Broadvood!

jamais je n'eprouvais pas un plus grand Plaisir de ce que me
causa votre Annonce de l'arrivée de cette Piano, avec qui vous
m'honorez de m'en faire présent; je regarderai coñe un Autel,
ou je deposerai les plus belles offrandes de mon esprit au divine
Apollon. Aussitôt coñe je recevrai votre Excellent instrument,
je vous enverrai d'en abord les Fruits de l'inspiration des
premiers moments, que j'y passerai, pour vous servir d'un
souvenir de moi à vous mon très cher B., et je ne souhaits ce que,
qu'ils soient dignes de votre instrument.

Mon cher Monsieur et ami recevéz ma plus grande con-

[1] B. & H. 224, 247, 255.
[2] The compass of this instrument was 6 octaves, from C five lines below the
Bass stave. A sister piano, No. 7252, of the same compass and quality, was
made about the same time for the Princess Charlotte, and is now at Claremont.
The number of grand pianos (full and concert only) now (Feb. 1878) reached
by the firm is 21,150.
[3] This interesting autograph is in the possession of Mr. M. M. Holloway,
to whom I am indebted for its presence here.

sideration de votre ami et très humble serviteur Louis van
Beethoven. Vienne le 3ᵐᵉ du mois Fevrier 1818.'

The instrument in course of time reached [1] its destination,
was unpacked by Streicher, and first tried by Mr. Cipriani
Potter, at that time studying in Vienna. What the result of
Beethoven's own trial of it was is not known. At any rate no
further communication from him reached the Broadwoods.

A correspondence, however, took place through Ries with
the Philharmonic Society on the subject of his visiting England.
The proposal of the Society was that he should come to London
for the spring of 1818, bringing two new MS. symphonies to
be their property, and for which they were to give the sum of
300 guineas. He demanded 400, — 150 to be in advance.[2]
However, other causes put an end to the plan, and on the
5th of the following March he writes to say that health has
prevented his coming. He was soon to be effectually nailed
to Vienna. In the summer of 1818 the Archduke [3] had been
appointed Archbishop of Olmütz. Beethoven was then in the
middle of his great Sonata in B♭ (op. 106), and of another work
more gigantic still ; but he at once set to work with all his old
energy on a grand Mass for the installation, which was fixed
for March 20, 1820. The score was begun in the autumn of
1818, and the composition went on during the following year,
uninterrupted by any other musical work, for the B♭ Sonata
was completed for press by March 1819, and the only other
pieces attributable to that year are a short canon for 3 voices
(' Glück zum neuen Jahr '), and 10 Variations of National Airs
(op. 107). The Sonata just referred to, the greatest work yet
written for the piano, and not unjustly compared with the
Ninth Symphony, belonged in a special sense to the Archduke.
The first two movements were presented to him for his Name-
day ; [4] the whole work when published was dedicated to him,
and the sketch of a piece for solo and chorus [5] exists in which
the subject of the first Allegro is set to the words ' Vivat
Rodolphus.' In addition the Archduke is said to have been
able to play the Sonata. Beethoven may have hated his
' Dienstschaft,' but there is reason to believe that he was sin-

---

[1] The note from Broadwood's agent in Vienna which accompanied this
letter shows that all freight and charges were paid by the giver of the piano.
[2] Letter to Ries July 9, 1817 ; and Hogarth's *Philharmonic Society*, p. 18.
[3] Schindler, i. 269.   [4] Letter, Köchel, No. 49.
[5] Nottebohm, *N. B.* VII.

cerely attached to his clever, sympathetic, imperial pupil.

The summer and autumn of both 1818 and 1819 were spent at Mödling. His health at this time was excellent, and his devotion to the Mass extraordinary. Never had he been known to be so entirely abstracted from external things, so immersed in the struggle of composition. Schindler [1] has well described a strange scene which occurred during the elaboration of the Credo — the house deserted by the servants, and denuded of every comfort ; the master shut into his room, singing, shouting, stamping, as if in actual conflict of life and death over the fugue ' Et vitam venturi ' ; his sudden appearance wild, dishevelled, faint with toil and 24 hours fast ! These were indeed ' drangvollen Umständen ' [2] — wretched [harassing] conditions — but they are the conditions which accompany the production of great works. During the whole of this time the letters [3] show that his nephew occupied much of his thoughts. While at work on this sublime portion of the Mass [4] just mentioned, he was inspired to write the beautiful Sonata in E major (op. 109), the first of that unequalled trio which terminate that class of his compositions.

It is hardly necessary to say that the installation went by without Beethoven's Mass, which indeed was not completed till the beginning of 1822 [1823]. He announces its termination on February 27,[5] and the perfect copy of the score was delivered into his patron's hands on March 19, exactly two [three] years after the day for which it was projected. As the vast work came to an end [was proceeding], his thoughts reverted to his darling pianoforte, and the dates of December 25, 1821, and January 13, 1822, are affixed to the two immortal and most affecting Sonatas, which vie with each other in grandeur, beauty, and pathos, as they close the roll of his large compositions for the instrument which he so dearly loved and so greatly ennobled.

But neither Mass nor Sonatas were sufficient to absorb the energy of this most energetic and painstaking of musicians. The climax of his orchestral compositions had yet to be reached. We have seen that when engaged on his last pair of symphonies

[1] Schindler, i. 270.
[2] His own words to Ries in describing the production of the Sonata in B♭. *Briefe*, No. 212.   [3] To Blöchinger (Sept. 14), to Artaria (Oct. 12), etc.
[4] End of 1819 and beginning of 1820. Nottebohm, Op. 109, in Catalogue.
[5] Letter to the Archduke, Köchel.

in 1812, Beethoven contemplated a third, for which he had then fixed the key of D minor. To this he returned before many years were over, and it was destined in the end to be the Ninth Symphony. The very characteristic theme of the Scherzo actually occurs in the sketch-books as early as 1815,[1] as the subject of a ' fugued piece,' though without the rhythm which now characterises it. But the practical beginning of the Symphony was made in 1817, when large portions of the first movement — headed ' Zur Sinfonie in D,' and showing a considerable approach to the work as carried out — together with a further development of the subject of the Scherzo, are found in the sketch-books. There is also evidence [2] that the Finale was at that time intended to be orchestral, and that the idea of connecting the ' Hymn to Joy ' with his 9th Symphony had not at that time occurred to Beethoven. The sketches continue in 1818,[3] more or less mixed up with those for the Sonata in B♭; and, as if not satisfied with carrying on two such prodigious works together, Beethoven has left a note giving the scheme of a companion symphony which was to be choral in both the Adagio and Finale.[4] Still, however, there is no mention of the ' Ode to Joy,' and the text proposed in the last case is ecclesiastical.

We have seen how 1819, 1820, and 1821 were filled up. The summer and autumn of 1822 were spent at Baden, and were occupied with the Grand Overture in C (op. 124), for the open- ing of the Josephstadt Theatre at Vienna, whence it derives its title of ' Weihe des Hauses ' — and the arrangement of a March and Chorus from the ' Ruins of Athens ' for the same occasion, and was followed by the revival of ' Fidelio ' at the Kärnth- nerthor [5] Theatre in November. That the two symphonies were then occupying his mind — ' each different from the other and from any of his former ones ' — is evident from his con- versation with Rochlitz in July 1822, when that earnest critic submitted to him Breitkopf's proposition for music to Faust.[6] After the revival of ' Fidelio ' he resumed the Symphony, and here for the first time Schiller's hymn appears in this connexion. Through the summer of 1823 it occupied him incessantly, with the exception of a few extras — the 33 Variations (op. 120),

[1] Nottebohm, N. B. xxiii.   [2] Ibid.   [3] Ibid.   [4] Ibid.
[5] Schindler, ii. 11. A. M. Z. for 1822, 836.
[6] Rochlitz, Für Freunde der Tonkunst, iv. 357, 8.

which were taken up almost as a *jeu d'esprit*, and being published in June must have been completed some time previously, a dozen ' Bagatelles ' for the piano (op. 119, 1-6, and op. 126), which can be fixed to the end of 1822 and beginning of 1823, and a short cantata for the birthday of Prince Lobkowitz (April 13 [12]) for soprano solo and chorus, the autograph of which is dated the evening previous to the birthday.[1] He began the summer at Hetzendorf, but a sudden dislike to the civilities of the landlord drove him to forfeit 400 florins which he had paid in advance, and make off to Baden. But wherever he was, while at work he was fully absorbed ; insensible to sun and rain, to meals, to the discomforts of his house and the neglect of the servants, rushing in and out without his hat, and otherwise showing how completely his great symphony had taken possession of him. Into the details of the composition we cannot here enter, farther than to say that the subject of the vocal portion, and its connexion with the preceding instrumental movements were what gave him most trouble. The story may be read in Schindler and Nottebohm, and it is full of interest and instruction. At length, on September 5 [1823], writing from Baden to Ries, he announces that ' the copyist has finished the score of the Symphony,' but that it is too bulky to forward by post. Ries was then in London, and it is necessary to go back a little to mention that on November 10, 1822, the Philharmonic Society passed a resolution offering Beethoven £50 for a MS. symphony, to be delivered in the March following. This was communicated to Beethoven by Ries, and accepted by him on December 20. The money was advanced, and the MS. copy of the 9th Symphony in the Philharmonic library carries a statement in his autograph that it was ' written for the society.' How it came to pass notwithstanding this that the score was not received by the Philharmonic till after its performance in Vienna, and that when published it was dedicated to the King of Prussia, are facts difficult to reconcile with Beethoven's usual love of fairness and justice.

Notwithstanding the announcement to Ries the process of final polishing went on for some months longer. Shortly before he left Baden, on October 5, he received a visit from Weber [2] and his pupil young Benedict, then in Vienna for the production

[1] Printed by Nohl, *Neue Briefe*, No. 255.
[2] Max V. Weber, *C. M. von Weber*, ii. 505-511.

of 'Euryanthe.' The visit was in consequence of a kind wish for
the success of the work expressed by Beethoven to Haslinger,
and was in every way successful. In former times [1] he had
spoken very depreciatingly of Weber, but since the perusal of
'Freischütz' had changed his mind. [2] No allusion was made to
Weber's youthful censures on the 4th and 7th Symphonies;
Beethoven was cordial and even confidential, made some interesting remarks on opera books, and they parted mutually
impressed. He returned to town at the end of October to a
lodging in the Ungergasse, near the Landstrasse gate, and by
February 1824 began to appear in the streets again and enjoy
his favourite occupation of peering with his double eyeglass into
the shop windows, [3] and joking with his acquaintances.

The publications of 1823 consist of the Overture to the
'Ruins of Athens' (op. 114), and the 'Meeresstille' (op. 112),
both in February; and the Sonata (op. 111) in April.

The revival of 'Fidelio' in the previous winter had inspired
Beethoven with the idea of writing a new German opera, and
after many propositions he accepted the 'Melusina' ['Melu-
sine'] by Grillparzer, a highly romantic piece, containing
many effective situations, and a comic servant's part, which
took his fancy extremely. Grillparzer had many conferences
with him, and between the two the libretto was brought into
practical shape. While thus engaged he received a commission
from Count Brühl, intendant at the Berlin Theatre, for an opera
on his own terms. Beethoven forwarded him the MS. of
'Melusina' for his opinion, but on hearing that a ballet of
a somewhat similar character was then being played at Berlin,
he at once renounced all idea of a German opera, and broke
out in abuse of the German singers for their inferiority to the
Italians, who were then playing Rossini in Vienna. In fact
this season of 1823 had brought the Rossini fever to its height,
no operas but his were played. Beethoven had indeed heard
the 'Barbiere' in 1822, [4] and had even promised to write an
opera for the Italian company in the same style, a promise
which it is unnecessary to say was never redeemed. Like
Mendelssohn he was in earnest in pursuit of an opera book,
but, like Mendelssohn, he never succeeded in obtaining one to
his mind. What he wanted he told Breuning on his death-bed

---

[1] Seyfried, 22.   [2] *C. M. von Weber*, ii. 509.   [3] Schindler, ii. 56.
[4] Ibid. ii. 49.

was something to interest and absorb him, but of a moral and elevating tendency, of the nature of ' Les Deux Journées ' or ' Die Vestalin ' [' La Vestale '], which he thoroughly approved ; for dissolute stories like those of Mozart's operas had no attraction for him, and he could never be brought to set them. After his death a whole bundle of libretti was found which he had read and rejected.[1]

But opera or no, it was quite a different thing to find the public so taken up with Rossini that no one cared for either his Mass or his new Symphony.[2] He had written early in 1823 to Prussia, France, Saxony, Russia, proposing a subscription for the Mass of 50 ducats from the sovereigns of each of those countries — but the answers were slow and the subscriptions did not arrive, and he therefore made use of the opportunity afforded him by Count Brühl to propose the two works to him for production at Berlin. The answer was favourable, and there appeared good prospect of success. But the disgrace of driving their great composer to the northern capital for the production of his last and greatest works was too much for the music-loving aristocracy of Vienna — and an earnest memorial was drawn up, dated February 1824, signed by the Lichnowskys,[3] Fries, Dietrichstein, Palfy [Pálffy], and 25 others of the persons principally concerned with music in that city, beseeching him to produce the Mass and Symphony, and to write a second opera, which should vindicate the claim of classical music, and show that Germany could successfully compete with Italy. Such an address, so strongly signed, naturally gratified him extremely. The theatre ' an der Wien ' was chosen, and after an amount of bargaining and delay and vacillation which is quite incredible — partly arising from the cupidity of the manager, partly from the extraordinary obstinacy and suspiciousness of Beethoven, from the regulation of the censorship, and from the difficulties of the music — but which was all in time surmounted by the tact and devotion of Lichnowsky, Schindler, and Schuppanzigh, the concert took place in the Kärnthnerthor theatre on May 7.[4] The programme consisted of the Overture in C — ' Weihe des Hauses ' — the Kyrie, Credo, Agnus and Dona, of the Mass in D, in the form of three

---

[1] Breuning, 96, 50 *note*. He thought the two libretti mentioned the best in existence.   [2] Dietrichstein in Schindler.
[3] The Archduke was away, and so also must Lobkowitz have been.
[4] Schindler, ii. 62-68.

hymns,[1] and the 9th Symphony. The house was crowded, and the music, especially the Symphony, excited the greatest enthusiasm. It was on this occasion that the affecting incident occurred of the deaf composer being turned round by Mlle. Ungher that he might *see* the applause he and his music were evoking. But financially the concert was a failure. The use of the theatre, including band and chorus, cost 1000 florins, and the copying 800 more, but the prices remained as usual, so that the net result to Beethoven was but 420 florins, or under £40. Well might he say that 'after six weeks of such discussion he was boiled, stewed, and roasted.' He was profoundly distressed at the result, would eat nothing, and passed the night in his clothes. The concert, however, was repeated on the 23rd at noon, the theatre guaranteeing Beethoven 500 florins. On the second occasion all the Mass was suppressed but the Kyrie; the trio 'Tremate' and some Italian solos were introduced; the Overture and Symphony remained. The result of this was a loss to the management, and furnishes a curious trait of Beethoven's character. He could not without difficulty be induced to accept the guaranteed sum, but he invited Schindler, Schuppanzigh, and Umlauf to dinner, and then accused them in the most furious manner of having combined to cheat him over the whole transaction! This broke up the party; the three faithful friends went off elsewhere, and Beethoven was left to devour the dinner with his nephew. The immediate effect of the outbreak was to put an end to a promising negotiation which he was carrying on with Neate, who in a letter of December 20, 1823, had, on the part of the Philharmonic Society, offered him 300 guineas and a benefit guaranteed at £500 for a visit to London with a symphony and a concerto. The terms had been accepted, and the arrangements for the journey were in a forward state; and although it is probably true that Beethoven's attachment to his nephew was too strong to allow of his leaving him when it came to the point, yet it is equally true that the event just related was the ostensible cause. Four days after he was at his beloved Baden, and craving for music paper.[2]

The subscriptions to the Mass had come in slowly, and in

---

[1] These were thus announced, and sung to German words, owing to the interference of the *Censur* and the clergy. A similar stipulation is still made at Exeter Hall. A mass must be announced as a 'Service.' Thus extremes meet.

[2] Letter to Steiner, May 27.

nine months amounted only to 350 ducats (£175) for seven copies.[1] This was too slow to satisfy the wishes of the composer. Indeed he had for some time past been negotiating in a much more mercantile style than before for the sale of Mass, Symphony, and Overture. He offered them to various publishers.[2] It is an unexpected trait in his character, and one for which we may thank his devotion to his nephew, to whom he was now sacrificing everything, that he might leave him well provided for. It resulted in his dealing for the first time with Schott, of Mayence, who purchased the Mass and the Symphony for 1000 and 600 florins respectively on July 19, 1824. He appears at this time to have taken generally a more commercial view of his position than usual, to have been occupied with plans [3] for new collected editions of his works (which however came to nothing), and generally to have shown an anxiety to make money very unlike anything before observable in him. In such calculations he was much assisted by a young man named Carl Holtz [Holz], a government employé, a good player on the violin and cello, a clever caricaturist, a bon vivant, and generally a lively agreeable fellow.[4] Holtz obtained an extraordinary influence over Beethoven. He drew him into society, induced him to be godfather to his child, to appoint him his biographer,[5] and amongst other things to forsake his usual sobriety, and to do that which has been absurdly exaggerated into a devotion to drink. That these commercial aims — too absurd if one reflects on the simple unbusinesslike character of Beethoven — and the occasional indulgence to which we have alluded, did not impair his invention or his imagination is evident from the fact that at this time he composed his last Quartets, works which, though misunderstood and naturally unappreciated at the time, are now by common consent of those who are able to judge placed at the head of Beethoven's compositions for individuality, depth of feeling, and expression. The relations with Russia, which Beethoven had originally cultivated through the Count de Browne, and the works dedicated to the Emperor of Russia and the Prince

---

[1] Schindler, ii. 17. The subscribers were the courts of Prussia, France, Saxony, Darmstadt, and Russia; Prince Radziwill, and Mr. Schelble, the founder of the Cäcilien Verein at Frankfort.

[2] See *Briefe* Nos. 237, 238, 285; and *Neue Briefe*, No. 269 *note*.

[3] Letter to Peters, June 5, 1822.

[4] *Briefe*, Nos. 363, 377.   [5] Ibid. No. 379.

Rasoumoffsky, and which had been deepened by the personal attention shown him in 1814 by the Empress were now to bear their full fruit. Early in 1824 he received a letter from Prince Galitzin [Galitsin], a Russian nobleman living at Petersburg, and subsequently others, requesting him to compose three string quartets to be dedicated to the Prince and handsomely paid for. The first of these, that in E♭, sketched at Baden in the autumn of 1824, was sold to Schott [1] in advance for the sum of 50 ducats, and was completed after his return to Vienna early in October. It was first played on March 6, 1825, and published in the following March. With the Quartet Schott received the Overture op. 124, the ' Opferlied ' (op. 121), and ' Bundeslied ' (op. 122), an air ' An Chloe ', [' Der Kuss '] (op. 128), and 11 Bagatelles (op. 126), for which he paid the sum of 130 ducats. The Quartet was played by Schuppanzigh, Weiss, Linke, and Holtz, and it was a humorous idea of the Master to make each player, after so long an interval, sign a compact ' pledging his honour to do his best, and vie with his comrades in zeal.' [2]

The second Quartet was that which now stands third — in A minor, op. 132. It was first played on November 6, 1825, and was published on September 27 by Schlesinger. For this he seems to have obtained 80 ducats. In a letter to Peters it is mentioned as ' a Quartet, and a grand one too.'

The third, in B flat (op. 130), originally ended with a fugue of immense length and still greater obscurity, which was afterwards published separately as op. 133. It was completed in 1825, and was played in its first form on March 21, 1826. The new finale — so gay and full of spirit — was written (at Artaria's instance) in great discomfort at his brother's house at Gneixendorf on November 26 [in November], just before leaving on the journey which cost him his life. It is his last completed composition. The Quartet was published by Artaria, May 7, 1827. The relations between Beethoven and Prince Galitzin have been the subject of much controversy. It will be sufficient here to say that Beethoven is not known to have received the promised payment, and that the quartets were sold by him to the publishers already named.

[1] Letter of Sept. 17. Here again we are puzzled by the fact that the quartet was sold to Schotts before Prince Galitzin had either paid, or declined to pay, the sum he promised.
[2] *Briefe*, 322.

Beethoven remained at Baden till October 1824. On his return to Vienna his nephew entered the University as a student in philology. The career of this worthy may be summed up in a few lines. He went in for his degree and was plucked, abandoned literature for trade, stood for the necessary examination in the Polytechnic School, and was plucked again; in despair attempted to shoot himself, and failed even to do that. He was then, as a suicide, taken charge of by the police, and after a time ordered out of Vienna at a day's notice, and at last joined the army.[1] And through it all his old uncle clung to him with truly touching affection. He, most simple-minded of men, could not believe that any one should really not desire to do his best; and so on the least appearance of contrition or amendment he forgives and embraces him, he bathes him in tenderness and confidence, only each time to find himself again deceived. The letters which this more than father wrote to his unworthy prodigal son are most affecting — injudicious no doubt, but full of tenderness and simplicity.

The first few weeks of the winter of 1824 were occupied in scoring the E flat Quartet, the composition of which had been the work of the summer, but it was hardly complete before Beethoven was taken with a severe illness in the lower part of the stomach.[2] For this he called in Staudenheim, a surgeon of eminence, who however was soon cashiered as too brusque, and replaced by Braunhofer. The malady hung about him till his next visit to the country; and its disappearance is commemorated in the *canzona di ringraziamento in modo lidico offerta alla divinita* [*divinità*] *da un guarito*, which forms so noble a feature in the A minor Quartet. His stay at Baden in 1825 was of unusual length, lasting from May 2 [3] till October 15,[3] by which date that Quartet was completely finished. It had already been tried, strictly in private, as early as August at the desire of the publisher, Beethoven sitting close to the players, and perhaps profiting by the rehearsal to make many alterations; and on November 6 was played, still in private but to a densely crowded room,[4] by Schuppanzigh and Linke's quartet party.

The B♭ Quartet was his next work, and it was first performed in public by the party just mentioned on March 21,

---

[1] He died in Vienna, April 13, 1858.   [2] Schindler, ii. 111, 112.
[3] *Briefe*, Nos. 329 and 372.   [4] *A. M. Z.* Dec. 21, 1825.

1826. The *Presto* and *danza tedesca* [1] were encored, but the Cavatina seems to have made no impression, and the fugue, which then served as finale, was universally condemned. In the case of the fugue his judgment agreed with that of his critics; it was published separately (op. 133) and a new finale written; but he did not often give way to the judgments of his contemporaries. 'Your new quartet did not please,' was one of the bits of news brought to him on his death-bed by some officious friend. 'It will please them some day,' was the answer.[2]

Between the date last-mentioned and October 1826 occurred the series of disasters with young Carl already alluded to; and the latter month found both uncle and nephew at Johann Beethoven's residence at Gneixendorf. It is a village near Krems, on the Danube, about 50 miles west of Vienna, and here his brother had settled on the property (*Gut*) which gave occasion to Ludwig's famous joke (see p. 27). The party must have been a curiously ill-assorted one. The somewhat pompous money-loving *Gutsbesitzer*; his wife, a common frivolous woman of questionable character;[3] the ne'er-do-well nephew, intensely selfish and ready to make game of his uncle or make love to his aunt; and in the midst of them all the great composer — deaf, untidy, unpresentable, setting every household rule and household propriety at defiance, by turns entirely absorbed and pertinaciously boisterous, exploding in rough jokes and horse-laughter, or bursting into sudden fury at some absolute misconception; — such a group had few elements of permanence in it. But nothing could stop the wonderful flow of Beethoven's thoughts. In fact, music being to him the language of his emotions, the more agitated he was the more he composed, and his very deafness, which fortunately must have made him insensible to much that went on around him, drove him more completely into himself and compelled him to listen to the workings of his own heart unalloyed by anything external. To his deafness we no doubt mainly owe the very individual and original style of the later quartets. Thanks to Michael Kren [Krenn],[4] who was engaged by Frau Johann to wait on him, we can see him with our own eyes. 'At half-past 5

---

[1] Originally written in A, and intended for the A minor Quartet.
[2] Breuning, 95.   [3] Schindler, in Wallace ii. 148.
[4] Nohl, *Leben*, iii. 716. *Deutsche Musik-Zeitung*, Mar. 8, 1862.

he was up and at his table, beating time with hands and
feet, singing, humming, and writing. At half-past 7 was the
family breakfast, and directly after it he hurried out of doors,
and would saunter about the fields, calling out, waving his
hands, going now very slowly, then very fast, and then suddenly standing still and writing in a kind of pocket-book. At
half-past 12 he came into the house to dinner, and after dinner
he went to his own room till 3 or so ; then again in the fields
till about sunset, for later than that he might not go out. At
half-past 7 was supper, and then he went to his room, wrote
till 10, and so to bed.'

During the last three years he had been composing incessantly, and yet all that he had done seemed to him as nothing
— as a mere prelude to what he was yet to do. As Newton
before his death spoke of himself as ' a child picking up a few
shells on the shore while the great ocean of truth lay undis-
covered before him,' so does Beethoven in somewhat similar
strain express himself at the close of his life : — ' I feel as if I
had written scarcely more than a few notes.' [1] And again — ' I
hope still to bring a few great works into the world, and then,
like an old child, to end my earthly course somewhere amongst
good people.' [2] His wish, however, was not fulfilled ; he was
to die in harness. Either before leaving Vienna or immediately
after it he had completed the C♯ minor Quartet, and before
the end of October had finished another, that in F, which is
dated with his own hand ' Gneixendorf [3] am 30 Oktober,
1826 [am Oktober 26].' This is the work the finale of which
embodies the strange dialogue between Beethoven and his
cook, ' Muss es sein? — Es muss sein,' and shows how he could
rise from the particular to the universal. A week or two later
and he had written a fresh finale to replace the enormously long
fugue which originally terminated the B♭ Quartet, and dated
it ' November 1826.' And this was his last work. By that time
the fine weather, of which he speaks shortly after his arrival,[4]
had departed. The economical *Gutsbesitzer* had forbidden his
infirm brother a fire in his room, the food was not to his taste,
and he was informed that for both food and lodging a charge

[1] Letter to Schott, Sept. 17, 1824.
[2] Letter to Wegeler, Vienna, Oct. 7, 1826.
[3] ' I am at Gneixendorf,' says he to Haslinger. ' The name is something
like the breaking of an axletree ' (*Briefe*, No. 383).
[4] Letter to Haslinger, Oct. 13.

would be made ; so that he determined to brave the police and return with his nephew to Vienna on December 2. The journey from Gneixendorf to Krems, the post town, is not far,[1] but the close carriage could not be had, and Beethoven was obliged to perform it in an open chaise — the weather was cold and damp, and the result was a violent cold in the stomach, which was the beginning of the end. He took to his bed on reaching the Schwarzspanierhaus. His former physicians, Braunhofer and Staudenheim, refused to attend him, and he was in the hands of a Dr. Wawruch who had been casually called to him by a billiard-marker at the rooms frequented by young Carl Beethoven. The cold had developed into an inflammation of the lungs, and on this dropsy supervened. Wawruch, who appears to have been a poor practitioner and a pompous pedant,[2] drenched his patient with herb decoctions, but the malady would probably have ended fatally whatever treatment had been adopted. What the poor patient most required was good nursing and comfort, and this he could not obtain till after the departure of his nephew for his regiment in the latter half of December. Then Schindler and Stephen Breuning came to his bedside, and from this time to the end Gerhard Breuning, the son of Stephen, a boy of eleven [fourteen], was his constant attendant. He was first tapped on December 18 [20], then again on January 8, and a third time on January 28. It was during one of these operations that on seeing the water he made the characteristic remark ' Better from my belly than from my pen.' The confidence both of Beethoven and his friends in Wawruch now became much shaken, and an application was made to Malfatti, who had attended him years before, but like so many others had parted from him in anger. It was long before Malfatti would answer the appeal, and even then he would only act in conjunction with Wawruch. The treatment was now changed, and iced punch administered in large quantities as a restorative. His faith in Malfatti was only equalled by his disgust at Wawruch. He would watch for the arrival of the former with eagerness, and welcome him as if he were an angel — whereas when Wawruch appeared he would immediately stop talking, turn his face to the wall with the exclamation ' Ach, der Esel ! ' and only answer his enquiries

---

[1] Gneixendorf is on the high ground which rises above Krems, two miles due north of it.   [2] Breuning, 90.

in the most grumpy manner.[1] Under the change Beethoven's
spirits greatly improved, and if permitted he would at once
have begun to work. This however was forbidden, and reading
only allowed. Walter Scott was recommended him, and he
began ' Kenilworth,' [2] but soon threw it down with the exclamation ' the man writes only for money.' He now made
acquaintance with some of Schubert's songs [3] for the first time,
and was delighted with them — ' Truly Schubert has the divine
fire,' were his words. Handel's works, in 40 volumes,[4] a
present from Stumpff, arrived at this date, and were an unfailing source of interest to him [5] as he lay in bed. A lithograph
[Artaria's print of an engraving] of Haydn's birthplace gave
him the liveliest satisfaction; his delight at receiving it, his
wrath at the mis-spelling of the name, and his curious care in
paying for it, may be read in Breuning's narrative (pp. 98-100).
During the four months of his last illness he wrote and dictated
many letters — 24 are published, some of them of considerable
length, and others no doubt remain in MS.

His nephew still retained his hold on his affections. A letter
to Dr. Bach, his old advocate, of January 3, declares the lad
his sole heir, and commits him to Bach's special care. He
was continually tormented with anxiety as to their future
maintenance. Notwithstanding Prince Galitzin's promise, dated
November 10/22, 1826, no portion of the money due from
him on the 3 Quartets had yet been received. The seven bank
shares he would not allow to be touched, regarding them
as the property of his nephew. He therefore wrote to his
friends [6] in London, urging the Philharmonic Society to carry
out their old intention of giving a concert for his benefit. The
reply to this was a letter from Moscheles,[7] dated March 1,
sending £100 from the Philharmonic Society on account of the
proceeds of a concert shortly to be given. His delight at this
response was great, and his answer, dated March 18 (forwarding
also the metronome marks of the 9th Symphony), is full of
warmth and enthusiasm. Meantime a fourth tapping had taken

[1] Ibid. 92, 90.
[2] Schindler ii. 135; but see his letter in Moscheles' *Leben*, i. 144.
[3] The ' Junge Nonne,' ' Die Burgschaft,' ' Der Taucher,' ' Elisium,' and the
Ossian Songs are mentioned by Schindler. But of these the only one published
before Beethoven's death was the first.
[4] See the Sale Catalogue.   [5] Breuning, 94.
[6] Feb. 8 to Stumpff; Feb. 22 to Moscheles and to Smart; March 6 to Smart;
and Mar. 14 to Moscheles.
[7] See the account in Moscheles' *Leben*, i. 138–175.

place on February 27, and a great discharge was caused by his
emotion at the receipt of Moscheles' letter on March 17.

During his illness he had a few visitors besides Schindler
and the two Breunings, who were his daily attendants, and
Holtz, who came frequently. Breuning mentions Johann
Beethoven and the nephew (in the early part of the time
only), Tobias and Carl Haslinger, Diabelli, Baron Eskeles,
Rauch, Dolezalek, Clement. Strangers occasionally arrived,
amongst whom Hummel with his pupil Ferdinand Hiller,
then a boy of 15, who saw him on March 8,[1] are worthy
of note. But the friends of his earlier days — Fries, Erdödy,
Ertmann, Brunswick, Gleichenstein, Zmeskall, Seyfried, the
Streichers, Czerny, Schuppanzigh, Linke — those who had
been honoured by his dedications, or had reaped the glory of
producing his compositions — were either dead or otherwise
occupied; at any rate none appeared. The absence of all
trace of the Archduke Rudolph at this time, or of any reference
to him in the correspondence of the last few years, is very
remarkable.

Neither Beethoven himself nor any of his friends seem to
have been aware that death was near. His letter to Moscheles
of March 18 is full of projects, and a conversation reported by
Breuning (p. 97) shows that he contemplated a tenth Symphony, a Requiem, music to Faust, and an instruction book
for the piano — ' to be something quite different from that of
any one else.' To Moscheles he speaks of the symphony as
lying ' in his desk fully sketched,' — much as Coleridge used to
talk of works as complete of which the title pages only had been
put on paper; for nothing which can be identified with the
description has been found. Indeed, the time of both projects
and fulfilment was over — the night was come in which no
man can work. The accumulation of water increased alarmingly, the wounds inflamed, lying became painful, and it was
evident that the end was near. On the 10th he wrote to Schott
desiring the dedication of the C# minor Quartet to be altered
in favour of Baron von Stutterheim, in token of his obligation
to him as colonel of his nephew's regiment. On the 18th [17th],
after dictating his letter to Moscheles, he settled the dedication
of his last Quartet (in F, op. 135) to Johann Wolfmayer,[2] a
Vienna merchant for whom he had much respect. On the

    [1] Hiller's *Beethoven* (1871), p. 73.   [2] Schindler, ii. 142.

following day he spoke of writing to Stumpff and Smart, but was compelled to relinquish the task to Schindler. '*Plaudite amici, comoedia finita est*,' said he to his two faithful friends, with a touch of his old good humour — the play was over, the lifelong symphony ended, and it was time to draw the curtain. On the 23rd, with the help of Breuning, he added with his own hand a codicil to his will, appointing his nephew Carl his sole heir, but without power over the capital of the property bequeathed. Thus two of his latest acts were inspired by his nephew. Several people appear to have come in and out during the last few days to look once more at the departing composer. Amongst these Schubert is said to have remained a long time, and to have been recognised by Beethoven, though he failed to understand the signs made by the dying man. He left the room at length deeply moved. On the 24th Beethoven received the Sacraments of the Roman Church, and at about one in the afternoon of the same day he sank into apparent unconsciousness, and a distressing conflict with death began which lasted the rest of that day, the whole of the next, and until a quarter to six on the evening of the 26th, the constant convulsive struggle and the hard rattle in the throat testifying at once too painfully to the strength of his constitution and the fact that he was still alive. Stephen Breuning and Schindler had gone to the Währinger cemetery to choose the spot for the grave; the little Breuning was away at his lessons; Johann Beethoven's wife and Anselm Hüttenbrenner (the friend of Schubert) alone [1] were in the sick room. As the evening closed in, at a quarter to six, there came a sudden storm of hail and snow, covering the ground and roofs of the Schwarzspanierplatz, and followed by a flash of lightning, and an instant clap of thunder. So great was the crash as to rouse even the dying man. He opened his eyes, clenched his fist, and shook it in the air above him. This lasted a few seconds while the hail rushed down outside, and then the hand fell, and the great composer was no more.

He was 56 years old on the 16th of the previous December.

The seven bank shares (for 1000 florins each) were discovered the next day after long search in a secret drawer in the writing desk, together with the two passionate and mysterious letters so often supposed — though to all appearance

[1] See the *Wiener Abendpost*, 24 Oct. 1868.

inaccurately — to be addressed to the Countess Giulietta Guicciardi.

The post mortem examination was made on the evening of the 27th by Dr. Wagner in the presence of Wawruch. During the 28th the body lay in one of the rooms, and a sketch [1] of the face was made by Danhauser.

The funeral took place on the 29th at 3 p.m., and was attended by an immense mass of people, including all the musicians of the city. From the house to the Church of the Minorites, in the Alsergasse on the glacis, a procession was formed, in which Breuning, Johann van Beethoven, and Mosel, were chief mourners; the coffin was borne by eight members of the Opera, with Eybler, Hummel, Seyfried, Kreutzer, Weigl, Gyrowetz, Gänsbacher, and Würfel, and 32 [36] torch bearers — including Czerny, Lablache, and Schubert — round it. A choir of 16 men singers and 4 trombones alternately sang and played two *Equali* of Beethoven's, originally written for trombones for All Souls Day during his stay in Linz, and arranged to the words of the ' Miserere ' and ' Amplius ' by Seyfried. The crowd was enormous,[2] soldiers had to be called in to force the way, and it took an hour and a half to pass the short distance from the house to the church. From the church the body was taken in a hearse drawn by four horses, and without music, to the Währinger cemetery, followed by a long string of carriages and many people.

At the gate of the cemetery an address by Grillparzer was recited by Anschütz — who being an actor was not permitted to speak on consecrated ground — and two poems by Castelli and Schlechta were read and distributed. Before the earth was filled in three laurel wreaths were placed on the coffin by Hummel. The grave is against the south wall of the cemetery, near the middle. Schubert is three places off, and Clement and Seyfried lie nearly opposite.

On April 3, the furniture and clothes, with the pianos by Graf and Broadwood, were sold by auction [3] at the lodgings. The same day a solemn mass was performed in the Hofpfarrkirche of the Augustines; Mozart's Requiem was sung, Lablache not only taking the bass part but paying Barbaja a

---

[1] Breuning, 113. Afterwards lithographed, but now rare owing to the stone having broken.

[2] 20,000, says Breuning.   [3] Breuning, 123.

sum of 200 gulden for the cost of the singers. Two days later
Cherubini's Requiem was sung at the Karlskirche.

In November [1] the sale of his musical effects took place by
auction. Thayer has reprinted the catalogue in his *Verzeichniss*,
p. 173. There were 50 lots of sketch and note-books; 19 autographs of unpublished and 73 autographs of published pieces;
5 MS. copies of published pieces; 40 copies of unpublished
works; 10 sets of MS. parts; 17 MS. copies of music by various
authors — including Cherubini's 'Faniska' and Mozart's
'Zauberflöte'; 26 lots of printed music; 6 of works on music;
1 autograph symphony of Haydn's; a pianoforte; a medal;
and two violins. The produce of the sale was 1193 florins,
curiously little [2] when compared with the prices which such
treasures would fetch now. This sum, added to the value of
the bank shares and the Philharmonic £100, made in all,
according to Schindler,[3] a total of 10,232 florins (in silver), or
a little over £1000.

In course of time the grave fell into neglect, and in 1863
the Gesellschaft der Musik-freunde undertook to exhume and
re-bury [4] the remains of both Beethoven and Schubert. This
was done on October 13, and Beethoven's monument now
consists of a large flat stone covering the grave, surrounded by
an iron railing, and headed by an obelisk in stone bearing a
lyre, the usual emblems of eternity, and the simple name
BEETHOVEN.

Beethoven's music has been divided by Herr von Lenz [5]
into three styles, and the division has evidently some justice
in it, or it would not have been so widely accepted as it is even
by those who differ about its details. That the division is not
chronological is evident from the fact that M. Lenz includes
the 2nd Symphony (op. 36), written in 1802, in the first period,
while he places the Sonatas op. 26 and 27, which were completed a year earlier, and the 3 Sonatas op. 31, which were
written in company with the 2nd Symphony, in the second

---

[1] Ibid. 125. The catalogue and valuation are dated August 16.
[2] Autographs of symphonies fetched 5 florins each; overtures 2½; sonatas 2;
the Mass in D 7; and so on.
[3] *Biographie*, ii. 147.
[4] See the *Actenmässige Darstellung der Ausgrabung und Wiederbeisetzung der irdischen
Reste von Beethoven und Schubert*, Vienna, 1863.
[5] *Beethoven et ses trois styles*. Petersburg, 1852.

period. As far as the sonatas are concerned he ends the first period with op. 22.

But we may go further than that. The first movement of the Solo Sonata in E♭ (op. 7) and the Finale of the Quartet in F, op. 18, No. 1, contain examples of the episodes which form one of Beethoven's main characteristics, such as even the first movement of the 'Eroica' can hardly surpass for independence and originality. The Scherzo of Symphony No. 1 and the Scherzo and Finale of Symphony No. 2 contain passages which would be found original and characteristic if met with in the compositions of many years later. Some will find it hard to place the Quartet in F minor, which Mendelssohn thought the most *Beethovenish* of all Beethoven's works, in anything but the third style; while the Overture in C, op. 124, written in 1822, might be classed with the works of an earlier period. And yet on the whole the division is just, as an expression of the fact that Beethoven was always in progress; and that, to an extent greater than any other musician, his style matured and altered as he grew in life. He began, as it was natural and inevitable he should, with the best style of his day — the style of Mozart and Haydn; with melodies and passages that might be almost mistaken for theirs, with compositions apparently moulded in intention [1] on them. And yet even during this Mozartian epoch we meet with works or single movements which are not Mozart, which Mozart perhaps could not have written, and which very fully reveal the future Beethoven. Such are the first two movements of the Sonata in A (op. 2), the Sonatas in E♭ (op. 7) and D (op. 10, No. 3) and B♭ (op. 22), the Scherzos of the 1st and 2nd Symphonies already mentioned, and the Coda of the Finale to the 2nd Symphony. From this youthful period he passes by the 3 Sonatas op. 31— which we have seen him speaking of as a change in his style — by the Kreutzer Sonata (March 1803), by the Pianoforte Concerto in C minor,[2] and by the 'Eroica' (1804), to his mature period, a time of extraordinary greatness, full of individuality, character, and humour, but still more full of power and mastery and pregnant strong sense.

This splendid and truly astonishing period contains the

[1] Sonata, op. 10, No. 1; melody in working out of 1st movement of Septet; Adagio of op. 31, No. 1; Quintet, op. 16.
[2] In the Finale of this work we almost surprise the change of style in the act of being made.

opera of Leonora-Fidelio, with its 4 overtures; the Mass in C; six symphonies, from the 'Eroica' to the No. 8 inclusive; the overture to 'Coriolan'; the Egmont music; the Pianoforte Concertos in G and E flat; the Violin Concerto; the Rassoumoffsky Quartets, and those in E♭ and F minor; the 3 later Pianoforte Trios; the Liederkreis; and last not least, a dozen sonatas for piano solo, of which the chiefs are the D minor and the 'Appassionata,' though the others are closely akin and hardly inferior.

From this period of extraordinary force and mastery — though abounding also in beauty and sentiment — he passes by a second transition to his third and final style. This transition is perhaps more obvious than the former. The difference between the 9th Symphony and its predecessors — not only in dimensions and in the use of the chorus, but in elevation and sentiment, and in the total impression produced — is unmistakable. The five Pianoforte Sonatas, op. 101 to 111, are perfectly distinct from any of the earlier ones, not only in individuality — for all Beethoven's works are distinct — but in a certain wistful yearning, a sort of sense of the invisible and vision of the infinite, mingled with their power. The last Quartets, op. 127 to op. 135, have the same characteristics as the Sonatas; but they are also longer, full of changes of time, less observant than before of the traditional forms of expression, less careful to make obvious the links of connection, and still more full of intense personality and of a wild unimprisoned spirit. All the sentiment and earnestness of Schumann, all the grace and individuality of Schubert, are there; with an intensity, breadth, and completeness, which those masters might perhaps have attained if they had bestowed the time and pains on their work which Beethoven did. In this period he passes from being the greatest musician to be a great teacher, and in a manner which no one ever did before and possibly no one will ever do again, conveys lessons which by their intense suggestiveness have almost the force of moral teaching. The cause of this is not far to seek. As we have seen in the preceding portion of this sketch the year 1814 was the culminating period of Beethoven's prosperity. He had produced his latest and then greatest works under such favourable circumstances as no musician had before enjoyed. He had been fêted and caressed by emperors and empresses, and others of the greatest

of this world's great; he had for the first time in his life been
able to put by money, and feel at all independent of daily
labour.   Immediately on this came an equally great and
sudden reverse — and that not a material reverse so much as
a blow to his spirit, and a series of misfortunes to mind and
heart such as left all his former sufferings far behind.   His
brother's death; the charge of the nephew; the collision with
the widow and with his other relatives and friends; the lawsuits; the attempts to form a home of his own, and the domestic
worries and wretchedness consequent thereon; the last stages
of his deafness; the appearance of chronic bad health; the
actual want of money — all these things, which lasted for many
years, formed a Valley of the Shadow of Death, such as few
men have been called to traverse, and which must inevitably
have exercised a great influence on a nature so sensitive and
in some respects so morbid.   That this fiery trial did not injure
his power of production is evident from the list of the great
works which form the third period — from op. 101 inclusive.
That it altered the tone and colour of his utterance is equally
evident from the works themselves.   'He passes,' as Mr.
Dannreuther has finely said,[1] 'beyond the horizon of a mere
singer and poet, and touches upon the domain of the seer and
the prophet; where, in unison with all genuine mystics and
ethical teachers, he delivers a message of religious love and
resignation, identification with the sufferings of all living
creatures, deprecation of self, negation of personality, release
from the world.'

Beyond the individual and peculiar character which distinguishes his works and makes them Beethovenish, as Haydn's
are Haydnish and Mozart's Mozartish, though in a greater
degree because of the stronger character of the man — there
are definite peculiarities in Beethoven's way of working which
should be specified as far as possible.   That he was no wild
radical, altering for the mere pleasure of alteration, or in the
mere search for originality, is evident from the length of time
during which he abstained from publishing or even composing
works of pretension, and from the likeness which his early works
possess to those of his predecessors.   He began naturally with
the forms which were in use in his days, and his alteration of
them grew very gradually with the necessities of his expression.

[1] *Macmillan's Magazine*, July, 1876.

The form of the sonata is ' the transparent veil through which Beethoven seems to have looked at all music.' [1]   And the good points of that form he retained to the last — the ' triune symmetry of exposition, illustration, and repetition,' [2] which that admirable method allowed and enforced — but he permitted himself a much greater liberty than his predecessors had done in the relationship of the keys of the different movements and parts of movements, and in the proportion of the clauses and sections with which he built them up.   In other words, he was less bound by the forms and musical rules, and more swayed by the thought which he had to express, and the directions which that thought took in his mind.

1. The range of keys within which the composers of sonatas and symphonies before Beethoven confined themselves was very narrow.   Taking the first movement as an example of the practice, the first theme was of course given out in the tonic, and this, if major, was almost invariably answered in due course by a second theme in the ' dominant ' or fifth above ; for instance, if the sonata was in C the second subject would be in G, if in D it would be in A.   If the movement were in minor, the answer was in the relative major — C minor would be answered by Eb, A minor by C♯, and so on. This is the case 19 times out of 20 in the sonatas and symphonies of Haydn and Mozart.   A similar restriction governed the key of the second movement.   It was usually in the ' subdominant ' or fifth below — in F if the key of the piece were C, in Bb if the key were F, and so on.   If the piece were in a minor key the second movement was in the third below.   A little more latitude was allowed here than in the former case ; the subdominant now and then became the dominant, or, very rarely, the ' mediant ' or third above ; and the relative major was occasionally exchanged for the tonic major.

Beethoven, as already remarked, adopted very different relations in respect of the change of key from one movement to another.   Out of 81 works in sonata form he makes the transition to the dominant only 3 times ; to the subdominant 19 times ; to the mediant or 3rd above 4 times ; and to the submediant or 3rd below 30 times.   From tonic major to tonic minor he changes 12, and from minor to major 8 times.   His favourite change was evidently to the submediant or third

[1] Ibid.   [2] Ibid.

below — that is to say, to a key less closely related to the tonic and more remote than the usual key. He makes it in his first work (op. 1, No. 2). In his B♭ trio (op. 97) he has it twice, and in his Variations on an original theme (op. 34), each of the first 5 variations is a third below the preceding.

In the relation of his first and second subjects he is more orthodox. Out of 26 of the pianoforte sonatas the usual change to the dominant occurs 17 times, to the mediant 3, and to the submediant 3.

2. Another of his innovations had respect to the connection of the different subjects or clauses. His predecessors were in the habit rather of separating their clauses than of connecting them; and this they did by conventional passages of entirely different character from the melodious themes themselves, stuffed in between the themes like so much hay or paper for mere packing. Any symphony of Mozart or Haydn will give examples of this, which Wagner [1] compares to the ' rattling of the dishes at a royal feast.' Mozart also has a way of drawing up and presenting arms before the appearance of the second subject, which tends to cut the movement up into very definite portions. Of these tiresome and provoking intermediate periods Beethoven got rid by the use of phrases which are either parts of the main theme or closely related to it; and he thus gives his movements a unity and consistency as if it were an organic growth, and not a piece of work cunningly put together by art or man's device. How he effects this, and the very tentative and gradual way in which he does it, may be seen in Symphonies 1 and 2 and the ' Eroica,' in which last all trace of the old plan has almost entirely disappeared.

3. The first movement of the ' Eroica ' supplies instances of other innovations on the established forms. Not only in the ' exposition ' (before the double bar) are other themes brought in besides the two main subjects, but in the ' illustration ', or, to use the more common term, the ' working out ', there is an unanticipated explosion which, to say the least, is entirely without precedent, followed by an entirely fresh episode as important as anything that has occurred before, and that again by a new feature (the staccato bass) which, while it accompanies and reinforces the main subject, adds materially to the interest of the music. Again, in the ' repetition ' we have not

[1] *Music of the Future*, translated by Dannreuther, 1873; p. 44.

only a great departure from regular rule in the keys which the music goes through, but we have a coda of no less than 140 bars long, proclaiming itself by its opening as an independent member of the movement, and though made almost entirely out of previous material, yet quite differently expressed from anything before, and full of fresh meaning. Now none of these alterations and additions to the usual forms were made by Beethoven for their own sake. They were made because he had something to say on his subject which the rules did not give him time and space to say, and which he could not leave unsaid. His work is a poem in which the thoughts and emotions are the first things, and the forms of expression second and subordinate. Still, even in his innovations, how careful he is to keep as near the rules as possible! His chief episodes occur in the working out, where a certain licence was always lawful; and codas were recognised, and had even, as in Mozart's 'Jupiter,' been turned to noble account. The same characteristics are found in the ninth Symphony as in the third, only the mood of mind being entirely different, the mode of expression is different too, but the principle of the perfect subordination of the expression to the thought, while adhering as closely to the 'form' as was consistent with perfect expression, is the same. One or two pieces of his second period may, however, be named, in which both thought and mode of expression are so entirely different from anything before them, that they stand quite by themselves. Such movements as the opening Adagio of the Sonata in C♯ minor, or the Con moto of the Pianoforte Concerto in G — in which Schumann used to see a picture of Orpheus taming brute-nature — have no prototypes; they are pure creations, founded on nothing previous, but absolutely new in style, idea, and form.

In the later quartets it must be admitted that he wandered further away from the old paths; the thought there seems everything and the form almost nothing. And this fact, as much as the obscurity and individuality of the thoughts themselves and their apparent want of connexion until they have become familiar, is perhaps the cause that these noble works are so difficult to understand. The forms, depend upon it, were founded in reason and nature. They grew through long periods to be what Haydn fixed them at; and as long as the thoughts of composers did not burst their limits they were perfect. Beethoven came, and he first enlarged and modified them, adhering however to their fundamental principle of recurrence and recapitulation, till in the end, withdrawn more and more into himself by his deafness, he wrote down what he felt, often without thinking of the exigences of those who were to hear him. This, however, only applies to the later quartets. The ninth Symphony and the last pianoforte sonatas are as strictly in form, and as coherent and intelligible, as could be desired.

4. A striking instance of this loyalty is found in Beethoven's treatment of the 'Introduction.' This — a movement in slow time, preceding the first Allegro — forms part of the original design of the overture by Lully, and is found in nine out of ten of Handel's overtures. Haydn often has one in his symphonies, usually 8 to 12 bars long, occasionally as much as 20. Mozart has prefixed similar prefaces to some of his works, such as the Symphony in E flat, the Quintet for piano and wind instruments, and the famous Quartet in C, dedicated to Haydn. Beethoven, besides placing one before his Quintet for piano and wind (op. 16), which, as already remarked, is like a challenge to Mozart, has one to the Sonata Pathétique and to the first Symphony. In the last of these cases it is 12 bars long. In the 2nd Symphony it expands to 33 bars long, and increases largely in development. But even this is a mere preface when compared with the noble and impressive movements which usher in the Allegros of the 4th and 7th Symphonies — long and independent movements, the latter no less than 80 bars in length, full of important and independent ideas, and of the grandest effect.

In all the instances mentioned — the Succession of Keys, the Episodes, the Coda, the Introduction — Beethoven's modifications seem to have sprung from the fact of his regarding his music less as a piece of technical performance than his predecessors had perhaps done, and more as the expression of the ideas with which his mind was charged. The ideas were too wide and too various to be contained in the usual limits, and therefore the limits had to be enlarged. He regards first what he has to say — his thought — and how he shall convey and enforce and reiterate that thought, so as to express it to his hearer exactly as he thinks it, without being careful to find an old formula in which to couch it. Even consecutive fifths were no hindrance to him — they gave the exact sound in which he wished to convey his idea of the moment; and therefore he used them as naturally, as a speaker might employ at a particular juncture, with the best effect, an expression usually quite inadmissible. No doubt other musicians had used similar liberties; but not to the same extent, because no one before had been gifted with so independent and original a nature. But in Beethoven the fact was connected with the peculiar position he had taken in society, and with the new ideas which the general movement of freedom at the end of the eighteenth century, and the French Revolution in particular, had forced even into such strongholds as the Austrian courts. People who were the servants of archbishops and princes, and moved about with the rest of the establishment in the train of their master, who wore powder and pigtail and red-heeled shoes, and were forced to wait in ante-rooms and regulate their conduct strictly by etiquette, and habitually keep down their passions under decorous rules and forms, could not give their thoughts and emotions the free and natural vent which they would have had without the perpetual curb of such restraints and the habits they must have engendered. But Beethoven, like Mirabeau, had 'swallowed the formulas' of the day; he had thrown over etiquette, and, *roturier* as he was, lived on absolute equality with the best aristocracy of Vienna. What he felt he said, both in society and in his music, and the result is before us. The great difference is, as we have already remarked, that whereas in his ordinary intercourse he was extremely abrupt and careless of effect, in his music he was exactly the reverse; painstaking, laborious, and never satisfied till he had conveyed his ideas in unmistakable language.

5. The Scherzo stands perhaps in a different category from the three features already mentioned. It is less of a modification and more of a distinct new creation. The word is met with in Haydn and Mozart, but in a different sense to that in which Beethoven uses it, and apparently neither of those masters have it in a symphony. To both of them the third movement of a symphony was a minuet. All that a minuet could be made they made of it, but it was never given them to go beyond. The minuet remained a dance tune to the end of its days, and is so even in Beethoven's No. 8 Symphony. In fact Haydn actually lamented that he could not make more of it than he

had. When discussing a rule of Albrechtsberger's by which
fourths were prohibited in strict composition, he said,[1] ' Such
trifling is absurd ; I wish, instead, that some one would try to
compose a really new minuet.' This Beethoven did. The third
movement of his first Symphony is what Haydn wished to see.[2]
Though labelled ' menuetto ' it is quite unlike a minuet. It is
in fact a scherzo, and in its little dimensions is the pattern and
model of those gigantic movements which in the ' Eroica,' the
C minor, the No. 7, and especially the No. 9 of the Symphonies ;
in the B flat trio ; in the Sonata, op. 106 ; and the first of the
Rassoumoffsky Quartets, are so truly astonishing, and so characteristic of their great author.

6. An innovation of great importance in the Finale, for
which no precedent can be found, was the introduction of the
Chorus. In the ' Eroica ' Symphony Beethoven showed how a
set of orchestral variations could be employed in a finale. In
the Choral Fantasia again he showed with what effect a chorus
could be employed in the same part of the work. But in the
9th Symphony he combined the two, by using the chorus in a
succession of variations. Mendelssohn has followed his example
in the ' Lobgesang,' the vocal portion of which is the last movement of a symphony ; but he has not adopted the Variation-
form.

7. One of the most striking characteristics of Beethoven's
music is the individual variety of each piece and each movement. In the symphonies every one of the 9 first movements
is entirely distinct from the other 8, and the same of the
andantes, scherzos, and finales. Each is based on a distinct
idea, and each leaves a separate image and impression on the
mind. And the same may be said of the majority of the smaller
works, of the concertos and quartets and pianoforte trios —
certainly of the sonatas, all but perhaps a very few. The themes
and passages have no family likeness, and have not the air of
having been taken out of a stock ready made, but are born for
the occasion. He thus very rarely repeats himself. The theme
of the slow movement of the Sonata in F minor and the second
theme in the first movement of the Sonata in C (op. 2, Nos. 1
and 3) are adapted from his early pianoforte quartets. The

---

[1] Griesinger, p. 114.
[2] One would like to know if Haydn ever heard the first or any other of
Beethoven's Symphonies, and what his real feelings were about them. He lived
on till 1809, and might thus have heard the ' Eroica ' and even the C minor.

minuet in the Septet is developed from that in the little Sonata in G (op. 49, No. 2). The Turkish March in the 'Ruins of Athens' had already appeared as a theme for Variations in D (op. 76). The theme of the Variations in the Choral Fantasia is a song of his own, 'Seufzer eines Ungeliebten' (No. 253), composed many years before. The melodies of two Contretänze (No. 17a) are employed in the Prometheus music, and one of them is also used in a set of Variations (op. 35) and in the Finale to the 'Eroica.' In the Finale to the Choral Fantasia there are some slight anticipations of the Finale to the Choral Symphony; the Prometheus music contains an anticipation of the storm in the Pastoral Symphony, and the subject of the Allegretto to the 8th Symphony is found in a humorous Canon (No. 256-2) — such are all the repetitions that have been detected. How far he employed *Volkslieder* and other tunes not invented by himself is not yet known. Certain melodies in the 'Eroica,' Pastoral, and No. 7 Symphonies, are said to have been thus adopted, but at present it is mere assertion.

This is perhaps the most convenient place for noticing a prominent fact about his own melodies, viz. that they often consist wholly or mainly of consecutive notes. This is the case with some of the very finest themes he has written, witness the Scherzo and Finale to the Choral Symphony; and that to the Choral Fantasia; the slow movements of the Bb Trio and the Symphony in the same key; the Adagio to the Quartet op. 127, and many others.

8. In the former part of this sketch we have mentioned the extraordinary manner in which Beethoven wrote and rewrote until he had arrived at the exact and most apt expression of his thought. The same extraordinary care not to be mistaken is found in the *nuances*, or marks of expression, with which his works are crowded, and which he was the first to introduce in such abundance. For instance, to compare the 'Jupiter' Symphony — Mozart's last — with Beethoven's first, we shall find that the violin part of the first half of the opening Allegro has in the former (120 bars long) 14 marks of expression, in the latter (95 bars) 42 marks. The Andante to Mozart's Symphony in G minor has 38 marks to 131 bars, while that to Beethoven's No. 2 has 155 marks to 276 bars. In the later works this attention to *nuance* increases. The Allegro agitato of the Quartet in F minor, 125 bars long, contains 95 marks;

the Cavatina in the Quartet in B♭, 66 bars long, contains 58
marks. It is part of the system of unwearied care and attention
by which this great man, whose genius was only equalled by
his assiduity, brought his works to their actual perfection, and
to the certainty that they would produce what he himself calls
il suo proprio proposto effetto [1] — their own special and intended
effect. How original and splendid the effect of such *nuances*
can be may be seen in the Vivace of the No. 7 Symphony, where
the sudden change from *ff* to *pp*, accompanying an equally
sudden plunge in the melody and abrupt change in the harmony, produces a wild romantic effect which once to hear is
never to forget.

In addition, Beethoven here and there gives indications
such as the ' Bitte um innern und äussern Frieden ' at the
' Dona ' in the Mass in D, the ' beklemmt ' in the Cavatina of
the B♭ Quartet, the ' Arioso dolente ' of Sonata op. 110, which
throw a very personal colour over the piece. The word
' Cantabile ' has a special meaning when he employs it.

9. Beethoven used Variations to a very great extent. For
the pianoforte, solo and in conjunction with other solo instruments, he has left 29 sets, some on original themes, some on
airs by other composers. But besides these several movements
in his sonatas, quartets, and trios are variations, so entitled
by him. Every one will remember those in the Septet, in the
' Harp ' Quartet, in the Kreutzer Sonata, in the Solo Sonata
in A flat, and in the two late Sonatas in E and C minor (op.
109 and 111). Many other movements in the same branches
of composition are variations, although not so named. The
slow movements in the Sonata ' appassionata ' and the op.
106 are splendid instances. In the symphonies the slow movements of the C minor, the Pastoral and the Ninth, are magnificent examples, the last the most splendid of all — while the
colossal Finales of the 'Eroica' and the Ninth Symphony are also
variations, though of a very different order from the rest and
from each other. Of the lowest and most obvious type of
variation, in which the tune remains in *statu quo* all through
the piece, with mere changes of accompaniment above, below,
and around it — the Herz-Thalberg type — the nearest
approach to be found in Beethoven's works, is the 5th variation
in op. 26. His favourite plan is to preserve the harmonic basis

[1] Preface to the 'Eroica.'

of the theme and to modify and embellish the melody. Of this type he makes use with astonishing ease and truly inexhaustible originality. It is to be found in some shape or other in nearly every work of his second and third periods. It is not his own invention, for fine instances of it exist in Mozart and Haydn, but no one practised it with such beauty and nobility as he did, unless it be Schubert, who at any rate approaches very near him in its use. Perhaps the finest instance of it is in the Adagio of the ninth Symphony, in which the melody is varied first in common time and then in 12-8, with a grace, beauty, and strength which are quite unparalleled. There is, however, a third [1] kind of variation which is all Beethoven's own, in which everything undergoes a change — rhythm, melody, and har- mony — and yet the individual theme remains clearly present. 'Perhaps one melodious step only of the subject is taken (op. 109; var. 1 and 5); perhaps the fundamental progressions of the harmony alone are retained; perhaps some thorough rhythmical alteration is made, with an entire change of key, as in the *poco andante*, finale of Eroica; in the B♭ variation *alla marcia*, of the ninth Symphony; and in many of the 33 Variations. This is no mere change of dress and decoration, but an actual creation of something new out of the old germ — we see the chrysalis change into the butterfly, and we know it to be the same creature despite the change.' 'In no other form than that of the Variation,' continues Mr. Dannreuther, ' does Beethoven's creative power appear more wonderful, and its effect on the art more difficult to measure.'

10. Of Fugues Beethoven wrote but few, and those near the end of his career, but he always knew how to introduce a *fugato* or bit of contrapuntal work with the happiest effect. Witness a passage in the working out of the first movement of the 'Eroica' Symphony, and another in the Finale of the same work; or in the middle portion of the Allegretto of No. 7; or the lovely counterpoint for the Bassoon in the opening of the Finale of No. 9. Of complete fugues the only instrumental ones are the Finale to the 3rd of the Rassoumoffsky Quartets; the Finales to the Cello Sonata op. 102, No. 2, and the Solo Sonatas op. 101, 106, and 110; and the enormous movement in B flat which originally formed the termination to the great String Quartet in the same key. Of the last-named fugue one

---

[1] Mr. Dannreuther in *Macmillan*.

has no opportunity of judging, as it is never played; but of the others, especially those in the Solo Sonatas, it may be safely said that nothing in the whole of Beethoven's music is associated with a more distinct dramatic intention, whether it be, as has been suggested,[1] a resolution to throw off an affection which was enthralling him, or some other great mental effort.

11. Beethoven did not originate 'programme music,' for Bach left a sonata [capriccio] describing the departure of his brother; and two symphonies are in existence by Knecht — a countryman of Beethoven's, and a few years his senior — entitled ' Tableau musical de la nature,' and ' La joie des Bergers interrompue par l'orage,' which are not only founded on the same idea with his Pastoral Symphony, but are said [2] to contain somewhat similar themes and passages. But, though he did not invent it, he raised it at once to a higher level than before, and his programme pieces have exercised a great effect on the art. ' When Beethoven had once opened the road,' said Mendelssohn, ' every one was bound to follow '; and it is probable that without his example we should not have had Mendelssohn's overtures to ' The Hebrides ' or to the ' Meeresstille und glückliche Fahrt.' His works in this line, omitting all which did not receive their titles from himself, are: — the ' Sonata pathétique '; ' La Malinconia,' an adagio in the String Quartet, No 6; the ' Eroica ' Symphony; the Pastoral ditto; the Battle of Vittoria; the Sonata ' Les Adieux, l'Absence et le Retour '; the movements in the A minor Quartet (op. 132) entitled ' Canzona di ringraziamento in modo lidico offerta alla divinita [divinità] da un guarito,' and ' Sentendo nuova forza '; the movement in the F major Quartet (op. 135), entitled ' Der schwergefasste Entschluss — Muss es sein? Es muss sein '; and a Rondo a capriccio for piano (op. 129), the MS. of which is entitled by the composer ' Die Wuth über den verlornen Groschen ausgetobt in einer Caprice.' Beyond these Beethoven made no acknowledged attempts to depict definite scenes or moods of mind in instrumental music. We have already (p. 45) quoted Schindler's statement that Beethoven intended the Sonatas in op. 14 to be a dialogue between two lovers, and to represent the ' entreating and resisting principle '; and the Sonata in E minor (op. 90) is said to have had direct reference to the difficulties attending Moritz Lichnowsky's

[1] Mr. Davison's Analysis of the Sonata op. 106.   [2] Fétis, *Biographie*, s. v. Knecht.

passion for the actress whom he ultimately married. The first movement was to have been called ' Kampf zwischen Kopf und Herz,' and the second, ' Conversation mit der Geliebten.' But none of these titles were directly sanctioned by Beethoven himself. In the programme of the concert of December 22, 1808, at which the Pastoral Symphony was produced, he prefixed the following words to the description of the Symphony : —' Pastoral Symphonie : mehr Ausdruck der Empfindung als Malerei ' — ' more expression of emotions than portraiture,' a canon which should surely be taken as the guide in interpreting all similar works of his.

We have now endeavoured to give the main external characteristics of Beethoven's music ; but the music itself, though it resides in them, is beyond and above them all. ' While listening,' says Mr. Dannreuther, ' to such works as the Overture to Leonora, the Sinfonia Eroica, or the Ninth Symphony, we feel that we are in the presence of something far wider and higher than the mere development of musical themes. The execution in detail of each movement and each succeeding work is modified more and more with the prevailing poetic sentiment. A religious passion and elevation are present in the utterances. The mental and moral horizon of the music grows upon us with each renewed hearing. The different movements — like the different particles of each movement — have as close a connection with one another as the acts of a tragedy, and a characteristic significance to be understood only in relation to the whole ; each work is in the full sense of the word a revelation. Beethoven speaks a language no one has spoken before, and treats of things no one has dreamt of before : yet it seems as though he were speaking of matters long familiar, in one's mother tongue ; as though he touched upon emotions one had lived through in some former existence. . . . The warmth and depth of his ethical sentiment is now felt all the world over, and it will ere long be universally recognised that he has leavened and widened the sphere of men's emotions in a manner akin to that in which the conceptions of great philosophers and poets have widened the sphere of men's intellectual activity.' [1]

[1] I have been much indebted in this part of my work to an admirable paper by Mr. Dannreuther in *Macmillan's Magazine* for July, 1876. I have quoted from it more than once, and if I have not done so still more it is because the style of his remarks is not suited to the bald rigidity of a Dictionary article.

SCHUBERT

FRANZ PETER SCHUBERT[1]

THE one great composer native to Vienna was born
January 31, 1797, in the district called Lichtenthal
[Liechtenthal] at the house which is now numbered 54 of
the Nussdorfer Strasse,[2] on the right, going out from Vienna.
There is now a grey marble tablet over the door, with the
words ' Franz Schuberts Geburtshaus ' in the centre ; on the
left side a lyre crowned with a star, and on the right a chaplet
of leaves containing the words, ' 31 Jänner 1797.' He came
of a country stock, originally belonging to Zukmantel in
Austrian Silesia. His father, Franz, the son of a peasant at
Neudorf in Moravia, was born about 1764 [July 11, 1763],
studied in Vienna, and in 1784 became assistant to his brother,
who kept a school in the Leopoldstadt. His ability and
integrity raised him in 1786 to be parish schoolmaster in the
parish of the ' Twelve [Fourteen] holy helpers ' in the Lichtenthal, a post which he kept till 1817 or 18 [1817], when [on
December 24] he was appointed to the parish school in the
adjoining district of the Rossau, and there he remained till his
death, July 9, 1830. He married early, while still helping his
brother, probably in 1783 [on January 17, 1785], Elisabeth
Vitz, or Fitz, a Silesian, who was in service in Vienna, and was,
like Beethoven's mother, a cook. Their first child, Ignaz, was
born in 1784 [on March 8, 1785]. Then came a long gap,

---

[1] The following abbreviations are used in the notes to this article :—
K.H. = Kreissle von Hellhorn. The first reference to the German edition ;
the second, in brackets, to Coleridge's translation.
Ferd. = Ferdinand Schubert, in his biographical sketch in Schumann's Neue
Zeitschrift für die Musik, x. p. 129, etc.
A.M.Z. = ' Allgemeine Musikalische Zeitung.'
N.Z.M. = ' Neue Zeitschrift für Musik.'
W.Z.K. = ' Wiener Zeitschrift für Kunst,' etc.
[2] The Nussdorfer Strasse runs north and south. At the time of Schubert's
birth it was called ' Auf dem Himmelpfortgrund,' and the house was No. 72.
The ' Himmelpfortgrund ' itself (the ' [ground of] gate of heaven ') was a
short street running out of it westwards towards the fortifications—the same
which is now the ' Säulengasse.' The present Schubertgasse did not then exist
beyond the opening into the main street. I find all this on a large map of the date
in the British Museum.

possibly filled by children who died in infancy — of which they lost nine in all; then, October 19, 1794, another boy, Ferdinand; then in 1796, Karl, then Franz, and lastly, a daughter, Theresia, September 17, 1801, who died August 7, 1878. The hard-worked mother of these 14 children lived till 1812. Soon after her death her husband was married again, to Anna Klayenbök [Kleyenböck], a Viennese, and had a second family of 5 children, of whom 3 grew up, viz. Josefa (+ 1861), Andreas, an accountant in one of the public offices, and Anton, a Benedictine priest, ' Father Hermann ' [1] — the last two still living (1881).

Ignaz and Ferdinand followed their father's calling, and inherited with it the integrity, frugality, and modesty, which had gained him such respect. Of the former we do not hear much; the one letter by him that is preserved (October 12, 1818), shows him very free-thinking, very tired of schoolmastering, very much attached to his home and his brother.[2] He remained at the Rossau school till his death in 1844. Ferdinand, on the other hand, rose to be director of the chief normal school of St. Anna in Vienna, and played a considerable part in the life of his celebrated brother, by whom he was fondly loved, to whom he was deeply attached, and whose eyes it was given to him to close in death.

Little Franz was no doubt well grounded by his father, and to that early training probably owed the methodical habit which stuck to him more or less closely through life, of dating his pieces, a practice which makes the investigation of them doubly interesting.[3] As schoolmasters the father and his two eldest sons were all more or less musical. Ignaz and Ferdinand had learned the violin with other rudiments from the father, and Franz was also taught it by him in his turn, and the ' clavier ' (i.e. probably the pianoforte — for Beethoven's op. 31

[1] Author of a sermon on the 1400th anniversary of the birth of St. Benedict (Vienna, 1880), in which he is styled ' Capitularpriester des Stiftes Schotten; Curat und Prediger an der Stiftspfarre; Besitzer des gold. Verdienstkreuzes m. d. Krone.'

[2] K. H.146 (i. 149).

[3] His usual practice was to write the title of the piece, the date, and his name, ' Frz Schubert Mpia.' [(manu propria)] at the head of the first page, on beginning to compose. In his earlier years he added the full date of completion at the end, even when it was the same day. See nos. 1, 2, and 5 of the ' 6 Lieder ' (Müller) —all three belonging to 1813, as given in Nottebohm's Catalogue, p. 243. Sometimes he has dated each movement, as in the String Quartet in Bb (op. 168), described under 1814. With 1815, however, this minute dating in great measure ceases, and as a rule we find the year or at most the month stated.

was published before Schubert had passed his 6th year) by
Ignaz, who was twelve years his senior. But his high vocation
quickly revealed itself; he soon outstripped these simple
teachers, and was put under Michael Holzer, the choirmaster
of the parish, for both violin and piano, as well as for singing,
the organ, and thorough bass. On this good man, who long
outlived him, he made a deep impression. 'When I wished
to teach him anything fresh,' he would say, ' he always knew
it already. I have often listened to him in astonishment.' [1]
Holzer would give him subjects to extemporise upon, and then
his joy would know no bounds, and he would cry ' the lad has
got harmony at his fingers' ends.' [2] Such astonishment was
natural enough, but it would have been far better if he had
taught him counterpoint. Ignaz too — and an elder brother
is not always a lenient judge of his junior — bears similar testimony. ' I was much astonished,' says he, ' when after a few
months he told me that he had no more need of any help from
me, but would go on by himself; and indeed I soon had to
acknowledge that he had far surpassed me, beyond hope of
competition.'

Before he became eleven he was first soprano in the
Lichtenthal choir, noted for the beauty of his voice and the
appropriateness of his expression. He played the violin solos
when they occurred in the service, and at home composed little
songs, and pieces for strings or for pianoforte. For a child so
gifted, of people in the position of the Schuberts, the next step
was naturally the Imperial *Convict*, or school [seminary] [3] for
educating the choristers for the Court-chapel; and to the
Convict accordingly Franz was sent in October 1808, when
11 years and 8 months old. He went up with a batch of other
boys, who, while waiting, made themselves merry over his grey
suit, calling him a miller, and otherwise cracking jokes. But the
laugh soon ceased when the ' miller ' came under the examiners,
the Court-capellmeisters Salieri and Eybler, and Korner the
singing-master. He sang the trial-pieces in such a style that
he was at once received, and henceforth the grey frock was
exchanged for the gold-laced uniform of the imperial choristers.
The music in the *Convict* had been a good deal dropt in conse-

---

[1] N.Z.M.   [2] K.H. 5 (i. 5).
[3] In the Piaristengasse in the Josephstadt. See a very full and interesting
account of this school in Hanslick's excellent book, *Geschichte des Concertwesens
in Wien* (Vienna, 1869), p. 141.

quence of the war, but after the signing of the treaty of peace, October 14, 1809, it regained its old footing, and then Franz soon took his right place in the music-school. There was an orchestra formed from the boys, which practised daily symphonies and overtures of Haydn, Mozart, Krommer, Kozeluch, Méhul, Cherubini, etc., and occasionally Beethoven. Here his home practice put him on a level with older boys than himself. The leader of the band, behind whom he sat, several years his senior, turned round the first day to see who it was that was playing so cleverly, and found it to be ' a small boy in spectacles named Franz Schubert.' [1] The big fellow's name was Spaun, and he soon became intimate with his little neighbour. Franz was extremely sensitive, and one day admitted to his friend, very confused and blushing deeply, that he had already composed much ; that indeed he could not help it, and should do it every day if he could afford to get music-paper. Spaun saw the state of matters, and took care that music-paper should be forthcoming ; for which and other kindnesses his name will be long remembered. Franz in time became first violin, and when Ruzicka, the regular conductor, was absent, he took his place. The orchestral music must have been a great delight to him, but we only hear that he preferred Kozeluch to Krommer, and that his particular favourites were some adagios of Haydn's, Mozart's G minor Symphony, in which he said ' you could hear the angels singing,' and the overtures to ' Figaro' and the ' Zauberflöte.' It is also evident from his earliest symphonies that the overture to ' Prometheus' had made its mark on his mind. On Sundays and holidays he went home, and then the great delight of the family was to play quartets, his own or those of other writers, in which the father took the cello, Ferdinand and Ignaz the first and second violins, and Franz the viola, as Mozart did before him, and Mendelssohn after him. The father would now and then make a mistake ; on the first occasion Franz took no notice, but if it recurred he would say with a smile, in a timid way, ' Herr Vater, something must be wrong there.'

From a very early date Beethoven was an object of his deepest reverence. Shortly before he entered the School the boys' orchestra had been taken to Schönbrunn for a perform-

---

[1] From a sketch by von Köchel, entitled *Nachruf an Joseph von Spaun*, Vienna (privately printed), 1866. I owe the sight of this to my excellent friend Mr. Pohl.

ance in Beethoven's presence, and Franz was never tired of hearing the details of the story from those who were there. A few months later, after some of his boyish songs to Klopstock's words had been sung, he asked a friend if it was possible that he himself ever would do anything; and on the friend replying that he could already do a great deal, answered, ' Perhaps : I sometimes have dreams of that sort ; but who can do anything after Beethoven? ' [1] With this feeling it is doubly strange that his juvenile works should show so few traces of Beethoven's direct influence.

The instruction in the *Convict* was by no means only musical. There was a Curator, a Director (Rev. Innocenz Lang), a Sub-director, an Inspector, a staff of preachers and catechists ; and there were teachers of mathematics, history and geography, poetry, writing, drawing [elementary Greek and Latin], French and Italian.[2] In fact it was a school, apart from its music department. Franz of course took his part in all this instruction, and for the first year is said to have acquitted himself with credit, but his reputation in the school fell off as it increased in the musical department. The extraordinary thirst for composition, which is so remarkable throughout his life, began to assert itself at this time, and appears to have been limited only by his power of obtaining paper ; and it not unnaturally interfered with his general lessons. His first pianoforte piece of any dimensions, and apparently his earliest existing composition, was a 4-hand phantasia, containing more than a dozen movements, all of different characters, and occupying 32 pages of very small writing. It is dated 8 April – 1 May 1810, and was followed by two smaller ones.[3] His brother remarks that not one of the three ends in the key in which it began. The next is a long vocal piece for voice and pianoforte, called ' Hagars Klage ' — Hagar's lament over her dying son — dated March 30, 1811, also containing 12 movements, with curious unconnected changes of key ; and another, of even grimmer character, attributed to the same year, is called ' Leichenfantasie,' or Corpse-fantasia, to the words of Schiller's gruesome juvenile poem of the same name :—

---

[1] See K.H. 258 (i. 260).
[2] See the list of names in K.H. 13 (i. 13).
[3] Ferd. p. 133. Reissmann (p. 7) gives the inscriptions—' Den 8. Aprill angefangen. Den 1. May vollbracht, 1810.'

Mit erstorbnem Scheinen
Steht der Mond auf todtenstillen Hainen,
   Seufzend streicht der Nachtgeist durch die Luft —
      Nebenwolken schauern,
      Sterne trauern
Bleich herab, wie Lampen in der Gruft.

With a deathlike glimmer
Stands the moon above the dying trees,
   Sighing wails the Spirit through the night;
      Mists are creeping,
      Stars are peeping
Pale aloft like torches in a cave.

and so forth. This has 17 movements, and is quite as erratic
in its changes of key and disregard of the compass of the voice
as the preceding.[1] The reminiscences of Haydn's ' Creation,'
Mozart's opera airs, and Beethoven's Andantes, are frequent
in both. A fourth is ' Der Vatermörder ' — the Parricide —
for voice and pianoforte, ' 26 December, 1811,' a pleasant
Christmas piece! a decided advance on the two previous songs
in individuality of style, and connection. 1811 also saw the
composition of a quintet-overture, a string quartet, a second
phantasia for 4 hands, and many songs.[2] For 1812 the list is
more instrumental. It contains an overture for orchestra in D;
a quartet overture in B♭; string quartets in C, B♭, and D;[3] a
sonata for pianoforte, violin, and cello; variations in E♭, and
an andante, both for pianoforte; a Salve Regina and a Kyrie.
In 1813 an octet[4] for wind; 3 [4] string quartets in C, B♭, E♭
and D; minuets and trios for orchestra and for pianoforte;
a third phantasia for the pianoforte 4 hands; several songs,
terzets, and canons; a cantata in two movements, for 3 male
voices and guitar, for his father's birthday, September 27 —
both words and music his own; and his first symphony in
D,[5] intended to celebrate the birthday of Dr. Lang, and
finished on October 28. With this very important work his

---

[1] The autographs of both are in possession of Herr Nicholas Dumba of Vienna.
[2] Ferd. p. 138.
[3] Kreissle expressly states this (p. 550) and gives the date—' Nov. 19, 1812.'
[4] This octet, dated Sept. 19, is said to be mentioned by Ferdinand Schubert
as ' Franz Schubert's Leichenbegängniss ' (funeral ceremony). It is supposed
by Kreissle (p. 31) to have been composed for the funeral of his mother; but
it is difficult to believe that the words which he wrote for his father's birthday
ode, eight days later, would have had no reference to the mother's death—which
they certainly have not—if it had occurred at that date.
[5] Adagio and Allegro vivace (D); Andante (G); Minuet and Trio (D);
Finale, Allegro vivace (D). The work was played from MS. at the Crystal
Palace, Feb. 5, 1881. The autograph is in possession of Herr Dumba, Vienna.

time at the *Convict* ended. He might have remained longer;
for it is said that the Emperor, who took an interest in the
lads of his chapel, had specially watched the progress of this
gifted boy with the lovely voice and fine expression, and
that a special decision had been registered in his favour on
October 21, assuring him a foundation scholarship in the
school, provided that during the vacation he should study
sufficiently to pass an examination.[1] This however he declined,
possibly at the instigation of Körner the poet, who was in
Vienna at this time, and is known to have influenced him in
deciding to throw himself entirely into music.[2] He accordingly
left the *Convict* (between October 26 and November 6), and
returned home. His mother died in 1812, but we hear nothing
of the event, unless the octet just named refers to it. The father
married again in about a year, and the new wife, as we shall
see, did her duty to her stepson Franz fully, and apparently
with affection.

Franz was now just completing his seventeenth year, and
what has been rightly called the first period of his life. The
Convict has much to answer for in regard to Schubert. It was
entrusted with the most poetical genius of modern times, and
it appears to have allowed him to take his own course in the
matter of composition almost unrestrained. Had but a portion
of the pains been spent on the musical education of Schubert
that was lavished on that of Mozart or of Mendelssohn, we can
hardly doubt that even his transcendent ability would have
been enhanced by it, that he would have gained that control
over the prodigious spontaneity of his genius which is his only
want, and have risen to the very highest level in all departments
of composition, as he did in song-writing. But though Eybler
and Salieri were the conductors of the choir in chapel, it does
not appear that they had any duties in the school, and Ruzicka,
the thorough-bass master, like Holzer, was so prostrated by
Schubert's facility as to content himself with exclaiming that
his pupil already knew all he could teach him, and must have
' learned direct from heaven.' If all masters adopted this attitude towards their pupils, what would have become of some of
the greatest geniuses? The discomforts of the school appear to

[1] K.H. 33 (i. 33).
[2] On Spaun's authority. There is no mention of Schubert in Körner's letters
from Vienna.

have been great even for that day of roughness. One of the pupils speaks of the cold of the practice-room as ' dreadful ' (*schauerlich*) ; and Schubert's own earliest letter, dated November 24, 1812, to his brother Ferdinand, shows that these young growing lads were allowed to go without food for 8½ hours, between ' a poor dinner and a wretched supper.' There was not even sufficient music paper provided for the scholars, and Schubert was, as we have seen, dependent on the bounty of the richer pupils.

On the other hand, the motets and masses in the service, the rehearsals in the school, such teaching as there was, and the daily practisings, must have been both stimulating and improving, and with all its roughness a good deal of knowledge could not but have been obtainable. One advantage Schubert reaped from the *Convict* — the friends which he made there, many of them for life, Spaun, Senn, Holzapfel, Stadler, and others, all afterwards, more or less eminent, who attached themselves to him as every one did who came into contact with him ; a band of young adorers, eager to play, or sing, or copy anything that he composed ; the earnest of the devoted friends who surrounded him in later years, and helped to force his music on an ignorant and preoccupied public. Nor did the enthusiasm cease with his departure ; for some years afterwards the orchestral pieces which he had written while at the school were still played by the boys from his own MS. copies. Outside the school he had sometimes opportunities of going to the opera. The first opera which he is said to have heard was Weigl's ' Waisenhaus,' played December 12, 1810 ; but this was eclipsed by the ' Schweitzer-familie [Schweizerfamilie] ' of the same composer, July 8, 1811 ; that again by Spontini's ' Vestalin,' with Milder, October 1, 1812 ; and all of them by Gluck's ' Iphigenie auf Tauris,' which he probably heard first April 5, 1815, with Milder and Vogl in the two principal parts, and which made a deep and ineffaceable impression upon him, and drove him to the study of Gluck's scores.[1] During the same years there were also many concerts, including those at which Beethoven produced his 5th, 6th, and 7th Symphonies, the Choral Fantasia, portions of the Mass in C, the Overture to ' Coriolan,' and others of his greatest compositions. Schubert probably heard all these works, but it is very doubtful whether

---

[1] From Bauernfeld, in W.Z.K.

he heard them with the same predilection as the operas just
mentioned. We might infer with certainty from the three
earliest of his symphonies, that Beethoven's style had as yet
taken but little hold on him, notwithstanding the personal
fascination which he seems to have felt for the great master
from first to last. But, indeed, we have his own express declaration to that effect. Coming home after a performance of an
oratorio of Salieri's, June 16, 1816, he speaks of the music in
terms which can only refer to Beethoven, as ' of simple natural
expression, free from all that *bizarrerie* which prevails in most
of the composers of our time, and for which we have almost
solely to thank one of our greatest German artists; that
bizarrerie which unites the tragic and the comic, the agreeable
and the repulsive, the heroic and the petty, the Holiest and a
harlequin; infuriates those who hear it instead of dissolving
them in love, and makes them laugh instead of raising them
heavenwards.' Mozart was at the time his ideal composer;
this too is plain from the symphonies, but here also he leaves
us in no doubt. Three days earlier we find in the same diary,[1]
à propos to one of the quintets of that great master : — ' Gently,
as if out of the distance, did the magic tones of Mozart's music
strike my ears. With what inconceivable alternate force and
tenderness did Schlesinger's masterly playing impress it deep,
deep, into my heart! Such lovely impressions remain on the
soul, there to work for good, past all power of time or circumstances. In the darkness of this life they reveal a clear, bright,
beautiful prospect, inspiring confidence and hope. O Mozart,
immortal Mozart! what countless consolatory images of a
bright better world hast thou stamped on our souls.' There
is no doubt to which of these two great masters he was most
attached at the time he wrote this.

We have seen what a scourge the conscription proved in
the case of Ries (iii. 131*a*)*, and the uneasiness of Mendelssohn's family till the risk of it was over in his case (p. 280).
To avoid a similar danger [2] Schubert elected to enter his
father's school, and after the necessary study for a few months
at the Normal School of St. Anna, did so, and actually remained
there for three years as teacher of the lowest class. The duties

---

[1] Quoted by K.H. 103, 101 (i. 105, 103).
* [Reference to a passage in another article in the first edition of Grove's
Dictionary.]
[2] He was three times summoned to enlist. See Ferd. p. 133.

were odious, but he discharged them with strict regularity, and not with greater severity than might reasonably be expected from the irritable temperament of a musician condemned to such drudgery. The picture of Pegasus thus in vile harness, and the absence of any remark on the anomaly, throws a curious light on the beginnings of a great composer. Out of school hours, however, he had his relaxations. There was a family in the Lichtenthal named Grob — a mother, son, and daughter — whose relations to him were somewhat like those of the Breunings to Beethoven (p. 8). The house was higher in the scale than his father's, and he was quite at home there. Therese, the daughter, had a fine high soprano voice, and Heinrich Grob played both pianoforte and cello; the mother was a woman of taste, and a great deal of music was made. It is not impossible that Therese inspired him with a softer feeling.[1] The choir of the Lichtenthal church, where his old friend Holzer was still choirmaster, was his resort on Sundays and feast days, and for it he wrote his first mass, in F — begun May 17, finished July 22, 1814—a fitting pendant to the symphony of the previous October. He was not yet eighteen, and the mass is pronounced by a trustworthy critic[2] to be the most remarkable first mass ever produced excepting Beethoven's in C, and as striking an instance of the precocity of genius as Mendelssohn's Overture to the 'Midsummer Night's Dream.' It seems to have been first performed on October 16, the first Sunday after St. Theresa's day, 1814 — Mayseder, then 25, and an acknowledged virtuoso, leading the first violins; and was repeated at the Augustine Church ten days after. This second performance was quite an event. Franz conducted, Holzer led the choir, Ferdinand took the organ, Therese Grob sang, the enthusiasm of the family and friends was great, and the proud father presented his happy son with a five-octave piano.[3] Salieri was present and loud in his praises, and claimed Schubert as his pupil. He had indeed began to take some interest in the lad before he left the *Convict*,[4] and continued it by daily lessons for a long time.'[5] That interest was probably much the same that he had shown to Beethoven 15 years before, making him write to Metastasio's words, and

[1] See K.H. 141 (i. 144).
[2] Mr. Prout, in *Monthly Musical Record*, Jan. and Feb. 1871.
[3] Ferd. 133 *b*.   [4] K.H. i. 27 *note*.
[5] Bauernfeld, in W.Z.K. June 9, 1829.

correcting the prosody of his music. But there must have been
some curious attraction about the old man, to attach two such
original geniuses as Beethoven and Schubert to him, and make
them willing to style themselves 'scholars of Salieri.'[1] His
permanent influence on Schubert may be measured by the fact
that he warned him against Goethe and Schiller, a warning
which Schubert attended to so far as to compose 67 [71] songs
of the one poet, and 54 [42] of the other!

Franz's next effort was an opera — a light and absurd
supernatural 'opéra comique' in 3 acts, 'Des Teufels Lustschloss,' words by Kotzebue. He probably began it while at the
Convict, the first act having been completed January 11, 1814;
the second, March 16; and the third, May 15. Two days
afterwards he began the mass. That over, he had leisure to
look again at the earlier work. The experience gained in
writing the mass probably revealed many an imperfection in
the opera. He at once rewrote it, and finished the redaction
of it on October 22. The work has never been performed,
nor can it now ever be so, since the second act, like the MS.
of the first volume of Carlyle's French Revolution, was used
by an officious maid-servant for lighting the fires as late as
1848. With all these and other labours he found time to visit
the *Convict* in the evenings,[2] take part in the practices, and try
over his new compositions. Besides the pieces already mentioned, the productions of 1814 embrace a Salve Regina for
tenor and orchestra. Also 2 string quartets in D and C [G]
minor, still in MS, and a third in Bb, published as op. 168,
and remarkable for the circumstances of its composition. It
was begun as a string trio, and ten lines were written in that
form. It was then begun again and finished as a quartet. The
movements are more fully dated than usual.[3] Also 5 minuets
and 6 Deutsche (or waltzes) for strings and horns; and 17
songs, among them 'Gretchen am Spinnrade' (October 19),
and Schiller's 'Der Taucher,' a composition of enormous
length, begun September 1813, and finished in the following

[1] For Beethoven see p. 18. Schubert so styles himself on the title-pages of his
'Fernando' and 'Claudine von Villabella.'
[2] E.H. 18 (i. 19).
[3] The Allegro has at beginning '5 Sept. 1814,' at end 'den 6 Sept. in 4½
Stunden angefertigt,' apparently implying that it was dashed off before and
after 12 o'clock at night. Andante, at beginning 'den 6 Sept. 1814,' at end
'den 10 Sept. 1814.' Minuet, at end '11 Sept. 1814.' Finale, at end 'den
13 Sept. 1814.' Autograph with Spina.

August. On December 10 he began his second symphony, in
Bb.[1] The autograph shows that the short Introduction and
Allegro vivace were finished by the 26th of the same month,
but its completion falls in 1815. Before the year closed he
made the acquaintance of Mayrhofer, a man of eccentric,
almost hypochondriac character, and a poet of grand and
gloomy cast, who became his firm friend, and 54 of whose
poems[2] (besides the operas of ' Adrast ' and ' Die beiden
Freunde von Salamanca '), fortunately for Mayrhofer's immortality, he set to music — some of them among his very
finest songs. The acquaintance began by Schubert's setting
Mayrhofer's ' Am See.' He composed it on the 7th December,
and a few days afterwards visited the poet at his lodgings in the
Wipplinger Strasse 420 (since destroyed), a small dark room
rendered illustrious by being the residence of Theodore Körner,
and afterwards of Schubert, who lived there in 1819 and 20.
The visit was the beginning of a friendship which ended only
with Schubert's death.

1815 is literally crowded with compositions. Two orchestral
symphonies of full dimensions, Nos. 2 and 3 (that in Bb ended
March 24, that in D,[3] May 24–July 19) ; a string quartet in G
minor (March 25–April 1) ; pianoforte sonatas in C, F, E
(Feb. 11) and E (Feb. 18) ; an adagio in G (April 8), 12 Wiener
Deutsche, 8 Ecossaises (October 3), and 10 variations for piano-
forte solo ; 2 masses, in G[4] (March 2–7) and B (November 11–) ;
a new ' Dona '[5] for the mass in F ; a Stabat Mater in G minor
(April 4) ; a Salve Regina (July 5) ; 5 large dramatic pieces
— ' Der vierjährige Posten,' 1-act operetta (ended May 16) ;
' Fernando,' 1-act Singspiel (July 3–9) ; ' Claudine von Villa-

[1] At beginning, ' 10 Dec. 1814 '; at end of Allegro, ' 26 Dec. 1814 '; at
beginning of Finale, ' 25 Feb. 1815,' and at end, ' 24 March 1815.' The movements are Largo and Allegro vivace (Bb) ; Andante (Eb) ; Minuet and Trio
(C minor) ; Finale, Presto vivace (Bb). Played from MS. at the Crystal Palace,
Oct. 20, 1877. Autograph with Herr Dumba.
[2] 48 published, and 6 in MS.
[3] It is in the usual number of movements : Adagio maestoso and Allegro con
brio (D) ; Allegretto (G) ; Minuet and Trio (D) ; Finale, Presto vivace (D).
Dates :—Allegro, at beginning, ' 24 May 1815 '; end, ' July 12, 1815.' Allegretto, at beginning, ' July 15, 1815.' End of Finale, ' July 19, 1815.' Autograph with Herr Dumba.
[4] Published by M. Berra, of Prague, in 1846, as the composition of R. Führer.
The fraud was not exposed till 1847, when it was announced by Ferd. Schubert
in the Allg. Wiener Musikzeitung of Dec. 14. Ferdinand mentions this mass in his
list under 1815. A copy, evidently copied closely from the autograph, but with
the addition of oboes (or clarinets) and bassoons by Ferd. Schubert (July 23, 1847),
is in the Library of the Gesellschaft der Musikfreunde.
[5] Mentioned by Ferdinand, 139 a.

bella,' 3-act Singspiel (Act 1, July 26–August 5), originally
composed complete, but Acts 2 and 3 perished in the same
manner as the ' Teufels Lustschloss '; ' Die beiden Freunde
von Salamanca ['Die Freunde von Salamanka '], a 2-act Singspiel by Mayrhofer (November 18–December 31); ' Der
Spiegelritter,' 3-act opera, of which 8 numbers are with the
Gesellschaft der Musikfreunde at Vienna; perhaps also a
Singspiel called ' Die Minnesänger,' and ' Adrast,' an opera by
Mayrhofer of which but two numbers exist.[1] In addition to
all these there are no less than 137 [146] songs — 67 printed,
and 70 still in MS. In August alone there are 29, of which
8 are dated the 15th, and 7 the 19th! And of these 137 songs
some are of such enormous length as would seem to have prevented their publication. ' Minona ' (MS., February 8), the
first one of the year, contains 16, and ' Adelwold and Emma '
(MS., June 5) no less than 55 closely written sides. Of those
published, ' Die Bürgschaft ' (' August 1815 ') fills 22 pages of
Litolff's edition, ' Elysium ' 13, and ' Loda's Gespenst ' 15 of
the same. It was the length of such compositions as these —
' pas une histoire, mais des histoires ' — that caused Beethoven's
exclamation on his deathbed : ' Such long poems, many of
them containing ten others,' by which he meant as long as ten
(p. 192). And this mass of music was produced in the mere
intervals of his school drudgery! Well might his brother say
that the rapidity of his writing was marvellous.

Amidst all this work and, one might be tempted to believe,
all this hurry, it is astonishing to find that some of the songs
of these boyish years are amongst the most permanent of his
productions. ' Gretchen am Spinnrade,' a song full of the
passion and experience of a lifetime, was written (as we have
said) in October 1814, when he was 17. The ' Erl King ' itself
in its original form (with a few slight differences [2]) belongs to
the winter of 1815, and the immortal songs of the ' Heidenröslein,' ' Rastlose Liebe,' ' Schäfers Klagelied,' the grand
Ossian songs, and others of his better-known works, fall within
this year. The Mass in G, too, though composed for a very
limited orchestra, and not without tokens of hurry, is a master-

[1] Autographs of Fernando, Teufels Lustschloss, and Adrast, are with Herr
Dumba.
[2] The Berlin Library possesses an autograph of the earlier form, and Mme.
Schumann one of the later (with triplet accompaniment). The former was
published in fascimile by Espagne (Berlin, Müller).

piece. The dramatic works contain many beautiful movements, and are full of striking things, but the librettos are so bad, that in their present condition they can never be put on the stage. The symphonies, though not original, are not without original points; and are so sustained throughout, so full of fresh melody and interesting harmony, and so extraordinarily scored considering their date, that in these respects a man of double Schubert's age might be proud to claim them.

The habit of writing to whatever words came in his way was one of Schubert's characteristics, especially in the earlier part of his career. With his incessant desire to sing; with an abundant fountain of melody and harmony always welling up in him and endeavouring to escape, no wonder that he grasped at any words, and tried any forms, that came in his way, and seemed to afford a channel for his thoughts. If good, well; if bad, well too. The reason why he wrote 8 operas in one year was no doubt in great measure because he happened to meet with 8 librettos; had it been 4 or 12 instead of 8 the result would have been the same. The variety in the productions even of this early year is truly extraordinary. A glance at the list is sufficient to show that he tried nearly every form of composition, while the songs he set range from gems like Goethe's 'Meeresstille' and Schiller's [the same poet's] 'Freudvoll und leidvoll,' to the noisy ballads of Bertrand; from Mayrhofer's stern classicality and the gloomy romance of Ossian, to the mild sentiment of Klopstock. No doubt, as Schumann says, he could have set a placard to music.[1] The spectacle of so insatiable a desire to produce has never before been seen; of a genius thrown naked into the world and compelled to explore for himself all paths and channels in order to discover by exhaustion which was the best — and then to die.

During this year he taught diligently and punctually in his father's school, and attended Salieri's lessons. His relations to the Lichtenthal remained as before. The Mass in G, like that in F, was written for the parish church, and according to the testimony of one of his old friends [2] was especially intended

[1] 'Qu'on me donne la Gazette de Hollande,' says Rameau. But Schubert could have thrown poetry into an advertisement! 'Give me the words,' said Mozart, 'and I'll put the poetry to them.'

[2] Herr Doppler. I cannot refrain from mentioning this gentleman, who in 1867 was shopman at Spina's (formerly Diabelli's). I shall never forget the droll shock I received when on asking him if he knew Schubert, he replied, 'Know him? I was at his christening!' Kreissle's Life is indebted to him for many a trait which would otherwise have been lost.

for those of his companions who had been pupils of Holzer
with him. A pleasant relic of his home life exists in a piece of
music written for his father's birthday, September 27, 1815,
for 4 voices and orchestra — ' Erhabner, verehrter Freund der
Jugend.'[1] He kept up his intercourse also with the *Convict*,
and when he had written anything special it was one of the
first places to which he would take it. There possibly his symphonies were tried, though it is doubtful if a juvenile orchestra
would contain clarinets, bassoons, trumpets, and horns, all
which are present in the scores of the first four symphonies.
There, thanks to the memorandum of another old ' Convicter,'
we can assist at the first hearing of the Erl King. Spaun happened to call one afternoon, in this very winter, at the elder
Schubert's house in the Himmelpfortgrund, and found Franz
in his room, in a state of inspiration over Goethe's ballad, which
he had just seen for the first time. A few times reading had
been sufficient to evoke the music, which in the rage of inspiration he was whelming down[2] on to the paper at the moment
of Spaun's arrival; indeed it was already perfect except the
mere filling in of the accompaniment. This was quickly done;
and it was finished in the form in which we can now see it in
the Berlin Library.[3] In the evening Schubert brought it to
the *Convict*, and there first he and then Holzapfel sang it through.
It was not altogether well received. No wonder; the form was
too new, the dramatic spirit too strong, even for that circle
of young Schubert-admirers. At the words ' Mein Vater,
mein Vater, jetzt fasst er mich an!' where Gb, F♮ and Eb
all come together, there was some dissent, and Ruzicka, as
teacher of harmony, had to explain to his pupils, as best he
might, a combination which now seems perfectly natural and
appropriate.

1816 was passed much as 1815 had been, in a marvellous
round of incessant work. The drudgery of the school, however,
had become so insupportable that Schubert seized the opportunity of the opening of a government school of music at
Laibach, near Trieste, to apply for the post of director, with a
salary of 500 Vienna florins — £21 a year. The testimonials

[1] Now in the Imperial Library, Berlin. No doubt there was one every year,
though that of 1814 has been lost.
[2] *Hinzuwühlend* is Kreissle's word, doubtless from Spaun's lips.
[3] If indeed this be the actually first original. The omission of bar 8, and its
subsequent insertion, however, as well as the clean regular look of the whole,
seem to point to its being a transcript.

K

which he sent in in April from Salieri, and from Joseph
Spendou, Chief Superintendent of Schools, were so cold in
tone as to imply that however much they valued Schubert,
they believed his qualifications not to be those of the head of
a large establishment.[1] At any rate he failed, and the post was
given, on the recommendation of Salieri, to a certain Jacob
Schaufl [Schauff]. Schubert found compensation, however, in
the friendship of Franz von Schober, a young man of good
birth and some small means, who had met with his songs at
the house of the Spauns at Linz, and had ever since longed to
make his personal acquaintance. Coming to Vienna to enter
the University, apparently soon after the Laibach rebuff, he
called on Schubert, found him in his father's house, over-
whelmed with his school duties, and with apparently no time
for music. There, however, were the piles of manuscript —
operas, masses, symphonies, songs, heaped up around the young
schoolmaster composer, and Schober saw at once that some
step must be taken to put an end to this cruel anomaly, and
give Schubert time to devote himself wholly to the Art of which
he was so full. Schober proposed that his new friend should
live with him; Franz's father — possibly not oversatisfied[2]
with his son's performance as a teacher of the alphabet to
infants — consented to the plan, and the two young men
(Schober was some four months Franz's junior) went off to
keep house together at Schober's lodgings in the Landkron-
gasse. A trace of this change is found on two MS. songs in the
Musik Verein at Vienna, ' Leiden der Trennung ' and ' Lebens-
lied,' inscribed ' In Herr v. Schober's lodging,' and dated
November 1816. Schubert began to give a few lessons, but
soon threw them up,[3] and the household must have been
maintained at Schober's expense, since there was obviously as
yet no sale for Schubert's compositions. He had good friends,
as Beethoven had had at the same age, though not so high in
rank — Hofrath von Kiesewetter, Matthäus von Collin, Graf
Moritz Dietrichstein, Hofrath Hammer von Purgstall, Pyrker,
afterwards Patriarch of Venice and Archbishop of Erlau, Frau
Caroline Pichler — all ready and anxious to help him had they
had the opportunity. But Schubert never gave them the
opportunity. He was a true Viennese, born in the lowest

---

[1] K.H. 107 (i. 109).   [2] There is ground for this supposition.
[3] Bauernfeld, W.Z.K.

ranks, without either the art or the taste for ' imposing ' on
[' impressing '] the aristocracy (Beethoven's favourite phrase) [1]
that Beethoven had ; loving the society of his own class, shrink-
ing from praise or notice of any kind, and with an absolute
detestation of teaching or any other stated duties.

But to know him was to love and value him.   Three little
events, which slightly diversify the course of this year, are of
moment as showing the position which Schubert took amongst
his acquaintances.   The first was the 50th anniversary of
Salieri's arrival in Vienna, which he had entered as a boy on
June 16, 1766. [See SALIERI, iii. 218*b*.] * On Sunday, July 16,
1816, the old Italian was invested with the Imperial gold medal
and chain of honour, in the presence of the whole body of
Court-musicians ; and in the evening a concert took place at
his own house, in which, surrounded by his pupils, Weigl,
Assmayer, Anna Fröhlich, Schubert, and many others,[2] both
male and female, he snuffed up the incense of his worshippers,
and listened to compositions in his honour by his scholars past
and present.   Among these were pieces sent by Hummel and
Moscheles, and a short cantata, both words and music by
Schubert.[3]

Eight days afterwards, on July 24, there was another festivity in honour of the birthday of a certain Herr Heinrich
Watteroth,[4] a distinguished official person, for which Schubert
had been employed to write a cantata on the subject of Prometheus, words by Philipp Dräxler, another official person.
The cantata has disappeared ; but from a description of it by
Leopold Sonnleithner, communicated to ' Zellner's Blätter für
Theater,' etc. (no. 19), and reprinted [5] separately, it seems to
have been written for two solo voices, soprano (Gäa) and bass

---

[1] *Imponiren.* Thayer, ii. 313.
    * [Reference to the first edition of Grove's Dictionary.]
[2] There was a Liszt among Salieri's pupils at this time, but hardly the future
Abbé, who was then but five years old.   Franz Liszt and Schubert met once—
in the curious collection of variations on Diabelli's waltz, to which 50 Austrian
composers contributed, Beethoven's contribution being the 33 variations, op.
120.   Liszt's variation is No. 24, and Schubert's No. 38.   Liszt has been throughout
an indefatigable champion for Schubert.
[3] The autograph of this little curiosity was sold in Paris, by auction, May 14,
1881.   The words are given by Kreissle, p. 82 (i. 83), but are not worth quoting.
They do not possess the individuality of thought which makes Schubert's later
verses so interesting, in spite of the crudity of their expression.
[4] His birthday was July 12, but the performance was put off on account
of the weather.
[5] I am indebted for this reprint to my ever-kind friend Mr. C. F. Pohl, of
the Gesellschaft der Musikfreunde, Vienna.

(Prometheus), chorus, and orchestra, and to have contained a duet in recitative, two choruses for mixed and one for male voices (the disciples of Prometheus). This last is described as having been in the form of a slow march, with original and interesting treatment. The performance took place in the garden of Watteroth's house in the Erdberg suburb of Vienna. As all the persons concerned in the festivity were people of some consideration, and as the music was very well received, it may have been an important introduction for the young composer. A congratulatory poem by von Schlechta, addressed to Schubert, appeared a day or two later in the ' Theater-zeitung.' Schubert had already, in the previous year, set a song of Schlechta's — ' Auf einem Kirchhof ' (Lief. 49, no. 2), and he promptly acknowledged the compliment by adopting one of more moment from Schlechta's ' Diego Manzanares,' ' Wo irrst du durch einsame Schatten ? ' (40 Lieder, no. 25), his setting of which is dated July 30, 1816.[1] Schubert evidently was fond of his cantata. It was performed at Innspruck [Innsbruck] by Gänsbacher, and at Vienna by Sonnleithner in 1819. Schubert wished to give it at the Augarten in 1820, and had sent it somewhere for performance at the time of his death. He was paid 100 florins, Vienna currency (or £4), for it, and he notes in his journal that it was the first time he had composed for money.

The third event was the composition of a cantata on a larger scale than either of the others. It was addressed to Dr. Joseph Spendou, in his character of Founder and Principal of the Schoolmasters' Widows' Fund, and contained 8 numbers, with solos for two sopranos and bass, a quartet and choruses, all with orchestral accompaniment. Whether it was performed or not is uncertain, but it was published in 1830 in pianoforte score by Diabelli, as op. 128. The other compositions of the year 1816 are as numerous as usual. A fine trio for S.S.A. and pianoforte to the words of Klopstock's ' grosses Halleluja ' (Lf. 41, no. 2) ; a Salve Regina in F, to German words, for 4 voices and organ [2] (February 21, 1816) ; the Angels' chorus from Faust, ' Christ ist erstanden,' [3] dated June 1816 — are also among the printed works. A Stabat Mater in F minor, to Klopstock's German

---

[1] He returned to this poet in 1820, 1825, 1826, 1828.
[2] Nottebohm's Catalogue, p. 226.
[3] First printed by Schumann as Appendix to his newspaper, the N.Z.M., for June 18, 1839.

words, dated February 28, 1816, is still in MS. It is written for
soprano, tenor, and bass solo, and chorus, and for an orchestra
of the usual strings, 2 flutes, 2 oboes, 2 bassoons, 1 contra-
bassoon, 2 horns, 3 trombones, 2 trumpets and drums. These,
however, are not uniformly employed : the trumpets and drums
only appear for a few chords in Nos. 9 and 12 ; No. 5, an
8-part chorus, is accompanied by the wind alone, and No. 6,
a tenor air, by the strings, with oboe solo. This interesting-
looking work was performed in 1841 by the Musik-Verein of
Vienna, and in 1863 at the Altlerchenfelder church there, but
has not yet been published. Two other MS. works are a
Magnificat in C for solos, chorus, and orchestra, dated October
1816, and a duet for soprano and tenor with orchestra, to Latin
words, 'Auguste jam Cœlestium,' dated September 1816, both
much tinctured by Mozart. There is also a ' Tantum ergo '
in C for 4 voices and orchestra, August 1816, and a fragment
of a Requiem in E♭, July 1816 ; the first pages are wanting,
and it ends with the 2nd bar of the 2nd Kyrie.[1]

Of operas we find only one in 1816, probably because only
one libretto came in his way. It is called ' Die Bürgschaft '
[after Schiller's ballad], and is in 3 acts. The author of the
words is not known [was Freiherr von Biedenfeld] ; and the
quotations in Kreissle show that they are in great part absolute
rubbish. Schubert continued his task to the 3rd act, 15 numbers, and there stopped. The autograph, in Herr Dumba's
possession, is dated May 1816, and no portion of it is printed.

The symphonies of 1816 are two — the 4th, in C minor,[2]
entitled ' Tragic Symphony,' and dated April 1816 ; and the
5th, in B♭, for small orchestra,[3] dated September 1816—October
3, 1816. The first of these — hardly ' tragic ' so much as
' pathetic ' — is a great advance on its predecessors ; the
Andante is individual and very beautiful, and the Finale
wonderfully spirited. The other, though full of Mozart, is as
gay and untrammelled as all Schubert's orchestral music of
that day. It is sometimes entitled ' without Trumpets or

[1] In Mr. Brahms's possession. The date is quoted from the Catalogue of the
accurate Nottebohm. I am bound to say that I saw no date, and Mr. Brahms
judged it to be later than 1816.
[2] April 1816.—Adagio molto and Allegretto vivace in C minor; Andante
in A♭ ; Minuet and Trio in E♭ ; Finale in C.—The autograph has vanished.
[3] Sept. 1816.—Fine den 3 Oct. 1816. Allegro B♭ ; Andante con moto E♭ ;
Minuet and Trio G minor and G major; Finale Allegretto vivace B♭. Autograph with Peters & Co.

Drums,' and is said to have been composed for the orchestra
at the Gundelhof, which grew out of the Schubert Sunday
afternoon quartets.[1] Neither work has yet been published in
score,[2] but they have often been played at the Crystal Palace,
under Mr. Manns's direction, and are among the favourite
works in the *répertoire* of that establishment. A string quartet
in F ; a string trio in B♭, apparently very good ; a rondo in
A for violin solo and quartet (June 1816) ; a violin concerto
in C ; 3 sonatinas for pianoforte and violin (op. 137) ; a
pianoforte sonata in F, two movements of another in E ; various
marches for pianoforte ; 12 Deutsche (waltzes) ; 6 Ecossaises,
with the inscriptions ' Composed while a prisoner in my room
at Erdberg ' and ' Thank God ' — probably the relic of some
practical joke — are still existing.

Very little of the above, however interesting, can be said
to be of real, first-rate, permanent value. But when we
approach the songs of 1816 the case is altered. There are not
quite so many with this date as there were with that of 1815,
but there are 99 in all [over 100] — 41 printed and 58 in MS.
Of Goethe there are splendid specimens, the three songs of
the Harper, in ' Wilhelm Meister ' (op. 12, Sept.), Mignon's
' Sehnsucht ' song (op. 62, no. 4) ; Der Fischer ; Der König
in Thule (op. 5, no. 5), Jägers Abendlied, and Schäfersklagelied
(op. 3), Wanderer's Nachtlied (op. 4), Schwager Kronos (op.
19). Of Schiller there are the beautiful Ritter Toggenburg,
Thekla's song (op. 58), etc., and to name only one other, the
far-famed ' Wanderer,' by Schmidt of Lübeck.

These magnificent pieces are well known to every lover of
Schubert, but they are not more valued than such exquisitely
simple and touching little effusions as ' An eine Quelle ' of
Claudius (op. 109, no. 3), ' Der Abend ' of Kosegarten (op.
118, no. 2), or ' Der Leidende ' of Hölty (Lief. 50, no. 2), all
equally bearing his stamp.

The lists of the songs of these two years throw a curious
light on Schubert's musical activity and mode of proceeding.
Dr. Johnson was said when he got hold of a book to ' tear the
heart out of it,' and with Schubert it was very much the same.
To read a poem, and at once to fasten upon it and transcribe
it in music, seems to have been his natural course ; and having

[1] Hanslick, *Concertwesen*, 142.
[2] Except the Andante of the ' Tragic,' which is published in score by Peters,
No. 1004.

done one he went at once to the next. A volume of Hölty,
or Claudius, or Kosegarten came into his hands; he tore from
it in a moment what struck him, and was not content with
one song, but must have three, four, or five. Thus, in October
[the summer of] 1815, he evidently meets with Kosegarten's
poems, and between the 15th and 19th sets seven [in July sets
twenty] of them. In March 1816 he sets five songs by Salis,
in May, six by Hölty; in November, four by Claudius, three
by Mayrhofer, and so on. To read these lists gives one a kind
of visible image of the almost fierce eagerness with which he
attacked his poetry, and of the inspiration with which the music
rushed from his heart and through his pen — ' everything that
he touched,' says Schumann, ' turning into music.' Thus, at
a later date, calling accidentally on Randhartinger, and his
friend being summoned from the room, Schubert, to amuse
himself in the interval, took up a little volume which lay on
the table. It interested him; and as his friend did not return
he carried it off with him. Anxious for his book, Randhartinger
called next morning at Schubert's lodgings, and found that he
had already set several pieces in it to music. The volume was
Wilhelm Müller's poems; the songs were part of the ' Schöne
Müllerin.' A year or two after this, in July 1826 — it is his
old friend Doppler who tells the story — returning from a
Sunday stroll with some friends through the village of Währing,
he saw a friend sitting at a table in the beer-garden of one of
the taverns. The friend, when they joined him, had a volume
of Shakespeare on the table. Schubert seized it, and began
to read; but before he had turned over many pages pointed
to ' Hark, hark, the lark,' and exclaimed, ' Such a lovely
melody has come into my head, if I had but some music paper.'
Some one drew a few staves on the back of a bill of fare, and
there, amid the hubbub of the beer-garden, that beautiful song,
so perfectly fitting the words, so skilful and so happy in its
accompaniment, came into perfect existence. Two others from
the same poet not improbably followed in the evening.[1]

It has been said that Schubert never heard his symphonies
played. This is no doubt true of the beautiful unfinished one
in B minor, of the Gastein Symphony, and of the great one in
C, no. 10; but of the first six it is not so correct. There was

[1] The drinking-song from *Antony and Cleopatra* (marked ' Währing, July 26 '), and
the lovely ' Sylvia ' [' Silvia '], July 1826 '). The anecdote is in Kreissle.

always the pupils' band at the *Convict*, where, as we have seen, parts in his handwriting are said to have lingered ; and there was also a flourishing amateur society, which, though their execution may not have had the precision of first-rate artists, yet probably played well enough to enable a composer to judge if his effects were what he intended them to be. Vienna amateurs were by no means contemptible. A society who met at the Mehlgrube even ventured on bringing out such works as Beethoven's Overture to ' Coriolan ' for the first time. Another, assembling at the Römische Kaiser, performed the ' Mount of Olives,' Beethoven himself conducting.

It seems that the Quartet afternoons at the house of Schubert the elder had gradually extended themselves into performances of Haydn's symphonies, arranged as quartets and played with doubled parts, players of ability and name joined, and a few hearers were admitted. After a time the modest room became inconveniently crowded, and then the little society migrated to the house of a tradesman named Frischling (Dorotheengasse 1105), wind instruments were added, and the smaller works of Pleyel, Haydn, and Mozart were attacked. In the winter of 1815 another move became necessary, to the house of Otto Hatwig, one of the violins of the Burgtheater, at the Schottenthor, and in the spring of 1818, to his new residence in the Gundelhof, and later still at Petten-kofer's house in the Bauernmarkt. The band now contained some good professional players, and could venture even on Beethoven's two first symphonies, and the overtures of Cheru-bini, Spontini, Boieldieu, Weigl, etc. Schubert belonged to it all through, playing the viola, and it was probably with the view to their performance by the society that he wrote the two symphonies of 1816 (nos. 4 and 5), two overtures in the winter of 1817, and his 6th symphony in the spring of 1818.

Schober and Mayrhofer were Schubert's first friends out-side the immediate circle of his youthful associates. He was now to acquire a third, destined to be of more active service than either of the others. This was Vogl. He was 20 years Franz's senior, and at the time of their meeting was a famous singer at the Vienna Opera, admired more for his intellectual gifts than for the technical perfection of his singing, and really great in such parts as Orestes in ' Iphigenie,' Almaviva in ' Figaro,' Creon in ' Medea,' and Telasko in the ' Vestalin.'

About the year 1816 — the date is not precisely given —[in February or March 1817] Vogl was induced by Schober to come to their lodgings and see the young fellow of whom Schober was always raving, but who had no access to any of the circles which Vogl adorned and beautified by his presence. The room as usual was strewed with music. Schubert was confused and awkward ; Vogl, the great actor and man of the world, gay, and at his ease. The first song he took up — probably the first music of Schubert's he had ever seen — was Schubert's ' Augenlied ' (Lf. 50, no. 3). He hummed it through, and thought it melodious, but slight — which it is. ' Ganymed ' and the ' Schäfersklage ' made a deeper impression ; others followed, and he left with the somewhat patronising but true remark, ' There is stuff in you ; but you squander your fine thoughts instead of making the most of them.' But the impression remained, he talked of Schubert with astonishment, soon returned, and the acquaintance grew and ripened till they became almost inseparable, and until in their performances of Schubert's songs, ' the two seemed,' in Schubert's own words, ' for the moment to be one.' In those days songs were rarely if ever sung in concert-rooms ; but Vogl had the entrée to all the great musical houses of Vienna, and before long his performances of the Erl King, the Wanderer, Ganymed, Der Kampf, etc., with the composer's accompaniment, were well known. What Vogl's opinion of him ultimately became, may be learnt from a passage in his diary : — ' Nothing shows so plainly the want of a good school of singing as Schubert's songs. Otherwise, what an enormous and universal effect must have been produced throughout the world, wherever the German language is understood, by these truly divine inspirations, these utterances of a musical *clairvoyance* ! How many would have comprehended, probably for the first time, the meaning of such expressions as ' speech and poetry in music,' ' words in harmony,' ' ideas clothed in music,' etc., and would have learnt that the finest poems of our greatest poets may be enhanced and even transcended when translated into musical language ? Numberless examples may be named, but I will only mention The Erl King, Gretchen, Schwager Kronos, the Mignon and Harper's songs, Schiller's Sehnsucht, Der Pilgrim, and Die Bürgschaft.'

This extract shows how justly Vogl estimated Schubert,

and how, at that early date, his discernment enabled him to pass a judgment which even now it would be difficult to excel. The word *clairvoyance*, too, shows that he thoroughly entered into Schubert's great characteristic. In hearing Schubert's compositions it is often as if one were brought more immediately and closely into contact with music itself than is the case in the works of others; as if in his pieces the stream from the great heavenly reservoir were dashing over us, or flowing through us, more directly, with less admixture of any medium or channel, than it does in those of any other writer — even of Beethoven himself. And this immediate communication with the origin of music really seems to have happened to him. No sketches, no delay, no anxious period of preparation, no revision, appear to have been necessary. He had but to read the poem, to surrender himself to the torrent, and to put down what was given him to say, as it rushed through his mind. This was the true 'inspiration of dictation,' as much so as in the utterance of any Hebrew prophet or seer. We have seen one instance in the case of the Erl King. The poem of the Wanderer attracted him in the same way, and the song was completed in one evening. In a third case, that of Goethe's 'Rastlose Liebe,' the paroxysm of inspiration was so fierce that Schubert never forgot it, but reticent as he often was, talked of it years afterwards.[1] It would seem that the results did not always fix themselves in the composer's memory as permanently as if they had been the effect of longer and more painful elaboration. Vogl tells an anecdote [2] about this which is very much to the point. On one occasion he received from Schubert some new songs, but being otherwise occupied could not try them over at the moment. When he was able to do so he was particularly pleased with one of them, but as it was too high for his voice, he had it copied in a lower key. About a fortnight afterwards they were again making music together, and Vogl placed the transposed song before Schubert on the desk of the piano. Schubert tried it through, liked it, and said, in his Vienna dialect, 'I say! the song's not so bad; *whose is it?*' so completely, in a fortnight, had it vanished from his mind! Sir Walter Scott attributed a song of his own to Byron; but this was in 1828, after his mind had begun to fail.[3]

[1] Bauernfeld, W.Z.K.   [2] In Kreissle, 119 (i. 123).
[3] Lockhart's Life of Scott, vii. 129.

1817 was comparatively an idle year. Its great musical event was the arrival of Rossini's music in Vienna. 'L' Inganno felice' was produced at the Hof theatre, November 26, 1816, and 'Tancredi,' December 17; 'L' Italiana in Algeri,' February 1 [15], 1817, and 'Ciro in Babilonia,' June 18; and the enthusiasm of the Viennese — like that of all to whom these fresh and animated strains were brought — knew no bounds. Schubert admired Rossini's melody and spirit, but rather made fun of his orchestral music, and a story is told — not impossibly apocryphal [1] — of his having written an overture in imitation of Rossini, before supper, after returning from 'Tancredi.' At any rate he has left two 'Overtures in the Italian style' in D and C, dated September [2] and November 1817 respectively, which were much played at the time. Schubert made 4-hand pianoforte arrangements of both, and that in C has been since published in score and parts as op. 170, and has been played at the Crystal Palace (December 1, 1866, etc.) and elsewhere. Its caricature of Rossini's salient points, including of course the inevitable *crescendo*, is obvious enough; but nothing could transform Schubert into an Italian, and the overture has individual and characteristic beauties which are immediately recognisable. The influence of Rossini was no mere passing fancy, but may be traced in the 6th Symphony, mentioned below, and in music of his later life — in the two Marches (op. 121), the Finale to the Quartet in G (op. 161), and elsewhere.

A third Overture in D belongs to 1817, and though still in MS., has also been played at the Crystal Palace (February 6, 1869, etc.). It is in two movements, Adagio, and Allegro giusto, and the former is almost a draft of the analogous movement in the overture known as 'Rosamunde' (op. 26), though really the 'Zauberharfe.' There the resemblance ceases.—What led Schubert to the pianoforte this year in so marked a manner is not known, but his devotion to it is obvious, for no fewer than 6 sonatas belong to this period. Of these, 3 are published — op. 122, in Eb; op. 147,[3] in B (August); op. 164, in A minor.[4] Those still in MS. are in F, Ab, and E minor (June).

[1] K.H. 129 (i. 133).
[2] Kreissle says May. September is Mr. Nottebohm's date; but there is another Overture in D, and it seems doubtful which of the two is dated May and which September.
[3] Autograph in possession of Mr. Brahms.
[4] Published, by Spina, as '7th Sonata.'

Schubert's 6th Symphony, in C,[1] completed in February 1818, appears to have been begun in the preceding October. It is the first one which he has marked as ' Grand ' — ' Grosse Sinfonie ' — though hardly with reason, as both in form and orchestra it is the same as the early ones. It is an advance on the others, and the Scherzo shows the first decided signs of Beethoven's influence. Passages may also be traced to Rossini and the Italian opera.

The catalogue of the instrumental compositions of this year closes with 2 sonatas for pianoforte and violin, op. 137, nos. 1 (March) and 2 ; a string Trio[2] and a Polonaise for the violin, both in MS. In the number of the vocal compositions of 1817 there is an equal falling off. Rossini's popularity for the time shut the door against all other composers, and even Schubert's appetite for bad librettos was compelled to wait. Not only, how-ever, are there no operas this year, there is no church music ; and but 47 songs (32 printed, and 15 in MS.). In quality, however, there is no deterioration in the songs. The astonishing ' Gruppe aus dem Tartarus,' and the ' Pilgrim ' of Schiller ; the ' Gany-med ' of Goethe ; the ' Fahrt zum Hades,' ' Memnon,' and ' Erlafsee ' of Mayrhofer ; and ' an die Musik ' of Schober, are equal to any that come before them. Among the MS. songs is one showing the straits to which Schubert was sometimes put, either by the want of materials or by the sudden call of his inspiration. It is the beginning of a setting of Schiller's ' Entzückung an Laura,' and is written on the front page of the 2nd violin part of a duet-fugue by Fux, the words ' Fuga. Duetto. Violino Secundo. Del : Sing : [3] Fux.' appearing in the copyist's formal handwriting through Schubert's hasty notes. It is superscribed ' Entzückung an Laura Abschied August 1817.   Schubert Mpia ' — interesting as showing that in ' Abschied,' he has added his own comment to Schiller's words ; that he dated his pieces at the moment of beginning them ; and that he sometimes signed his name without the ' Franz.'

His circle of intimate friends was increased about this date by Anselm and Joseph Hüttenbrenner and Joseph Gahy. Anselm, four years his senior, was a pupil of Salieri's, and there they had met in 1815. With the younger brother, Joseph, he

---

[1] Adagio and Allegro in C; Andante in F; Scherzo in C, and Trio in E major ; Finale in C.
[2] In B♭. Played at the Monday Popular Concert of Feb. 15, 1869.
[3] For ' Sign.' A facsimile is given by Reissmann.

became acquainted in the summer of 1817.[1] Both were men of independent means, and Anselm was a musician by profession. Gahy was in the government employment, an excellent pianoforte player, of whom Schubert was for long very fond. The younger Hüttenbrenner was bewitched by Schubert, much as Krumpholz and Schindler were by Beethoven; and was ever ready to fetch and carry for his idol, and to praise whatever he did, till the idol would turn on his worshipper, and be so cruel as to get the nickname of ' The Tyrant ' from the rest of the set.

How Schubert existed since he threw up his place at the school and left his father's house is a point on which we are in entire ignorance. His wants were few, but how even those few were supplied is a mystery. We have seen that he lived rent-free with Schober for a few months in 1816, but the return of Schober's brother put an end to the arrangement,[2] and from that date he must have been indebted to Spaun, or some friend better off than himself, for lodgings, for existence, and for his visits to the theatre, for there is no trace of his earning anything by teaching in 1817, and the few pounds paid him for the Watteroth cantata is the only sum which he seems to have earned up to this date.

In the summer of 1818, however, on the recommendation of Unger, the father of Mme. Unger-Sabatier, the great singer, Schubert accepted an engagement as teacher of music in the family of Count Johann Esterházy, to pass the summer at his country seat at Zelész [Zseliz], in Hungary, on the Waag [Gran], some distance east of Vienna, and the winter in town. He was to be a member of the establishment and to receive two gulden for every lesson. The family consisted of the Count and Countess, two daughters, Marie, 13, and Caroline, 11, and a boy of 5. All were musical. The Count sang bass, the Countess and Caroline contralto, Marie had a fine soprano, and both daughters played the piano. Baron von Schönstein, their intimate friend, slightly older than Schubert, a singer of the highest qualities, with a noble baritone [tenor] voice, made up the party, which certainly promised all the elements of enjoyment. It was a pang to Schubert to part from the circle of his

[1] So Kreissle, i. 128. But does not the dedication of the song, ' Die Erwartung,' composed Feb. 27, 1815—' to his friend ' J. H.—show that the acquaintance was of much earlier date? True, it was not published till the April after Schubert's death ; and the song may have been prepared by him for publication shortly before, and the dedication added then.

[2] K.H. 109 (i. 112).

companions, to whom he was devoted, but it is not difficult to imagine how pleasant he must have found the comfort and generous living of the Esterházy house, while at the same time there would be opportunities of retirement, and abundant means of diversion in a beautiful country, a new people, and the Hungarian and gipsy melodies.

When they left town does not appear.[1] Schubert's Mass in C,[2] his 4th, written like the others, for Holzer, is dated ' July, 1818 ' ; but there is nothing to show whether it was finished in Vienna or in the country. A set of MS. Solfeggi for the Countess Marie, also dated July, is perhaps evidence that by that time they were settled at Zelész. Two letters to Schober are printed by Bauernfeld,[3] and are dated August 3 and September 18, 1818. The first is addressed to his home circle, his ' dearest fondest friends . . . Spaun, Schober, Mayrhofer, and Senn . . . you who are everything to me.' There are messages also to Vogl, and to Schober's mother and sister, and to ' all possible acquaintances,' and an urgent entreaty to write soon — ' every syllable of yours is dear to me.' He is thoroughly well and happy, and ' composing like a god. . . . Mayrhofer's Einsamkeit is ready, and I believe it to be the best thing I have yet done, for I was *without anxiety* ' (*ohne Sorge* — the italics are his own). ' Einsamkeit ' (Lf. 32) is a long ballad, filling 19 close pages of print, with a dozen changes of tempo and as many of signature ; perhaps not quite coming up to his own estimate of it, though both words and music are often very striking. The length of this and other ballads will probably always hinder their wealth of melody, dramatic effects, and other striking beauties, from being known by the world at large.

The other letter, seven weeks later, throws more light on his position at Zelész ' as composer, manager, audience, everything, in one.' ' No one here cares for true Art, unless it be now and then the Countess ; so I am left alone with my beloved, and have to hide her in my room, or my piano, or

---

[1] There is an interesting autograph copy of the ' Forelle ' song dated at A. Hüttenbrenner's Lodgings (in Vienna) midnight Feb. 21, 1818, and besprinkled with ink instead of sand. It has been published in photography. But the ' Forelle ' really dates from 1817. (Nottebohm, in the Them. Catalogue.)

[2] Published in 1826 as op. 48. Schubert wrote a new and most beautiful Benedictus to it in 1828, only a few months before his death.

[3] In *Die Presse*, Vienna, Ap. 17, 1869. Reprinted in the *Signale*, Nov. 15, 1869.

my own breast. If this often makes me sad, on the other hand it often elevates me all the more. Several songs have lately come into existence, and I hope very successful ones.' He is evidently more at home in the servants' hall than the drawing-room. ' The cook is a pleasant fellow; the ladies'-maid is thirty; the housemaid very pretty, and often pays me a visit; the nurse is somewhat ancient; the butler is my rival; the two grooms get on better with the horses than with us. The Count is a little rough; the Countess proud, but not without heart; the young ladies good children. I need not tell you, who know me so well, that with my natural frankness I am good friends with everybody.' The letter ends with an affectionate message to his parents.

The only songs which can be fixed to this autumn, and which are therefore doubtless those just referred to, besides the great ' Einsamkeit,' are the ' Blumenbrief' (Lief. 21, no. 1), ' Blondel und Maria,' ' Das Marienbild ' and ' Litaney,' ' Das Abendroth ' — for a contralto, evidently composed for the Countess; ' Vom Mitleiden Mariä,' and three Sonnets from Petrarch (MS.). The Hungarian national songs left their mark in the ' 36 original dances,' or ' First Waltzes ' (op. 9), some of which were written down in the course of the next year. The ' Divertissement à la hongroise,' and the Quartet in A minor (op. 29), in which the Hungarian influence is so strong, belong — the first apparently, the second certainly — to a much later period.

A third letter of this date, hitherto unprinted, with which the writer has been honoured by the granddaughter [1] of Ferdinand Schubert, to whom it was addressed, is not without interest, and is here printed entire. The Requiem referred to was by Ferdinand, and had evidently been sent to his brother for revision. The letter throws a pleasant light on the strong link existing between Franz and his old home, and suggests that assistance more solid than ' linen ' may often have reached him from his fond stepmother in his poverty in Vienna. In considering the pecuniary result of the engagement, it must be remembered that the florin was at that time only worth a franc, instead of two shillings. The month's pay therefore, instead of being £20, was really only about £8. Still, for Schubert that was a fortune.

[1] Fräulein Caroline Geisler, daughter of Linus Geisler and Ferdinand's second daughter, Elise.

24 *Aug.* 1818.

DEAR BROTHER FERDINAND,

It is half-past 11 at night, and your Requiem is ready. It has made me sorrowful, as you may believe, for I sang it with all my heart. What is wanting you can fill in, and put the words under the music and the signs above. And if you want much rehearsal you must do it yourself, without asking me in Zelész. Things are not going well with you; I wish you could change with me, so that for once you might be happy. You should find all your heavy burdens gone, dear brother; I heartily wish it could be so.— My foot is asleep, and I am mad with it. If the fool could only write it wouldn't go to sleep!

Good morning, my boy, I have been asleep with my foot, and now go on with my letter at 8 o'clock on the 25th. I have one request to make in answer to yours. Give my love to my dear parents, brothers, sisters, friends, and acquaintances, especially not forgetting Carl. Didn't he mention me in his letter? As for my friends in the town, bully them, or get some one to bully them well, till they write to me. Tell my mother that my linen is well looked after, and that I am well off, thanks to her motherly care. If I could have some more linen I should very much like her to send me a second batch of pocket-handkerchiefs, cravats, and stockings. Also I am much in want of two pairs of kerseymere trowsers. Hart can get the measure whenever he likes. I would send the money very soon. For July, with the journey-money, I got 200 florins.

It is beginning already to be cold, and yet we shall not start for Vienna before the middle of October. Next month I hope to have a few weeks at Freystadt, which belongs to Count Erdödy, the uncle of my count. The country there is said to be extraordinarily beautiful. Also I hope to get to Pesth while we are at the vintage at Bosczmedj, which is not far off. It would be delightful if I should happen to meet Herr Administrator Taigele there. I am delighted at the thought of the vintage, for I have heard so much that is pleasant about it. The harvest also is beautiful here. They don't stow the corn into barns as they do in Austria, but make immense heaps out in the fields, which they call *Tristen*. They are often 80 to 100 yards long, and 30 to 40 high, and are laid together so cleverly that the rain all runs off without doing any harm. Oats and so on they bury in the ground.

Though I am so well and happy, and every one so good to me, yet I shall be immensely glad when the moment arrives for going to Vienna. Beloved Vienna, all that is dear and valuable to me is there, and nothing but the actual sight of it will stop my longing! Again entreating you to attend to all my requests, I remain, with much love to all, your true and sincere,

FRANZ Mpia.

A thousand greetings to your good wife and dear Resi, and a very hearty one to aunt Schubert and her daughter.

The inscription ' Zelész, November 1818 ' on the song ' Das Abendroth ' shows that the return to Vienna was not till nearly the end of the year. He found the theatre more than ever in possession of Rossini. To the former operas, ' Elisabetta ' was added in the autumn, and ' Otello ' early in January [on January 19] 1819. But one of the good traits in Schubert's character was his freedom from jealousy, and his determination to enjoy what was good, from whatever quarter it came, or however much it was against his own interest. A letter of his to Hüttenbrenner, written just after the production of ' Otello,' puts this in very good light. ' Otello is far better and more characteristic than Tancredi. Extraordinary genius it is impossible to deny him. His orchestration is often most original, and so is his melody ; and except the usual Italian gallopades, and a few reminiscences of Tancredi, there is nothing to object to.' But he was not content to be excluded from the theatre by every one, and the letter goes on to abuse the ' canaille of Weigls and Treitschkes,' and ' other rubbish, enough to make your hair stand on end,' all which were keeping his operettas off the boards. Still, it is very good-natured abuse, and so little is he really disheartened, that he ends by begging Hüttenbrenner for a libretto ; nay, he had actually just completed a little piece called ' Die Zwillingsbrüder ' (' the Twins '), translated by Hofmann from the French — a Singspiel in one act, containing an overture and 10 numbers. He finished it on January 19, 1819, and it came to performance before many months were over.

Of his daily life at this time we know nothing. We must suppose that he had regular duties with his pupils at the Esterházys' town house, but there is nothing to say so. We gather [1] that he joined Mayrhofer in his lodgings, 420 in the Wipplingerstrasse, early in the year. It was not a prepossessing apartment. ' The lane was gloomy ; both room and furniture were the worse for wear ; the ceiling drooped ; the light was shut out by a big building opposite — a worn-out piano, and a shabby bookcase.' The only relief is the name of the landlady

---

[1] In a letter to Mayrhofer from Linz, dated Aug. 19, 1819, he says, ' Let the bearer have my bed while he stays with you.' K.H. 159 (i. 160). The bed must have been his before he left town.

— Sanssouci, a Frenchwoman. No wonder that Mayrhofer's poems — he was ten years Schubert's senior — were of a gloomy cast.

The two friends were on the most intimate terms, and addressed each other by nicknames. What Mayrhofer's appellation may have been we do not know, but Schubert, now and later, was called ' the Tyrant,' for his treatment of Hütten-brenner; also ' Bertl,' ' Schwammerl,' and, best of all, ' Kanevas ' — because when a stranger came into their circle his first question always was, ' Kann er was? ' ' Can he do anything? ' Their humour took all sorts of shapes, and odd stories are told of their sham fights, their howls, their rough jokes and repartees.[1] Mayrhofer was a Government employé, and went to his office early, leaving his fellow-lodger behind. Schubert began work directly he awoke, and even slept in his spectacles to save trouble; he got at once to his writing, sometimes in bed, but usually at his desk. It was so still, when Hiller [2] called on him eight years later. ' Do you write much? ' said the boy, looking at the manuscript on the standing desk — they evidently knew little in North Germany of Schubert's fertility. ' I compose every morning,' was the reply; ' and when one piece is done, I begin another.' And yet this was the *musicien le plus poète que jamais* — it might have been the answer of a mere Czerny! Add to this a trait, communicated to the writer by Schubert's friend, Franz Lachner, of Munich, that when he had completed a piece, and heard it sung or played, he locked it up in a drawer, and often never thought about it again.

This close work went on till dinner-time — two o'clock — after which, as a rule, he was free for the day, and spent the remainder either in a country walk with friends, or in visits — as to Sofie Müller, and Mme. Lacsny [Lászny] — Buchwieser, whom we shall encounter further on; or at Schober's rooms, or some coffee-house — in his later days it was Bogner's Café in the Singerstrasse, where the droll cry of a waiter was a never-ending pleasure to him. But no hour or place was proof against the sudden attack of inspiration when anything happened to excite it. An instance occurs at this very time, November 1819, in an overture for 4 hands in F (op. 34), which he has inscribed as ' written in Joseph Hüttenbrenner's room at the City

---

[1] K.H. 51 (i. 51).   [2] In Hiller's *Künstlerleben* p. 49.

Hospital in the inside of three hours; and dinner missed in consequence.'[1] If the weather was fine he would stay in the country till late, regardless of any engagement that he might have made in town.

The only compositions that can be fixed to the spring of 1819 are 5 songs dated February, and one dated March; a very fine quintet for equal voices, to the ' Sehnsucht ' song in ' Wilhelm Meister ' — a song which he had already set for a single voice in 1816, and was to set twice more in the course of his life (thus rivalling Beethoven, who also set the same words four times); an equally fine quartet for men's voices, ' Ruhe, schönstes Glück der Erde,' dated April; and four sacred songs by Novalis, dated May.

The earnings of the previous summer allowed him to make an expedition this year on his own account. Mayrhofer remained in Vienna, and Vogl and Schubert appear to have gone together to Upper Austria. Steyr was the first point in the journey, a town beautifully situated on the Enns, not far south of Linz. They reached it early in July; it was Vogl's native place, and he had the pleasure of introducing his friend to the chief amateurs of the town, Paumgartner, Koller, Dornfeld, Schellmann — substantial citizens of the town, with wives and daughters, ' Pepi Koller,' ' Frizi Dornfeld,' ' the eight Schellmann girls,' etc., who all welcomed the musician with real Austrian hospitality, heard his songs with enthusiasm, and themselves helped to make music with him. His friend Albert Stadler was there also with his sister Kathi. How thoroughly Schubert enjoyed himself in this congenial *bourgeois* society, and in such lovely country — he mentions its beauties each time he writes — we have ample proof in two letters.[2] Among other drolleries the Erl King was sung with the parts distributed amongst Vogl, Schubert, and Pepi Koller. Perhaps, too, Schubert gave them his favourite version of it on a comb. Vogl's birthday (August 10) was celebrated by a cantata in C, containing a terzet, 2 soprano and 2 tenor solos, and a finale in canon, pointed by allusions to his various operatic triumphs, words by Stadler, and music by Schubert.[3] After this the two friends strolled on to Linz, the home of the Spauns, and of Kenner and Ottenwald [Ottenwalt], whose verses Franz had

[1] K.H. 160 (i. 162). [2] Ibid. 158–159 (i. 159–160).
[3] Published to other words, ' Herrlich prangt,' as op. 158.

set in his earlier days; and thence perhaps to Salzburg, returning to Steyr about the end of the month. Nor did the
joviality of these good Austrians interfere with composition.
Besides the impromptu cantata just mentioned, the well-known
pianoforte quintet (op. 114), in which the air of ' Die Forelle ' is
used as the theme of the Andantino, was written at Steyr,
possibly as a commission from the good Paumgartner, and was
performed by the Paumgartner party. Schubert achieved in it
the same feat which is somewhere ascribed to Mozart, of writing
out the separate parts without first making a score, and no doubt
played the pianoforte part by heart. The date of their departure, September 14, is marked by an entry in the album
of Miss Stadler, when Schubert delivered himself of the following highly correct sentiment : — ' Enjoy the present so wisely,
that the past may be pleasant to recollect, and the future not
alarming to contemplate.' This may pair off with a sentence
written by Mozart, in English, in the album of an English
Freemason, which has not yet been printed : — ' Patience and
tranquility of mind contribute more to cure our distempers as
the whole art of medicine. Wien, den 30te März 1787.' [1]

A few days more saw them again settled in Vienna. Each
of the two letters preserved from the journey contains an
obvious allusion to some love affair ; but nothing is known of
it. He could hardly have adopted a more effectual diversion
from such sorrows than the composition of a mass, on an
extended scale ; that namely in A♭ — his 5th — which he
began this month under the serious title of ' Missa Solemnis ' ;
but he seems to have dawdled over it more than over any other
of his works ; as it was not finished till September 1822, and
contains many marks of indecision.

The most pregnant musical event of this year is the fact
that on February 28, 1819, a song of Schubert's was sung in
public — the ' Schäfers Klagelied,' sung by Jäger at Jäll's
[Jaëll's] concert, at 5 p.m. at the ' Römische Kaiser,' Vienna.
It was Schubert's first appearance before the public in any
capacity [as a song-writer], and is noticed by the Leipzig
A.M.Z. in these terms : — ' Goethe's Schäfers Klagelied set to
music by Herr Franz Schubert — the touching and feeling
composition of this talented young man was sung by Herr
Jäger in a similar spirit.' Such is the first utterance of the press

[1] I owe this to my good friend Mr. Pohl, of Vienna.

on one who has since evoked so much enthusiasm! In the
course of this year Schubert appears to have forwarded the
three songs, ' Schwager Kronos,' ' Ueber Thal ' (Mignon)
[' An Mignon '], and ' Ganymed,' — afterwards published as
op. 19, — to Goethe ; but no notice was taken by the poet of
one who was to give some of his songs a wider popularity than
they could otherwise have enjoyed, a popularity independent
of country or language ; nor does Schubert's name once occur
in all the 6 volumes of Goethe's correspondence with Zelter.[1]

1820 was again a year of great activity. Owing to Vogl's
influence, Schubert was gradually attracting the attention of
the managers. The ' Zwillingsbrüder ' had been written for
the Kärnthnerthor theatre (see p. 151), and it was not long
before the *régisseur* of the rival opera-house, the Theatre an-der-
Wien, suggested to him a libretto called the ' Zauberharfe,'
or ' Magic harp,' a melodrama in 3 acts, by the same Hofmann
who had translated the former piece. To receive such a proposal and to act upon it was a matter of course with Schubert,
and the ' Zauberharfe ' is said to have been completed in a
fortnight.[2] But before this, early in the year, he had met with
the works of A. H. Niemeyer, Professor of Theology at Halle,
and had adopted the poem of ' Lazarus, or the Feast of the
Resurrection,' for an Easter Cantata. Easter fell that year on
April 2, and his work is dated ' February,' so that he was in
ample time. The poem — or drama, for there are seven
distinct characters — is in three parts. 1. The sickness and
death. 2. The burial and elegy. 3. The resurrection. Of
these, the 1st and a large portion of the 2nd were completed
by Schubert, apparently without the knowledge of any of his
friends. Ferdinand mentions the first part in his list,[3] but the
existence of the second was unknown, till, through the instru-
mentality of Mr. Thayer, it was unearthed in 1861. These
have been published,[4] but no trace of the 3rd act has yet been
found, and the work was not performed till long after the composer's death — viz. in 1863.

On June 14 the ' Zwillingsbrüder ' or ' Zwillinge ' was
produced at the Kärnthnerthor theatre. It is a comic operetta
(' Posse '), with spoken dialogue, in one act, containing an

---

[1] Search should be made in the *Goethe Archiv* at Weimar for the autograph
of these songs, and the letter which doubtless accompanied them.
[2] Autograph in Herr Dumba's collection.
[3] N.Z.M. 139 *a*.   [4] In 1866, by Spina.

overture and 10 numbers, and turns on the same plot that has done duty in ' Box and Cox ' and a dozen other farces, the confusion between two twin-brothers, who were both acted by Vogl. The overture was encored on the first night, and Vogl's two songs were much applauded, but the piece was virtually a *fiasco*, and was withdrawn after six representations. Schubert took so little interest in its production that, like Mendelssohn at the ' Wedding of Camacho,' he did not even stay in the house, and Vogl had to appear instead of him in front of the curtain. The libretto, though overburdened with characters, is sadly deficient in proportion, and contains very little action. Schubert's music, on the other hand, is light, fresh, and melodious, pointed, unusually compact, and interesting through-out. In the concerted numbers there is evidence of great dramatic power. To condemn it, as the critics of the day do, as wanting in melody, and constantly striving after originality, is to contradict Schubert's most marked characteristics, and is contrary to the facts. There is possibly more justice in the complaint that the accompaniments were too loud, though that is certainly not the fault in his masses, his only other published works with orchestral accompaniments anterior to this date. The work has been published in vocal score by Peters (1872).

On August 19 the Zauberharfe was produced at the Theatre an-der-Wien. It is said to consist chiefly of chorus and melo-drama, with only a few solos, among them a romance for tenor which was highly praised. There is a fine overture (in C), original, characteristic, and full of beauty, which was published before 1828 as op. 26, under the name of ' Rosamunde,' to which it seems to have no claim.[1] The piece was occasionally brought forward till the winter, and was then dropped. These three vocal works appear so far to have whetted Schubert's appetite that in the autumn he attacked the more important libretto of ' Sakontala,' a regular opera in 3 acts, by P. H. Neumann, founded on the Indian drama of that name. He sketched 2 acts, and there it remains; the MS. is in Herr Dumba's possession. Another important and very beautiful piece is the 23rd Psalm,[2] set for 2 sopranos and 2 altos with

[1] The overture played to the Rosamunde music is in D minor, and was afterwards published as ' Alfonso and Estrella.' There is perhaps another in existence. See the letter to von Mosel quoted further on.
[2] To Moses Mendelssohn's translation.

pianoforte accompaniment, at the instigation of the sisters Fröhlich, and dated at the beginning '23 December 1820' — perhaps with a view to some private concerts given, now or later, at the old hall of the Musikverein. Another is the 'Gesang der Geister über den Wassern' of Goethe (op. 167). This fine and mystical poem had a strong attraction for Schubert. He set it for 4 equal voices in 1817; then he reset it for 4 tenors and 4 basses with 2 violas, 2 cellos, and bass, in December 1820; and lastly revised this in February 1821. It was first produced on March 7, 1821, and found no favour, to Schubert's disgust. It was again performed on March 30, before a more receptive audience, with a far better result. It was revived at Vienna in 1858 by Herbeck, and in England was performed with success on March 22, 1881, under the direction of Mr. Prout. It is enormously difficult, and, though perfectly in character with the poem, will probably never be attractive to a mixed audience. Another work of 1820 were some anti-phons (op. 113) for Palm Sunday (March 26), composed for Ferdinand, who had been recently appointed Choirmaster at the Altlerchenfelder Church, and found the duties rather too much for him. They are written with black chalk, on coarse grey wrapping-paper; and the tradition is that they and two motets were written in great haste, just in time for the service. On Easter Sunday Franz attended and conducted the mass for his brother.

The Fantasie in C for pianoforte solo (op. 15), containing Variations on Schubert's own 'Wanderer,' is probably a work of this year. It was written for von Liebenberg, a pianoforte player, to whom Schubert dedicated it. This fine piece has lately been brought into vogue by Liszt's arrangement of it for pianoforte and orchestra as a concerto; but it is doubtful if it is improved by the process. Schubert never could play it; he always stuck fast in the last movement; and on one occasion jumped up and cried 'let the devil himself play it!' Another piece is an Allegro for strings in C minor, dated December 1820, the first movement of a quartet, of which there exist besides 41 bars of the Andante, in A♭. The Allegro is of first-rate quality, and Schubert in every bar. It was published in 1868 by Senff. The MS. is in Mr. Brahms's fine collection of autographs.

The songs of 1820, 17 in all, though not so numerous as those of previous years, are very fine. They contain 'Der

Jüngling auf dem Hügel' (op. 8, no. 1), 'Der Schiffer' (Lf. 33, no. 1), 'Liebeslauschen' (Lf. 15, no. 2), 3 grand songs to Mayrhofer's words, 'Orest auf Tauris,' 'Der entsühnte Orest,' and 'Freiwilliges Versinken' (Lf. 11), and 4 Italian Canti, written for Frl. von Romer, who afterwards married Schubert's friend Spaun, and since published with one which was probably written under Salieri's eye as early as 1813. The most remarkable of all is 'Im Walde,' or 'Waldesnacht' (Lf. 16), a very long song of extraordinary beauty, variety, force, and imagination.

With February 1821 Schubert entered his 25th year, and it was a good omen to receive such a birthday present as the three testimonials of this date which Kreissle has preserved.[1] The first is from von Mosel, then Court Secretary; the second from Weigl, Director of the Court Opera, Salieri, and von Eichthal; the third from Moritz Count Dietrichstein, whom Beethoven addresses as 'Hofmusikgraf,' and who appears to have been a sort of Jupiter-Apollo with general sway over all Court music. These influential personages warmly recognise his eminent ability, industry, knowledge, feeling, and taste, and profess the best intentions towards him. The three documents were enclosed by the Count in a letter to Vogl, full of good wishes for the future of his friend. Still more gratifying was the prospect, which now at last opened, of the publication of his songs. It was the first good epoch in Schubert's hitherto struggling life. He had now been writing for more than seven years, with an industry and disregard of consequences which are really fearful to contemplate; and yet, as far as fame or profit were concerned, might almost as well have remained absolutely idle. Here at length was a break in the cloud. It was not less welcome because it was mainly due to his faithful friends the Sonnleithners, who had made his acquaintance through the accident of Leopold Sonnleithner's being at school with him, and ever since cherished it in the most faithful and practical way—Ignaz, the father, having, since 1815, had large periodical music-meetings of artists and amateurs in his house at the Gundelberg [Gundelhof], which were nothing less than Schubert propaganda. Here, before large audiences of thoroughly musical people, Schubert's pieces were repeatedly performed, and at length, on December 1, 1820, the 'Erl King'

[1] K.H. 201 (i. 203).

was sung by Gymnich, a well-known amateur, with a spirit
which fired every one of the audience with the desire to possess
the song, and appears to have suggested to Leopold and
Gymnich the possibility of finding a publisher for the inspirations which had for so long been their delight and astonishment.
They applied to Diabelli and Haslinger, the leading houses of
Vienna, but without success; the main objections being the
insignificance of the composer, and the difficulty of his pianoforte accompaniments. On this they resolved to take the matter
into their own hands; and, probably not without misgivings,
had the ' Erl King ' engraved. The fact was announced at
the next concert at the Gundelberg, and a hundred copies were
at once subscribed for in the room — sufficient to defray the
cost of the engraving and printing, and of engraving a second
song as well. Meantime the ' Erl King ' had been sung in
public (for the concerts at the Gundelberg were, strictly speaking, private, limited to the friends of the host) by Gymnich,
at an evening concert of the Musikverein, in one of the public
rooms of the city, on January 25, 1821, Schubert himself
appearing on the platform, and playing the accompaniment.
Everything was done by the young enthusiasts to foster the
Schubert *furore*, even to the publication of a set of ' Erl King
waltzes ' by A. Hüttenbrenner, which at any rate must have
made the name familiar, though they provoked Schubert, and
drew from him [from Kanne] some satirical hexameters and
pentameters which may be read in Kreissle.[1] On February 8
the programme of the Musikverein concert included three
songs of his, the ' Sehnsucht ' by Schiller, ' Gretchen am
Spinnrade,' and ' Der Jüngling auf dem Hügel ': and on
March 8 the ' Gruppe aus dem Tartarus.' On March 7 the
' Erl King ' was again sung, this time by Vogl himself, at an
unmistakable public concert, at the Kärnthnerthor theatre,
a concert supported by all the most distinguished ladies of the
Court, who received the song with loud applause. Think what
the first appearance of these godlike pieces must have been!
It was the rising of the Sun! He is now an every-day sight to
us; but how was it the first time that he burst in all his brightness on the eyes of mortals? In the midst of all this enthusiasm
the ' Erl King ' was published on the 1st of April, 1821, by
Cappi and Diabelli, on commission. It was dedicated to Count

Moritz Dietrichstein, whose kindness well deserved that recognition. On April 30, ' Gretchen am Spinnrade ' appeared as op. 2. The succeeding publications — each made to depend on the success of the last — were as follows : —

May 29.   Op. 3. Schäfers Klagelied ; Meeres-Stille ; Heidenröslein ; Jägers Abendlied.
Do.   Op. 4. Der Wanderer ; Morgenlied ; Wanderers Nachtlied.
July 9.   Op. 5. Rastlose Liebe ; Nähe des Geliebten ; Der Fischer ; Erster Verlust ; Der König in Thule.
Aug. 23. Op. 6. Memnon ; Antigone und Oedip ; Am Grabe Anselmos.
Nov. 27. Op. 7. Die abgeblühte Linde ; Der Flug der Zeit ; Der Tod und das Mädchen.

Here the publication by commission stopped, the Diabellis being evidently convinced that the risk might be profitably assumed ; and accordingly op. 8 appears on May 9, 1822, as ' the property of the publishers.' The dedications of the first seven numbers no doubt furnish the names of Schubert's most influential supporters : 1. Graf von Dietrichstein ; 2. Reichsgraf Moritz von Fries ; 3. Ignaz von Mosel ; 4. Johann Ladislaus Pyrker, Patriarch of Venice ; 5. Salieri ; 6. Michael Vogl ; 7. Graf Ludwig Széchényi. It must be admitted that the above are very good lists, and that if Schubert had waited long for the publication of his works, the issue of twenty songs in eight months, under the patronage of seven such eminent personages, was a substantial compensation. We do not hear, however, that much money came into his hands from the publication. The favourable impression made by the publication may be gathered from the long, intelligent, and sympathetic criticism, ' Blick auf Schuberts Lieder,' by F. von Hentl, which appeared in the ' Wiener Zeitschrift für Kunst,' etc. — a periodical belonging to Diabelli's rivals, Steiner & Co. — for March 23, 1822.

Schubert was now a good deal about the theatre, and when it was determined to produce a German version of Hérold's ' Clochette,' as ' Das Zauberglöckchen,' at the Court-opera, he was not unnaturally called upon to insert a couple of pieces to suit the Vienna audience. It was what Mozart often did for the Italian operas of his day — what indeed we know Shakespeare to have done in more than one case. The opera was

produced on June 20. The interpolated pieces were a ong
air for tenor,[1] in 3 movements — Maestoso, Andante, and
Allegro — full of passion and imagination, and a comic duet
(said to be very comic) between the princes B flat and C natural
(Bedur and Cedur). They were more applauded than anything
else in the work, but Schubert's name was not divulged; the
opera as a whole did not please, and was soon withdrawn.

The little Variation which he contributed, as No. 38, to
Diabelli's collection of 50 Variations — the same for which
Beethoven wrote his 33 (op. 120) — should not be overlooked.
Though not published till 1823, the autograph, now in the
Hofbibliothek at Vienna, is dated 'March 1821.' The variation is fresh and pretty, in the minor of the theme, but is more
noticeable from its situation than from its own qualities. A few
dances for pianoforte solo are dated '8th March' and 'July'
in this year, and a collection of 36, containing those alluded
to, and others of 1816 and 1819, was published by Cappi and
Diabelli on November 29, as op. 18. Some of these are inscribed in the autograph 'Atzenbrucker Deutsche, July 1821,'
indicating a visit to Atzenbruck [Atzenbrugg], the seat of an
uncle of Schober's, near Abstetten, between Vienna and St.
Pölten, where a three days' annual festivity was held, to which
artists of all kinds were invited, and where Schubert's presence
and music were regarded as indispensable.

Whether after this he and Schober returned to Vienna we
know not, no letters remain; but the next event of which any
record remains is the composition of a symphony, his seventh,
in E, which is marked, without note of place, as begun in
August. He did not complete the writing of it, and indeed it is
probable that it did not occupy him more than a few hours;
but the autograph, which is in the writer's possession,[2] is a very
curious manuscript, probably quite unique, even among
Schubert's feats of composition. It occupies 167 pages of 42
sheets (10 quires of 4, and 1 of 2), and is in the usual movements
— Adagio in E minor, and Allegro in E major; Andante in
A; Scherzo in C, and Trio in A; and Allegro giusto in E
major. The Introduction and a portion of the Allegro are fully
scored and marked; but at the 110th bar — the end of a page

[1] Introduced into 'Alfonso und Estrella' in 1881 by Joh. Fuchs.
[2] I received it in 1868 from the late Paul Mendelssohn, Felix's brother,
into whose hands it came after his brother's death. Felix Mendelssohn had it
from Ferdinand Schubert direct.

— Schubert appears to have grown impatient of this regular proceeding, and from that point to the end of the work has made merely memoranda. But these memoranda are, in their way, perfectly complete and orderly to the end of the Finale. Every bar is drawn-in; the *tempi* and names of the instruments are fully written at the beginning of each movement; the *nuances* are all marked; the very double bars and flourishes are gravely added at the end of the sections, and ' Fine ' at the conclusion of the whole; and Schubert evidently regarded the work as no less complete on the paper than it was in his mind. And complete it virtually is; for each subject is given at full length, with a bit of bass or accompaniment-figure, or *fugato* passage. There is not a bar from beginning to end that does not contain the part of one or more instruments; at all crucial places the scoring is much fuller; and it would no doubt be possible to complete it as Schubert himself intended. It is said that Mendelssohn contemplated doing so, but this is probably a mere legend, and Mendelssohn was too practical to give his time to a work which at the best could only be regarded as a curiosity. Though containing much that is original, and as deeply imbued throughout with melody and spirit as any of the preceding six, this symphony is, like them, virtually a work of the old school, and it required another year before Schubert could break with the past, and in the two movements of his unfinished 8th Symphony in B minor, and the great Entr'acte to ' Rosamunde,' in the same key, appear in the orchestra in his own individual and native shape, as he had done in the Song so many years before.[1]

We next find the two friends at the castle of Ochsenburg, a few miles south of St. Pölten, the seat of the Bishop, who was a relative of Schober; and there and in St. Pölten itself they passed a thoroughly happy and healthy holiday of some weeks in September and October. The Bishop and Baron Mink, a local magnate, were congenial hosts, and the visit of the two clever young men was the signal for various festivities, in which all the aristocracy of the country-side — ' a princess, two countesses, and three baronesses,' in Schober's enumeration

---

[1] The change in this symphony from the Scherzo in C to the Trio in A, by an E in octaves in the oboes lasting 4 bars, is an anticipation of the similar change in the same place in the great C major Symphony of 1828, and a curious instance of the singular way in which many of Schubert's earlier symphonies lead up to his crowning effort.

— took part, and in which the music and drollery of Schubert and his friend delighted every one. The great result of the visit, however, was the composition of an opera to Schober's words, on a romantic subject of battles, love, conspiracy, hunting, peasant life, and everything else, so natural in opera librettos, so impossible in real life. It was called ' Alfonso and Estrella,' and two acts were completed before their return to town. The first act is dated at the end of the autograph September 20, and the second October 20. A week later they were back again in Vienna.

The songs composed in 1821 are very important, and comprise some of his very finest, and in the most various styles. It is sufficient to name among the published ones ' Grenzen der Menschheit ' (February, Lf. 14, no. 1) ; ' Geheimes ' (March, op. 14, no. 2) ; Suleika's two songs (ops. 14, 31) ; ' Sey mir gegrüsst ' (op. 20, no. 1) ; and ' Die Nachtigal ' [' Nachtigall '] for four men's voices (op. 11, no. 2) — all of the very highest excellence, of astonishing variety, and enough of themselves to make the fame of any ordinary composer. A fine setting of ' Mahomet's song,' by Goethe, for bass (possibly for Lablache), was begun in March, but remains a MS. fragment.

The third act of ' Alfonso and Estrella ' was finished on February 27, 1822. The fact that a thoroughly worldly, mercenary, money-making manager like Barbaja, who was at the same time a firm believer in Rossini, had become lessee of the two principal theatres of Vienna, augured badly for Schubert's chance of success in that direction. But indeed the new piece seems to have been calculated to baffle any manager, not only in Vienna, but everywhere else. It caused, as we shall see, a violent dispute, eighteen months later, between Schubert and Weber, which but for Schubert's good temper would have led to a permanent quarrel. Anna Milder, to whom Schubert sent a copy of the work in 1825, tells him, in a letter full of kindness and enthusiasm, that the libretto will not suit the taste of the Berliners, ' who are accustomed to the grand tragic opera, or the French opéra comique.' Nor was the libretto the only drawback. Schubert, like Beethoven in ' Fidelio,' was in advance of the modest execution of those days. At Gratz [Graz], the abode of the Hüttenbrenners, where there was a *foyer* of Schubert-enthusiasts, the opera got as far as rehearsal, and would probably have reached the stage, if the accompaniments had not proved impossible for the band.[1]   No performance took place until twenty-six years after poor Schubert's death, namely at Weimar, on June 24, 1854, under the direction of Liszt, who, with all his devotion to the master, had to reduce it much for performance.   It was very carefully studied, and yet the success, even in that classical town, and with all Liszt's enthusiasm and influence, seems to have been practically *nil*.   At last, however, its time came.   Twenty-five years later, in 1879, it was again taken in hand by Capellmeister Johann Fuchs of the Court opera, Vienna, who entirely rewrote the libretto, and greatly curtailed the work; and in this form it was brought to performance at Carlsruhe in March 1881, with great success. Several numbers were extremely applauded, and the opera now bids fair to become a stock piece in the German, and let us hope the English, theatres.

But to return to Schubert and 1822.   Early in the year he made the acquaintance of Weber,[2] who spent a few weeks of February and March in Vienna to arrange for the production of his 'Euryanthe.'   No particulars of their intercourse on this occasion survive.   With Beethoven Schubert had as yet hardly exchanged words.   And this is hardly to be wondered at, because, though Vienna was not a large city, yet the paths of the two men were quite separate.   Apart from the great difference in their ages, and from Beethoven's peculiar position in the town, his habits were fixed, his deafness was a great obstacle to intercourse, and, for the last five or six years, what with the lawsuits into which his nephew dragged him, and the severe labour entailed by the composition of the Mass in D, and of the Sonatas ops. 106, 109, 110, and 111 — works which by no means flowed from him with the ease that masses and sonatas did from Schubert — he was very inaccessible.   Any stranger arriving from abroad, with a letter of introduction, was seen and treated civilly.   But Schubert was a born Viennese, and at the time of which we speak, Beethoven was as much a part of Vienna as St. Stephen's tower, and to visit him required some special reason, and more than special resolution.

---

[1] K.H. 249 (i. 252).
[2] For their meeting we have the authority of Weber's son in his biography, ii. 420.   But his statement that Schubert was alienated from Weber by Weber's criticism on Rosamunde is more than doubtful, because Rosamunde was probably not composed till some 19 months later, and because it was not Schubert's habit to take offence at criticism.

A remark of Rochlitz [1] in the July of this year shows that
Schubert was in the habit of going to the same restaurant with
Beethoven, and worshipping at a distance; but the first direct
evidence of their coming into contact occurs at this date. On
April 19, 1822, he published a set of Variations on a French
air as op. 10, and dedicated them to Beethoven as ' his admirer
and worshipper ' (*sein Verehrer und Bewunderer*). The Variations
were written in the preceding winter [at Zseliz in 1818], and
Schubert presented them in person to the great master. There
are two versions of the interview, Schindler's [2] and J. Hüttenbrenner's. Schindler was constantly about Beethoven. He
was devoted to Schubert, and is very unlikely to have given a
depreciating account of him. There is therefore no reason for
doubting his statement, especially as his own interest or vanity
were not concerned. It is the first time we meet Schubert face
to face. He was accompanied by Diabelli, who was just beginning to find out his commercial value, and would naturally be
anxious for his success. Beethoven was at home, and we know
the somewhat overwhelming courtesy with which he welcomed
a stranger. Schubert was more bashful and retiring than ever;
and when the great man handed him the sheaf of paper and the
carpenter's pencil provided for the replies of his visitors, could
not collect himself sufficiently to write a word. Then the
Variations were produced, with their enthusiastic dedication,
which probably added to Beethoven's good humour. He
opened them and looked through them, and seeing something
that startled him, naturally pointed it out. At this Schubert's
last remnant of self-control seems to have deserted him, and
he rushed from the room. When he got into the street, and was
out of the magic of Beethoven's personality, his presence of
mind returned, and all that he might have said flashed upon
him, but it was too late. The story is perfectly natural, and
we ought to thank Beethoven's Boswell for it. Which of us
would not have done the same? Beethoven kept the Variations
and liked them; and it must have been some consolation to the
bashful Franz to hear that he often played them with his
nephew. Hüttenbrenner's story [3] is that Schubert called, but
found Beethoven out; which may have been an invention of
Diabelli's to shield his young client.

[1] *Für Freunde der Tonkunst*, iv. 352. See the lifelike and touching picture by
Braun von Braun given in Nohl's Beethoven, iii. 682.
[2] Schindler's *Beethoven*, ii. 176.   [3] K.H. 261 (i. 264).

This autumn Schubert again took up the Mass in A♭, which was begun in 1819; finished it, and inscribed it ' *im* 7ᵇ 8̅2̅2̅ *beendet.*' [1] Not that that was the final redaction; for, contrary to his usual practice — in fact it is almost a solitary instance — he took it up again before his death, and made material improvements [2] both in the position of the voice-parts and in the instrumentation, as may be seen from the autograph score now in the Library of the Gesellschaft der Musikfreunde.

This year seems to have been passed entirely in Vienna, at least there are no traces of any journey; and the imprisonment in the broiling city, away from the nature he so dearly loved, was not likely to improve his spirits. What events or circumstances are alluded to in the interesting piece called ' My dream,' [3] dated ' July 1822,' it is hard to guess. It may not improbably have been occasioned by some dispute on religious subjects of the nature of those hinted at in his brother Ignaz's letter [4] of October 12, 1818. At any rate it is deeply pathetic and poetical.

During this summer Joseph Hüttenbrenner was active in the cause of his friend. He made no less than four endeavours to bring out the ' Teufels Lustschloss ' — at the Josefstadt and Court theatres of Vienna, at Munich, and at Prague. At Prague alone was there a gleam of hope. Hollbein [Hollpein], the manager there, requests to have the score and parts sent to him, at the same time regretting that during a month which he had passed in Vienna, Schubert had not once come near him. Hüttenbrenner also urged Schubert on Peters, the publisher, of Leipzig, who in a tedious egotistical letter, dated November 14, 1822, gives the usual sound reasons of a cautious publisher against taking up with an unknown composer — for

---

[1] 7 *b* stands for September.

[2] This was kindly pointed out to the writer by Mr. Brahms, who has an early copy of the score, made by Ferdinand Schubert from the autograph in its original condition. In this shape Mr. Brahms rehearsed the mass, but found many portions unsatisfactory, and was interested to discover subsequently from the autograph that Schubert had altered the very passages alluded to, and made them practicable.—He made three attempts at the ' Cum Sancto ' before succeeding, each time in fugue, and always with a different subject. Of the first there are 4 bars; of the second 199; the third is that printed in Schreiber's edition. This edition is unfortunately very incorrect. Not only does it swarm with misprints, but whole passages, and those most important ones (as in the Horns and Trombones of the Dona), are clean omitted. The *nuances* also are shamefully treated.

[3] First printed by R. Schumann in the *Neue Zeitschrift für Musik* for Feb. 5, 1839. See also K.H. 333 (ii. 16).

[4] K.H. 146 (i. 148).

in North Germany Schubert was still all but unknown. One is
sorry to hear of a little rebuff which he sustained at this time
from the Gesellschaft der Musikfreunde of Vienna, to whom
he applied to be admitted as a practising member (on the
viola), but who refused him on the ground of his being a professional, and therefore outside their rules.[1] A somewhat similar
repulse was experienced by Haydn from the Tonkünstler
Societät. [See vol. i. 707a.] * On the other hand, the musical
societies both of Linz and Gratz [Graz] elected him an honorary
member. To the latter of these distinctions we owe the two
beautiful movements of the Symphony No. 8, in B minor,
which was begun at Vienna on October 30, 1822, and intended
as a return for the compliment. The Allegro and Andante
alone are finished, but these are of singular beauty and the
greatest originality. In them, for the first time in orchestral
composition, Schubert exhibits a style absolutely his own, un-
tinged by any predecessor, and full of that strangely direct
appeal to the hearer of which we have already spoken. It is
certain that he never heard the music played, and that the
new and delicate effects and orchestral combinations with
which it is crowded were the result of his imagination alone.
The first movement is sadly full of agitation and distress.
It lay hidden at Gratz for many years, until obtained from
Anselm Hüttenbrenner by Herbeck, who first produced it in
Vienna at one of the Gesellschaft concerts in 1865.[2] It was
published by the excellent Spina early in 1867; was played
at the Crystal Palace, Sydenham, April 6, 1867, and elsewhere
in England, and always with increasing success. In fact no
one can hear it without being captivated by it.

The songs composed in 1822 — 14 printed and 2 in MS.
— comprise ' Epistel von Collin ' (Lf. 46 ; January) ; ' Heliopolis ' (Lf. 37, no. 1 ; April) ; ' Todesmusik,' with a magnificent opening (op. 108, no. 2 ; September) ; ' Schatzgräbers
Begehr ' (op. 23, no. 4 ; November) with its stately bass ;
' Willkommen und Abschied ' (op. 56, no. 1 ; December) ;
' Die Rose ' (op. 73) and ' Der Musensohn ' (op. 92). The
concerted pieces, ' Constitutionslied ' (op. 157 ; January), ' Geist
der Liebe ' (op. 11, No. 3), ' Gott in der Natur ' (op. 133), and

---

[1] Ibid. 280 (i. 283).
* [Reference to the first edition of Grove's Dictionary.]
[2] See Hanslick, *Concertsaal*, 350.

M

'Des Tages Weihe' (op. 146), all belong to this year.

Publication went on in 1822, though not so briskly as before. The Variations dedicated to Beethoven (op. 10) were first to appear, on April 19. They were followed by op. 8 (4 songs) on May 9, and op. 11 (3 part-songs) on June 12. Then came a long gap till December 13, on which day ops. 12, 13, and 14, all songs, appeared at once. We have not space to name them. But with such accumulated treasures to draw upon, it is unnecessary to say that they are all of the first class. The pecuniary result of the publications of 1821 had been good; 2000 gulden were realised, and of the 'Erl King' alone more than 800 copies had been sold; and if Schubert had been provident enough to keep his works in his own possession he would soon have been out of the reach of want. This, however, he did not do. Pressed by the want of money, in an incautious moment he sold the first 12 of his works [1] to Diabelli for 800 silver gulden (£80), and entered into some injudicious arrangement with the same firm for future publications. His old and kind friend Count Dietrichstein about this time offered him a post as organist to the Court Chapel [?], but he refused it, and he was probably right, though in so doing he greatly distressed his methodical old father. His habits, like Beethoven's, made it absurd for him to undertake any duties requiring strict attendance.

The Vienna Theatre being closed to 'Alfonso and Estrella', Schubert turned his thoughts in the direction of Dresden, where his admirer Anna Milder was living, and where Weber was Director of the Opera; and we find him in a letter of February 28, 1823 (recently published [2] for the first time) asking his old patron Herr von Mosel for a letter of recommendation to Weber. He is confined to the house by illness, and apologises for not being able to call. There are no traces of reply to this application, but it probably led to nothing, for, as we shall see, the score of the opera was still in his hands in October. He was evidently now set upon opera. In the letter just mentioned he implores von Mosel to entrust him with a libretto 'suitable for his littleness'; and though he seems never to have obtained

---

[1] So say the books; but the works published on commission were ops. 1–7, containing 20 songs.

[2] In the *Neue Freie Presse* of Vienna, Nov. 19, 1881. The letter though formal in style, is curiously free in some of its expressions. It mentions the overture to the 1st Act of Alfonso and Estrella. What can this be? The overture known under that name (op. 69) is dated 'Dec. 1823,' and is said to have been written for Rosamunde.

this, he went on with the best he could get, and 1823 saw the birth of no less than three dramatic pieces. The first was a one-act play with dialogue, adapted from the French by Castelli, and called ' die Verschworenen,' or ' the Conspirators.' The play was published in the ' Dramatic Garland ' — an annual collection of dramas — for 1823. Schubert must have seen it soon after publication, and by April had finished the composition of it. The autograph, in the British Museum, has at the end the words ' Aprill 1823. F. Schubert, Ende der Oper.' It contains an overture and 11 numbers, and appears from Bauernfeld's testimony to have been composed with a view to representation at the Court-theatre. The libretto is a very poor one, with but few dramatic points, and confines the composer mainly to the chorus. The licensers changed its title to the less suspicious one of ' Die [Der] häusliche Krieg' or ' The domestic Struggle,' and it was duly sent in to the management, but it returned in twelve months without examination. It did not come to performance at all during Schubert's lifetime, nor till 1861. In that year it was given, under Herbeck's direction, by the Musikverein, Vienna, on March 1 and 22 ; and on the stage at Frankfort on August 29 ; since then at the Court-theatre, Vienna, at Munich, Salzburg, and other German towns ; in Paris, February 3, 1868, as ' La Croisade des Dames,' and at the Crystal Palace, Sydenham, March 2, 1872, as ' The Conspirators.' In less than two months after throwing off this lively Singspiel, Schubert had embarked in something far more serious, a regular 3-act opera of the ' heroico-romantic ' pattern — also with spoken dialogue — the scene laid in Spain, with Moors, knights, a king, a king's daughter, and all the usual furniture of these dreary compilations. The libretto of ' Fierabras,' by Josef Kupelwieser — enough of itself to justify all Wagner's charges[1] against the opera books of the old school — was commissioned by Barbaja for the Court-theatre. The book was passed by the *Censur* on July 21 ; but Schubert had by that time advanced far in his labours, and had in fact completed more than half of the piece. He began it, as his own date tells us, on May 25. Act 1, filling 304 pages of large oblong paper,[2] was completely scored by the 31st of the month ;

[1] Hanslick, *Concertsaal*, 150.
[2] The autograph was shown to Mr. Sullivan and the writer by that energetic Schubert apostle, Herr Johann Herbeck, in 1868.

Act 2, in 5 days more, by June 5; and the whole 3 acts, fully
1000 pages, and containing an overture and 23 numbers, were
entirely out of hand by October 2. And all for nothing!
Schubert was not even kept long in suspense, for early in the
following year he learnt that the work had been dismissed. The
ground for its rejection was the badness of the libretto; but
knowing Barbaja's character, and seeing that Kupelwieser was
secretary to a rival house (the Josefstadt), it is difficult not to
suspect that the commission had been given by the wily Italian
merely to facilitate the progress of some piece of business
between the two establishments.

It is, as Liszt has remarked, extraordinary that Schubert,
who was brought up from his youth on the finest poetry, should
have unhesitatingly accepted the absurd and impracticable
librettos which he did, and which have kept in oblivion so much
of his splendid music. His devotion to his friends, and his
irrepressible desire to utter what was in him, no doubt help to
explain the anomaly, but an anomaly it will always remain.
It is absolutely distressing to think of such extraordinary ability,
and such still more extraordinary powers of work, being so
cruelly thrown away, and of the sickening disappointment
which these repeated failures must have entailed on so simple
and sensitive a heart as his. Fortunately for us, the strains in
which he vents his griefs are as beautiful and endearing as
those in which he celebrates his joys : —

> He wore no less a loving face
> Because so broken-hearted.

His work this summer was not however to be all disappointment. If the theatre turned a deaf ear to his strains there were
always his beloved songs to confide in, and they never deceived
him. Of the Song in Schubert's hands we may say what
Wordsworth so well says of the Sonnet : —

> With this key
> Shakespeare unlocked his heart; the melody
> Of this small lute gave ease to Petrarch's wound.
> .   .   .   .
> .   .   .   .   . and when a damp
> Fell round the path of Milton, in his hand
> The thing became a trumpet, whence he blew
> Soul-animating strains, alas too few !

— with the notable difference that it was given to Schubert to

gather up and express, in his one person and his one art, all the
various moods and passions which Wordsworth has divided
amongst so many mighty poets.

And now, in the midst of the overwhelming tumult and
absorption which inevitably accompany the production of so
large a work of imagination as a three-act opera, brought into
being at so extraordinarily rapid a pace, he was to stop, and
to indite a set of songs which, though not of greater worth than
many others of his, are yet so intelligible, so expressive, address
themselves to such universal feelings, and form so attractive a
whole, that they have certainly become more popular, and are
more widely and permanently beloved, than any similar production by any other composer. We have already described
the incident through which Schubert made acquaintance with
the Müller-lieder [1] of Wilhelm Müller, twenty of which he
selected for the beautiful series or ' Cyclus,' so widely known
as the ' Schöne Müllerin.' We have seen the enduring impatience with which he attacked a book when it took his fancy,
and the eagerness with which he began upon this particular one.
We know that the Müller-lieder were all composed this year ;
that some of them were written in hospital ; that No. 15 is
dated ' October ' ; that a considerable interval elapsed between
the 2nd and 3rd Act of ' Fierabras ' — probably the best part
of July and August. Putting these facts together it seems to
follow that the call on Randhartinger (see p. 141) and the
composition of the first numbers of the ' Schöne Müllerin ' took
place in May, before he became immersed in ' Fierabras.'
Then came the first two Acts of that opera ; then his illness,
and his sojourn in the hospital, and more songs ; then the third
Act of the opera ; and lastly the completion of the Lieder.

Be this as it may, there was no lack of occupation for
Schubert after he had put ' Fierabras " out of hand. Weber
arrived in Vienna late in September 1823, and on October 3
began the rehearsals of ' Euryanthe ' ; and for a month the
musical world of Austria was in a ferment. After the first
performance, on October 25, Weber and Schubert came some-

[1] The Müller-lieder, 23 in number, with Prologue and Epilogue in addition,
are contained in the 1st vol. of the *Gedichte aus den hinterlassenen Papieren eines
reisenden Waldhornisten* (Poems found among the papers of a travelling French-
horn-player), which were first published at Dessau, 1821. Schubert has
omitted the Prologue and Epilogue, and 3 poems—' Das Mühlenleben ' after
' Der Neugierige ' ; ' Erster Schmerz, letzter Scherz,' after ' Eifersucht und
Stolz ' ; and ' Blümlein Vergissmein ' after ' Die böse Farbe.'

what into collision. Schubert, with characteristic frankness, asserted that the new work wanted the geniality and grace of 'Der Freischütz,' that its merit lay mainly in its harmony,[1] and that he was prepared to prove that the score did not contain a single original melody. Weber had been much tried by the rehearsals, by the growing conviction that his work was too long, and by the imperfect success of the performance; and with a combination of ignorance and insolence which does him no credit, replied, 'Let the fool learn something himself before he criticises me.' Schubert's answer to this was to go off to Weber with the score of 'Alfonso and Estrella.' When they had looked through this, Weber returned to Schubert's criticisms on 'Euryanthe,' and finding that the honest Franz stuck to his point, was absurd enough to lose his temper, and say, in the obvious belief that the score before him was Schubert's first attempt, 'I tell you the first puppies and the first operas are always drowned.' Franz, it is unnecessary to say, bore no malice, even for so galling a speech, and it is due to Weber to state that he took some pains later to have the work adopted at the Dresden theatre.[2]

Schubert did not yet know the fate which awaited 'Fierabras'; all was at present *couleur de rose*; and the fascination of the theatre, the desire innate in all musicians, even one so self-contained as Schubert, to address a large public, sharpened not improbably by the chance recently enjoyed by the stranger, was too strong to be resisted, and he again, for the third time in ten months, turned towards the stage. This time the temptation came in the shape of 'Rosamunde, Princess of Cyprus,' a play of ultra-romantic character, by Madame von Chézy, authoress of 'Euryanthe,' a librettist whose lot seems to have been to drag down the musicians connected with her. The book of 'Rosamunde' must have been at least as inefficient as that with which Weber had been struggling, to cause the failure of such magnificent and interesting music as Schubert made for it. The drama has disappeared, but Kreissle [3] gives the plot, and it is both tedious and improbable. It had moreover the disadvantage of competition with a sensational spectacular piece, written expressly to suit the taste of the suburban house, the Theatre an-der-Wien, at which 'Rosamunde' was pro-

---

[1] See Mendelssohn's opinion, in *The Mendelssohn Family*, i. 237.
[2] K.H. 246 (i. 249) *note*.   [3] Ibid. 285 (i. 288), etc.

duced, and which, since the time when Schikaneder induced Mozart to join him in the ' Magic Flute,' [1] had a reputation for such extravaganzas. Schubert completed the music in five days.[2] It consists of an Overture in D,[3] since published as ' Alfonso and Estrella,' op. 69; 3 Entr'actes; 2 numbers of ballet music; a little piece for clarinets, horns, and bassoons, called a ' Shepherds' Melody,' of bewitching beauty; a Romance for soprano solo, and 3 Choruses. The Romance (op. 26), the Shepherds' Chorus, the Entr'acte in B♭, and the Air de Ballet in G, are not only very beautiful but very attractive; and the Entr'acte in B minor, of a grand, gloomy, and highly imaginative cast, is one of the finest pieces of music existing. The play was brought out on December 20, 1823; the overture, though the entire orchestral part of the music had only one rehearsal of two hours, was twice redemanded, other numbers were loudly applauded, and Schubert himself was called for at the close; but it only survived one more representation, and then the parts were tied up and forgotten till the year 1867, when they were discovered by two English travellers in Vienna.*

Besides the Müller-lieder several independent songs of remarkable beauty belong to 1823. Conspicuous among these are ' Viola ' (Schneeglöcklein; op. 123), a long composition full of the most romantic tenderness and delicacy, with all the finish of Meissonnier's pictures, and all his breadth and dignity. Also the ' Zwerg ' (op. 22, no. 1), by Matthias [Matthäus] von Collin, in which Schubert has immortalised the one brother, as Beethoven, in his overture to ' Coriolan,' did the other. This long, dramatic, and most pathetic ballad, which but few can hear unmoved, was written absolutely à l'improviste, without note or sketch, at the top of his speed, talking all the while to Randhartinger, who was waiting to take him out for a walk.[4] Equal, if not superior, to these in merit, though of smaller dimensions, are ' Dass sie hier gewesen ' (op. 59, no. 2); ' Du bist die Ruh ' (do. no. 3); the Barcarolle, ' Auf dem Wasser zu singen ' (op. 72), to which no nearer date than ' 1823 ' can be given. Below these again, though still fine songs, are ' Der

---

[1] Produced at the Theatre an-der-Wien, Sept. 30, 1791.
[2] So says Wilhelm von Chézy, the son of the librettist, who was on terms with Schubert. See his Journal, *Erinnerungen*, etc., 1863.
[3] The autograph is dated ' Dec. 1823.'
[4] Kreissle, *Sketch*, p. 154 *note*.   * [Grove himself and Arthur Sullivan.]

zürnende Barde' (Lf. 9, no. 1; February); 'Drang in die
Ferne' (op. 71; March 25); 'Pilgerweise' (Lf. 18, no. 1;
April); 'Vergissmeinnicht' (Lf. 21, no. 2; May). The fine
Sonata in A minor for pianoforte solo, published as op. 143, is
dated February 1823, and the sketch of a scena for tenor solo
and chorus of men's voices with orchestra, dated May 1823.
The latter was completed by Herbeck, and published in 1868
by Spina as ' Rüdiger's Heimkehr.'

Ten works (op. 15-24) were published in 1823. The earliest
was a collection of dances, viz. 12 Waltzes, 9 Ecossaises, and
17 Ländler, op. 18, published February 5; the pianoforte
Fantasia, op. 15, followed on February 24. The rest are songs,
either solo — op. 20, April 10; op. 22, May 27; op. 23,
August 4; op. 24, October 7; op. 16, October 9; op. 19,
21 (no dates) — or part-songs, op. 17, October 9. With
op. 20, the names of Sauer & Leidesdorf first occur as
publishers.

The year 1824 began almost exclusively with instrumental
compositions. An Introduction and Variations for pianoforte
and flute (op. 160), on the 'Trockne Blumen' of the 'Schöne
Müllerin,' are dated 'January,' and were followed by the
famous Octet (op. 166), for clarinet, horn, bassoon, 2 violins,
viola, cello, and contrabass, which is marked as begun in
February, and finished on March 1. It was written — not, let
us hope, without adequate remuneration, though that was
probably the last thing of which its author thought — for Count
F. Troyer, chief officer of the household to the Archduke
Rudolph, Beethoven's patron. In this beautiful composition
Schubert indulges his love of extension. It contains, like
Beethoven's Septet, 8 [6] movements; but, unlike the Septet, it
occupies more than an hour in performance. But though long,
no one can call it tedious.[1] The Count played the clarinet,
and must have been delighted with the expressive melody
allotted to him in the Andante. The work was performed
immediately after its composition, with Schuppanzigh, Weiss,
and Linke, three of the famous Rassomofsky [Rasumovsky]
quartet, amongst the players. His association with the members of this celebrated party may well have led Schubert to
write string quartets; at any rate he himself tells us that he

---

[1] Published by Spina in 1854. It is a great favourite at the Popular Concerts
in London, having been played 18 times since Mar. 4, 1867.

had written two before the 31st March,[1] and these are doubtless those in E♭ and E (op. 125), since the only other quartet bearing the date of 1824 — that in A minor — has so strong a Hungarian flavour as to point to his visit to Zselész later in the year. How powerfully his thoughts were running at present on orchestral music is evident from the fact that he mentions both octet and quartets as studies [2] for 'the Grand Symphony,' which was then his goal, though he did not reach it till eighteen months later.

A bitter disappointment, however, was awaiting him in the rejection of 'Fierabras,' which, as already mentioned, was returned by Barbaja, ostensibly on account of the badness of its libretto. Two full-sized operas — this and 'Alfonso and Estrella' — to be laid on the shelf without even a rehearsal! Whatever the cause, the blow must have been equally severe to our simple, genuine composer, who had no doubt been expecting, not without reason, day by day for the last four months, to hear of the acceptance of his work. His picture of himself under this temporary eclipse of hope is mournful in the extreme, though natural enough to the easily depressed temperament of a man of genius. After speaking of himself as ' the most unfortunate, most miserable being on earth,' he goes on to say, ' think of a man whose health can never be restored, and who from sheer despair makes matters worse instead of better. Think, I say, of a man whose brightest hopes have come to nothing, to whom love and friendship are but torture, and whose enthusiasm for the beautiful is fast vanishing ; and ask yourself if such a man is not truly unhappy.

> My peace is gone, my heart is sore,
> Gone for ever and evermore.

This is my daily cry ; for every night I go to sleep hoping never again to wake, and every morning only brings back the torment of the day before. Thus joylessly and friendlessly would pass my days, if Schwind did not often look in, and give me a glimpse of the old happy times. . . . Your brother's opera ' — this is a letter to Kupelwieser the painter, and the allusion is to Fierabras — ' turns out to be impracticable, and my music is therefore wasted. Castelli's " Verschworenen " has been set in

---

[1] In his letter to Leopold Kupelwieser of Mar. 31. K.H. 321 (ii. 5).
[2] ' In this manner I shall prepare the way to the Grand Symphony (zur grossen Sinfonie).' Ibid.

Berlin by a composer there, and produced with success.   Thus
I have composed two operas for nothing.'   This sad mood,
real enough at the moment, was only natural after such re-
pulses.   It was assisted, as Schubert's depression always was, by
the absence of many of his friends, and also, as he himself
confesses, by his acquaintance with Leidesdorf the publisher
(in Beethoven's banter ' Dorf des Leides,' a very ' village of
sorrow '), whom he describes as a thoroughly good, trustworthy
fellow, ' but so very melancholy that I begin to fear I may
have learnt too much from him in that direction.'   It must
surely have been after an evening with this worthy that he
made the touching entries in his journal which have been
preserved ;   *e.g.*   ' Grief   sharpens   the   understanding   and
strengthens the soul : Joy on the other hand seldom troubles
itself about the one, and makes the other effeminate or frivolous.'   ' My musical works are the product of my genius and
my misery, and what the public most relish is that which has
given me the greatest distress.'   Fortunately, in men of the
genuine composer-temperament, the various moods of mind
follow one another rapidly.   As soon as they begin to compose
the demon flies and heaven opens.   That gloomy document
called ' Beethoven's Will,' to which even Schubert's most
wretched letters must yield the palm, was written at the very
time that he was pouring out the gay and healthy strains of
his 2nd Symphony.   Schubert left town with the Esterházys
in a few weeks after these distressing utterances, and for a time
forgot his troubles in the distractions of country life in Hungary.
At Zselész he remained for six months, but his life there is
almost entirely a blank to us.   We can only estimate it by the
compositions which are attributable to the period, and by
the scanty information conveyed by his letters, which, though
fuller of complaint than those of 1818, are even less communicative of facts and occurrences.   To this visit is to be ascribed
that noble composition known as the ' Grand Duo ' (op. 140),
though designated by himself as ' Sonata for the pianoforte
for four hands.   Zselés, June 1824 ' ; a piece which, though
recalling in one movement Beethoven's 2nd, and in another
his 7th Symphony, is yet full of the individuality of its author ;
a symphonic work in every sense of the word, which, through
Joachim's instrumentation, has now become an orchestral
symphony, and a very fine one.   To Zselész also is due the

Sonata in B♭ (op. 30, May or June), the Variations in A♭ (op.
35, 'middle of 1824'), 2 Waltzes (in op. 33, '1824, July'),
and 4 Ländler ('July, 1824,' Nott. p. 215) — all for pianoforte
4 hands; other Waltzes and Ländler in the same collections
for 2 hands; and the 'Gebet' of Lamotte [La Motte] Fouqué
(op. 139*a*), signed 'September 1824, at Zelész in Hungary'
— all evidently arising from the necessity of providing music
for the Count's family circle. The young Countesses were now
nineteen and seventeen, and doubtless good performers, as is
implied in the duet-form of the pianoforte works. We are
probably right in also attributing the lovely String Quartet
in A minor (op. 29), and the 4-hand 'Divertissement à la
hongroise' (op. 54), to this visit, at any rate to its immediate
influence. Both are steeped in the Hungarian spirit, and the
Divertissement contains a succession of real national tunes, one
of which he heard from the lips of a maidservant as he passed
the kitchen with Baron Schönstein in returning from a walk.
For the Baron was at Zselész on this as on the last occasion,
and frequent and exquisite must have been the performances
of the many fine songs which Schubert had written in the
interval since his former visit.

The circumstances attending the composition of the vocal
quartet ('Gebet,' op. 139) just mentioned are told by Kreissle,
probably on the authority of Schönstein, and they give a
good instance of Schubert's extraordinary facility. At breakfast one morning, in September 1824, the Countess produced
Lamotte Fouqué's poem, and proposed to Schubert to set it
for the family party. He withdrew after breakfast, taking the
book with him, and in the evening, less than ten hours afterwards, it was tried through from the score at the piano. The
next evening it was sung again, this time from separate parts,
which Schubert had written out during the day. The piece is
composed for quartet, with solos for Mme. Esterházy, Marie,
Schönstein, and the Count, and contains 209 bars. A MS.
letter of Ferdinand's,[1] dated July 3, full of that strong half-
reverential affection which was Ferdinand's habitual attitude
towards his gifted brother, and of curious details, mentions
having sent him Bach's fugues (never-cloying food of great
composers), and an opera-book, 'Der kurze Mantel.' Strange

---

[1] For which I again gladly acknowledge the kindness of Frl. Caroline Geisler,
of Vienna, Schubert's grandniece.

fascination of the stage, which thus, in despite of so many failures, could keep him still enthralled !

The country air of the Hungarian mountains, and no doubt the sound and healthy living and early hours of the château, restored Schubert's health completely, and in a letter of September 21 to Schober he says that for five months he had been well. But he felt his isolation, and the want of congenial Vienna society keenly ; speaks with regret of having been ' enticed ' into a second visit to Hungary, and complains of not having a single person near to whom he could say a sensible word. How different from the exuberant happiness of the visits to Steyr and St. Pölten, when every one he met was a demonstrative admirer, and every evening brought a fresh triumph !

Now, if ever, was the date of his tender feeling for his pupil Caroline Esterházy, which his biographers have probably much exaggerated. She was seventeen at the time, and Bauernfeld represents her as the object of an ideal devotion, which soothed, comforted, and inspirited Schubert to the end of his life. Ideal it can only have been, considering the etiquette of the time, and the wide distance between the stations of the two ; and the only occasion on which Schubert is ever alleged to have approached anything like a revelation of his feelings, is that told by Kreissle — on what authority he does not say, and it is hard to conceive — when on her jokingly reproaching him for not having dedicated anything to her, he replied, ' Why should I ? everything I ever did is dedicated to you.' True, the fine Fantasia in F minor, published in the March following his death as op. 103, is dedicated to her ' by Franz Schubert,' a step which the publishers would hardly have ventured upon unless the MS. — probably handed to them before his death — had been so inscribed by himself. But it is difficult to reconcile the complaints of isolation and neglect already quoted from his letter to Schober with the existence of a passion which must have been fed every time he met his pupil or sat down to the piano with her. We must be content to leave each reader to decide the question for himself.

Vocal composition he laid aside almost entirely in 1824. The only songs which we can ascertain to belong to it are four — the fine though gloomy ones called ' Auflösung ' (Lf. 34, no. 1), and ' Abendstern ' (Lf. 22, no. 4), both by Mayrhofer ; another evening song, ' Im Abendroth,' by Lappe (Lf. 20, no. 1),

all three in March; and the bass song, ' Lied eines Krieger's '
(Lf. 20, no. 2), with which he closed the last day of the year.[1]
Of part-songs there are two, both for men's voices; one a
' Salve regina,' written in April, before leaving town; and the
other, the ' Gondelfahrer,' or Gondolier, a very fine and picturesque composition, of which Lablache is said to have been
fond.—A Sonata for pianoforte and Arpeggione, in A minor,
dated November 1824, was probably one of his first compositions
after returning to town.[2]

The publications of 1824 embrace ops. 25 to 28 inclusive,
all issued by Sauer & Leidesdorf. Op. 25 is the ' Schöne
Müllerin,' 20 songs in five numbers, published March 25; op.
26 is the vocal music in ' Rosamunde,' [3] the romance and three
choruses; op. 27, three fine ' heroic marches,' for pianoforte
4 hands; op. 28, ' Der Gondelfahrer,' for four men's voices and
pianoforte, Aug. 12.

1825 was a happy year to our hero — happy and pro-
ductive. He was back again in his dear Vienna, and exchanged
the isolation of Zselész for the old familiar life, with his
congenial friends Vogl, Schwind, Jenger, Mayrhofer, etc.
(Schober was in Prussia, and Kupelwieser still at Rome), in
whose applause and sympathy and genial conviviality he rapidly
forgot the disappointments and depression that had troubled
him in the autumn. Sofie Müller, one of the great actresses
of that day, evidently a very accomplished, cultivated woman,
was then in Vienna, and during February and March her house
was the resort of Schubert, Jenger, and Vogl, who sang or
listened to her singing of his best and newest Lieder, — she
herself sang the ' Junge Nonne ' at sight on March 3 — and
lived a pleasant and thoroughly artistic life.[4] Others, which
she mentions as new, and which indeed had their birth at this
time, are ' Der Einsame,' and ' Ihr Grab.' The ' new songs
from the Pirate,' which she heard on March 1, may have been
some from ' The Lady of the Lake,' or ' Norna's song,' or even
' Anna Lyle,' usually placed two years later. Schubert published some important works early in this year, the Overture

[1] The autograph, so dated, belongs to Mr. C. J. Hargitt, London.
[2] Gotthard, 1871. Autograph in Musik Verein.
[3] Besides the vocal music, the overture was published about 1828 and the
Entr'actes and Ballet music in 1866.
[4] See her interesting Journal, in her *Leben und nachgelassene Papiere herausg. von
Johann Grafen Majláth* (Vienna 1832).

in F for 4 hands (op. 34) ; also the Sonata in B♭ (op. 30), and
the Variations in A♭ (op. 35), both for 4 hands ; and the String
Quartet in A minor (op. 29) — fruits of his sojourn in Hungary.
The last of these, the only quartet he was destined to publish
during his life, is dedicated ' to his friend I. Schuppanzigh,' a
pleasant memorial of the acquaintance cemented by the performance of the octet, a twelvemonth before. And as on such
publications some amount of money passes from the publisher
to the composer, this fact of itself would contribute to enliven
and inspirit him. In addition to these instrumental works some
noble songs were issued in the early part of 1825 — ' Der
zürnenden Diana,' and the ' Nachtstück,' of Mayrhofer ; ' Der
Pilgrim ' and ' Der Alpenjäger,' of Schiller ; and Zuleika's
second song. The two beautiful solo sonatas in A minor and
in C — the latter of which he never succeeded in completely
writing out, but the fragment of which is of first-rate quality
— also date from this time.

As if to revenge himself for his sufferings at the Esterházys',
he planned an extensive tour for this summer, in his favourite
district, and in the company of his favourite friend. Vogl on
March 31 started for his home at Steyr. Schubert soon [1]
followed him, and the next five months, to the end of October,
were passed in a delightful mixture of music, friends, fine
scenery, lovely weather, and absolute ease and comfort, in
Upper Austria and the Salzkammergut, partly amongst the
good people who had welcomed him so warmly in 1819, partly
among new friends and new enthusiasm. Taking Steyr as their
point d'appui they made excursions to Linz, Steyrock, Gmunden,
Salzburg, and even as far as Gastein, etc., heartily enjoying
the glorious scenery by day, received everywhere on arrival
with open arms, and making the best possible impression with
their joint performances. The songs from ' The Lady of the
Lake ' were either composed before starting or on the road.
At any rate they formed the chief programme during the excursion. If the whole seven were sung or not is uncertain ; [2]
but Schubert particularly mentions the ' Ave Maria,' *à propos*
to which he makes an interesting revelation. ' My new songs,'
says he, ' from Walter Scott's Lady of the Lake, have been very

---

[1] The dates of the early part of the tour are not to be made out.
[2] Schubert speaks of them as ' unsere sieben Sachen ' (letter to Ferdinand
Kreissle 363) ; but Nos. 3 and 4 are for chorus.

successful. People were greatly astonished at the devotion which I have thrown into the Hymn to the Blessed Virgin, and it seems to have seized and impressed everybody. I think that the reason of this is that I never force myself into devotion, or compose hymns or prayers unless I am really overpowered by the feeling; that alone is real, true devotion.' It is during this journey, at Salzburg, that he makes the remark, already noticed, as to the performance of Vogl and himself. At Salzburg too, it was the ' Ave Maria ' that so riveted his hearers. ' We produced our seven pieces before a select circle, and all were much impressed, especially by the Ave Maria, which I mentioned in my former letter. The way in which Vogl sings and I accompany, so that for the moment we seem to be one, is something quite new and unexpected to these good people.' Schubert sometimes performed alone. He had brought some variations and marches for 4 hands with him, and finding a good player at the convents [monasteries] of Florian and Kremsmünster, had made a great effect with them. But he was especially successful with the lovely variations from the solo Sonata in A minor (op. 42); and here again he lets us into his secret. ' There I played alone, and not without success, for I was assured that the keys under my hands sang like voices, which if true makes me very glad, because I cannot abide that accursed thumping, which even eminent players adopt, but which delights neither my ears nor my judgment.' He found his compositions well known throughout Upper Austria. The gentry fought for the honour of receiving him, and to this day old people are found to talk with equal enthusiasm of his lovely music, and of the unaffected gaiety and simplicity of his ways and manners.

The main feature of the tour was the excursion to Gastein in the mountains of East Tyrol. To Schubert this was new ground, and the delight in the scenery which animates his description is obvious. They reached it about August 18, and appear to have remained three or four weeks, returning to Gmunden about September 10. At Gastein, among other good people, he found his old ally Ladislaus Pyrker, Patriarch of Venice, and composed two songs to his poetry, ' Heimweh ' and ' Allmacht ' (op. 79). But the great work of this date was the ' Grand Symphony ' which had been before him for so long. We found him 18 months ago writing quartets and the octet

as preparation for it, and an allusion in a letter of Schwind's [1]
shows that at the beginning of August he spoke of the thing as
virtually done. That it was actually put on to paper at Gastein
at this date we know from the testimony of Bauernfeld,[2] who
also informs us that it was a special favourite with its composer.
Seven songs in all are dated in this autumn, amongst them two
fine scenes from a play by W. von Schütz called ' Lacrimas '
(op. 124), not so well known as they deserve.

The letters of this tour, though not all preserved, are unusually
numerous for one who so much disliked writing. One long
one to his father and [step-]mother ; another, much longer, to
Ferdinand ; a third to Spaun, and a fourth to Bauernfeld, are
printed by Kreissle, and contain passages of real interest, showing how keenly he observed and how thoroughly he enjoyed
nature, and displaying throughout a vein of good sense and
even practical sagacity,[3] and a facility of expression, which
are rare in him.

At length the summer and the money came to an end,
Vogl went off to Italy for his gout, and Schubert, meeting Gahy
at Linz, returned with him and the MS. Symphony to Vienna
in an *Einspänner*, to find Schober and Kupelwieser both once
more settled there. The first thing to be done was to replenish
his purse, and this he soon did by the sale of the seven songs
from ' The Lady of the Lake,' which he disposed of on October
29 to Artaria, for 200 silver gulden — just £20 ! Twenty
pounds, however, were a mine of wealth to Schubert ; and even
after repaying the money which had been advanced by his
father, and by Bauernfeld for the rent of the lodgings during
his absence, he would still have a few pounds in hand.

During Schubert's absence in the country his old friend
Salieri died, and was succeeded by Eybler. The Court organist
also fell ill, and Schwind wrote urging him to look after the
post ; but Schubert makes no sign, and evidently did nothing
in the matter, though the organist died on November 19. He
obviously knew much better than his friends that he was
absolutely unfit for any post requiring punctuality or restraint.

---

[1] K.H. 358 (ii. 43). ' To your Symphony we are looking forward eagerly,'
implying that Schubert had mentioned it in a former letter.
[2] W.Z.K., June 9–13, 1829.
[3] See his shrewd reasons for not at once accepting Bauernfeld's proposition
that he, Schwind and Schubert should all live together. K.H. 370 (ii. 57). Also
the whole letter to Spaun.

In the course of this year he was made ' Ersatzmann,' or substitute — whatever that may mean — by the Musik-Verein, or Gesellschaft der Musikfreunde. Of what happened from this time till the close of 1825 we have no certain information. He set two songs by Schulze (Lf. 13, nos. 1, 2) in December; and it is probable that the Piano Sonata in D (op. 53), and the noble funeral march for the Emperor of Russia (op. 55), whose death was known in Vienna on December 14, both belong to that month.* What gave him his interest in the death of Alexander is not known, but the march is an extraordinarily fine specimen. A piece for the piano in F, serving as accompaniment to a recitation from a poem by Pratobevera, a series of graceful modulations in arpeggio form, also dates from this year.[1]

The compositions of 1825 may be here summed up : — Sonata for pianoforte solo in A minor (op. 42) ; ditto in D (op. 53) ; ditto in A (op. 120) ; unfinished ditto in C (' Reliquie,' Nott. p. 211) ; a funeral march, 4 hands, for the Emperor Alexander of Russia (op. 55). Songs — ' Des Sängers Habe,' by Schlechta, and ' Im Walde,' by E. Schulze ; 7 from ' The Lady of the Lake ' (op. 52) ; another from Scott's ' Pirate '[2] ; ' Auf der Brücke [Bruck],' by Schulze ; ' Fülle der Liebe,' by Schlegel ; ' Allmacht ' and ' Heimweh,' by Pyrker ; two scenes from ' Lacrimas,' by W. von Schütz ; and ' Abendlied für die Entfernte,' by A. W. Schlegel ; ' Die junge Nonne,' ' Todtengräbers Heimweh,' and ' Der blinde Knabe,' all by Craigher [the last translated from Colley Cibber] ; ' Der Einsame,' by Lappe ; and, in December, ' An mein Herz ' and ' Der liebliche Stern,' both by Ernst Schulze. It is also more than probable that the String Quartet in D minor was at least begun before the end of the year.

The publications of 1825 are : — In January, ops. 32, 30, 34 ; February 11, ops. 36 and 37 ; May 9, op. 38 ; July 25, op. 43 ; August 12, op. 31 ; and, without note of date, ops. 29 and 33. Op. 29 is the lovely A minor Quartet ; and it is worthy of note that it is published as the first of ' Trois quatuors.' This was never carried out. The two others were written, as we have already seen (p. 175), but they remained unpublished till after the death of their author.

* [The Sonata is now known to have been written at Gastein in the summer.]
[1] Printed by Reissmann in his book.
[2] So says Sofie Müller (under date of Mar. 1) ; but perhaps it was her mistake for Norman's song in *The Lady of the Lake.*

N

1826 was hardly eventful in any sense of the word, though by no means unimportant in Schubert's history. It seems to have been passed entirely in Vienna. He contemplated a trip to Linz with Spaun and Schwind, but it did not come off. The weather of this spring was extraordinarily bad, and during April and May he composed nothing.[1] The music attributable to 1826 is, however, of first-rate quality. The String Quartet in D minor, by common consent placed at the head of Schubert's music of this class, was first played on January 29, and was therefore doubtless only just completed.[2] That in G (op. 161), Schubert himself has dated as being written in ten days (June 20 to June 30), a work teeming with fresh vigour after the inaction of the preceding two months, as full of melody, spirit, romance, variety, and individuality as anything he ever penned,[3] and only prevented from taking the same high position as the preceding, by its great length — due to the diffuseness which Schubert would no doubt have remedied had he given himself time to do so. One little point may be mentioned *en passant* in both these noble works — the evidence they afford of his lingering fondness for the past. In the D minor Quartet he goes back for the subject and feeling of the Andante to a song of his own of 1816, and the Finale of the G major is curiously tinged with reminiscences of the Rossini-fever of 1819.

The ' Rondeau brillant ' in B minor for pianoforte and violin (op. 70), now such a favourite in the concert-room, also belongs to this year, though it cannot be precisely dated ; and so does a piece of still higher quality, which is pronounced by Schumann to be its author's ' most perfect work both in form and conception,' the Sonata in G major for pianoforte solo, op. 78, usually called the ' Fantasia,' owing to a freak of the publisher. The autograph is inscribed, in the hand of its author, ' IV. Sonate für Pianoforte allein. October 1826, Franz Schubert ' ; above which, in the writing of Tobias Haslinger, stands the title ' Fantasie, Andante, Menuetto und Allegretto.' We may well say with Beethoven, ' O Tobias ! '

By the side of these undying productions the ' Marche

---

[1] See his letter to Bauernfeld and Mayrhofer, in *Die Presse*, Apr. 21, 1869.

[2] K.H. 391 (ii. 77). The finale was voted too long, to which Schubert, after a few minutes' consideration, agreed, and ' at once cut out a good part.' (Hauer's information.) The autograph has disappeared.

[3] Played at the Monday Popular Concerts of Dec. 14, 1868 and Jan. 13, 1879 ; Joachim leading on both occasions.

héroïque,' written to celebrate the accession of Nicholas I. of
Russia, and the Andantino and Rondo on French *motifs* — both
for pianoforte 4 hands, are not of great significance.

An attack of song-writing seems to have come upon him
in March, which date we find attached to six songs; or, if the
rest of those to Seidl's words forming ops. 105 and 80, and
marked merely ' 1826,' were written at the same time (as,
from Schubert's habit of eviscerating his books, they not improbably were) — twelve. Three Shakespeare songs are due
to this July — ' Hark! hark! the lark,' [1] from ' Cymbeline ';
' Who is Sylvia [Silvia]? ' from the ' Two Gentlemen of
Verona '; and the Drinking-song in ' Antony and Cleopatra '
— the first two perhaps as popular as any single songs of
Schubert's. The circumstances of the composition, or rather
creation, of the first of these has already been mentioned (p. 141).
The fact of three songs from the same volume belonging to one
month (not improbably to one day, if we only knew) is quite
à la Schubert.—A beautiful and most characteristic piece of this
year is the ' Nachthelle ' (or Lovely night), written to words of
Seidl's — not improbably for the Musikverein, through Anna
Fröhlich — for tenor solo, with accompaniment of 4 men's
voices and pianoforte, which would be a treasure to singing
societies, for its truly romantic loveliness, but for the inordinate
height to which the voices are taken, and the great difficulty
of executing it with sufficient delicacy. A song called ' Echo '
(op. 130), probably written in 1826, was intended to be the
first of six ' humorous songs ' for Weigl's firm.[2]

We hear nothing of the new symphony during the early
part of this year. No doubt it was often played from the MS.
score at the meetings of the Schubert set, but they say no more
about it than they do of the octet, or quartets, or sonatas,
which were all equally in existence; and for aught we know
it might have been ' locked in a drawer,' which was often
Schubert's custom after completing a work — ' locked in a
drawer and never thought about again.' [3] It was, however,
destined to a different fate. On the 9th September 1826, at
one of the first meetings of the Board of the Musik Verein after
the summer recess, Hofrath Kiesewetter reports that Schubert

---

[1] Entitled ' Serenade,' but more accurately an ' Aubade.'
[2] See Nottebohm's Catalogue under op. 130.
[3] Lachner's expression to my friend Mr. C. A. Barry in 1881.

desires to dedicate a symphony to the Society; upon which the sum of 100 silver florins (£10) is voted to him, not in payment for the work, but as a token of sympathy, and as an encouragement. The letter conveying the money is dated the 12th, and on or even before its receipt Schubert brought the manuscript and deposited it with the Society. His letter accompanying it may here be quoted : —

To the Committee of the Austrian Musical Society.— Convinced of the noble desire of the Society to give its best support to every effort in the cause of art, I venture, as a native artist, to dedicate this my Symphony to the Society, and most respectfully to recommend myself to its protection. With the highest esteem, Your obedt.   FRANZ SCHUBERT.

In accordance with this, the MS. probably bears his formal dedication to the Verein, and we may expect to find that though so long talked of, it bears marks of having been written down as rapidly as most of his other productions.[1] At present, however, all trace of it is gone; not even its key is known. There is no entry of it in the catalogue of the Society's Library, and except for the minute and letter given above, and the positive statements of Bauernfeld quoted below,[2] it might as well be non-existent. That it is an entirely distinct work from that in C, written 2½ years later, can hardly admit of a doubt.

[1] The documents on which these statements are based are given by Herr C. F. Pohl in his History of the Gesellschaft der Musikfreunde—or Musikverein —Vienna, 1871, p. 16; and by Ferdinand Schubert in the *Neue Zeitschrift für Musik* for April 30, 1839, p. 140.

[2] Bauernfeld, in an article ' Ueber Franz Schubert ' in the *Wiener Zeitschrift für Kunst, Literatur, Theater, und Mode*, for 9, 11, 13 June, 1829 (Nos. 69, 70, 71), says as follows :—' To the larger works of his latter years also belongs a symphony written in 1825 at Gastein, for which its author had an especial predilection. . . . At a great concert given by the Musik Verein shortly after his death a Symphony in C was performed, which was composed as early as 1817 (1818), and which he considered as one of his less successful works. . . . Perhaps the Society intends at some future time to make us acquainted with one of the later Symphonies, possibly the Gastein one already mentioned.' (N.B. The two movements of the B minor Symphony (1822) were not at this time known, so that by ' later Symphonies ' Bauernfeld must surely intend the two of 1825 and 1828.) At the end of the article he gives a ' chronological list of Schubert's principal works not yet generally known.' Amongst these are ' 1825, Grand Symphony ' . . . ' 1828, Last Symphony '—' Grand ' (*grosse*) being the word used by Schubert himself in his letter to Kupelwieser referred to above (p. 175). It is plain, therefore, that at this time, seven months after Schubert's death, the Gastein Symphony of 1825 and that in C major of 1828 were known as distinct works. The present writer has collected the evidence for the existence of the Symphony in a letter to the London *Athenæum* of Nov. 19, 1881.

Of the publications of 1826, the most remarkable are the seven songs from ' The Lady of the Lake,' for which Artaria had paid him 200 florins in the preceding October, and which appeared on the 5th of this April, in two parts, as op. 52. They were succeeded immediately, on April 8, by the pianoforte Sonata in D (op. 53), and the ' Divertissement à la hongroise ' (op. 54), both issued by the same firm. For these two splendid works Schubert received from the penurious Artaria only 300 Vienna florins, equal to £12. Songs issued fast from the press at this date; for on the 6th of April we find op. 56 (3 songs) announced by Pennauer, and ops. 57 and 58 (each 3 songs) by Weigl; on June 10, op. 60 (' Greisengesang ' and ' Dithy-rambe ') by Cappi and Czerny; in September op. 59 (4 songs, including ' Dass sie hier gewesen,' ' Du bist die Ruh,' and ' Lachen und Weinen ') by Leidesdorf; and op. 64 (3 part-songs for men's voices) by Pennauer; and on November 24, op. 65 (3 songs) by Cappi and Czerny. Some of these were composed as early as 1814, 15, 16; others again in 1820, 22, and 23. The Mass in C (op. 48), and three early pieces of church music, ' Tantum ergo ' (op. 45), ' Totus in corde ' (op. 46), and ' Salve Regina ' (op. 47), were all issued in this year by Diabelli. Of dances and marches for piano there are 8 numbers : — a Galop and 8 Ecossaises (op. 49) ; 34 Valses sentimentales (op. 50) ; ' Hommage aux belles Viennoises ' (16 Ländler and 2 Ecossaises, op. 67) ; 3 Marches (4 hands, op. 51) — all published by Diabelli ; the 2 Russian Marches (op. 55, 56), by Pennauer ; 6 Polonaises (op. 61), Cappi and Czerny ; and a Divertissement, or ' Marche brillante et raisonnée,' on French *motifs* (op. 63), Weigl. In all, 22 publi-cations, divided between 6 publishers, and containing 106 works.

We have been thus particular to name the numbers and publishers of these works, because they show conclusively how much Schubert's music was coming into demand. Pennauer and Leidesdorf were his personal friends, and may possibly have printed his pieces from chivalrous motives ; but no one can suspect hard and experienced men of business like Diabelli and Artaria of publishing the music of any one at their own risk unless they believed that there was a demand for it. The list is a remarkable one, and will compare for extent and variety with that of most years of Beethoven's life. And even at the incredibly low price [1] which his publishers gave for the exclusive copyright of his works, there is enough in the above to produce an income sufficient for Schubert's wants. But the fact is that he was mixed up with a set of young fellows who regarded him as a Crœsus,[2] and who virtually lived upon his carelessness and good-nature, under the guise of keeping house in common. Bauernfeld, in an article in the Vienna ' Presse ' of April 17, 1869, has given us the account with some naïveté. A league or partnership was made between himself, Schwind the painter, and Schubert. They had nominally their own lodgings, but often slept all together in the room of one. The affection between them was extraordinary. Schubert used to call Schwind ' seine Geliebte ' — his innamorata! A kind of common property was established in clothes and money ; hats, coats, boots, and cravats were worn in common, and the one who was in cash paid the score of the others. As Schwind and Bauernfeld were considerably younger than Schubert, that duty naturally fell on him. When he had sold a piece of music he seemed to this happy trio to ' swim in money,' which was then spent ' right and left ' in the most reckless manner, till it was all gone, and the period of reverse came. Under these circumstances life was a series of fluctuations, in which the party were never rich, and often very poor. On one occasion Bauernfeld and Schubert met in a coffee-house near the Kärnthnerthor theatre, and each detected the other in ordering a mélange (café au lait) and biscuits, because neither had the money to pay for dinner. And this in Schubert's 29th year, when he had already written immortal works quite sufficient to make a good livelihood! Outside the circle of this trio were a number of other young people, artists and literary men, Schober, Jenger, Kupelwieser, etc., attracted by Schubert's genius, good-nature, and love of fun, and all more or less profiting by the generosity of one who never knew what it was to deny a friend. The evenings of this jolly company were usually passed in the

[1] It is said by Schindler that the prices agreed on with him were 10 Vienna gulden per Heft of songs, and 12 per pianoforte piece. (The Vienna gulden was then worth just 1 franc. ' Heft ' meant then a single song, not a ' Part ' of two or three. This is conclusively proved by Ferdinand Schubert's letter of 1824.) These prices were not adhered to. Thus for the 7 ' Lady of the Lake ' songs he had 500 paper gulden = 20l., or nearly 3l. per song. Even that is low enough. On the other hand, F. Lachner told Mr. Barry that in the last year of Schubert's life he took half-a-dozen of the ' Winterreise ' songs to Haslinger at Schubert's request, and brought back 1 gulden apiece (= 10d.) for them !

[2] The expression is Bauernfeld's.

Gasthaus, and then they would wander about, till daybreak drove them to their several quarters, or to the room of one of the party. It would be absurd to judge Vienna manners from an English point of view. The Gasthaus took the place of a modern club, and the drink consumed probably did not much exceed that which some distinguished Vienna artists now imbibe night after night, and does not imply the excess that it would infallibly lead to in a Northern climate; but it must be obvious that few constitutions could stand such racket, and that the exertion of thus trying his strength by night and his brain by day, must have been more than any frame could stand. In fact his health did not stand the wear and tear. We have seen that in February 1823 he could not leave the house; that in the summer of the same year he was confined to the hospital; that in March 1824 he speaks of his health as irrecoverably gone; and the dedication of the six 4-hand Marches, op. 40, to his friend Bernhardt, doctor of medicine, ' as a token of gratitude,' is strong evidence that in 1826, the year of their publication, he had had another severe attack.

It was probably a sense of the precarious nature of such a life that led some of his friends in the autumn of [early in] 1826 to urge Schubert to stand for the post of Vice-Capellmeister in the Imperial Court, vacant by the promotion of Eybler to that of principal Capellmeister; but the application, like every other of the same kind made by him, was a failure, and the place was given to Joseph Weigl by the imperial decree of January 27, 1827.

Another opportunity of acquiring a fixed income was opened to him during the same autumn, by the removal of Karl August Krebs [1] from the conductorship of the Court-theatre to Hamburg. Vogl interested Duport, the administrator of the theatre, in his friend, and the appointment was made to depend on Schubert's success in composing some scenes for the stage. Madame [Nanette] Schechner, for whom the principal part was intended, and whose voice at that time was on the wane [and who was a beginner aged 20], at the pianoforte rehearsals objected to some passages in her air, but could not induce the composer to alter them. The same thing happened at the first orchestral rehearsal, when it also became evident that the accompaniments were too noisy for the voice.

[1] Father of Miss Mary Krebs the pianist.

Still Schubert was immovable. At the full-band rehearsal Schechner fairly broke down, and refused to sing any more. Duport then stepped forward, and formally requested Schubert to alter the music before the next meeting. This he refused to do; but taking the same course as Beethoven had done on a similar occasion, said loudly, ' I will alter nothing,' took up his score and left the house. After this the question of the conductorship was at an end. Schubert's behaviour in this matter has been strongly censured, but we do not see much in it. Such questions will always depend on the temperament of the composer. Had it been either Mozart or Mendelssohn we cannot doubt that all would have gone smoothly; the prima donna would not only not have been ruffled, but would have felt herself complimented, and the music would have been so altered as to meet every one's wish, and yet sound as well as before. On the other hand, had it been Beethoven or Schumann we may be equally sure that not a note would have been changed, and that everything would have ended in confusion. With all Schubert's good-nature, when his music was concerned he was of the same mind as Beethoven and Schumann. There are other instances of the same stubbornness, which will be noticed later.

Some set-off to these disappointments was afforded by the ready way in which his Gastein Symphony [?] was received by the Musik-Verein, and the sympathetic resolution and prompt donation which accompanied its acceptance, although no attempt to perform or even rehearse it can now be traced. The beautiful ' Nachthelle,' already referred to, which he composed in September, was rehearsed during the early winter months, and performed by the Society on January 25, 1827.

Some little gratification also he not improbably derived from the letters which during this year he began to receive from publishers in the north. Probst of Leipzig — one of Beethoven's publishers, predecessor of the present firm of Senff — was the first to write. His letter is dated August 26, and is followed by one from Breitkopf & Härtel of September 7. True, neither are very encouraging. Probst speaks of his music as too often ' peculiar and odd,' and ' not intelligible or satisfactory to the public '; and begs him to write so as to be easily understood; while Breitkopf stipulates that the only remuneration at first shall be some copies of the works. Still, even with this poor present result, the fact was obvious that he had begun to attract attention outside of Austria.

As to Schubert's life in the early part of 1827 we have little to guide us beyond the scanty inferences to be drawn from the dated compositions. The first of these of any moment are 8 Variations (the 8th very much extended) on a theme in Hérold's opera ' Marie,' for pianoforte 4 hands (op. 82). ' Marie ' was produced on the Vienna boards January 18, 1827 [December 18, 1826] ; and Schubert's Variations are dated ' February,' and are dedicated to one of his friends in Upper Austria, Prof. Cajetan Neuhaus of Linz. The next and still more important work is the first half of the ' Winterreise,' 12 songs (' Gute Nacht ' to ' Einsamkeit '), marked as begun in February 1827. Franz Lachner remembers that ' half a dozen ' of them were written in one morning, and that Diabelli [Haslinger] gave a gulden (that is a franc) apiece for them. The poems which form the basis of this work are by Wilhelm Müller, the poet of the ' Schöne Müllerin,' which the Winterreise closely approaches in popularity, and which it would probably equal if the maiden of the Winter-walk were as definite a creation as the miller's daughter is. They are 24 in all,[1] and appear under their now immortal name in the 2nd volume of the work of which vol. i. contained the ' Schöne Müllerin,' and which has the quaint title already quoted (p. 171 n.). The 2nd volume was published at Dessau in 1824, and did not at once attract Schubert's notice. When it did, he made short work of it. Another important composition of this month (dated February 28) is the Schlacht-lied (battle-song) of Klopstock, set for 2 choirs of male voices, sometimes answering, sometimes in 8 real parts, of immense force and vigour, and marked by that dogged adherence to rhythm so characteristic of Schubert.

He can scarcely have finished with this before the news that Beethoven was in danger spread through Vienna. The great musician got back to his rooms in the Schwarzspanierhaus from his fatal expedition to Gneixendorf in the first week of December, became very ill, and during January was tapped for the dropsy three times. Then Malfatti was called in, and there was a slight improvement. During this he was allowed to read, and it was then that Schindler, a zealous Schubert-propagandist, took the opportunity to put some of Schubert's

[1] The order of the songs is much changed in the music.

songs into his hands.[1] He made a selection of about 60, in
print and MS., including ' Iphigenie,' ' Grenzen der Menschheit,' ' Allmacht,' ' Die junge Nonne,' ' Viola,' the ' Müller-
lieder,' etc.[2] Beethoven up to this time probably did not know
half a dozen of Schubert's compositions, and his astonishment
was extreme, especially when he heard that there existed at least
500 of the same kind. ' How can he find time,' said he, ' to set
such long poems, many of them containing ten others? ' *i.e.*
as long as ten separate ones; and said over and over again,
' If I had had this poem I would have set it myself '; ' Truly,
Schubert has the divine fire in him.' He pored over them for
days, and asked to see Schubert's operas and pianoforte pieces,
but the illness returned and it was too late. But from this time
till his death he spoke often of Schubert, regretting that he had
not sooner known his worth, and prophesying that he would
make much stir in the world.[3] Schubert was sure to hear of
these gratifying utterances, and they would naturally increase
his desire to come into close contact with the master whom he
had long worshipped at a distance. It is possible that this
emboldened him to visit the dying man. He seems to have
gone twice; first with Anselm Hüttenbrenner and Schindler.
Schindler told Beethoven that they were there, and asked who
he would see first. ' Schubert may come in first,' was the
answer. At this visit perhaps, if ever,[4] it was, that he said, in
his affectionate way, ' You, Anselm, have my mind (*Geist*), but
Franz has my soul (*Seele*).' The second time he went with
Josef Hüttenbrenner and Teltscher the painter. They stood
round the bed. Beethoven was aware of their presence, and
fixing his eyes on them, made some signs with his hand. No
one, however, could explain what was meant, and no words
passed on either side. Schubert left the room overcome with
emotion. In about three weeks came the end, and then the
funeral. Schubert was one of the torch-bearers. Franz
Lachner and Randhartinger walked with him to and from the
cemetery. The way back lay by the Himmelpfortgrund, and

---

[1] Schindler, *Beethoven*, ii. 136.
[2] Schindler's list of the songs perused by Beethoven differs in his two accounts.
Compare his *Beethoven*, ii. 136, with K.H. 264 (i. 266).
[3] Schindler, in Bäuerle's *Theaterzeitung* (Vienna), May 3, 1831.
[4] See von Leitner, *Anselm Huttenbrenner*, Gratz [Graz], 1868, p. 5. The
story has an apocryphal air, but Hüttenbrenner was so thoroughly trustworthy
that it is difficult to reject it. At any rate, Beethoven is not likely to have thus
expressed himself before he had made acquaintance with Schubert's music.

close by the humble house in which he had drawn his first breath. They walked on into the town, and stopped at the ' Mehlgrube,' a tavern in the Kärnthnerthorstrasse, now the Hotel Munsch. There they called for wine, and Schubert drank off two glasses, one to the memory of Beethoven, the other to the first of the three friends who should follow him. It was destined to be himself.

Lablache was also one of the torch-bearers at the funeral. This and the part which he took in the Requiem for Beethoven (p. 102) may have induced Schubert to write for him the ' 3 Italian Songs for a Bass voice,' which form op. 83, and are dedicated to the great Italian basso.

Hummel and Hiller were in Vienna during March 1827, and Hiller describes meeting Schubert and Vogl at Madame Lacsny-Buchwieser's, and his astonishment at their joint performance. ' Schubert,' says Hiller,[1] ' had little technique, and Vogl but little voice; but they had both so much life and feeling, and went so thoroughly into the thing, that it would be impossible to render these wonderful compositions more clearly and more splendidly. Voice and piano became as nothing; the music seemed to want no material help, but the melodies appealed to the ear as a vision does to the eye.' Not only did the boy think it the deepest musical impression he had ever received, but the tears coursed down the cheeks even of the veteran Hummel. Either then or a few evenings afterwards Hummel showed his appreciation by extemporising on Schubert's ' Blinde Knabe,' which Vogl had just sung — to Franz's delight.

In April Schubert wrote the beautiful ' Nachtgesang im Walde ' (op. 139b) for 4 men's voices and 4 horns; and a ' Spring Song,' also for men's voices, still in MS. In July we have the very fine and characteristic serenade ' Zögernd leise ' (op. 135) for alto solo and female voices, a worthy pendant to the ' Nachthelle,' and written almost à l'improviste.[2] A fête was to be held for the birthday of a young lady of Döbling. Grillparzer had written some verses for the occasion, and Schubert, who was constantly in and out of the Fröhlichs' house, was asked by Anna to set them for her sister Josephine and her pupils. He took the lines, went aside into the window, pushed up his spectacles on to his brow, and then, with the paper close

---

[1] *Künstlerleben* (1880), p. 49.   [2] K.H. 474 (ii. 160).

to his face, read them carefully twice through.   It was enough :
' I have it,' said he, ' it's done, and will go famously.'   A day or
two afterwards he brought the score, but he had employed a
male chorus instead of a female one, and had to take it away
and transpose it.   It was sung in the garden by moonlight, to
the delight of every one, the villagers thronging round the gate.
He alone was absent.

    1827 witnessed another attempt at an opera — the ' Graf
von Gleichen,' written by Bauernfeld, apparently in concurrence with Mayrhofer.[1]   Schubert had the libretto in August
1826, submitted it to the management of the Royal Opera-
house, and arranged with Grillparzer, in case the *Censur*
should cause its rejection, to have it accepted by the Königstadt
Theatre.   Owing possibly to the delay of the *Censur* it was
nearly a year before he could begin the composition.   The
MS. sketch, now in Herr Dumba's collection, is dated at the
beginning ' 17 Juni 1827.'   The opera is sketched throughout,
and he played portions of it to Bauernfeld.   Forty years later
the sketch came into the hands of Herbeck, and he began to
score it after Schubert's indications — of which there are plenty
— but was prevented by death.

    A correspondence had been going on for long between the
Schubert circle at Vienna and the Pachler family in Gratz,
the capital of Styria, as to an expedition thither by Schubert,
and at length it was arranged for the autumn of this year.   Carl
Pachler was one of those cultivated men of business who are
such an honour to Germany ;   an advocate, and at the head
of his profession, yet not ashamed to be an enthusiastic lover
of music and musicians, and proud to have them at his house
and to admit them to his intimate friendship.   Amongst his
circle was Anselm Hüttenbrenner, the brother of Schubert's
friend Josef, himself an earnest admirer of Franz, whose last
visit to Vienna had been to close the eyes of his old friend
Beethoven.   The house was open to painters, singers, actors,
and poets, ' the scene of constant hospitalities, the headquarters
of every remarkable person visiting Gratz '.   Such was the
family whose one desire was to receive Schubert and Jenger.
The journey, now accomplished in 5½ hours, was an affair
of two days and a night, even in the fast coach.   They left

    [1] See Schubert's letter [May, 1826] with Bauernfeld's statement in the
Presse of Apr. 21, 1869, and *Signale*, Nov. 1869.

on Sunday morning, September 2, and reached Gratz on Monday night. The next three weeks were spent in the way which Schubert most enjoyed, excursions and picnics by day through a beautiful country, and at night incessant music; good eating and drinking, clever men and pretty women, no fuss, a little romping, a good piano, a sympathetic audience, and no notice taken of him — such were the elements of his enjoyment. The music was made mostly by themselves, Schubert singing, accompanying, and playing duets with Jenger, and extemporising endless dance tunes. He does not appear to have composed anything of great moment during the visit. A galop and twelve waltzes, published under the titles of the 'Grätzer Waltzer' (op. 91) and the 'Grätzer Galoppe'[1]; 3 songs (op. 106, 1, 2, 3 — the last a particularly fine one) to words by local poets — and the 'Old Scottish ballad' by Herder (op. 165, no. 5), were probably all that he penned during this festive fortnight; unless perhaps some of those exquisite little pieces published in 1828 and 1838 as 'Impromptus' and 'Momens musicals' ['Moments musicaux'] are the result of this time. Two songs, written a couple of years before, 'Im Walde,' and 'Auf der Brücke [Bruck],' of the purest Schubert, proved, and justly proved, such favourites that he had them lithographed and published in the place.[2] The visit is further perpetuated by the titles of the dances just mentioned, and by the dedication to Mme. Pachler of op. 106, a collection of four songs, the three already named, and the lovely 'Sylvia' ['Silvia']. Schubert seems to have had this set of songs lithographed without name of place or publisher, shortly after his return, on purpose for his hostess.[3]

The journey home was a triumphal progress, and by the 27th they were back in Vienna. Schubert then wrote the second part of the 'Winterreise' (nos. 13-24), completing that immortal work. The shadows lie much darker on the second than on the first part, and the 'Wegweiser,' 'Das Wirthshaus,' 'Die Krähe,' 'Die Nebensonnen,' and 'Der Leiermann,' are unsurpassed for melancholy among all the songs. Even in the extraordinary and picturesque energy of 'Die Post' there is a

---

[1] Published by Haslinger, as No. 10 of the 'Favorite Galops,' 1828.

[2] They stood originally in B♭ minor and A♭, but on republication by Diabelli after his death, as op. 93, the keys were changed to G minor and G major.

[3] Compare Jenger's letter in K.H. (ii. 103), note, with Nottebohm's notice under op. 103.

deep vein of sadness. Schubert here only followed faithfully, as he always does, the character of the words.

On October 12 he wrote a little 4-hand march as a souvenir for Faust Pachler, the son of his host, a trifle interesting only from the circumstances of its composition. In the same month he composed his first pianoforte trio, in B♭ (op. 99), and in November the second, in E♭ (op. 100). They were both written for Boklet, Schuppanzigh, and Linke, and were first heard in public, the one early in January, the other on March 26, 1828. The year was closed with an Italian cantata, dated December 26, ' alla bella Irene,' in honour of Miss Kiesewetter (after-wards Mme. Prokesch von Osten), the daughter of his friend the Hofrath, sponsor to the Gastein Symphony (p. 185-6). It is still in MS., and is probably more interesting for its accompani-ment for two pianos than for anything else.

The communications with Probst of Leipzig went on. There is a letter from him dated January 15, and he himself paid a visit to Vienna later in the season, and made Schubert's personal acquaintance,[1] but the negotiations were not destined to bear fruit till next year. But a proof that Schubert was making his mark in North Germany is afforded by a letter from Rochlitz, the critic — editor of the Leipzig Allgemeine Musika-lische Zeitung, and a great personage in the musical world of Saxony — dated November 7, 1827, proposing that Schubert should compose a poem by him, called ' Der erste Ton,' or ' The first Sound,' a poem which Weber had already set without success, and which Beethoven had refused. Rochlitz's letter was probably inspired by the receipt of three of his songs set by Schubert as op. 81, and published on May 27. The pro-position, however, came to nothing.

Coincident with these communications from abroad came a gratifying proof of the improvement in his position at home, in his election as a member of the representative body of the Musical Society of Vienna. The date of election is not men-tioned ; but Schubert's reply, as given by Herr Pohl,[2] is dated Vienna, June 12, 1827, and runs as follows : —

The Managing Committee of the Society of Friends of Music of the Austrian Empire having thought me worthy of election as a Member of the Representative Body of that excellent Society, I beg

---

[1] K.H. 421 (ii. 107).
[2] *Die Gesellschaft der Musikfreunde,* etc., p. 16.

herewith to state that I feel myself greatly honoured by their choice, and that I undertake the duties of the position with much satisfaction.   FRANZ SCHUBERT, Compositeur.

We have mentioned the more important compositions of 1827. There remain to be named two songs by Schober (op. 96, no. 2; Lf. 24, no. 1), and one by Reil (op. 115, no. 1); a comic trio, ' Die Hochzeitsbraten ' (op. 104), also by Schober ; and an Allegretto in C minor for pianoforte solo, written for his friend Walcher, 'in remembrance of April 26, 1827,' and not published till 1870.

The publications of 1827 are as follow : —the Overture to ' Alfonso and Estrella ' (op. 69) ; Rondeau brillant, for pianoforte and violin (op. 70) ; songs — ' Der Wachtelschlag' (op. 68, March 2), ' Drang in die Ferne ' (op. 71, February), ' Auf dem Wasser au singen ' (op. 72, February), ' Die Rose ' (op. 73, May 10) — all four songs previously published in the Vienna Zeitschrift für Kunst ; four Polonaises, for pianoforte 4 hands (op. 75) ; Overture to ' Fierabras,' for pianoforte 4 hands, arranged by Czerny (op. 76) ; 12 ' Valses Nobles,' for pianoforte solo (op. 77, January) ; Fantasie, etc. [Sonata] for pianoforte in G (op. 78) ; 2 songs, ' Das Heimweh,' ' Die Allmacht' (op. 79, 'May 16 ') ; 3 songs (op. 80, May 25) ; 3 ditto (op. 81, May 28) ; Variations on theme of Hérold's (op. 82, December) ; 3 Italian songs (op. 83, September 12) ; 4 songs (op. 88, December 12).

We have now arrived at Schubert's last year, 1828. It would be wrong to suppose that he had any presentiment of his end ; though, if a passion for work, an eager use of the ' day,' were any sign that the ' night ' was coming ' in which no man could work,' we might almost be justified in doing so. We hear of his suffering from blood to the head, but it was not yet enough to frighten any one. He returned to the extraordinary exertions, or rather to the superabundant productions of his earlier years, as the following full list of compositions of 1828, in order, as far as the dates permit, will show.

Jan.   Songs, ' Die Sterne ' (op. 96, no. 1) ; ' Der Winterabend ' (Lf. 26).
March Symphony in C, no. 9.
       Oratorio, ' Miriam's Siegesgesang.'
       Song, ' Auf dem Strom,' Voice and Horn (op. 119).

May   Lebensstürme, pianoforte duet (op. 144).

Hymn to the Holy Ghost (op. 154), for 2 Choirs and Wind.

2 Clavierstücke.

Song, ' Widerschein ' (Lief. 15, no. 1).

June   Mass in E♭ (begun).

Fugue in E minor, pianoforte duet, op. 152 (' Baden, Juny. 1828 ').

Grand Rondeau, pianoforte duet (op. 107).

July   Psalm 92, in Hebrew, for Baritone and Chorus.

August   Songs, ' Schwanengesang,' nos. 1–13.

Sept.   Pianoforte Sonata in C minor.

Ditto in A.

Ditto in B♭ (' Sept. 26 ').

Oct.   Song, ' Schwanengesang,' No. 14.

New Benedictus to Mass in C.

' Der Hirt auf den [dem] Felsen,' Voice and Clarinet (op. 129).

' 1828 ' only.   String Quintet in C (op. 163).

This truly extraordinary list includes his greatest known symphony, his greatest and longest mass, his first oratorio, his finest piece of chamber music, 3 noble pianoforte sonatas, and some astonishingly fine songs. The autograph of the symphony, 218 pages in oblong quarto, is now one of the treasures of the Library of the Musik-verein at Vienna. It has no title or dedication, nothing beyond the customary heading to the first page of the score, ' Symfonie März 1828, Frz. Schubert Mpia,' marking the date at which it was begun. If it may be taken as a specimen, he took more pains this year than he did formerly. In the first three movements of this great work there are more afterthoughts than usual. The subject of the Introduction and the first subject of the Allegro have both been altered. In several passages an extra bar has been stuck in — between the Scherzo and the Trio, 2 bars ; in the development of the Scherzo itself 16 bars of an exquisite episode — first sketched in the Octet — have been substituted. The Finale alone remains virtually untouched.[1] But such alterations, always rare in Schubert, are essentially different from the painful writing, and erasing, and rewriting, which we are familiar with in the case of Beethoven's finest and most spontaneous music. This, though the first draft, is no rough copy ;

[1] See details by the present writer in Appendix to the Life of Schubert, translated by A. D. Coleridge, Esq., vol. ii. p. 320.

there are no traces of sketches or preparation ; the music has evidently gone straight on to the paper without any intervention, and the alterations are merely a few improvements *en passant*.[1] It is impossible to look at the writing of the autograph, after Schubert has warmed to his work, especially that of the Finale, and not see that it was put down as an absolute *impromptu*, written as fast as the pen could travel on the paper.

It seems that Schubert's friends used to lecture him a good deal on the diffuseness and want of consideration which they discovered in his works, and were continually forcing Beethoven's laborious processes of composition down his throat. This often made him angry, and when repeated, evening after evening, he would say, ' So you're going to set upon me again to-day ! Go it, I beg you ! ' But, for all his annoyance, the remonstrances appear to have had some effect ; and after Beethoven's death he asked Schindler [2] to show him the MS. of ' Fidelio.' He took it to the piano, and pored over it a long time, making out the passages as they had been, and comparing them with what they were ; but it would not do ; and at last he broke out, and exclaimed that for such drudgery he could see no reason under any circumstances ; that he thought the music at first just as good as at last ; and that for his part he had really no time for such corrections. Whether the amendments to the Great Symphony were a remorseful attempt on Schubert's part to imitate Beethoven and satisfy the demands of his friends we cannot tell ; but if so, they are very unlike the pattern.

The autograph of the Eb Mass, in the Bibliothek at Berlin, does not show at all the same amount of corrections as that in Ab (see p. 166), nor do the fugal movements appear to have given any special trouble. True, the ' Cum Sancto ' was recommenced after the erasure of 7 bars,[3] but apparently merely for the sake of changing the tempo from c to ₵, and the larger part of the movement was evidently written with great rapidity. In the ' Et vitam ' there are barely a dozen corrections, and

[1] The original MS. orchestral parts show at any rate that the alterations in the score were made before they were copied from it. Mr. Stanford kindly examined them for me with that view.

[2] Schindler, ' Erinnerungen,' in *Niederrheinische Musikzeitung*, 1857, pp. 73-78 ; 81-85.

[3] The omission of the words ' Jesu Christe ' at the end of the ' Quoniam,' and other omissions, show that he had not conquered the carelessness as to the treatment of the words, so frequent in his early Masses.

O

the ' Osanna ' has every mark of extreme haste. Some of the erasures in this work are made with the penknife — surely an almost unique thing with Schubert! The 4-hand pianoforte fugue in E minor (op. 152, dated ' Baden, June 1828 ') is not improbably a trial of counterpoint with reference to this Mass.

The songs of 1828 are splendid. It does not appear that the 14 which were published after his death with the publisher's title of ' Schwanengesang ' — ' the Swan's song ' — were intended by him to form a series of the same kind as the Schöne Müllerin and Winterreise ; but no lover of Schubert can dissociate them, and in the Liebesbothschaft, Aufenthalt, Ständchen, etc., we have some of the most beautiful, and in the Atlas, Am Meer, Doppelgänger, etc., some of the most impressive, of his many songs. The words of some are by Rellstab, and the origin of these is thus told by Schindler.[1] Schubert had been much touched by Schindler's efforts to make Beethoven acquainted with his music, and after the great master's death the two gradually became intimate. Schindler had possession of many of Beethoven's papers, and Schubert used to visit him in familiar style, to look over them. Those which specially attracted him were the poems and dramas sent in at various times for consideration ; amongst others a bundle of some 20 anonymous [2] lyrics which Beethoven had intended to set, and which therefore attracted Schubert's particular notice. He took them away with him, and in two days brought back the Liebesbothschaft, Kriegers Ahnung, and Aufenthalt, set to music. This account, which is perfectly natural and consistent, and which Mr. Thayer allows me to say he sees no reason to question, has been exaggerated [3] into a desire expressed by Beethoven himself that Schubert should set these particular songs ; but for this there is no warrant. Ten more quickly followed the three just mentioned ; and these thirteen — 7 to Rellstab's and 6 to Heine's words (from the ' Buch der Lieder ' [4]), were, on Mr. Nottebohm's authority, written in

---

[1] Schindler, ' Erinnerungen,' etc., as before.
[2] They proved afterwards to be by Rellstab.
[3] See Rellstab's ' An m. Leben,' ii. 245.
[4] Baron Schönstein relates—K.H. 447 (ii. 135)—that he found Heine's *Buch der Lieder* on Schubert's table some years before this date, and that Schubert lent them to him with the remark ' that he should not want them again.' But such reminiscences are often wrong to point of date : the fact remains ineffaceable in the mind, the date easily gets altered. In fact Heine's *Buch der Lieder* was first published in 1827. The 6 songs which Schubert took from it are all from the section entitled ' Der Heimkehr.'

August.   The last is by Seidl; it is dated ' October 1828,' and
is probably Schubert's last song.

But it is time to return to the chronicle of his life during its
last ten months.   Of his doings in January we know little more
than can be gathered from the following letter to Anselm
Hüttenbrenner, the original of which is in the British Museum.

VIENNA, Jan. 18, 1828.

My dear old Hüttenbrenner,—You will wonder at my writing
now? So do I.   But if I write it is because I am to get something
by it.   Now just listen; a drawing-master's place near you at
Grätz is vacant, and competition is invited.   My brother Karl,
whom you probably know, wishes to get the place.   He is very
clever, both as a landscape painter and a draughtsman.   If you
could do anything for him in the matter I should be eternally
obliged to you.   You are a great man in Grätz, and probably
know some one in authority, or some one else who has a vote.   My
brother is married, and has a family, and would therefore be very
glad to obtain a permanent appointment.   I hope that things are
all right with you, as well as with your dear family, and your
brothers.   A Trio of mine, for Pianoforte, Violin, and Violoncello,
has been lately performed by Schuppanzigh, and was much liked.
It was splendidly executed by Boklet, Schuppanzigh, and Linke.
Have you done nothing new?   A propos, why doesn't Greiner,[1] or
whatever his name is, publish the two songs?   What's the reason?
Sapperment!

I repeat my request: recollect, what you do for my brother,
you do for me.   Hoping for a favourable answer, I remain your
true friend, till death,

FRANZ SCHUBERT Mpia.
of Vienna.

The expression ' till death,' which appears here for the first
time in his letters, and the words ' of Vienna,' added to his
name, are both singular.

On the 24th, at an evening concert at the Musik-Verein,
the serenade for contralto solo and female chorus just mentioned
was performed, and is spoken of by the correspondent of the
Leipzig A.M.Z. as ' one of the most charming works of this
favourite writer.'   In February we find three letters from North
Germany, one from Probst of Leipzig, and two from Schott.
They show how deep an impression Schubert was making outside Austria.   Both firms express warm appreciation of his

---

[1] A publisher in Grätz [Graz]. His name was Kienreich, and the two songs,
Im Walde and Auf der Brücke [Bruck] (op. 93), appeared in May.

music, both leave the terms to be named by him, and Schott
orders a list of 9 important pieces.

On March 26 Schubert gave, what we wonder he never
gave before, an evening concert on his own account in the Hall
of the Musik-Verein. The following is the programme exactly
reprinted from the original.

Einladung
zu dem Privat Concerte, welches Franz Schubert am
26. März, Abends 7 Uhr im Locale des oesterreichischen Musikvereins
unter den Tuchlauben No. 558 zu geben die Ehre haben wird.
Vorkommende Stücke.

1. Erster Satz eines neuen Streich Quartetts vorgetragen von
   den Herren Böhm, Holz, Weiss, und Linke.
2. a. Der Kreutzzug, von Leitner ⎫ Gesänge mit Begleitung des
   b. Die Sterne, von demselben ⎪ Piano Forte, vorgetragen von
   c. Fischerweise, von Bar. Schlechta ⎬ Herrn Vogl, k. k. pensionirten
   d. Fragment aus dem Aeschylus ⎭ Hofopernsänger.
3. Ständchen von Grillparzer, Sopran-Solo und Chor, vorgetragen von
   Fräulein Josephine Fröhlich und den Schülerinnen des Conservatoriums.
4. Neues Trio für das Piano Forte, Violin und Violoncelle,
   vorgetragen von den Herren Carl Maria von Boklet, Böhm und Linke.
5. Auf dem Strome von Rellstab. Gesang mit Begleitung
   des Horns und Piano Forte, vorgetragen von den Herren
   Tietze, und Lewy dem Jüngeren.
6. Die Allmacht, von Ladislaus Pyrker, Gesang mit Begleitung
   des Piano Forte, vorgetragen von Herren Vogl.
7. Schlachtgesang von Klopfstock, Doppelchor für Männerstimmen.
Sämmtliche Musikstücke sind von der Composition des Concertgebers.
Eintrittskarten zu fl. 3. W. W. sind in den Kunsthandlungen
der Herren Haslinger, Diabelli und Leidesdorf zu haben.

This programme attracted ' more people than the hall had
ever before been known to hold,' and the applause was very
great. The net result to Schubert was 800 gulden, Vienna
currency, equal to about £32. This put him in funds for the
moment, and the money flowed freely. Thus, when, three days
later, Paganini gave his first concert in Vienna, Schubert was
there, undeterred, in his wealth, by a charge of 5 gulden. Nay,
he went a second time, not that he cared to go again, but that
he wished to treat Bauernfeld, who had not 5 farthings, while
with him ' money was as plenty as blackberries.' [1]

This month he wrote, or began to write, his last and greatest
Symphony, in C. He is said to have offered it to the Society
for performance, and in so doing to have expressed himself to

[1] See Bauernfeld's letter in the *Presse*, April 17, 1869. *Häckerling*, chaff, is
Schubert's word.

the effect that henceforth he wished to have nothing more to do with songs, as he was now planted firmly in opera and symphony. This rests on the authority of Kreissle;[1] the silence of Herr Pohl in his history of the Society shows that its minute-books contain no express mention of the reception of the work, as they do that of the symphony in October 1826. There is no doubt, however, that it was adopted by the Society, and is entered in the Catalogue, under the year 1828, as xiii. 8024.[2] But this prodigious work was far beyond the then powers of the chief musical institution of Vienna. The parts were copied, and some rehearsals held; but both length and difficulty were against it, and it was soon withdrawn, on Schubert's own advice, in favour of his earlier symphony, No. 6, also in C. Neither the one nor the other was performed till after his death.

March also saw the birth of the interesting Oratorio ' Miriam's Song of Victory,' to Grillparzer's words.[3] It is written, as so many of Schubert's choral pieces are, for a simple pianoforte accompaniment; but this was merely to suit the means at his disposal and is an instance of his practical sagacity. It is unfortunate, however, since the oratorio has become a favourite, that we have no other orchestral accompaniment than that afterwards adapted by Lachner, which is greatly wanting in character, and in the picturesque elements so native to Schubert.[4] A song to Rellstab's words, ' Auf dem Strom ' (op. 119), for soprano, with obbligato horn and pianoforte accompaniment, written for Lewy, a Dresden horn-player, belongs to this month, and was indeed first heard at Schubert's own concert, on the 26th, and afterwards repeated at a concert of Lewy's, on April 20, Schubert himself playing the accompaniment each time.

To April no compositions can be ascribed, unless it be the Quintet in C for strings (op. 163), which bears only the date ' 1828.' This is now universally accepted not only as Schubert's finest piece of chamber music, but as one of the very finest of

---

[1] K.H. 445 (ii. 132).

[2] See Herr Pohl's letter to *The Times* of Oct. 17, 1881.

[3] Kreissle, 609 (ii. 285), says that it was produced in the Schubert Concert, Mar. 1828. But this is contradicted by the Programme which is printed above. It was first performed Jan. 30, 1829, at a concert for erecting Schubert's headstone.

[4] It has been performed (with Lachner's orchestration) at the Crystal Palace several times, at the Leeds Festival 1880, and elsewhere in England.

its class. The two cellos alone give a distinction ; it has all the
poetry and romance of the G major Quartet, without the extravagant length which will always stand in the way of that noble
production ; while the Adagio is so solemn and yet so beautiful
in its tone, so entrancing in its melodies, and so incessant in its
interest, and the Trio of the Scherzo, both from itself and its
place in the movement, is so eminently dramatic, that it is
difficult to speak of either too highly.

In May we have a grand battle-piece, the ' Hymn to the
Holy Ghost,' for 8 male voices, written for the Concert Spirituel
of Vienna, at first with pianoforte in October scored by the
composer for a wind band, and in 1847 published as op. 154.
Also a ' Characteristic Allegro ' for the pianoforte 4 hands,
virtually the first movement of a sonata — issued some years
later with the title ' Lebensstürme ' (op. 144) ; an Allegro
vivace and Allegretto in E♭ minor and major, for pianoforte
solo, published in 1868 as 1st and 2nd of ' 3 Clavierstücke ' ;
and a song ' Widerschein ' (Lf. 15, 1).

In June, probably at the request of the publisher, he wrote
a 4-hand Rondo for pianoforte in A, since issued as ' Grand
Rondeau, op. 107 ' ; and began his sixth Mass, that in E♭. In
this month he paid a visit to Baden — Beethoven's Baden ;
since a fugue for 4 hands in E minor is marked as written
there in ' June 1828.' In the midst of all this work a letter [1]
from Mosewius of Breslau, a prominent Prussian musician,
full of sympathy and admiration, must have been doubly
gratifying as coming from North Germany.

In July he wrote the 92nd Psalm in Hebrew for the syna-
gogue at Vienna, of which Sulzer was precentor. In August,
notwithstanding his declaration on completing his last Symphony, we find him (under circumstances already described)
composing 7 songs of Rellstab's, and 6 of Heine's, afterwards
issued as ' Schwanengesang.'

He opened September with a trifle in the shape of a short
chorus,[2] with accompaniment of wind band, for the consecra-
tion of a bell in the church of the Alservorstadt. A few days
after, the memory of Hummel's visit in the spring of 1827 seems
to have come upon him like a lion, and he wrote off 3 fine

---

[1] K.H. 428 (ii. 114).
[2] K.H. 443 (ii. 131). This piece, ' Glaube, Hoffnung, und Liebe,' is not to
be confounded with one of similar title for a solo voice, published, Oct. 6, 1828,
as op. 97.

pianoforte solo sonatas, with the view of dedicating them to that master. These pieces, though very unequal and in parts extraordinarily diffuse, are yet highly characteristic of Schubert. They contain some of his finest and most original music, and also his most affecting (e.g. Andantino, Scherzo and Trio of the A minor [major] Sonata) ; and if full of disappointment and wrath, and the gathering gloom of these last few weeks of his life, they are also saturated with that nameless personal charm that is at once so strong and so indescribable. The third of the three, that in Bb, dated September 26, has perhaps more of grace and finish than the other two, and has now, from the playing of Mme. Schumann, Mr. Charles Hallé, and others, become a great favourite. The sonatas were not published till a year after Hummel's death, and were then dedicated by Diabelli-Spina to Robert Schumann, who acknowledges the dedication by a genial though hardly adequate article in his ' Gesammelte Schriften,' ii. 239. The second part of the Winterreise was put into Haslinger's hands for engraving before the end of this month.[1]

In October, prompted by some occasion which has eluded record, he wrote a new ' Benedictus ' to his early Mass in C, a chorus of great beauty and originality in A minor, of which a competent critic [2] has said that ' its only fault consists in its immeasurable superiority to the rest of the Mass.' For some other occasion, which has also vanished, he wrote accompaniments for 13 wind instruments to his grand ' Hymn to the Holy Ghost ' ; a long scena or song for soprano — probably his old admirer, Anna Milder — with pianoforte and obbligato clarinet (op. 129) ; and a song called ' Die Taubenpost ' (' The carrier pigeon ') to Seidl's words. The succession of these pieces is not known. It is always assumed that the Taubenpost, which now closes the Schwanengesang, was the last. Whichever of them was the last, was the last piece he ever wrote.

The negotiations with Probst and Schott, and also with Brüggemann of Halberstadt, a publisher anxious for some easy pianoforte pieces for a series called ' Mühling's Museum,' by no means fulfilled the promise of their commencement. The magnificent style in which the Schotts desired Schubert to

---

[1] Schubert's letter to Jenger, Sept. 25. K.H. 437 (ii. 124).
[2] Mr. E. Prout in the *Monthly Musical Record* for 1871, p. 56.

name his own terms [1] contrasts badly with their ultimate refusal
(October 30) to pay more than 30 florins (or about 25*s.*) for
the Pianoforte Quintet (op. 114) instead of the modest 60
demanded by him. In fact the sole result was an arrangement
with Probst to publish the long and splendid E♭ Trio, which
he did, according to Nottebohm,[2] in September, and for which
the composer received the incredibly small sum of 21 Vienna
florins, or just 17*s.* 6*d.*! Schubert's answer to Probst's enquiry
as to the 'Dedication' is so characteristic as to deserve
reprinting :—

VIENNA, *Aug.* 1.

Euer Wohlgeboren, the opus of the Trio is 100. I entreat you
to make the edition correct; I am extremely anxious about it.
The work will be dedicated to no one but those who like it. That
is the most profitable dedication. With all esteem,

FRANZ SCHUBERT.

The home publications of 1828 are not so important as
those of former years. The first part of the Winterreise (op. 89)
was issued in January by Haslinger; March 14, 3 songs by
Sir W. Scott (ops. 85, 86) by Diabelli; at Easter (April 6)
6 songs (ops. 92 and 108), and one set of 'Momens musicals'
['Moments musicaux'], by Liedesdorf; in May, 2 songs (op.
93) by Kienreich [3] of Gratz; in June or July ('Sommer') 4 songs
(op. 96) by Diabelli; August 13, 4 Refrain-Lieder (op. 95)
Weigl. Also the following, to which no month can be fixed :—
'Andantino varié and Rondeau brillant' (op. 84), pianoforte
4 hands, on French *motifs*, forming a continuation of op. 63,
Weigl; 3 songs (op. 87), Pennauer; 4 impromptus (op. 90),
and 12 Grätzer Walzer (op. 91) for pianoforte solo, Diabelli;
Grätzer Galopp, do. Haslinger; 4 songs (op. 106) lithographed
without publisher's name.

There is nothing in the events already catalogued to have
prevented Schubert's taking an excursion this summer. In
either Styria or Upper Austria he would have been welcomed
with open arms, and the journey might have given him a stock
of health sufficient to carry him on for years. And he appears

---

[1] K.H. 424 (ii. 109).
[2] Probst announces two long lists of new music in the A.M.Z. for Oct., but
no mention of the Trio. It is reviewed most favourably in the A.M.Z. for Dec.
10, 1828. Alas! he was then beyond the reach of praise or blame.
[3] Whom Schubert parodies as 'Greiner,' *i.e.* grumbler.

to have entertained the idea of both.[1]   But the real obstacle,
as he constantly repeats, was his poverty.[2]   ' It's all over with
Gratz for the present,' he says, with a touch of his old
fun, ' for money and weather are both against me.'   Herr
Franz Lachner, at that time his constant companion, told the
writer, that he had taken half-a-dozen of the ' Winterreise '
songs to Haslinger and brought back half-a-dozen gulden —
each gulden being then worth a franc.   Let the lover of Schubert
pause a moment, and think of the ' Post ' or the ' Wirthshaus '
being sold for tenpence ! of that unrivalled imagination and
genius producing those deathless strains and being thus re-
warded !   When this was the case, when even a great work
like the E♭ Trio, after months and months of negotiation and
heavy postage, realises the truly microscopic amount of ' 20
florins 60 kreutzers ' (as with true Prussian businesslike minute-
ness Herr Probst specifies it), of 17s. 6d. as our modern currency
has it — not even Schubert's fluency and rapidity could do
more than keep body and soul together.   It must have been
hard not to apply the words of Müller's ' Leiermann ' to his
own case—

> Barfuss auf dem Eise
> Wankt er hin und her,
> *Und sein kleiner Teller*
> *Bleibt ihm immer leer.*

> Wandering barefoot to and fro
> On the icy ground,
> In his little empty tray
> Not a copper to be found.

In fact so empty was his little tray that he could not even afford
the diligence-fare to Pesth, where Lachner's ' Bürgschaft ' was
to be brought out, and where, as Schindler reminds him, he
would be safe to have a lucrative concert of his own music, as
profitable as that of March 26.   Escape from Vienna by *that*
road was impossible for him this year.

Schubert had for some time past been living with Schober
at the ' Blaue Igel ' (or Blue Hedgehog), still a well-known
tavern and resort of musicians in the Tuchlauben ; but at the
end of August he left, and took up his quarters with Ferdinand
in a new house in the Neue Wieden suburb, then known as

---

[1] Jenger's and Traweger's letters, K.H. 416, 427, 431, etc.
[2] Letters, K.H. 437 (ii. 124), etc.

No. 694 Firmian, or Lumpert,[1] or Neugebaute Gasse, now (1881) No. 6 Kettenbrücken Gasse; a long house with three rows of nine windows in front; a brown sloping tiled roof; an entry in the middle to a quadrangle behind; a quiet, clean, inoffensive place.[2] Here, on the second floor, to the right hand, lived Schubert for the last five weeks of his life, and his death is commemorated by a stone tablet over the entry, placed there by the Männergesang Verein in November 1869, and containing these words : — ' In diesem Hause starb am 19 November 1828 der Tondichter Franz Schubert ' : — In this house died on November 19, 1828, the composer Franz Schubert. Ferdinand had removed there, and Franz, perhaps to help his brother with the rent, went there too. He made the move with the concurrence of his doctor, von Rinna, in the hope that as it was nearer the country — it was just over the river in the direction of the Belvedere — Schubert would be able to reach fresh air and exercise more easily than he could from the heart of the city. The old attacks of giddiness and blood to the head had of late been frequent, and soon after taking up his new quarters he became seriously unwell. However, this was so far relieved that at the beginning of October he made a short walking tour with Ferdinand and two other friends to Ueber-Waltersdorf, and thence to Haydn's old residence and grave at Eisenstadt, some 25 miles from Vienna. It took them three days, and during that time he was very careful as to eating and drinking, regained his old cheerfulness, and was often very gay. Still he was far from well, and after his return the bad symptoms revived, to the great alarm of his friends. At length, on the evening of October 31, while at supper at the Rothes Kreuz in the Himmelpfortgrund, an eating-house much frequented by himself and his friends, he took some fish on his plate, but at the first mouthful threw down the knife and fork, and exclaimed that it tasted like poison. From that moment hardly anything but medicine passed his lips; but he still walked a good deal. About this time Lachner returned from Pesth in all the glory of the success of his opera; and though only in Vienna for a few days, he called on his friend, and they had two hours' conversation. Schubert was full of plans for

---

[1] K.H. 453 note.

[2] It is quite a musical spot. ' Franz Haydn ' has a shop for comestibles at the corner of the next house to Schubert's.

the future, especially for the completion of ' Graf von Gleichen,' which, as already mentioned, he had sketched in the summer of 1827. He discussed it also with Bauernfeld during the next few days, and spoke of the brilliant style in which he intended to score it. About this time Carl Holz, Beethoven's old friend, at Schubert's urgent request, took him to hear the great master's C♯ minor Quartet, still a novelty in Vienna. It agitated him extremely. ' He got (says Holz) into such a state of excitement and enthusiasm that we were all afraid for him.' [1] On the 3rd November, the morrow of All Souls' day, he walked early in the morning to Hernals — then a village, now a thickly built suburb outside the Gürtelstrasse — to hear his brother's Latin Requiem in the church there. He thought it simple, and at the same time effective, and on the whole was much pleased with it. After the service he walked for three hours, and on reaching home complained of great weariness.

Shortly before this time the scores of Handel's oratorios had come into his hands — not impossibly some of the set of Arnold's edition given to Beethoven before his death, and sold in his sale for 102 florins; and the study of them had brought home to him his deficiencies in the department of counterpoint. ' I see now,' said he [2] to the Fröhlichs, ' how much I have still to learn; but I am going to work hard with Sechter, and make up for lost time ' — Sechter being the recognized authority of the day on counterpoint. So much was he bent on this, that on the day after his walk to Hernals, i.e. on November 4, notwithstanding his weakness, he went into Vienna and, with another musician named Lanz, called on Sechter, to consult him on the matter, and they actually decided on Marpurg as the text-book, and on the number and dates of the lessons. [3] But he never began the course. During the next few days he grew weaker and weaker; and when the doctor was called in, it was too late. About the 11th he wrote a note [4] to Schober — doubtless his last letter.

DEAR SCHOBER,
    I am ill. I have eaten and drunk nothing for eleven days, and am so tired and shaky that I can only get from the bed to the chair,

[1] Quoted by Nohl, *Beethoven*, iii, 964. Holz says it was the last music that poor Schubert heard, Ferdinand claims the same for his Requiem. At any rate, both were very near the end.
    [2] Kreissle's *Sketch*, p. 152.   [3] K.H. 451 (ii. 138), expressly on Sechter's authority.
    [4] Given by Bauernfeld, in *Die Presse*, Apr. 21, 1869.

and back.   Rinna is attending me.   If I taste anything, I bring it up again directly.

In this distressing condition, be so kind as to help me to some reading.   Of Cooper's I have read the Last of the Mohicans, the Spy, the Pilot, and the Pioneers.   If you have anything else of his, I entreat you to leave it with Frau von Bogner at the Coffee house. My brother, who is conscientiousness itself, will bring it to me in the most conscientious way.   Or anything else.   Your friend,

SCHUBERT.

What answer Schober made to this appeal is not known.   He is said to have had a daily report of Schubert's condition from the doctor, but there is no mention of his having called.   Spaun, Randhartinger,[1] Bauernfeld, and Josef Hüttenbrunner, are all said to have visited him ; but in those days there was great dread of infection, his new residence was out of the way, and dangerous illness was such a novelty with Schubert that his friends may be excused for not thinking the case so grave as it was.   After a few days Rinna himself fell ill, and his place was filled by a staff-surgeon named Behring.

On the 14th Schubert took to his bed.[2]   He was able to sit up a little for a few days longer, and thus to correct the proofs of the 2nd part of the ' Winterreise,' probably the last occupation of those inspired and busy fingers.   He appears to have had no pain, only increasing weakness, want of sleep, and great depression.   Poor fellow!   no wonder he was depressed! everything was against him, his weakness, his poverty, the dreary house, the long lonely hours, the cheerless future — all concentrated and embodied in the hopeless images of Müller's poems, and the sad gloomy strains in which he has clothed them for ever and ever — the Letzte Hoffnung, the Krähe, the Wegweiser, the Wirthshaus, the Nebensonnen, the Leiermann — all breathing of solitude, broken hopes, illusions, strange omens, poverty, death, the grave!   As he went through the pages, they must have seemed like pictures of his own life ; and such passages as the following, from the Wegweiser (or Signpost), can hardly have failed to strike the dying man as aimed at himself :—

[1] Fräulein Geisler informs me that Ferdinand's wife (still living, 1882) maintains that Randhartinger was the only one who visited him during his illness ; but it is difficult to resist the statements of Bauernfield (*Presse*, Apr. 21, 1869) and of Kreissle's informants, p. 452 (ii. 140).
[2] Ferdinand, in the *Neue Zeitschrift für Musik*, p. 143.

Einen Weiser seh' ich stehen,
Unverrückt vor meinem Blick,
Eine Strasse muss ich gehen,
Die noch keiner ging zurück.

Straight before me stands a signpost,
Steadfast in my very gaze;
'Tis the road none e'er retraces,
'Tis the road that I must tread.

Alas! he was indeed going the road which no one e'er
retraces! On Sunday the 16th the doctors had a consultation;
they predicted a nervous fever, but had still hopes of their
patient. On the afternoon of Monday, Bauernfeld saw him
for the last time. He was in very bad spirits, and complained
of great weakness, and of heat in his head, but his mind was
still clear, and there was no sign of wandering; he spoke of his
earnest wish for a good opera-book. Later in the day, however,
when the doctor arrived, he was quite delirious, and typhus
[typhoid] had unmistakably broken out. The next day,
Tuesday, he was very restless throughout, trying continually to
get out of bed, and constantly fancying himself in a strange
room. That evening he called Ferdinand on to the bed, made
him put his ear close to his mouth, and whispered mysteri-
ously ' What are they doing with me?' ' Dear Franz,' was
the reply, ' they are doing all they can to get you well again,
and the doctor assures us you will soon be right, only you
must do your best to stay in bed.' He returned to the idea in
his wandering — ' I implore you to put me in my own room,
and not to leave me in this corner under the earth; don't I
deserve a place above ground?' ' Dear Franz,' said the
agonised brother, ' be calm; trust your brother Ferdinand,
whom you have always trusted, and who loves you so dearly.
You are in the room which you always had, and lying on your
own bed.' ' No' said the dying man, ' that's not true; Beethoven is not here.' So strongly had the great composer taken
possession of him! An hour or two later the doctor came,
and spoke to him in the same style. Schubert looked him full
in the face and made no answer: but turning round clutched
at the wall with his poor tired hands, and said in a slow earnest
voice, ' Here, here, is my end.' At 3 in the afternoon of
Wednesday the 19th November 1828 he breathed his last, and
his simple earnest soul took its flight from the world. He was
31 years, 9 months, and 19 days old. There never has been

one like him, and there never will be another.

His death, and the letters of the elder Franz and of Ferdi-nand, bring out the family relations in a very pleasant light. The poor pious bereaved father, still at his drudgery as ' school teacher in the Rossau,' ' afflicted, yet strengthened by faith in God and the Blessed Sacraments,' writing to announce the loss of his ' beloved son, Franz Schubert, musician and com-poser ' ; the good innocent Ferdinand, evidently recognised as Franz's peculiar property, clinging to his brother as the one great man he had ever known ; thinking only of him, and of fulfilling his last wish to lie near Beethoven, and ready to sacrifice all his scanty savings to do it — these form a pair of interesting figures. Neither Ignaz nor Carl appear at all in connexion with the event, the father and Ferdinand alone are visible.

The funeral took place on Friday November 21. It was bad weather, but a number of friends and sympathisers assembled. He lay in his coffin, dressed, as the custom then was, like a hermit, with a crown of laurel round his brows. The face was calm, and looked more like sleep than death. By desire of the family Schober was chief mourner. The coffin left the house at half-past two, and was borne by a group of young men, students and others, in red cloaks and flowers, to the little church of S. Joseph in Margarethen, where the funeral service was said, and a motet by Gänsbacher, and a hymn of Schober's, ' Der Friede sey mit dir, du engelreine Seele ' — written that morning in substitution for his own earlier words, to the music of Schubert's ' Pax vobiscum ' — were sung over the coffin. It was then taken to the Ortsfriedhof in the village of Währing, and committed to the ground, three [1] places higher up than the grave of Beethoven. In ordinary course he would have been buried in the cemetery at Matzleinsdorf, but the appeal which he made almost with his dying breath was naturally a law to the tender heart of Ferdinand, and through his piety and self-denial his dear brother rests, if not next, yet near to the great musician, whom he so deeply reverenced and admired. Late in the afternoon Wilhelm von Chézy, son of the authoress of ' Euryanthe' and 'Rosamunde,' who though not in Schubert's intimate circle was yet one of his acquaintances,

---

[1] Next to Beethoven comes ' Freiherr von Wsserd [Wssehrd] '; then ' Joh. Graf O'Donel and Gräfin O'Donnell [sic],' and then Schubert.

by some accident remembered that he had not seen him for
many months, and he walked down to Bogner's coffee-house,
where the composer was usually to be found between 5 and 7,
smoking his pipe and joking with his friends, and where the
Cooper's novels mentioned in his note to Schober were not
improbably still waiting for him. He found the little room
almost empty, and the familiar round table deserted. On
entering he was accosted by the waiter — 'Your honour is
soon back from the funeral!' 'Whose funeral?' said Chézy
in astonishment. 'Franz Schubert's,' replied the waiter, 'he
died two days ago, and is buried this afternoon.' [1]

He left no will. The official inventory [2] of his possessions
at the time of his death, in which he is described as 'Tonkünstler und Compositeur' — musician and composer — is as
follows: — 'Three dress coats, 3 walking coats, 10 pairs of
trowsers, 9 waistcoats — together worth 37 florins; 1 hat,
5 pairs of shoes and 2 of boots — valued at 2 florins; 4 shirts,
9 cravats and pocket handkerchiefs, 13 pairs of socks, 1 towel,
1 sheet, 2 bed-cases — 8 florins; 1 mattress, 1 bolster, 1 quilt
— 6 florins; a quantity of old music valued at 10 florins — 63
florins (say £2 : 10s.) in all. Beyond the above there were no
effects.' Is it possible, then, that in the 'old music, valued at
8s. 6d.,' are included the whole of his unpublished manuscripts?
Where else could they be but in the house he was inhabiting?

The expenses of the illness and funeral, though the latter is
especially mentioned as 'second class,' amounted in all to
269 silver florins, 19 kr. (say £27) — a heavy sum for people
in the poverty of Ferdinand and his father. Of this the preliminary service cost 84 fl. 35 kr.; the burial 44 fl. 45 kr.; and
the ground 70 fl.; leaving the rest for the doctor's fees and
incidental disbursements. Illness and death were truly expensive luxuries in those days.

On the 27th November the Kirchen-musikverein performed
Mozart's Requiem in his honour; and on December 23 a
requiem by Anselm Hüttenbrenner was given in the Augustine
church. On the 14th December his early Symphony in C,
No. 6, was played at the Gesellschafts concert, and again on
March 12, 1829. At Linz on Christmas Day there was a funeral

---

[1] Wilhelm von Chézy, *Erinnerungen aus meinem Leben* (1863), 182, 183.
[2] Given at length by Kreissle (p. 457) — but entirely omitted in the translation
—and materially misquoted by Gumprecht (p. 15).

ceremony with speeches and music. Articles in his honour
appeared in the 'Wiener Zeitschrift' of December 25 (by von
Zedlitz), in the 'Theaterzeitung' of Vienna of the 20th and
27th (by Blahetka); in the Vienna 'Zeitschrift für Kunst' of
June 9, 11, 13, 1829 (by Bauernfeld); in the Vienna 'Archiv
für Geschichte' (by Mayrhofer); and memorial poems were
published by Seidl, Schober and others. On January 30, 1829,
a concert was given by the arrangement of Anna Fröhlich in
the hall of the Musikverein; the programme included
'Miriam,' and consisted entirely of Schubert's music, excepting a set of flute variations by Gabrielsky, and the first Finale in
'Don Juan'; and the crowd was so great that the performance
had to be repeated shortly afterwards. The proceeds of these
concerts and the subscriptions of a few friends sufficed to erect
the monument which now stands at the back of the grave. It
was carried out by Anna Fröhlich, Grillparzer, and Jenger.
The bust was by Franz Dialler [Josef Alois Dialer], and the
cost of the whole was 360 silver florins, 46 kr. The inscription [1]
is from the pen of Grillparzer : —

DIE TONKUNST BEGRUB HIER EINEN REICHEN BESITZ
ABER NOCH VIEL SCHOENERE HOFFNUNGEN.
FRANZ SCHUBERT LIEGT HIER.
GEBOREN AM XXXI. JÆNNER MDCCXCVII.
GESTORBEN AM XIX. NOV. MDCCCXXVIII.
XXXI JAHRE ALT.

MUSIC HAS HERE ENTOMBED A RICH TREASURE,
BUT STILL FAIRER HOPES.
FRANZ SCHUBERT LIES HERE.
BORN JAN. 31, 1797;
DIED NOV. 19, 1828,
31 YEARS OLD.

The allusion to fairer hopes has been much criticised, but
surely without reason. When we remember in how many
departments of music Schubert's latest productions were his
best, we are undoubtedly warranted in believing that he would
have gone on progressing for many years, had it been the will
of God to spare him.

In 1863, owing to the state of dilapidation at which the
graves of both Beethoven and Schubert had arrived, the repair

[1] We have given the inscription exactly as it stands on the monument. Kreissle's
version (463), followed by Gumprecht and others, is incorrect in almost every line.

of the tombs, and the exhumation and reburial of both, were undertaken by the Gesellschaft der Musikfreunde. The operation was begun on the 12th October and completed on the 13th. The opportunity was embraced of taking a cast and a photograph of Schubert's skull, and of measuring the principal bones of both skeletons. The lengths in Schubert's case were to those in Beethoven's as 27 to 29,[1] which implies that as Beethoven was 5 ft. 5 in. high, he was only 5 ft. and $\frac{1}{2}$ an inch.

Various memorials have been set up to him in Vienna. The tablets on the houses in which he was born and died have been noticed. They were both carried out by the Männergesang Verein, and completed, the former October 7, 1858, the latter in November 1869. The same Society erected by subscription a monument to him in the Stadt Park; a sitting figure in Carrara marble by Carl Kuntmann, with the inscription ' Franz Schubert, seinem Andenken der Wiener Männergesangverein, 1872.' It cost 42,000 florins, and was unveiled May 15, 1872.

Outside of Austria his death created at first but little sensation. Robert Schumann, then 18, is said to have been deeply affected, and to have burst into tears when the news reached him at Leipzig; Mendelssohn too, though unlike Schubert in temperament, circumstances and education, doubtless fully estimated his loss; and Rellstab, Anna Milder, and others in Berlin who knew him, must have mourned him deeply; but the world at large did not yet know enough of his works to understand either what it possessed or what it had lost in that modest reserved young musician of 31. But Death always brings a man, especially a young man, into notoriety, and increases public curiosity about his works: and so it was now; the stream of publication at once began, and is even yet flowing, neither the supply of works nor the eagerness to obtain them having ceased. The world has not yet recovered from its astonishment as, one after another, the stores accumulated in those dusty heaps of music paper (valued at 8s. 6d.) were made public, each so astonishingly fresh, copious, and different from the last. As songs, masses, part-songs, operas, chamber-music of all sorts and all dimensions — pianoforte sonatas, im-

---

[1] See *Actenmässige Darstellung der Augsrabung und Weiderbeeinsetzung der irdischen Reste von Beethoven und Schubert.* Vienna, Gerold, 1863.

promptus and fantasias, duets, trios, quartets, quintet, octet, issued from the press or were heard in manuscript; as each season brought its new symphony, overture, entr'acte, or ballet music, people began to be staggered by the amount. 'A deep shade of suspicion,' said a leading musical periodical in 1839, 'is beginning to be cast over the authenticity of posthumous compositions. All Paris has been in a state of amazement at the posthumous diligence of the song-writer, F. Schubert, who, while one would think that his ashes repose in peace in Vienna, is still making eternal new songs.' We know better now, but it must be confessed that the doubt was not so unnatural then.

Of the MS. music — an incredible quantity, of which no one then knew the amount or the particulars, partly because there was so much of it, partly because Schubert concealed, or rather forgot, a great deal of his work — a certain number of songs and pianoforte pieces were probably in the hands of publishers at the time of his death, but the great bulk was in the possession of Ferdinand, as his heir. A set of 4 songs (op. 105) was issued on the day of his funeral. Other songs — ops. 101, 104, 106, 110-112, 116-118; and two pianoforte duets, the Fantasia in F minor (op. 103) and the 'Grand Rondeau' (op. 107) — followed up to April 1829. But the first important publication was the well-known 'Schwanengesang,' so entitled by Haslinger — a collection of 14 songs, 7 by Rellstab, 6 by Heine, and 1 by Seidl — unquestionably Schubert's last. They were issued in May 1829, and, to judge by the lists of arrangements and editions given by Nottebohm, have been as much appreciated as the Schöne Müllerin or the Winterreise. A stream of songs followed — for which we must refer the student to Mr. Nottebohm's catalogue. The early part [1] of 1830 saw the execution of a bargain between Diabelli and Ferdinand, by which that firm was guaranteed the property of the following works : — op. 1-32, 35, 39-59, 62, 63, 64, 66-69, 71-77, 84-88, 92-99, 101-104, 106, 108, 109, 113, 115, 116, 119, 121-124, 127, 128, 130, 132-140, 142-153; also 154 songs; 14 vocal quartets; the canons of 1813; a cantata in C for 3

---

[1] The list which follows is taken from Kreissle, p. 566 (ii. 245), who apparently had the original document before him. The only date given by Kreissle is 1830, but it must have been early in that year, since op. 121, which forms part of the bargain, was issued in February. Some of the numbers in the list had already been issued as the property of the publishers.

voices; the Hymn to the Holy Ghost; Klopstock's Stabat Mater in F minor, and Grosses Halleluja; Magnificat in C; the String Quintet in C; 4 string quartets in C, B♭, G, B♭; a string trio in B♭; 2 sonatas in A and A minor, variations in F, an Adagio in D♭, and Allegretto in C♯ — all for pianoforte solo; Sonata for pianoforte and Arpeggione; Sonata in A, and Fantasie in C — both for pianoforte and violin; Rondo in A for violin and quartet; Adagio and Rondo in F, for pianoforte and quartet; a concert-piece in D for violin and orchestra; Overture in D for orchestra; Overture to 3rd Act of the ' Zauberharfe '; Lazarus; a Tantum ergo in E♭ for 4 voices and orchestra; an Offertorium in B♭ for tenor solo, chorus and orchestra.

Another large portion of Ferdinand's possessions came, sooner or later, into the hands of Dr. Eduard Schneider, son of Franz's sister Theresia. They comprised the autographs of Symphonies 1, 2, 3, and 6, and copies of 4 and 5; autographs of operas: — the ' Teufel's Lustschloss,' ' Fernando,' ' Der Vierjährige Posten,' ' Die Freunde von Salamanka,' ' Die Bürgschaft,' ' Fierabras,' and ' Sakontala '; the Mass in F; and the original orchestral parts of the whole of the music to ' Rosamunde.' The greater part of these are now (1882) safe in the possession of Herr Nicholas Dumba of Vienna.

On July 10, 1830, Diabelli began the issue of what was termed Schubert's 'Musical Remains' (*musikalischer Nachlass*), though confined to songs; and continued it at intervals till 1850, by which time 50 Parts (*Lieferungen*), containing 137 songs, had appeared. In 1830 he also issued the two astonishing 4-hand marches (op. 121); and a set of 20 waltzes (op. 127); whilst other houses published the pianoforte Sonatas in A and E♭ (op. 120, 122); two string quartets of the year 1824 (op. 125); the D minor Quartet, etc. For the progress of the publication after this date we must again refer the reader to Mr. Nottebohm's invaluable Thematic Catalogue (Vienna, Schreiber, 1874), which contains every detail, and may be implicitly relied on; merely mentioning the principal works, and the year of publication: — Miriam, Mass in B♭, 3 last Sonatas and the Grand Duo, 1838; Symphony in C, 1840; Phantasie in C, pianoforte and violin, 1850; Quartet in G, 1852; Quintet in C, and Octet, 1854; Gesang der Geister, 1858; Verschworenen, 1862; Mass in E♭, 1865; Lazarus, 1866;

Symphony in B minor, 1867; Mass in A♭, 1875.

No complete critical edition of Schubert's works has yet been undertaken. Of the pianoforte pieces and songs there are numberless publications, for which the reader is referred to Mr. Nottebohm's Thematic Catalogue. Of the songs two collections may be signalised as founded on the order of opus numbers : — that of Senff of Leipzig, edited by Julius Rietz, 361 songs in 20 volumes, and that of Litolff of Brunswick — songs in 10 volumes. But neither of these, though styled 'complete,' are so. For instance, each omits ops. 83, 110, 129, 165, 172, 173; the 6 songs published by Müller, the 40 by Gotthard; and Litolff also omits ops. 21, 60. Still, as the nearest to completeness, these have been used as the basis of List No. I. at the end of this article.*

Schumann's visit to Vienna in the late autumn of 1838 formed an epoch in the history of the Schubert music. He saw the immense heap of MSS. which remained in Ferdinand's hands even after the mass bought by Diabelli had been taken away, and amongst them several symphonies. Such sympathy and enthusiasm as his must have been a rare delight to the poor desponding brother. His eagle eye soon discovered the worth of these treasures. He picked out several works to be recommended to publishers, but meantime one beyond all the rest riveted his attention — the great symphony of March 1828 (was it the autograph, not yet deposited in the safe-keeping of the Gesellschaft der Musikfreunde, or a copy?) and he arranged with Ferdinand to send a transcript of it to Leipzig to Mendelssohn for the Gewandhaus concerts, where it was produced March 21, 1839,[1] and repeated no less than 3 times during the following season. His chamber music was becoming gradually known in the North, and as early as 1833 is occasionally met with in the Berlin and Leipzig programmes. David, who led the taste in chamber music at the latter place, was devoted to Schubert. He gradually introduced his works, until there were few seasons in which the Quartets in A minor, D minor (the score of which he edited for Senff), and G, the String Quintet

* [Omitted in this edition. This list has been superseded by the publication of the complete edition of Schubert's works between 1885–97.].

[1] Mar. 22 in the *Allg. Mus. Zeitung.* Mar. 21 in Schumann's paper. Misled by the former the date is given in the biography of Mendelssohn as the 22nd. The reader will please correct this. The Symphony was repeated Dec. 12, 1839, Mar. 12 and Apr. 3, 1840. Mendelssohn made a few cuts in the work for performance.

SCHUBERT

SCHUBERT   219

in C (a special favourite), the Octet, both Trios, the Pianoforte
Quintet, and the Rondeau brillant, were not performed amid
great applause, at his concerts. Schumann had long been a
zealous Schubert propagandist. From an early date his *Zeitschrift*
contains articles of more or less length, always inspired by an
ardent admiration; Schubert's letters and poems and his
brother's excellent short sketch of his life, printed in vol. x
(Ap. 23 to May 3, 1839) — obvious fruits of Schumann's Vienna
visit — are indispensable materials for Schubert's biography;
when the Symphony was performed he dedicated to it one of
his longest and most genial effusions,[1] and each fresh piece was
greeted with a hearty welcome as it fell from the press. One
of Schumann's especial favourites was the E♭ Trio; he liked it
even better than that in B♭, and has left a memorandum of
his fondness in the opening of the Adagio of his Symphony in
C, which is identical, in key and intervals, with that of Schubert's Andante. The enthusiasm of these prominent musicians,
the repeated performances of the Symphony, and its publication by Breitkopfs (in January 1850), naturally gave Schubert
a strong hold on Leipzig, at that time the most active musical
centre of Europe; and after the foundation of the Conservatorium in 1843 many English and American students must
have carried back the love of his romantic and tuneful music to
their own countries.

Several performances of large works had taken place in
Vienna since Schubert's death, chiefly through the exertions of
Ferdinand, and of a certain Leitermayer, one of Franz's early
friends; such as the E♭ Mass at the parish church of Maria
Trost on November 15, 1829; Miriam, with Lachner's orchestration, at a Gesellschaft concert in 1830; two new overtures
in 1833; an overture in E, the Chorus of Spirits from Rosamunde, the Grosses Halleluja, etc., early in 1835, and four large
concerted pieces from Fierabras later in the year; an overture
in D; the finale of the last Symphony; a march and chorus,
and an air and chorus, from Fierabras, in April 1836; another
new overture, and several new compositions from the
'Remains,' in the winter of 1837–8. As far as can be judged
by the silence of the Vienna newspapers these passed almost

---

[1] *Ges. Schriften*, iii. 195. Schumann's expressions leave no doubt that the
Symphony in C was in Ferdinand's possession at the time of his visit. This
and many other of his articles on Schubert have been translated into English
by Miss M. E. von Glehn and Mrs. Ritter.

unnoticed. Even the competition with North Germany failed to produce the effect which might have been expected. It did indeed excite the Viennese to one effort. On the 15th of the December following the production of the Symphony at Leipzig its performance was attempted at Vienna, but though the whole work was announced,[1] such had been the difficulties at rehearsal that the first two movements alone were given, and they were only carried off by the interpolation of an air from ' Lucia ' between them.

But symphonies and symphonic works can hardly be expected to float rapidly ; songs are more buoyant, and Schubert's songs soon began to make their way outside, as they had long since done in his native place. Wherever they once penetrated their success was certain. In Paris, where spirit, melody, and romance are the certain criterions of success, and where nothing dull or obscure is tolerated, they were introduced by Nourrit, and were so much liked as actually to find a transient place in the programmes of the concerts of the Conservatoire, the stronghold of musical Toryism.[2] The first French collection was published in 1834, by Richault, with translation by Bélanger. It contained 6 songs — Die Post, Ständchen, Am Meer, Das Fischermädchen, Der Tod und das Mädchen, and Schlummerlied. The Erl King and others followed. A larger collection, with translation by Emil [Émile] Deschamps, was issued by Brandus in 1838 or 39. It is entitled ' Collection des Lieder de Franz Schubert,' and contains 16 — La jeune religieuse ; Marguérite ; Le roi des aulnes ; La rose ; La sérénade ; La poste ; Ave Maria ; La cloche des agonisants ; La jeune fille et la mort ; Rosemonde ; Les plaintes de la jeune fille ; Adieu ; Les astres ; La jeune mère ; La berceuse ; Eloge des larmes.[3] Except that one — Adieu [4] — is spurious, the selection does great credit to Parisian taste. This led the

[1] The MS. parts in the possession of the Musik Verein show the most cruel cuts, possibly with a view to this performance. In the Finale, one of the most essential and effective sections of the movement is clean expunged.
[2] ' La jeune Religieuse ' and ' Le roi des Aulnes ' were sung by Nourrit, at the concerts of Jan. 18 and Apr. 26, 1835, respectively — the latter with orchestral accompaniment. On March 20, 1836, Marguérite was sung by Mlle. Falcon, and there the list stops. Schubert's name has never again appeared in these programmes, to any piece, vocal or instrumental.
[3] This list is copied from the Paris correspondence of the A.M.Z., 1839, p. 394.
[4] This song is made up of phrases from Schubert's songs, and will probably always be attributed to him. It stands even in Pauer's edition. But it is by A. H. von Weyrauch, who published it himself in 1824. See Nottebohm's Catalogue, p. 254.

way to the ' Quarante mélodies de Schubert ' of Richault,
Launer, etc., a thin octavo volume, to which many an English
amateur is indebted for his first acquaintance with these
treasures of life. By 1845 Richault had published as many as
150 with French words.

Some of the chamber music also soon obtained a certain
popularity in Paris, through the playing of Tilmant, Urhan,
and Alkan, and later of Alard and Franchomme. The Trio
in B♭, issued by Richault in 1838, was the first instrumental
work of Schubert's published in France. There is a ' Collection
complète ' of the solo pianoforte works, published by Richault
in octavo, containing the Fantaisie (op. 15), 10 sonatas,
the two Russian marches, Impromptus, Momens musicals
[Moments musicaux] 5 single pieces, and 9 sets of dances.
Liszt and Heller kept the flame alive by their transcriptions of
the songs and waltzes. But beyond this the French hardly
know more of Schubert now than they did then ; none of his
large works have become popular with them. Habeneck
attempted to rehearse the Symphony in C (No. 10) in 1842,
but the band refused to go beyond the first movement, and
Schubert's name up to this date (1881) appears in the programmes of the concerts of the Conservatoire attached to three
songs only. M. Pasdeloup has introduced the Symphony in
C and the fragments of that in B minor, but they have taken
no hold on the Parisian amateurs.

Liszt's devotion to Schubert has been great and unceasing.
We have already mentioned his production of Alfonso and
Estrella at Weimar in 1854, but it is right to give a list of his
transcriptions, which have done a very great deal to introduce
Schubert into many quarters where his compositions would
otherwise have been a sealed book. His first transcription —
Die Rose, op. 73 — was made in 1834,[1] and appeared in Paris
the same year. It was followed in 1838 by the Ständchen,
Post, and Lob der Thränen, and in 1839 by the Erl King and
by 12 Lieder. These again by 6 Lieder ; 4 Geistliche Lieder ;
6 of the Müllerlieder ; the Schwanengesang, and the Winterreise. Liszt has also transcribed the Divertissement à la
hongroise, 3 Marches and 9 ' Valses-caprices,' or ' Soirées de

---

[1] These particulars are taken partly from Miss Ramann's Life of Liszt, and
partly from Liszt's Thematic Catalogue. The third No. of the ' Apparitions '
is founded on a Waltz melody of Schubert's.

Vienne,' after Schubert's op. 67. All the above are for pianoforte solo. He has also scored the accompaniment to the Junge
Nonne, Gretchen am Spinnrade, So lasst mich scheinen, and
the Erl King, for a small orchestra ; has adapted the Allmacht
for tenor solo, male chorus, and orchestra, and has converted
the Fantasie in C (op. 15) into a concerto for pianoforte and
orchestra. Some will think these changes indefensible, but
there is no doubt that they are done in a masterly manner,
and that many of them have become very popular.—Heller's
arrangements are confined to 6 favourite songs.

England made an appearance in the field with 2 songs,
' The Letter of flowers ' and ' The Secret,' which were published by Mr. Ayrton in 1836 in the Musical Library, to
Oxenford's translation. Mr. Wessel (Ashdown & Parry) had
begun his ' Series of German Songs ' earlier than this, and by
1840, out of a total of 197, the list included 38 of Schubert's,
remarkably well chosen, and including several of the finest
though less known ones, *e.g.* Ganymed, An den Tod, Sei mir
gegrüsst, Die Rose, etc., etc. Ewer's ' Gems of German Song,'
containing many of Schubert's, were begun in 1836 [September
1837]. Schubert's music took a long time before it obtained
any public footing in this country. The first time it appears
in the Philharmonic programmes — then so ready to welcome
novelties — is on May 20, 1839, when Ivanoff sang the Serenade
in the Schwanengesang to Italian words, ' Quando avvolto.'
Staudigl gave the Wanderer, May 8, 1843. On June 10, 1844,
the Overture to Fierabras was played under Mendelssohn's
direction, and on June 17 the Junge Nonne was sung to French
words by M. de Revial, Mendelssohn playing the magnificent
accompaniment. We blush to say, however, that neither piece
met with approval. The leading critic says that ' the overture
is literally beneath criticism : perhaps a more overrated man
never existed than this same Schubert.' His dictum on the
song is even more unfortunate. He tells us that ' it is a very
good exemplification of much ado about nothing — as un-
meaningly mysterious as could be desired by the most devoted
lover of bombast.' Mendelssohn conducted the last five Philharmonic concerts of that season (1844) ; and amongst other
orchestral music new to England had brought with him
Schubert's Symphony in C, and his own overture to Ruy Blas.
At the rehearsal, however, the behaviour of the band towards

the symphony — excited, it is said, by the continual triplets
in the Finale — was so insulting that he refused either to go
on with it or to allow his own overture to be tried.[1] But the
misbehaviour of our leading orchestra did not produce the
effect which it had done in Paris; others were found to take
up the treasures thus rudely rejected, and Schubert has had an
ample revenge. The centres for his music in England have
been — for the orchestral and choral works, the Crystal Palace,
Sydenham, and Mr. Charles Hallé's Concerts, Manchester;
and for the chamber music, the Monday and Saturday Popular
Concerts and Mr. Hallé's Recitals. At the Crystal Palace
the Symphony in C (No. 10) has been in the répertoire of
the Saturday Concerts since April 5, 1856; the two movements of the B minor Symphony were first played April 6,
1867, and have been constantly repeated. The 6 other MS.
symphonies were obtained from Dr. Schneider in 1867 and
since, and have been played at various dates, a performance
of the whole eight in chronological order forming a feature in
the series of 1880–81. The Rosamunde music was first played
November 10, 1866, and has been frequently repeated since.
Joachim's orchestration of the Grand Duo (op. 140) was given
March 4, 1876. The overtures to Alfonso and Estrella, Fierabras, Freunde von Salamanka, Teufels Lustschloss, and that
'in the Italian style' are continually heard. Miriam's song
was first given November 14, 1868 (and three times since);
the Conspirators, March 2, 1872; the 23rd Psalm, Feb. 21,
1874; the Eb Mass, March 29, 1879. At the Popular Concerts
a beginning was made May 16, 1859, with the A minor Quartet,
the D major Sonata, and the Rondeau brillant. Since then
the D minor and G major Quartets, many sonatas and other
pianoforte pieces have been added, and the Octet, the Quintet
in C, and the two Trios are repeated season by season, and
enthusiastically received. The Quartet in Bb, a MS. trio in the
same key, the Sonata for pianoforte and Arpeggione, etc. have
been brought to a hearing. A large number of songs are familiar

[1] Even 15 years later, when played at the Musical Society of London, the
same periodical that we have already quoted says of it, 'The ideas throughout
it are all of a minute character, and the instrumentation is of a piece with the
ideas. There is no breadth, there is no grandeur, there is no dignity in either;
clearness, and contrast, and beautiful finish are always apparent, but the orchestra,
though loud, is never massive and sonorous, and the music, though always correct,
is never serious or imposing.' Is it possible for criticism to be more hopelessly
wrong?

to the subscribers to these concerts through the fine interpreta-
tion of Stockhausen, Mme. Joachim, Miss Regan, Miss Sophie
Löwe, Mr. Santley, Mr. Henschel, and other singers. At
Mr. Hallé's admirable recitals at St. James's Hall, since their
commencement in 1863 all the published sonatas have been
repeatedly played ; not only the popular ones, but of those less
known none have been given less than twice ; the Fantasia in
C, op. 15, three times ; the pianoforte Quintet, the Fantasia for
pianoforte and Violin, the Impromptus and Momens musicals,
the ' 5 pieces,' the ' 3 pieces,' the Adagio and Rondo, the
Valses nobles, and other numbers of this fascinating music have
been heard again and again.

The other principal publications in England are the vocal
scores of the six Masses, the pianoforte accompaniment arranged
from the full score by Ebenezer Prout, published by Augener
& Co. — the 1st, 2nd, 3rd, 4th in 1871, the 6th (E♭) in 1872,
and the 5th (A♭) in 1875.[1] The Masses have been also published
by Novellos, both with Latin and English words (' Communion
Service ') ; and the same firm has published Miriam, in two
forms, and the Rosamunde music, both vocal score and orchestral parts. Messrs. Augener have also published editions of the
pianoforte works, and of a large number of songs, by Pauer.

Schubert was not sufficiently important during his lifetime
to attract the attention of painters, and although he had more
than one artist in his circle, there are but three [contemporary]
portraits of him known [six, or ten if groups are included].
1. A poor stiff head by Leopold Kupelwieser, full face, taken
July 10, 1821, photographed by Mietke [Miedke] and Wawra
of Vienna, and wretchedly engraved as the frontispiece to
Kreissle's biography. 2. A very characteristic half-length,
3-quarter-face, in water colours, by W. A. Rieder, taken in
1825, and now in possession of Dr. Granitsch of Vienna.[2] A
replica by the artist, dated 1840, is now in the Musik-Verein.
It has been engraved by Passini, and we here give the head,
from a photograph expressly taken from the original. 3. The
bust on the tomb, which gives a very prosaic version of his
features.

His exterior by no means answered to his genius. His
general appearance was insignificant. As we have already said,

[1] Reviewed by Mr. E. Prout in *Concordia* for 1875, pp. 8, 29, 109, etc.
[2] He bought it in Feb. 1881 for 1,205 florins, or about 120*l*. It is about
8 inches high, by 6 wide.

he was probably not more
than 5 feet and 1 inch high,
his figure was stout and
clumsy, with a round back
and shoulders (perhaps due
to incessant writing), fleshy
arms, and thick short fingers. His complexion was
pasty, nay even tallowy ; his
cheeks were full, his eye-
brows bushy, and his nose
insignificant. But there were
two things that to a great extent redeemed these insignificant traits—his hair, which
was black [? brown] and re-

markably thick and vigorous,[1] as if rooted in the brain within ;
and his eyes, which were truly ' the windows of his soul,' and
even through the spectacles he constantly wore were so bright
as at once to attract attention.[2] If Rieder's portrait may be
trusted — and it is said to be very faithful, though perhaps a
little too *fine* — they had a peculiarly steadfast penetrating look,
which irresistibly reminds one of the firm rhythm of his music.
His glasses are inseparable from his face. One of our earliest
glimpses of him is ' a little boy in spectacles ' at the *Convict* ;
he habitually slept in them ; and within 18 months of his
death we see him standing in the window at Döbling, his glasses
pushed up over his forehead, and Grillparzer's verses held close
to his searching eyes. He had the broad strong jaw of all great
men, and a marked assertive prominence of the lips. When at
rest the expression of his face was uninteresting, but it bright-
ened up at the mention of music, especially that of Beethoven.
His voice was something between a soft tenor and a baritone.
He sang ' like a composer,' without the least affectation or
attempt.[3]

His general disposition was in accordance with his counte-
nance. His sensibility, though his music shows it was extreme,

[1] All three portraits agree in this. An eminent surgeon of our own day is
accustomed to say, ' Never trust a man with a great head of black hair, he is
sure to be an enthusiast.'

[2] W. v. Chézy, *Erinnerungen*—' with eyes so brilliant as at the first glance
to betray the fire within.'

[3] Bauernfeld.

was not roused by the small things of life. He had little of that jealous susceptibility which too often distinguishes musicians, more irritable even than the 'irritable race of poets.' His attitude towards Rossini and Weber proves this. When a post which he much coveted was given to another,[1] he expressed his satisfaction at its being bestowed on so competent a man. Transparent truthfulness, good-humour, a cheerful contented evenness, fondness for a joke, and a desire to remain in the background — such were his prominent characteristics in ordinary life. But we have seen how this apparently impassive man could be moved by a poem which appealed to him, or by such music as Beethoven's C♯ minor Quartet.[2] This unfailing good-nature, this sweet lovableness, doubtless enhanced by his reserve, was what attached Schubert to his friends. They admired him; but they loved him still more. Ferdinand perfectly adored him, and even the derisive Ignaz melts when he takes leave.[3] Hardly a letter from Schwind, Schober, or Bauernfeld, that does not amply testify to this. Their only complaint is that he will not return their passion, that 'the affection of years is not enough to overcome his distrust and fear of seeing himself appreciated and beloved.'[4] Even strangers who met him in this *entourage* were as much captivated as his friends. J. A. Berg of Stockholm, who was in Vienna in 1827, as a young man of 24, and met him at the Bogners, speaks of him [5] with the clinging affection which such personal charm inspires.

He was a born *bourgeois*, never really at his ease except among his equals and chosen associates. When with them he was genial and compliant. At the dances of his friends he would extemporise the most lovely waltzes for hours together, or accompany song after song. He was even boisterous — playing the Erl King on a comb, fencing, howling, and making many practical jokes. But in good society he was shy and silent, his face grave; a word of praise distressed him, he would repel the admiration when it came, and escape into the next room, or out of the house, at the first possible moment. In consequence he was overlooked, and of his important friends few knew, or showed that they knew, what a treasure they had

[1] Weigl.
[2] See pages 135, 209.
[3] K.H. 149 (i. 151).
[4] Schwind, in K.H. 345 (ii. 28).
[5] In a letter to the writer.

within their reach. A great player like Boklet, after performing
the B♭ Trio, could kneel to kiss the composer's hand in rapture,
and with broken voice stammer forth his homage, but there is
no trace of such tribute from the upper classes. What a contrast to Beethoven's position among his aristocratic friends
— their devotion and patience, his contemptuous behaviour,
the amount of pressing necessary to make him play, his scorn
of emotion, and love of applause after he had finished! (See
p. 19.) The same contrast is visible in the dedications of the
music of the two — Beethoven's chiefly to crowned heads and
nobility, Schubert's in large proportion to his friends. It is also
evident in the music itself, as we shall endeavour presently to
bring out.

He played, as he sang, ' like a composer,' that is, with less
of *technique* than of knowledge and expression. Of the virtuoso
he had absolutely nothing. He improvised in the intervals of
throwing on his clothes, or at other times when the music
within was too strong to be resisted, but as an exhibition or
performance never, and there is no record of his playing any
music but his own. He occasionally accompanied his songs at
concerts (always keeping very strict time), but we never hear
of his having extemporised or played a piece in public in Vienna.
Notwithstanding the shortness of his fingers, which sometimes
got tired,[1] he could play most of his own pieces, and with such
force and beauty as to compel a musician [2] who was listening
to one of his latest sonatas to exclaim, ' I admire your playing
more than your music,' an exclamation susceptible of two
interpretations, of which Schubert is said to have taken the
unfavourable one. But accompaniment was his *forte*, and of
this we have already spoken (see pp. 181, 193). Duet-playing
was a favourite recreation with him. Schober, Gahy, and
others, were his companions in this, and Gahy has left on record
his admiration of the clean rapid playing, the bold conception
and perfect grasp of expression, and the clever droll remarks
that would drop from him during the piece.

His life as a rule was regular, even monotonous. He composed or studied habitually for six or seven hours every morning. This was one of the methodical habits which he had
learned from his good old father ; others were the old-fashioned

[1] Bauernfeld.
[2] Horzalka. K.H. 128 (i. 132).

punctilious style of addressing strangers, which struck Hiller [1]
with such consternation, and the dating of his music. He was
ready to write directly he tumbled out of bed, and remained
steadily at work till two. ' When I have done one piece I
begin the next ' was his explanation to a visitor in 1827 ; and
one of these mornings produced six of the songs in the ' Winterreise ' ! At two he dined — when there was money enough
for dinner — either at the Gasthaus, where in those days it
cost a ' Zwanziger ' ($8\frac{1}{2}d.$), or with a friend or patron ; and the
afternoon was spent in making music, as at Mme. Lacsny-
Buchwieser's (p. 193), or in walking in the environs of
Vienna. If the weather was fine the walk was often prolonged till late, regardless of engagements in town ; but if this
was not the case, he was at the coffee-house by five, smoking
his pipe and ready to joke with any of his set ; then came an
hour's music, as at Sofie Müller's (p. 179) ; then the theatre,
and supper at the Gasthaus again, and the coffee-house, sometimes till far into the morning. In those days no Viennese,
certainly no young bachelor, dined at home ; so that the
repeated visits to the Gasthaus need not shock the sensibilities
of any English lover of Schubert. (See p. 189). Nor let any
one be led away with the notion that he was a sot, as some
seem prone to believe. How could a sot — how could any one
who even lived freely, and woke with a heavy head or a dis-
ordered stomach — have worked as he worked, and have
composed nearly 1000 such works as his in 18 years, or have
performed the feats of rapidity that Schubert did in the way
of opera, symphony, quartet, song, which we have enumerated ?
No sot could write six of the ' Winterreise ' songs — perfect,
enduring works of art — in one morning, and that no singular
feat ! Your Morlands and Poes are obliged to wait their time,
and produce a few works as their brain and their digestion
will allow them, instead of being always ready for their greatest
efforts, as Mozart and Schubert were. Schubert — like
Mozart — loved society and its accompaniments ; he would
have been no Viennese if he had not ; and he may have been
occasionally led away ; but such escapades were rare. He
does not appear to have cared for the other sex, or to have

---

[1] *Künstlerleben*, p. 49. ' Schubert I find mentioned in my journal as a
quiet man — possibly not always so, though it was only amongst his intimates that
he broke out. When I visited him in his modest lodging he received me kindly,
but so respectfully as quite to frighten me.'

been attractive to them as Beethoven was, notwithstanding his ugliness. This simplicity curiously characterises his whole life ; no feats of memory are recorded of him as they so often are of other great musicians ; the records of his life contain nothing to quote. His letters, some forty [71] in all, are evidently forced from him. ' Heavens and Earth,' says he, ' it's frightful having to describe one's travels ; I cannot write any more.' ' Dearest friend ' — on another occasion — ' you will be astonished at my writing : I am so myself.' [1] Strange contrast to the many interesting epistles of Mozart and Mendelssohn, and the numberless notes of Beethoven ! Beethoven was well read, a politician, thought much, and talked eagerly on many subjects. Mozart and Mendelssohn both drew ; travelling was a part of their lives ; they were men of the world, and Mendelssohn was master of many accomplishments. Schumann too, though a Saxon of Saxons, had travelled much, and while a most prolific composer, was a practised literary man. But Schubert has nothing of the kind to show. He not only never travelled out of Austria [-Hungary], but he never proposed it, and it is difficult to conceive of his doing so. To picture or work of art he very rarely refers. He expressed himself with such difficulty that it was all but impossible to argue with him.[2] Besides the letters just mentioned, a few pages of diary and four or five [7] poems are all that he produced except his music. In literature his range was wide indeed, but it all went into his music ; and he was strangely uncritical. He seems to have been hardly able — at any rate he did not care — to discriminate between the magnificent songs of Goethe, Schiller, and Mayrhofer, the feeble domesticities of Kosegarten and Hölty, and the turgid couplets of the authors of his librettos. All came alike to his omnivorous appetite. But the fact is that, apart from his music, Schubert's life was little or nothing, and that is its most peculiar and most interesting fact. Music and music alone was to him all in all. It was not his *principal* mode of expression, it was his *only* one ; it swallowed up every other. His afternoon walks, his evening amusements, were all so many preparations for the creations of the following morning. No doubt he enjoyed the country, but the effect of the walk is to be found in his music and his music only. He left, as we have

[1] K.H. 368 (ii. 55) ; 417 (ii, 104).
[2] Seyfried, in Schilling's Lexicon.

said, no letters to speak of, no journal; there is no record of his ever having poured out his soul in confidence, as Beethoven did in the ' Will,' in the three mysterious letters to some unknown Beloved, or in his conversations with Bettina. He made no impression even on his closest friends beyond that of natural kindness, goodness, truth, and reserve. His life is all summed up in his music. No memoir of Schubert can ever be satisfactory, because no relation can be established between his life and his music; or rather, properly speaking, because there is no life to establish a relation with. The one scale of the balance is absolutely empty, the other is full to overflowing.

For when we come to the music we find everything that was wanting elsewhere. There we have fluency, depth, acuteness and variety of expression, unbounded imagination, the happiest thoughts, never-tiring energy, and a sympathetic tenderness beyond belief. And these were the result of natural gifts and of the incessant practice to which they forced him; for it seems certain that of education in music — meaning by education the severe course of training in the mechanical portions of their art to which Mozart and Mendelssohn were subjected—he had little or nothing. As we have already mentioned, the two musicians who professed to instruct him, Holzer and Ruczicka [Ruzicka], were so astonished at his ability that they contented themselves with wondering, and allowing him to go his own way. And they are responsible for that want of counterpoint which was an embarrassment to him all his life, and drove him, during his last illness, to seek lessons. (See p. 209.) What he learned, he learned mostly for himself, from playing in the *Convict* orchestra, from incessant writing, and from reading the best scores he could obtain; and, to use the expressive term of his friend Mayrhofer, remained a ' Naturalist ' to the end of his life. From the operas of the Italian masters, which were recommended to him by Salieri, he advanced to those of Mozart, and of Mozart abundant traces appear in his earlier instrumental works. In 1814 Beethoven was probably still tabooed in the *Convict*; and beyond the Prometheus music, and the first two symphonies, a pupil there would not be likely to encounter anything of his.

To speak first of the orchestral works.

The 1st Symphony dates from 1814 (his 18th year), and between that and 1818 we have five more. These are all much tinctured by what he was hearing and reading — Haydn, Mozart, Rossini, Beethoven (the last but slightly, for reasons just hinted at). Now and then — as in the second subjects of the first and last Allegros of Symphony 1, the first subject of the opening Allegro of Symphony 2, and the Andante of Symphony 5, the themes are virtually reproduced — no doubt unconsciously. The treatment is more his own, especially in regard to the use of the wind instruments, and to the ' working out' of the movements, where his want of education drives him to the repetition of the subject in various keys, and similar artifices, in place of contrapuntal treatment. In the slow movement and Finale of the Tragic Symphony, No. 4, we have exceedingly happy examples, in which, without absolutely breaking away from the old world, Schubert has revealed an amount of original feeling and an extraordinary beauty of treatment which already stamp him as a great orchestral composer. But whether always original or not in their subjects, no one can listen to these first six symphonies without being impressed with their *individuality*. Single phrases may remind us of other composers, the treatment may often be traditional, but there is a fluency and continuity, a happy cheerfulness, an earnestness and want of triviality, and an absence of labour, which proclaim a new composer. The writer is evidently writing because what he has to say must come out, even though he may occasionally couch it in the phrases of his predecessors. Beauty and profusion of melody reign throughout. The tone is often plaintive but never obscure, and there is always the irrepressible gaiety of youth and of Schubert's own Viennese nature, ready and willing to burst forth. His treatment of particular instruments, especially the wind, is already quite his own — a happy *conversational way* which at a later period becomes highly characteristic. At length, in the B minor Symphony (October 30, 1822), we meet with something which never existed in the world before in orchestral music — a new class of thoughts and a new mode of expression which distinguish him entirely from his predecessors, characteristics which are fully maintained in the Rosamunde music (Christmas 1823), and culminate in the great C major Symphony (March 1828).

The same general remarks apply to the other instrumental compositions — the quartets and pianoforte sonatas. These

Q

often show a close adherence to the style of the old school, but
are always effective and individual, and occasionally, like
the symphonies, varied by original and charming movements,
as the Trio in the Eb Quartet, or the Minuet and Trio in
the E major one (op. 125, 1 and 2), the Sonata in A minor
(1817) etc. The visit to Zelész in 1824, with its Hungarian
experiences, and the pianoforte proclivities of the Esterházys,
seems to have given him a new impetus in the direction of
chamber music. It was the immediate or proximate cause of
the ' Grand Duo ' — that splendid work in which, with Beethoven in his eye, Schubert was never more himself — and the
Divertissement à la hongroise; as well as the beautiful and
intensely personal String Quartet in A minor, which has been
not wrongly said to be the most characteristic work of any
composer; ultimately also of the D minor and G major
Quartets, the String Quintet in C, and the three last sonatas,
in all of which the Hungarian element is strongly perceptible
— all the more strongly because we do not detect it at all in the
songs and vocal works.

Here then, at 1822 in the orchestral works, and 1824 in
the chamber music, we may perhaps draw the line between
Schubert's mature and immature compositions. The step from
the Symphony in C of 1818 to the Unfinished Symphony in
B minor, or to the Rosamunde Entr'acte in the same key, is
quite as great as Beethoven's was from No. 2 to the Eroica, or
Mendelssohn's from the C minor to the Italian Symphony.
All trace of his predecessors is gone, and he stands alone in
his own undisguised and pervading personality. All trace of
his youth has gone too. Life has become serious, nay cruel ;
and a deep earnestness and pathos animate all his utterances.
Similarly in the chamber-music, the Octet stands on the line,
and all the works which have made their position and are
acknowledged as great are on this side of it — the Grand Duo,
the Divertissement [à la] Hongroise, the Pianoforte Sonatas in
A minor, D, and Bb, the Fantasie-Sonata in G ; the Impromptus
and Momens musicals [Moments musicaux]; the String
Quartets in A minor, D minor, and G ; the String Quintet in
C ; the Rondo brillant, — in short, all the works which the
world thinks of when it mentions ' Schubert ' (we are speaking
now of instrumental music only) are on this side of 1822. On
the other side of the line, in both cases, orchestra and chamber,

are a vast number of works full of beauty, interest, and life; breathing youth in every bar, absolute Schubert in many move-ments or passages, but not completely saturated with him, not of sufficiently independent power to assert their rank with the others, or to compensate for the diffuseness and repetition which remained characteristics of their author to the last, but which in the later works are hidden or atoned for by the astonishing force, beauty, romance, and personality inherent in the contents of the music. These early works will always be more than interesting; and no lover of Schubert but must regard them with the strong affection and fascination which his followers feel for every bar he wrote. But the judgment of the world at large will probably always remain what it now is.

He was, as Liszt so finely said,[1] '*le musicien le plus poète que jamais*' — the most poetical musician that ever was; and the main characteristics of his music will always be its vivid per-sonality, fullness, and poetry. In the case of other great com-posers, the mechanical skill and ingenuity, the very ease and absence of effort with which many of their effects are produced or their pieces constructed, is a great element in the pleasure produced by their music. Not so with Schubert. In listening to him one is never betrayed into exclaiming 'how clever!' but very often 'how poetical, how beautiful, how intensely Schubert!' The impression produced by his great works is that the means are nothing and the effect everything. Not that he had no technical skill. Counterpoint he was deficient in, but the power of writing whatever he wanted he had absolutely at his fingers' end. No one had ever written more, and the notation of his ideas must have been done without an effort. In the words of Mr. Macfarren,[2] 'the committing his works to paper was a process that accompanied their composition like the writing of an ordinary letter that is indited at the very paper.' In fact we know, if we had not the manuscripts to prove it, that he wrote with the greatest ease and rapidity, and could keep up a conversation, not only while writing down but while inventing his best works; that he never hesitated; very rarely revised — it would often have been better if he had; and never seems to have aimed at making innovations or doing things for effect. For instance, in the number and

[1] Liszt's worst enemies will pardon him much for this sentence.
[2] Philharmonic programme, May 22, 1871.

arrangement of the movements, his symphonies and sonatas never depart from the regular Haydn pattern. They show no [rarely show] aesthetic artifices, such as quoting the theme of one movement in another movement, or running them into each other; changing their order, or introducing extra ones; mixing various times simultaneously — or similar mechanical means of producing unity or making novel effects, which often surprise and please us in Beethoven, Schumann, Mendelssohn and Spohr. Not an instance of this is to be found in Schubert. Nor has he ever indicated a programme, or prefixed a motto to any of his works. His matter is so abundant and so full of variety and interest that he never seems to think of enhancing it by any devices. He did nothing to extend the formal limits of Symphony or Sonata, but he endowed them with a magic, a romance, a sweet naturalness, which no one has yet approached. And as in the general structure so in the single movements. A simple canon, as in the Eb Trio, the Andante of the B minor or the Scherzo of the C major Symphonies; an occasional round, as in the Masses and Part-songs; — such is pretty nearly all the science that he affords. His vocal fugues are notoriously weak, and the symphonies rarely show those piquant *fugatos* which are so delightful in Beethoven and Mendelssohn. On the other hand, in all that is necessary to express his thoughts and feelings, and to convey them to the hearer, he is inferior to none. Such passages as the return to the subject in the Andante of the B minor Symphony, or in the ballet air in G of Rosamunde; as the famous horn passage in the Andante of the C major Symphony (No. 10) — which Schumann happily compares to a being from the other world gliding about the orchestra — or the equally beautiful cello solo further on in the same movement, are unsurpassed in orchestral music for felicity and beauty, and have an emotional effect which no learning could give. There is a place in the working-out of the Rosamunde Entr'acte in B minor (change into G♯), in which the combination of modulation and scoring produces a weird and overpowering feeling quite exceptional, and the change to the major near the end of the same great work will always astonish. One of the most prominent beauties in these orchestral works is the exquisite and entirely fresh manner in which the wind instruments are combined. Even in his earliest symphonies he begins that method of dialogue by interchange of phrases,

which rises at last to the well-known and lovely passages in the
Overture to Rosamunde (2nd subject), the Trios of the B♭
Entr'acte, and the *Air de Ballet* in the same music, and in the
Andantes of the 8th and 10th Symphonies.   No one has ever
combined wind instruments as these are combined.   To quote
Schumann once more — they talk and intertalk like human
beings.   It is no artful concealment of art.   The artist vanishes
altogether, and the loving, simple, human friend remains.   It
were well to be dumb in articulate speech with such a power of
utterance at command !   If anything were wanting to convince
us of the absolute *inspiration* of such music as this it would be
the fact that Schubert never can have heard either of the two
symphonies which we have just been citing.—But to return to
the orchestra.   The trombones were favourite instruments with
Schubert in his later life.   In the fugal movements of his two
last Masses he makes them accompany the voices in unison,
with a persistence which is sometimes almost unbearable for its
monotony.   In portions of the C major Symphony also (No. 10)
some may possibly find them too much used.[1]   But in other
parts of the Masses they are beautifully employed, and in the
Introduction and Allegro of the Symphony they are used with
a noble effect, which not improbably suggested to Schumann
the equally impressive use of them in his B♭ Symphony.   The
accompaniments to his subjects are always of great ingenuity
and originality, and full of life and character.   The triplets in
the Finale to the 10th Symphony, which excited the *mal à
propos* merriment of the Philharmonic orchestra (see p. 223)
are a very striking instance.   Another is the incessant run of
semiquavers in the second violins and violas which accompany
the second theme in the Finale of the Tragic Symphony.
Another, of which he is very fond, is the employment of a
recurring monotonous figure in the inner parts : —

often running to great length, as in the Andantes of the Tragic

---

[1] There is a tradition that he doubted this himself, and referred the score
to Lachner for his opinion.

and B minor Symphonies; the Moderato of the B♭ Sonata; the fine song ' Viola ' (op. 123, at the return to A♭ in the middle of the song), etc. etc. In his best pianoforte music, the accompaniments are most happily fitted to the leading part, so as never to clash or produce discord. Rapidly as he wrote he did these things as if they were calculated. But they never obtrude themselves or become prominent. They are all merged and absorbed in the gaiety, pathos and personal interest of the music itself, and of the man who is uttering through it his griefs and joys, his hopes and fears, in so direct and touching a manner as no composer ever did before or since, and with no thought of an audience, of fame, or success, or any other external thing. No one who listens to it can doubt that Schubert wrote for himself alone. His music is the simple utterance of the feelings with which his mind is full. If he had thought of his audience, or the effect he would produce, or the capabilities of the means he was employing, he would have taken more pains in the revision of his works. Indeed the most affectionate disciple of Schubert must admit that the want of revision is often but too apparent.

In his instrumental music he is often very diffuse. When a passage pleases him he generally repeats it at once, almost note for note. He will reiterate a passage over and over in different keys, as if he could never have done. In the songs this does not offend ; and even here, if we knew what he was thinking of, as we do in the songs, we might possibly find the repetitions just. In the E♭ Trio he repeats in the Finale a characteristic accompaniment which is very prominent in the first movement and which originally belongs perhaps to the A♭ Impromptu (op. 90, no. 4) — and a dozen other instances of the same kind might be quoted.[1] This arose in great part from his imperfect education, but in great part also from the furious pace at which he dashed down his thoughts and feelings, apparently without previous sketch, note, or preparation; and from his habit of never correcting a piece after it was once on paper. Had he done so he would doubtless have taken out many a repetition, and some trivialities which seem terribly out of place amid the usual nobility and taste of his thoughts. It was doubtless this diffuseness and apparent want of aim, as

[1] For a comparison of his sonatas with those of other masters see SONATA. [Reference to that article in the first edition of Grove's Dictionary.]

well as the jolly, untutored, *naïveté* of some of his subjects
(Rondo of D major Sonata, etc.), and the incalculable amount
of modulation, that made Mendelssohn shrink from some of
Schubert's instrumental works, and even go so far as to call
the D minor quartet *schlechte Musik* — *i.e.* ' nasty music.' But
unless to musicians whose fastidiousness is somewhat abnormal
— as Mendelssohn's was — such criticisms only occur afterwards, on reflection; for during the progress of the work all is
absorbed in the intense life and personality of the music. And
what beauties there are to put against these redundances!
Take such movements as the first Allegro of the A minor Sonata
or the B♭ Sonata; the G major Fantasia-Sonata; the two
Characteristic Marches; the Impromptus and Momens musicals [Moments musicaux]; the Minuet of the A minor Quartet;
the Variations of the D minor Quartet; the Finale of the B♭
Trio; the first two movements, or the Trio, of the String
Quintet; the two movements of the B minor Symphony, or
the wonderful Entr'acte in the same key in Rosamunde; the
Finale of the 10th Symphony — think of the abundance of the
thoughts, the sudden surprises, the wonderful transitions, the
extraordinary pathos of the turns of melody and modulation,
the absolute manner (to repeat once more) in which they bring
you into contact with the affectionate, tender, suffering personality of the composer, — and who in the whole realm of music
has ever approached them? For the magical expression of
such a piece as the Andantino in A♭ (op. 94, no. 2), any
redundance may be pardoned.

In Schumann's words,[1] ' he has strains for the most subtle
thoughts and feelings, nay even for the events and conditions
of life; and innumerable as are the shades of human thought
and action, so various is his music.' Another equally true saying
of Schumann is that, compared with Beethoven, Schubert is
as a woman to a man. For it must be confessed that one's
attitude towards him is almost always that of sympathy, attraction, and love, rarely that of embarrassment or fear. Here
and there only, as in the Rosamunde B minor Entr'acte, or the
Finale of the 10th Symphony, does he compel his hearers with
an irresistible power; and yet how different is this compulsion
from the strong, fierce, merciless coercion, with which Beethoven
forces you along, and bows and bends you to his will, in the

[1] *Ges. Schriften,* i. 206.

Finale of the 8th or still more that of the 7th Symphony.

We have mentioned the gradual manner in which Schubert reached his own style in instrumental music (see p. 231). In this, except perhaps as to quantity, there is nothing singular, or radically different from the early career of other composers. Beethoven began on the lines of Mozart, and Mendelssohn on those of Weber, and gradually found their own independent style. But the thing in which Schubert stands alone is that while he was thus arriving by degrees at individuality in sonatas, quartets, and symphonies, he was pouring forth songs by the dozen, many of which were of the greatest possible novelty, originality, and mastery, while all of them have that peculiar *cachet* which is immediately recognisable as his. The chronological list of his works given at the end of this article* shows that such masterpieces as the Gretchen am Spinnrade, the Erl King, the Ossian Songs, Gretchen im Dom, Der Taucher, Die Bürgschaft, were written before he was 19, and were contemporary with his very early efforts in the orchestra and chamber music; and that by 1822 — in the October of which he wrote the two movements of his 8th Symphony, which we have named as his first absolutely original instrumental music — he had produced in addition such ballads as Ritter Toggenburg (1816), and Einsamkeit (1818); such classical songs as Memnon (1817), Antigone und Œdip (1817), Iphigenia (1817), Ganymed (1817), Fahrt zum Hades (1817), Prometheus (1819), Gruppe aus dem Tartarus (1817); Goethe's Wilhelm Meister songs, An Schwager Kronos (1816), Grenzen der Menschheit (1821), Suleika's two songs (1821), Geheimes (1821); as well as the 'Wanderer' (1816), 'Sei mir gegrüsst' (1821), Waldesnacht (1820), Greisengesang (1822), and many more of his very greatest and most immortal songs.

And this is very confirmatory of the view already taken in this article (p. 144 of Schubert's relation to music. The reservoir of music was within him from his earliest years, and songs being so much more direct a channel than the more complicated and artificial courses and conditions of the symphony or the sonata, music came to the surface in them so much the more quickly. Had the orchestra or the piano been as direct a mode of utterance as the voice, and the forms of

* [In the first edition of the Dictionary, but not here.]

symphony or sonata as simple as that of the song, there seems
no reason why he should not have written instrumental music
as characteristic as his 8th Symphony, his Sonata in A minor,
and his Quartet in the same key, eight years earlier than he
did ; for the songs of that early date prove that he had then
all the original power, imagination, and feeling, that he ever
had. That it should have been given to a comparative boy
to produce strains which seem to breathe the emotion and
experience of a long life is only part of the wonder which will
also [? always] surround Schubert's songs. After 1822, when
his youth was gone, and health had begun to fail, and life had
become a terrible reality, his thoughts turned inwards, and he
wrote the two great cycles of the ' Müllerlieder ' (1823) and the
'Winterreise' (1827) ; the Walter Scott and Shakespeare songs ;
the splendid single songs of ' Im Walde ' and ' Auf der Brücke
[Bruck],' ' Todtengräbers Heimweh,' ' Der Zwerg,' ' Die junge
Nonne'; the Barcarolle, 'Du bist die Ruh,' and the lovely 'Dass
sie hier gewesen'; the 'Schiffers Scheidelied,' those which were
collected into the so-called ' Schwanengesang,' and many more.

It is very difficult to draw a comparison between the songs
of this later period and those of the earlier one, but the difference
must strike every one, and it resides mainly perhaps in the
subjects themselves. Subjects of romance — of ancient times
and remote scenes, and strange adventures, and desperate
emotion — are natural to the imagination of youth. But in
maturer life the mind is calmer, and dwells more strongly on
personal subjects. And this is the case with Schubert. After
1822 the classical songs and ballads are rare, and the themes
which he chooses belong chiefly to modern life and individual
feeling, such as the ' Müllerlieder ' and the ' Winterreise,' and
others in the list just given. Walter Scott's and Shakespeare's
form an exception, but it is an exception which explains itself.
We no longer have the exuberant dramatic force of the Erl
King, Ganymed, the Gruppe aus dem Tartarus, Cronnan, or
Kolmas Klage ; but we have instead the condensation and
personal point of ' Pause,' ' Die Post,' ' Das Wirthshaus,' ' Die
Nebensonnen,' the ' Doppelgänger,' and the ' Junge Nonne.'
And there is more maturity in the treatment. His modulations
are fewer. His accompaniments are always interesting and
suggestive, but they gain in force and variety and quality of
ideas in the later songs.

In considering the songs themselves somewhat more closely, their most obvious characteristics are : — Their number ; their length ; the variety of the words ; their expression, and their other musical and poetical peculiarities.

1. Their number. The published songs, that is to say the compositions for one and two voices, including Offertories and songs in operas, amount to just 455. In addition there are, say, 150 unpublished songs, a few of them unfinished. The chronological list at the end of this article [omitted] shows that a very large number of these were written before the year 1818.

2. Their length. This varies very much. The shortest, like ' Klage um Aly Bey ' (Lf. 45, 3), ' Der Goldschmiedsgesell ' (Lf. 48, 6), and ' Die Spinnerin ' (op. 118, 6), are strophe songs (that is, with the same melody and harmony unchanged verse after verse), in each of which the voice part is only 8 bars long, with a bar or two of introduction or ritornel. The longest is Bertrand's ' Adelwold und Emma ' (MS., June 5, 1815), a ballad the autograph of which contains 55 pages. Others of almost equal length and of about the same date are also still in MS. — ' Minona,' ' Die Nonne,' ' Amphiaraos,' etc. The longest printed one is Schiller's ' Der Taucher ' — the diver. This fills 36 pages of close print. Schiller's ' Bürgschaft ' and the Ossian-songs are all long, though not of the same extent as ' Der Taucher.' These vast ballads are extremely dramatic ; they contain many changes of tempo and of signature, dialogues, recitatives, and airs. The ' Ritter Toggenburg ' ends with a strophe-song in five stanzas. ' Der Taucher ' contains a long pianoforte passage of 60 bars, during the suspense after the diver's last descent. ' Der Liedler ' contains a march. The ballads mostly belong to the early years, 1815, 1816. The last is Mayrhofer's ' Einsamkeit,' the date of which Schubert has fixed in his letter of August 3, 1818. There are long songs of later years, such as Collin's ' Der Zwerg ' of 1823 ; Schober's ' Viola ' and ' Vergissmeinnicht ' of 1823, and ' Schiffers Scheidelied ' of 1827, and Leitner's ' Der Winterabend ' of 1828 ; but these are essentially different to the ballads ; they are lyrical, and evince comparatively few mechanical changes.

It stands to reason that in 650 [just over 600] songs collected from all the great German poets, from Klopstock to Heine, there must be an infinite variety of material, form, sentiment, and expression. And one of the most obvious characteristics in

Schubert's setting of this immense collection is the close way in which he adheres to the words.[1] Setting a song was no casual operation with him, rapidly as it was often done ; but he identi-fied himself with the poem, and the poet's mood for the time was his. Indeed he complains of the influence which the gloom of the ' Winterreise ' had had upon his spirits. He does not, as is the manner of some song-composers, set the poet at naught by repeating his words over and over again. This he rarely does ; but he goes through his poem and confines himself to enforcing the expression as music alone can do to poetry. The music changes with the words as a landscape does when sun and cloud pass over it. And in this Schubert has anticipated Wagner, since the words to which he writes are as much the absolute basis of his songs, as Wagner's librettos are of his operas. What this has brought him to in such cases as the Erl King, the Wanderer, Schwager Kronos, the Gruppe aus dem Tartarus, the Shakespeare songs of ' Sylvia [Silvia] ' and ' Hark, hark, the lark ! ' those of Ellen and the Huntsman in ' The Lady of the Lake ' even Englishmen can judge ; but what he did in the German literature generally may be gathered from the striking passage already quoted from Vogl (p. 143), and from Mayrhofer's confession — doubly remarkable when coming from a man of such strong individuality — who some-where says that he did not understand the full force even of his own poems until he had heard Schubert's setting of them.

One of his great means of expression is modulation. What magic this alone can work may be seen in the Trio of the Sonata in D. As in his pianoforte works, so in the songs, he sometimes carries it to an exaggerated degree. Thus in the short song ' Liedesend ' of Mayrhofer (September 1816), he begins in C minor, and then goes quickly through E♭ into C♭ major. The signature then changes and we are at once in D major ; then C major. Then the signature again changes to that of A♭, in which we remain for 15 bars. From A♭ it is an easy transition to F minor, but a very sudden one from that again to A minor. Then for the breaking of the harp we are forced into D♭, and immediately, with a further change of signature, into F♯. Then for the King's song, with a fifth change of signature, into B

[1] It is strange to find his practice in the Masses so different. There—a critic has pointed out— in every one of the six, words are either omitted or incorrectly jumbled together (Mr. Prout, in *Concordia*, 1875, p. 110 *a*). Was this because he understood the Latin words imperfectly ?

major; and lastly, for the concluding words,

> Und immer näher schreitet
> Vergänglichkeit und Grab—
> And always nearer hasten
> Oblivion and the tomb—

a sixth change, with 8 bars in E minor, thus ending the song a third higher than it began.

In Schiller's ' Der Pilgrim ' (1825), after two strophes (four stanzas) of a chorale-like melody in D major, we come, with the description of the difficulties of the pilgrim's road — mountains, torrents, ravines — to a change into D minor, followed by much extraneous modulation, reaching Ab minor, and ending in F, in which key the first melody is repeated. At the words ' näher bin ich nicht zum Ziel ' — ' still no nearer to my goal ' — we have a similar phrase and similar harmony (though in a different key) to the well-known complaint in ' The Wanderer,' ' Und immer fragt der Seufzer, Wo ? ' — ' Sighing I utter where ? oh where ? ' The signature then changes, and the song ends very impressively in B minor.

These two are quoted, the first as an instance rather of exaggeration, the second of the mechanical use of modulations to convey the natural difficulties depicted in the poem. But if we want examples of the extraordinary power with which Schubert wields this great engine of emotion, we would mention another song which contains one of the best instances to be found of propriety of modulation. I allude to Schubert's short poem to Death, ' An den Tod,' where the gloomy subject and images of the poet have tempted the composer to a series of successive changes so grand, so sudden, and yet so easy, and so thoroughly in keeping with the subject, that it is impossible to hear them unmoved.

But modulation, though an all-pervading means of expression in Schubert's hands, is only one out of many. Scarcely inferior to the wealth of his modulation is the wealth of his melodies. The beauty of these is not more astonishing than their variety and their fitness to the words. Such tunes as those of Ave Maria, or the Serenade in the Schwanengesang, or Ungeduld, or the Grünen Lautenband, or Anna [Annot] Lyle, or the Dithyrambe, or Geheimes, or Sylvia, or the Lindenbaum, or Du bist die Ruh, or the Barcarolle, are not more lovely and more appropriate to the text than they are

entirely different from one another. One quality only, spontaneity, they have in common. With Beethoven, spontaneity
was the result of labour, and the more he polished the more
natural were his tunes. But Schubert read the poem, and the
appropriate tune, married to immortal verse (a marriage, in
his case, truly made in heaven), rushed into his mind, and to
the end of his pen. It must be confessed that he did not
always think of the compass of his voices. In his latest songs,
as in his earliest (see p. 126), we find him taking the singer
from the low B♭ to F, and even higher.

The tune, however, in a Schubert song is by no means an
exclusive feature. The accompaniments are as varied and as
different as the voice-parts, and as important for the general
effect. They are often extremely elaborate, and the publishers'
letters contain many complaints of their difficulty.[1] They are
often most extraordinarily suitable to the words, as in the Erl
King, or the beautiful ' Dass sie hier gewesen,' the ' Gruppe
aus dem Tartarus,' the ' Waldesnacht ' (and many others) ;
where it is almost impossible to imagine any atmosphere more
exactly suitable to make the words grow in one's mind, than is
supplied by the accompaniment. Their unerring certainty is
astonishing. Often, as in Heliopolis, or Auflösung, he seizes
at once on a characteristic impetuous figure, which is then
carried on without intermission to the end. In ' Anna Lyle,'
how exactly does the sweet monotony of the repeated figure
fall in with the dreamy sadness of Scott's touching little lament !
Another very charming example of the same thing, though in
a different direction, is found in ' Der Einsame,' a fireside piece,
where the frequently recurring group of four semiquavers im-
parts an indescribable air of domesticity to the picture.[2] In
the ' Winterabend ' — the picture of a calm moonlit evening
— the accompaniment, aided by a somewhat similar little
figure, conveys inimitably the very breath of the scene. Such
atmospheric effects as these are very characteristic of Schubert.

The voice-part and the accompaniment sometimes form
so perfect a whole, that it is impossible to disentangle the
two ; as in ' Sylvia,' where the persistent dotted quaver in
the bass, and the rare but delicious ritornel of two notes in

[1] Op. 57, containing three songs by no means difficult, was published with
a notice on the title-page that care had been taken (we trust with Schubert's
consent) to omit everything that was too hard.
[2] A similar mood is evoked in the Andante of the Grand Duo (op. 140).

the treble of the piano-part (bars 7, 14, etc.), are essential to the grace and sweetness of the portrait, and help to place the lovely English figure before us. This is the case also in ' Anna Lyle ' just mentioned, where the ritornel in the piano-part (bar 20, etc.) is inexpressibly soothing and tender in its effect, and sounds like the echo of the girl's sorrow. The beautiful Serenade in the Schwanengesang, again, combines an incessant rhythmical accompaniment with ritornels (longer than those in the last case), both uniting with the lovely melody in a song of surpassing beauty. In the ' Liebesbothschaft,' the rhythm is not so strongly marked, but the ritornels are longer and more frequent, and form a charming feature in that exquisite love-poem. Schubert's passion for rhythm comes out as strongly in many of the songs as it does in his marches and scherzos. In the two just named, though persistent throughout, the rhythm is subordinated to the general effect. But in others, as ' Suleika,' ' Die Sterne,' the ' Nachtgesang im Walde,' ' Erstarrung,' or ' Frühlingssehnsucht,' it forces itself more on the attention.

Schubert's basses are always splendid, and are so used as not only to be the basis of the harmony but to add essentially to the variety and effect of the songs. Sometimes, as in ' Die Krähe,' they are in unison with the voice-part. Often they share with the voice-part itself in the melody and structure of the whole. The wealth of ideas which they display is often astonishing. Thus in ' Waldesnacht,' a very long song of 1820, to a fine imaginative poem by F. Schlegel, describing the impressions produced by a night in the forest, we have a splendid example of the *organic life* which Schubert can infuse into a song. The pace is rapid throughout ; the accompaniment for the right hand is in arpeggios of semiquavers throughout, never once leaving off ; the left hand, where not in semiquavers also, has a succession of noble and varied rhythmical melodies, independent of the voice, and the whole is so blended with the voice-part — itself extraordinarily broad and dignified throughout ; the spirit and variety, and the poetry of the whole are so remarkable, and the mystery of the situation is so perfectly conveyed, as to make the song one of the finest of that class in the whole Schubert collection. The same qualities will be found in Auf der Brücke [Bruck] (1815).

We do not say that this is the highest class of his songs. The highest class of poetry, and of music illustrating and enforcing poetry, must always deal with human joys and sorrows, in their most individual form, with the soul loving or longing, in contact with another soul, or with its Maker; and the greatest of Schubert's songs will lie amongst those which are occupied with those topics, such as 'Gretchen am Spinnrade,' the Mignon songs, the 'Wanderer,' the 'Müllerlieder,' and 'Winterreise,' and perhaps highest of all, owing to the strong religious element which it contains, the 'Junge Nonne.' [1] In that wonderful song, which fortunately is so well known that no attempt at describing it is necessary, the personal feelings and the surroundings are so blended — the fear, the faith, the rapture, the storm, the swaying of the house, are so given that for the time the hearer becomes the Young Nun herself. Even the convent bell, which in other hands might be a burlesque, is an instrument of the greatest beauty.

We have spoken of the mental atmosphere which Schubert throws round his poems; but he does not neglect the representation of physical objects. He seems to confine himself to the imitation of natural noises, and not to attempt things which have no sound. The triplets in the Lindenbaum may be intended to convey the fluttering leaves of the lime-tree, and the accompaniment-figure in 'Die Forelle' may represent the leaps of the Trout; but there are other objects about which no mistake can be made. One imitation of the bell we have just referred to. Another is in the 'Abendbilder,' where an F♯ sounds through 16 bars to represent the 'evening bell'; in the Zügenglöcklein the upper E is heard through the whole piece; and the bell of St. Mark's is a well-known feature in the part-song of the 'Gondelfahrer.' The post-horn forms a natural feature in 'Die Post,' and the hurdy-gurdy in 'Der Leiermann.' Of birds he gives several instances; the Nightingale in 'Ganymed' and 'Die gefangene Sänger'; the Raven in 'Abendbilder,' and perhaps in 'Frühlingstraum'; the Cuckoo in 'Einsamkeit,' the Quail in 'Der Wachtelschlag'; and the Cock in 'Frühlingstraum.'

That hesitation between major and minor which is so marked in Beethoven is characteristic also of Schubert, and may be found in nearly every piece of his. A beautiful instance

[1] Who was Craigher, the author of this splendid song? and would he ever have been heard of but for Schubert?

may be mentioned *en passant* in the trio of the G major Fantasia
Sonata (op. 78), where the two bars in E minor which precede
the E major have a peculiarly charming effect. Another is
supplied by the four bars in A minor, for the question which
begins and ends the beautiful fragment from Schiller's ' Gods
of ancient Greece.' He also has an especially happy way —
surely peculiarly his own — of bringing a minor piece to a conclusion in the major. Two instances of it, which all will
remember, are in the Romance from ' Rosamunde ' :—

Du süs-ses Herz, es ist so schön,wenn treu die Treu-e küsst.

and in the ' Moment musical,' No. 3, in F minor. This and
the ritornels already spoken of strike one like personal features
or traits of the composer. But apart from these idiosyncrasies,
the changes from minor to major in the songs are often superb.
That in the ' Schwager Kronos ' (astonishing [1] production for
a lad under 20), where the key changes into D major, and
further on into F major, to welcome the girl on the threshold,
with the sudden return to D minor for the onward journey,
and the sinking sun — can be forgotten by no one who hears
it, nor can that almost more beautiful change to D major in
the ' Gute Nacht ' on the mention of the dream. This latter,
and the noble transition to F major in the ' Junge Nonne ' are
too familiar to need more than a passing reference, or that to
G major in the ' Rückblick,' for the lark and nightingale and
the girl's eyes, or to D major in the Serenade. ' Irdisches
Glück ' is in alternate stanzas of major and minor. In Schiller's
' Rose ' (op. 73) every shade in the fate of the flower is thus
indicated ; and this is no solitary instance, but in almost every
song some example of such faithful painting may be found.
A word will often do it. With Schubert the minor mode seems
to be synonymous with trouble, and the major with relief ;
and the mere mention of the sun, or a smile, or any other
emblem of gladness, is sure to make him modulate. Some
such image was floating before his mind when he made the
beautiful change to A major near the beginning of the A minor
Quartet (bar 23).

The foregoing remarks, which only attempt to deal with a

[1] Why is this wonderful song never sung in public in England?

few of the external characteristics of these astonishing songs, will be of use if they only encourage the knowledge and study of them. The chronological list (No. II) of Schubert's productions, which is here attempted * in this form for the first time, will, it is hoped, throw much light on the progress of his genius, by facilitating the search where alone it can be made with profit, namely in the works themselves. All are worth knowing, though all are by no means of equal excellence.

I end my imperfect sketch of the life and works of this wonderful musician, by recalling the fact that Schubert's songs, regarded as a department of music, are absolutely and entirely his own. Songs there were before him, those of Schulz for instance, and of Zumsteeg, which he so greatly admired, and of Haydn and Mozart — touching, beautiful expressions of simple thought and feeling. But the Song, as we know it in his hands; full of dramatic fire, poetry, and pathos; set to no simple Volkslieder, but to long complex poems, the best poetry of the greatest poets, and an absolute reflection of every change and breath of sentiment in that poetry; with an accompaniment of the utmost force, fitness, and variety — such songs were his and his alone. With one exception. Beethoven left but one song of importance, his ' Liederkreis ' (op. 98), but that is of superlative excellence. The Liederkreis, however, was not published till December 1816, and even if Schubert made its acquaintance immediately, yet a reference to the Chronological List will show that by that time his style was formed, and many of his finest songs written. He may have gained the idea of a connected series of songs from Beethoven, though neither the ' Schöne Müllerin ' nor the ' Winterreise ' have the same intimate internal connexion as the Liederkreis; but the character and merits of the single songs remain his own. When he wrote ' Loda's Gespenst ' and ' Kolma's Klage ' in 1815, he wrote what no one had ever attempted before. There is nothing to detract from his just claim to be the creator of German Song, as we know it, and the direct progenitor of those priceless treasures in which Schumann, Mendelssohn, and Brahms have followed his example.

---

* [Not reproduced in this reprint.]

R

Of Schubert's religion it is still more difficult to say anything than it was of Beethoven's, because he is so much more
reticent. A little poem of September 1820, one of two preserved
by Robert Schumann (Neue Zeitschrift für Musik, February 5,
1839) is as vague a confession of faith as can well be imagined.

THE SPIRIT OF THE WORLD

Leave them, leave them, to their dream,
  I hear the Spirit say :—
It and only it can keep them
  Near me on their darkling way.

Leave them racing, hurrying on
  To some distant goal,
Building creeds and proofs upon
  Half-seen flashes in the soul.

Not a word of it is true.
  Yet what loss is theirs or mine?
In the maze of human systems
  I can trace the thought divine.

The other, three years later, May 8, 1823, is somewhat more
definite. It calls upon a ' mighty father ' to look upon his son
lying in the dust; and implores Him to pour upon him the
everlasting beams of His love; and, even though He kill him,
to preserve him for a purer and more vigorous existence. It
expresses — very imperfectly, it is true, but still unmistakably
— the same faith that has been put into undying words by the
great poet of our own day : —

Thou wilt not leave us in the dust;
  Thou madest man, he knows not why;
  He thinks he was not made to die;
And Thou hast made him : Thou art just.

    .   .   .   .   .   .

Let knowledge grow from more to more,
  But more of reverence in us dwell.
  That mind and soul, according well,
May make one music as before,

  But vaster.[1]

Franz may not have gone the length of his brother Ignaz [2] in
vulgar scoffing at religious forms and persons, which no doubt
were very empty in Vienna at that date; but still of formal
or dogmatic religion we can find no traces, and we must content

[1] Tennyson, 'In Memoriam' (Prologue).
[2] See his letter in Kreissle, 147 (i. 149).

ourselves with the practical piety displayed in his love for his
father and Ferdinand, and testified to by them in their touching
words and acts at the time of his death (p. 211-2) ; and with the
certainty that, though irregular after the irregularity of his
time, Schubert was neither selfish, sensual, nor immoral. What
he was in his inner man we have the abundant evidence of his
music to assure us. Whatever the music of other composers
may do, no one ever rose from hearing a piece by Schubert
without being benefited by it. Of his good-nature to those who
took the bread out of his mouth we have already spoken. Of
his modesty we may be allowed to say that he was one of the
very few musicians who ever lived who did not behave as if he
thought himself the greatest man in the world.[1] And these
things are all intrinsic parts of his character and genius.

That he died at an earlier age [2] even than Mozart or
Mendelssohn, or our own Purcell, must be accounted for on
the ground partly of his extraordinary exertions, but still more
of the privations to which he was subjected from his very earliest
years. His productions are enormous, even when measured by
those of the two great German composers just named, or even
of Beethoven, who lived to nearly double his years. At an age
when Beethoven had produced one symphony, he had written
ten [seven and two unfinished *] besides all the mass of works
great and small which form the extraordinary list in the
Appendix to this article †. 'Fairer hopes'? Had he lived, who
can doubt that he would have thrown into the shade all his
former achievements? But as we have endeavoured to explain,
his music came so easily and rapidly that it was probably not
exhausting. It was his privations, his absolute poverty, and
the distress which he naturally felt at finding that no exertions
could improve his circumstances, or raise him in the scale of

[1] This modesty comes out in a letter to Ferdinand of July 16–18, 1824,
where Schubert says, ' it would be better to play some other quartets than mine '
(probably referring to those in E and E♭), ' since there is nothing in them except
perhaps the fact that they please you, as everything of mine pleases you. True,'
he goes on, ' you do not appear to have liked them so much as the waltzes at the
Ungarische Krone,' alluding to a clock at that eating-house of which Ferdinand
had told him, which was set to play Franz's waltzes. The clock shows how
popular Schubert was amongst his own set, and I regret having overlooked the
fact in its proper place.
[2] The following are among the musicians, poets, and painters who have died
in the fourth decade of their lives. Shelley, 30; Sir Philip Sidney, 32; Bellini
33; Mozart, 35; Byron, 36; Rafaelle, 37; Burns, 37; Purcell, 37; Mendelssohn, 38; Weber, 39; Chopin, 40.
  * [Not counting the problematical ' Gastein ' Symphony.]
  † [Not reproduced.]

existence, that in the end dragged him down. His poverty is
shocking to think of. Nearly the first distinct glimpse we catch
of him is in the winter of 1812, supplicating his brother for a
roll, some apples, or a few halfpence, to keep off the hunger
of the long fast in the freezing rooms of the *Convict*. Within a
year of his death we catch sight of him again, putting up with
coffee and biscuits because he has not 8½d. to buy his dinner
with; selling his great Trio for 17s. 6d. and his songs at 10d.
each, and dying the possessor of effects which were valued at
little more than two pounds. Beside this the poverty of Mozart
— the first of the two great musicians whom Vienna has
allowed to starve — was wealth.

Such facts as these reduce the so-called friendship of his
associates to its right level. With his astonishing power of
production the commonest care would have ensured him a
good living; and that no one of his set was found devoted
enough to take this care for him, and exercise that watch over
ways and means which Nature had denied to his own genius,
is a discredit to them all. They prate of their devotion to their
friend, when not one of them had the will or the wit to prevent
him from starving; for such want as he often endured must
inevitably have injured him, and we cannot doubt that his
death was hastened by the absence of those comforts, not to
say necessaries, which should have nursed and restored the
prodigal expenditure of his brain and nerves.

We are accustomed to think of Beethoven's end as solitary
and his death as miserable, but what was his last illness compared to Schubert's ? Officious friends, like Pasqualati, sending
him wine and delicacies ; worshipping musicians, like Hummel
and Hiller, coming to his deathbed as if to a shrine ; his faithful
attendants, Schindler, Hüttenbrenner and Breuning waiting on
his every wish ; the sense of a long life of honour and renown ;
of great works appreciated and beloved ; the homage of distant
countries, expressed in the most substantial forms — what a
contrast to the lonely early deathbed, and the apparent wreck
of such an end as Schubert's ! Time has so altered the public
sense of his merits that it is all but impossible to place oneself in
the forlorn condition in which he must have resigned himself
to his departure, and to realise the darkness of the valley of the
shadow of death through which his simple sincere guileless soul
passed to its last rest, and to the joyful resurrection and glorious

renown which have since attended it. *Then* an intelligent and well-informed foreign musician could visit the Austrian capital and live in its musical circles, without so much as hearing Schubert's name.[1] *Now* memorials are erected to him in the most public places of Vienna, institutions are proud to bear his name, his works go through countless editions, and publishers grow rich upon the proceeds even of single songs, while faces brighten and soften, and hands are clasped, as we drink in the gay and pathetic accents of his music.

For even his privations and his obscurity have now been forgotten in the justice since done to him, and in the universal affection with which he was regarded as soon as his works reached the outside world — an affection which, as we have conclusively shown, has gone on increasing ever since his death. In the whole range of composers it may be truly said that no one is now so dearly loved as he, no one has the happy power so completely of attracting both the admiration and the affection of his hearers. To each one he is not only a great musician, not only a great enchanter, but a dear personal friend. If in his ' second state sublime ' he can know this, we may feel sure that it is a full compensation to his affectionate spirit for the many wrongs and disappointments that he endured while on earth.

The very wide field over which Schubert ranged in poetry has been more than once alluded to in the foregoing. It would be both interesting and profitable to give a list of the poems which he has set. Such a list, not without inaccuracies, will be found in Wurzbach's ' Biographical Lexicon,' vol. xxxii. p. 94. Here we can only say that it includes 634 poems, by 100 authors, of whom the principal are : —

Goethe 71 ; Schiller 42 ; Mayrhofer 47 ; Hölty 21 ; Matthisson 26 ; Kosegarten 21 ; F. Schlegel 16 ; Klopstock 13 ; Körner 13 ; Schober 12 ; Seidl 11 ; Salis 16 ; Claudius 12 ; Walter Scott 8 ; Rellstab 10 ; Uz 5 ; Ossian 9 ; Heine 6 ; Shakespeare 3 ; Pope 1 ; Colley Cibber 1 ; etc. etc.

[1] The allusion is to E. Holmes, the biographer of Mozart, who passed some time in Vienna in the spring of 1827, evidently with the view of finding out all that was best worth knowing in music, and yet does not mention Schubert's name. (See his *Ramble among the Musicians of Germany*.)

MENDELSSOHN

FELIX MENDELSSOHN

JAKOB LUDWIG FELIX MENDELSSOHN-BARTHOLDY was born at Hamburg, in the Grosse Michaelisstrasse No. 14,[1] Friday, February 3, 1809. *That* was, at all events, a lucky Friday. The family was already well known from Moses Mendelssohn, the grandfather of Felix, ' The Modern Plato,' whose ' Phädon,' a dialogue upon the immortality of the soul, based on the Phædo of Plato, was translated, long before the birth of his illustrious grandson, into almost every European [2] (and at least one Asiatic) language. Moses was the son of Mendel, a poor Jewish schoolmaster of Dessau, on the Elbe, and was born there September 6, 1729. The name Mendelssohn, *i.e.* ' son of Mendel,' is the ordinary Jewish, oriental, way of forming a name. Moses migrated at 14 years old to Berlin, settled there in 1762, married Fromet, daughter of Abraham Gugenheim, of Hamburg, had 6 [many] children, 3 sons and 3 daughters [of whom attained maturity], published his

N.B. The following abbreviations are used for the references in this article :— F.M. =' Die Familie Mendelssohn,' Berlin 1879; Dev. =' Devrient's Recollections,' London 1869; L. i. = Letters from Italy and Switzerland—' Reisebriefe '; L. ii. = Letters from 1833 to 47. When the original is referred to the title 'Briefe,' i. or ii. is used; H. = Hiller's Mendelssohn, London 1874; G. & M. = Goethe and Mendelssohn, 2nd ed., London 1874; B. = Benedict's Sketch, London 1853; Mos. = Moscheles's Life, London 1873; C. = Chorley's Life, London 1873; P. = Polko's Reminiscences, London 1869; Sch. = Schubring's Erinnerungen, in ' Daheim,' 1866, No. 26; C.E.H. = C. E. Horsley's Reminiscences, in ' The Choir ' for Jan. and Feb. 1873; Dorn = Recollections of Mendelssohn and his friends by Dr. Heinrich Dorn, in ' Temple Bar ' for Feb. 1872; A.M.Z. = ' Allgemeine musikalische Zeitung ' (Leipzig); N.M.Z. =' Neue musikalische Zeitung,' Schumann's paper (Leipzig).

[1] Ferdinand David, destined to become so great a friend of Mendelssohn, was born in the same house the year after. The house is at the corner of the Brunnenstrasse, and is now, through the affectionate care of Mr. and Madame Otto Goldschmidt, decorated with a memorial tablet over the front door.

[2] Dutch (Hague 1769) ; French, 2 versions (Paris 1772, Berlin 1772) ; Italian, 2 do. (Chur 1773, Parma 1800) ; Danish (Copenhagen 1779) ; Hebrew (Berlin 1786) ; English (London 1789) ; also Russian, Polish, and Hungarian. It is a curious evidence of the slowness with which music penetrates into literary circles in England, that the excellent article on Moses Mendelssohn in the Penny Cyclopædia, from which the words in the text are quoted, though published in 1839, makes no mention of Felix, though he had then been four times in this country. The ' Phädon' attracted the notice of no less a person than Mirabeau— *Sur M. Mendelssohn*, etc., London 1787.

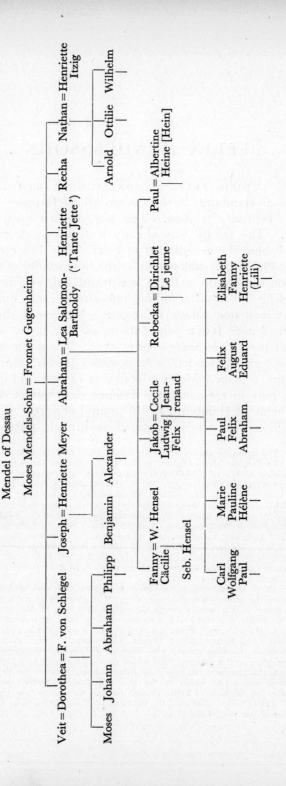

Mendel of Dessau

Moses Mendels-Sohn = Fromet Gugenheim

Veit = Dorothea = F. von Schlegel   Joseph = Henriette Meyer   Benjamin   Alexander   Abraham = Lea Salomon-Bartholdy   Henriette ('Tante Jette')   Recha   Nathan = Henriette Itzig

Moses   Johann   Abraham   Philipp

Benjamin   Alexander

Fanny = W. Hensel (Cäcilie)   Jakob Ludwig Felix = Cecile Jeanrenaud   Rebecka = Dirichlet Le jeune   Paul = Albertine Heine [Hein]

Seb. Hensel

Carl Wolfgang Paul   Marie Pauline Hélène   Paul Felix Abraham   Felix August Eduard   Elisabeth Fanny Henriette (Lili)

Arnold   Ottilie   Wilhelm

Phädon at Berlin in 1767, and died there January 4, 1786. He was a small humpbacked man with a keen eager face, bright eyes, and a humorous mouth. The first peculiarity was traceable in his grandchild Fanny, and the bright eyes were one of Felix's most noticeable characteristics. After the death of Moses his widow left Berlin with Joseph, the eldest son, and returned to her native city.

Abraham, the second son, born December 11, 1776, went to Paris, and in 1803 was cashier to Fould's bank there. In 1804 he resigned this post and went into partnership with his elder brother Joseph; married December 26, 1804, Lea Salomon (born March 15 [26], 1777), of a Jewish family in Berlin, and settled in Hamburg, carrying on his business at the house above mentioned, and having also a house out of town called ' Marten's Mühle.' He remained in Hamburg till 1811, and there were born to him Fanny Cäcilie (November 14, 1805), Jakob Ludwig Felix (February 3, 1809), and Rebecka (April 11, 1811). During the French occupation of Hamburg, life became intolerable, and shortly after Rebecka's birth the whole family escaped in disguise to Berlin, where they started the eminent banking-house, and lived in a large house on the Neue Promenade, in the N.E. quarter of the town, a broad open street or place between the Spree and the Haacksche Markt, with houses on one side only, the other side lying open to a canal with trees, a sufficiently retired spot as late as 1820 for Felix and his friends to play in front of it.[1] There, ten [eleven] days after the battle of Leipzig, Abraham's second son and youngest child Paul was born (October 30, 1813). The daughters of Moses Mendelssohn, Dorothea and Henriette, became Catholics. Dorothea married Friedrich von Schlegel, and Henriette was governess to [Fanny] the only daughter of General Sebastiani, afterwards (1847) so unfortunate as the Duchesse de Praslin. The sons remained Jews, but at length Abraham saw that the change was inevitable, and decided [2] to have his children baptised and brought up as Protestant Christians. This decision was taken on the advice and example of his wife's brother, Salomon Bartholdy, to whom also is due the adoption of the name Bartholdy. He himself had taken it, and he urged it on his brother-in-law as a means of distinction from the rest of the family. Salomon was a man of mark. He

[1] Dev. 2.   [2] F.M. i. 83.

resided in Rome for some time as Prussian Consul-General;
had his villa [on Monte Pincio] (Casa Bartholdy) decorated
with frescoes,¹ by Veit, Schadow, Cornelius, Overbeck, and
Schnorr, collected objects of art, and died there in 1827, leaving
his fortune to his sister Lea. He was cast off by his mother for
his conversion, and was only reconciled long after at the entreaty of Fanny.² At a later date Abraham and Lea were
received into the Christian Church at Frankfort, and Lea took
the additional names of Felicia Paulina, from her sons.

Abraham Mendelssohn was accustomed to describe his
position in life by saying ' formerly ³ I was the son of my father,
now I am the father of my son.' ⁴ But though not so prominent
as either, he was a man of strong character, wise judgment,
and very remarkable ability. These qualities are strikingly
obvious in the success of his method for the education of his
children, and in the few of his letters ⁵ which are published ;
and they are testified to in a very remarkable manner by his
son in many passages of his letters, and in the thorough deference
which he always pays to the judgment of his father, not only on
matters relating to the conduct of life, but on points of art.
Though not, like Leopold Mozart, a technical musician, and
apparently having no acquaintance with the art, he had yet
an insight into it which many musicians might envy. ' I am
often,' says his son, ' quite unable to understand how it is
possible to have so accurate a judgment about music without
being a technical musician, and if I could only say what I feel
in the same clear and intelligent manner that you always do,
I would certainly never make another confused speech as long
as I live.' ⁶ Or again, this time after his death, ' not only my
father, but . . . my teacher both in art and in life.' ⁷

Though apparently cold in his manners, and somewhat
stern in his tone, and towards the end perhaps unduly irritable,
Abraham Mendelssohn was greatly beloved by his wife and
children. Felix, in particular, is described by the latest bio-

¹ Felix's letter, Feb. 1, 1831 ; Fanny's do., F.M. ii. 127.   ² F.M. i. 83.
³ ' Früher war ich der Sohn meines Vaters, jetzt bin ich der Vater meines
Sohnes ' (F.M. i. 77). Said Talleyrand :—' L'on disait il y a douze ans que
M. de St. Aulaire étoit beau père de M. de Cazes; l'on dit maintenant que
M. de Cazes est gendre de M. de St. Aulaire.'—Macaulay's Life, i. 232.
⁴ Elsewhere he describes himself as a mere dash, a *gedankenstrich* (—) between
father and son. (F.M. i. 367.)
⁵ Letters, ii. 66, 83 ; F.M. i. 84, 87, 91 ; 347-386.
⁶ Letter, March 23, 1835.   ⁷ Briefe, ii. 106 ; Dec. 9. 1835.

grapher [1] as ' enthusiastically, almost fanatically, fond of him,'
and the letters show how close was the confidence which existed
between them. Hardly less remarkable was the mother. She
was one of those rare persons whose influence seems to be
almost in proportion to the absence of any attempt to exert it.
Hiller, when a boy, saw her once, and the impression made
upon him by the power of her quiet kindness and gentleness
remained fresh in his mind after more than half a century.[2]
When her house was thronged with the intellect and wit of
Berlin, she was the centre of the circle and the leader of the
conversation.[3] Her letters, of which large numbers exist in
manuscript, are full of cleverness and character. The education
of her children was her great object in life. She was strict —
we may now think over strict; [4] but no one who looks at the
result in the character of her children can say that her method
was not a wise one. They loved her dearly to the end, and the
last letters which Felix wrote to her are full of an overflowing
tenderness and a natural confidential intimacy which nothing
can surpass. Calm and reserved like her husband, she was full
of feeling, and had on occasion bursts of passion. Felix's
intention to leave Berlin affected her to a ' terrible ' degree — a
degree which surprised him. He confesses that his yielding to
the wishes of the King, after having made up his mind to retire,
was due solely to her. ' You think that in my official position
I *could* do nothing else. It was not that. It was my mother.' [5]

How far she was herself a pianoforte-player we are not told,
but the remark which she made after Fanny's birth, ' that the
child had got Bach-fugue fingers,' shows that she knew a good
deal about the matter. We learn also [6] that she herself for
some time taught the two eldest children music, beginning with
lessons five minutes long, and gradually increasing the time until
they went through a regular course of instruction. For many
years Felix and Fanny never practised or played without the
mother sitting by them, knitting in hand.

Felix was scarcely three when his family escaped to Berlin.
The first definite event of which we hear after this is a visit to
Paris by Joseph and Abraham in 1816, for the liquidation of
the indemnity to be paid by France to Prussia on account of
the war. Abraham took his family with him, and Felix and

[1] F.M. i. 424. Compare 349.   [2] Hiller, p. 3.   [3] Dev. 38.
[4] Devrient gives an instance or two of it; see p. 8, and 57 note.
[5] Letter, Jan. 13, 1843. See too Nov. 4, 1834.   [6] Benedict, p. 6.

Fanny, then 7 and 11 respectively, were taught the piano by Madame Bigot, a remarkable musician, and apparently an excellent teacher. She was the daughter of a Madame Kiéné, and in 1816 was 30 years old. Miniatures of the four children were taken during this visit, which are still in existence. Soon after their return from Paris to the grandmother's house at the Neue Promenade, where the family still lived, the children's education seems to have begun systematically. Heyse [1] was their tutor for general subjects, Ludwig Berger for the piano, Zelter for thorough bass and composition, Henning for the violin, and Rösel for landscape. Greek Felix learned with Rebecka, two years his junior, and advanced as far as Æschylus.[2] On October 24 [28], 1818, he made his first appearance in public at a concert given by a certain Herr Gugel, in which he played the pianoforte part of a Trio for pianoforte and 2 horns by Woelfl, and was much applauded.[3] The children were kept very closely to their lessons, and Felix is remembered in after-life to have said how much they enjoyed the Sundays, because then they were not forced to get up at 5 o'clock to work. Early in his 11th year, on April 11, 1819, he entered the singing class of the Singakademie as an alto, for the Friday practisings. There and elsewhere ' he took his place,' says Devrient,[4] ' amongst the grown people in his child's suit, a tight-fitting jacket cut very low at the neck, and with full trowsers buttoned over it. Into the slanting pockets of these he liked to thrust his hands, rocking his curly head (he had long brown curls) from side to side, and shifting restlessly from one foot to the other.'

With 1820, that is to say with his 12th year, Felix seems to have begun systematically to compose ; at least with that year begins the invaluable series of 44 volumes, in which Mendelssohn's methodical habits have preserved a collection of autographs or copies of a great part of his works, published and unpublished, down to the time of his death, the majority carefully inscribed with both date and place — which are now deposited in the Imperial Library at Berlin.

To the year 1820 are attributable between 50 and 60 movements, including amongst them a Trio for pianoforte and strings (3 movements) ; a sonata for pianoforte and violin in F (3 do.) ; 2 movements for the same in D minor ; 2 full sonatas

---

[1] Father of Paul Heyse the novelist.   [2] Schubring, 374 a.
A.M.Z. 1818, p. 791.   [4] Dev. p. 2.

for pianoforte solo; the beginning of a 3rd in G minor, finished the next year, and published in 1868 (as op. 105); 6 pieces for pianoforte solo; 3 do. for do., 4 hands; 4 pieces for organ; 3 songs for single voice; 2 do. for 4 men's voices; a cantata, 'In rührend feierlichen Tönen'; and a Lustspiel, or little comedy, for voices and pianoforte in 3 scenes, beginning 'Ich J. Mendelssohn.' The earliest date is that to the cantata — January 13, 1820. The extraordinary neatness and finish, which characterise Mendelssohn's MSS. to the end, are observable in the earliest of these childish productions, and the mysterious letters L. e g. G. or H. d. m., so familiar to those who know his latest scores, are usually at the head of each.

Among the pieces for 1821 are 5 sinfonies for string quartet, each in 3 movements; 9 fugues for ditto; the completion of the G minor Pianoforte Sonata (op. 105); motets for 4 voices; a couple of songs; a couple of études for pianoforte solo; 2 one-act operas, 'Soldatenliebschaft' and 'Die beiden Pädagogen'; [1] and half a third, 'Die wandernde[n] Comödianten.' This was the year of his acquaintance with Weber, then in Berlin for the production of Freischütz, and of an enthusiasm on the part of the boy for that romantic composer which he never lost.[2] This too was the year of his first visit to Goethe. Zelter took his pupil to Weimar in November, and they passed sixteen days under the old poet's roof.[3]

The same incessant and varied production marks 1822 and 1823. In the summer of 1822 the whole family made a tour in Switzerland. Starting on July 6, they went by Cassel (for Spohr), Frankfort, Darmstadt, Schaffhausen, Amsteg, Interlachen [Interlaken], Vevey, and Chamounix; a large and merry party of ten, besides servants. The tour was taken at great leisure, and on the return two important halts were made — first at Frankfort, to make the acquaintance of Schelble, the conductor of the famous Cäcilien-Verein, whom Felix astonished by extemporising on Bach's motets; and at Weimar, for a second visit to Goethe.[4]

At Secheron, near Geneva, 2 songs were written (September 18); and the Pianoforte Quartet in C minor, afterwards published as op. 1, was begun to be put on paper (the auto-

---

[1] Words by Dr. Caspar (Dev. p. 5).   [2] H. 32.
[3] See details in *Goethe and Mendelssohn*. See also Rellstab, *Aus meinem Leben*, ii. 135; and Lobe, in *Once a Week* for 1867.
[4] G. & M. 33.

graph being marked ' Begun at Secheron 20 September 1822 '),
and was finished after the return home. Besides this, the
records of these two years (1822 and 23) contain 6 more
symphonies, Nos. 7, 8, 9, 10, 11, 12 ; 5 [6] detached pieces for
strings ; 5 concertos for solo instruments with quartet accompaniment, viz. 1 for violin solo, 1 for pianoforte solo, 1 for
pianoforte and violin, and 2 for two pianofortes ; 2 quartets
for pianoforte and strings, viz. in C minor (op. 1) and in
F minor (op. 2) ; sonatas for pianoforte and violin (op. 4)
and for pianoforte and viola (MS.) ; a fantasia and 3 other
pieces for the organ ; a fugue and fantasia for pianoforte ; a
Kyrie for two choirs ; a psalm, 3 songs, a piece for contralto
solo and strings in 3 movements to Italian text (No. 167),
2 songs for men's voices, and the completion of the fourth
opera, ' Die beiden Neffen,' or ' Der Onkel aus Boston,' which
was a full-grown piece in three acts. The symphonies show a
similar advance. They are in four movements instead of three,
as before, and the length of the movements increases. No. 8,
in D, written November 6 — November 27, after the return
from Switzerland, has an *Adagio e grave* before the opening
Allegro. The slow movement is for 3 violas and bass, and the
finale has a prominent part for the cello. This symphony must
have pleased the composer or some of his audience in whose
judgment he believed, since within a month he began to rescore
it for full orchestra. He wrote a new trio for the minuet, and
in this form it became Symphony No. 9. The three last of the
six are for quintet, and the Scherzos of Nos. 10 and 12 are
founded on Swiss tunes, in No. 12 with the addition of triangles,
cymbals, and drums. The independent cello part is conspicuous throughout. This advance in his music is in keeping
with the change going on in Felix himself. He was now nearly
15 [14], was growing fast,[1] his features and his expression were
altering and maturing, his hair was cut short,[2] and he was put
into jackets and trousers. His extemporising — which he had
begun to practise early in 1821 [3] — was already remarkable,[4]
and there was a dash of audacity in it hardly characteristic of
the mature man. Thus Goethe wished to hear a certain fugue
of Bach's, and as Felix could not remember it all he developed it
himself at great length, which he would hardly have done later.[5]

[1] Zelter, in G. & M. 35.   [2] F.M. i. 130 ; Dev. 10.
[3] F.M. 100.   [4] Dev. 11.   [5] F.M. i. 129.

In 1822 he made a second appearance in public of a more serious nature than before, viz. on March 31, at a concert of Aloys Schmitt's, in which he played with Schmitt a duet of Dussek's for 2 pianos; and on December 5 he again appeared at a concert of Anna Milder's, in a pianoforte concerto of his own, probably that in A minor with quintet accompaniment.[1]

It must not be supposed that the symphonies, operas, quartets, concertos, and other words mentioned were written for exercise only. It had been the custom in the Mendelssohn house for some time past to have musical parties on alternate Sunday mornings, with a small orchestra, in the large dining-room of the house, and the programmes included one or more of Felix's compositions. As a rule the pianoforte part was taken by himself or Fanny, or both, while Rebecka sang, and Paul played the cello.[2] But Felix always conducted, even when so small as to have to stand on a stool to be seen; and thus enjoyed the benefit not only of hearing his compositions played (a benefit for which less fortunate composers — Schubert, for example — have sighed in vain) but of the practice in conduct-ing and in playing before an audience.[3] The size of the room was not sufficient for a large audience, but on these occasions it was always full, and few musicians of note passed through Berlin without being present.[4] In performing the operettas and operas, no attempt was made to act them. The characters were distributed as far as the music went, but the dialogue was read out from the piano, and the chorus sat round the dining-table. Zelter, in strong contrast to his usual habit of impartial neglect of his pupils,[5] was not only regularly there, but would criticise the piece at the close of the performance, and if he often praised would sometimes blame. The comments of his hearers, however, were received by Felix with perfect simplicity. De-vrient has well described how entirely the music itself was his aim, and how completely subordinated were self-conscious-ness and vanity to the desire of learning, testing, and progressing in his art. These Sunday performances, however, were only

[1] A.M.Z. 1822, 273; 1823, 55.   [2] F. M. ii. 45.
[3] It seems that he accompanied the quartet symphonies on the piano. Dorn, in his Recollections, expressly says so, and the slow movement of the Symphony No. 10 contains a note in Mendelssohn's own writing, ' Das Klavier mit dem Basse,' which seems to prove it. The practice, therefore, did not end with last century, as has been supposed (On the Growth of the Modern Orchestra, Mus. Association 1878-9, p. 37). Indeed, as we shall see, Mendelssohn conducted from the piano at the Philharmonic in 1829.
[4] F.M. i. 137.   [5] Dev. 4.

S

one feature of the artistic and intellectual life of the house.
Music went on every evening more or less, theatricals, impromptu or studied, were often got up, and there was a constant
flux and reflux of young, clever, distinguished people, who
made the suppers delightfully gay and noisy, and among whom
Felix was the favourite.

The full rehearsal of his fourth opera, ' Die beiden Neffen,'
on his birthday, February 3, 1824, was an event in the boy's life.
At supper, after the conclusion of the work, Zelter, adopting
freemason phraseology, raised him from the grade of ' appren-
tice,' and pronounced him an ' assistant,' ' in the name of
Mozart, and of Haydn, and of old Bach.' [1] A great incentive
to his progress had been given shortly before this in the score
of Bach's Passion, copied by Zelter's express permission from
the MS. in the Singakademie, and given him by his grandmother at Christmas, 1823. The copy was made by Eduard
Rietz,[2] who had succeeded Henning as his violin teacher, and
to whom he was deeply attached. His confirmation took place
about this date, under Wilmsen, a well-known clergyman of
Berlin. Preparation for confirmation in Germany is often a
long and severe process, and though it may not [3] in Felix's
case have led to any increase in church-going, as it probably
would in that of an English lad similarly situated, yet we may
be sure that it deepened that natural religious feeling which
was so strong an element in the foundation of his character.

In the compositions of 1824 there is a great advance. The
Symphony in C minor (op. 11) — which we know as ' No. I,'
but which on the autograph in the library of the Philharmonic
Society is marked ' No. XIII ' — was composed between
March 3 and 31. The Sestet for pianoforte and strings (op.
110), the Quartet in B minor [4] (op. 3), a fantasia for 4 hands
on the pianoforte, and a motet in 5 numbers, are all amongst
the works of this year. An important event in the summer of
1824 was a visit of the father, Felix, and Rebecka, to Dobberan,
a bathing place on the shores of the Baltic near Rostock. For
the wind-band at the bath-establishment Felix wrote an overture, which he afterwards scored for a full military band and
published as Op. 24. But the chief result of the visit was that

---

[1] F.M. i. 140; Dorn, 399.
[2] Or Ritz, as Mendelssohn always spells it. He seems to have been on the
whole Felix's most intimate early friend.
[3] Sch. 375.   [4] Finished Jan. 18, 1825.

he there for the first time saw the sea, and received those
impressions and images which afterwards found their tangible
shape in the Meeresstille Overture.

Among the great artists who came into contact with Felix
at this time was Moscheles, then on his way from Vienna to
Paris and London. He was already famous as a player, and
Madame Mendelssohn calls him ' the prince of pianists.' He
remained in Berlin for six weeks in November and December,
1824, and was almost daily at the Mendelssohns'; and after
a time, at the urgent request of the parents, and with great
hesitation on his own part, gave Felix regular lessons on the
pianoforte every other day. Moscheles was now just turned
thirty. It is pleasant to read of his unfeigned love and admiration for Felix and his home — ' a family such as I have never
known before; Felix a mature artist, and yet but fifteen;
Fanny extraordinarily gifted, playing Bach's fugues by heart
and with astonishing correctness — in fact, a thorough musician. The parents give me the impression of people of the
highest cultivation. They are very far from being over-proud
of their children; indeed, they are in anxiety about Felix's
future, whether his gifts are lasting, and will lead to a solid,
permanent future, or whether he may not suddenly collapse,
like so many other gifted children.' ' He has no need of lessons;
if he wishes to take a hint from me as to anything new to him,
he can easily do so.' Such remarks as these do honour to all
concerned, and it is delightful to find Mendelssohn years
afterwards, in the full glory of his great fame, referring to these
very lessons as having fanned the sacred fire within him and
urged him on to enthusiasm.[1]

Moscheles has preserved two of the Sunday morning
programmes : —

' November 28. Morning music at the Mendelssohns' :—
Felix's C minor Quartet; D major Symphony; Concerto by
Bach (Fanny); Duet for 2 pianos in D minor, Arnold.'

' December 12. Sunday music at Mendelssohns' :—Felix's
F minor Quartet. I played my Duet for 2 Pianos in G. Little
Schilling played Hummel's Trio in G.'

Moscheles was followed by Spohr, who came to superintend
the production of his ' Jessonda ' (February 14, 1825). He
was often at the house, and on very intimate terms,[2] though he

[1] Moscheles Leben, i. 93; ii. 161.   [2] F.M. i. 144.

does not mention the fact in his Autobiography.

One or two accounts by competent judges of Felix's style of playing at this time have survived. Hiller was with him in Frankfort in the spring of 1825, and speaks [1] both of his extemporising, and of his playing the music of others. With the latter he delighted both Hiller and André (who relished neither his face, his ideas, nor his manners) by playing the *Allegretto* of Beethoven's 7th Symphony in such a ' powerful orchestral style ' as fairly to stop André's mouth. With the former he carried Hiller away by extemporising on Handel's choruses in ' Judas,' as he had done Schelble, in the same room, three years before, on subjects from Bach's motets. This time his playing was quite in the vein of his subject, ' the figures thoroughly Handelian, the force and clearness of the passages in thirds and sixths and octaves really grand, and yet all belonging to the subject-matter, thoroughly true, genuine, living music, with no trace of display.' Dorn is more explicit as to his accompanying — the duet in Fidelio. ' He astonished me in the passage, Du wieder nun in meinen Armen, Gott ! by the way in which he represented the cello and the basso parts on the piano, playing them two octaves apart. I asked him why he chose that striking way of rendering the passage, and he explained it all to me in the kindest manner. How many times since, says Dorn, has that duet been sung, but how seldom has it been so accompanied ! ' [2] He rarely played from book, either at this or any other time of his life. Even works like Beethoven's 9th Symphony, and the Sonata in B♭ (op. 106), he knew by heart.[3] One of the grounds of Spontini's enmity to him is said to have been a performance of the 9th Symphony by Felix, without book, before Spontini himself had even heard it, and it is known on the best authority that he played the Symphony through by heart only a few months before his death. Here we may say that he had a passion for Beethoven's latest works, his acquaintance with which dated from their publication, Beethoven's last years (1820–27) exactly corresponding with his own growth to maturity. It was almost the only subject on which he disagreed with his father.[4] On the other hand, the devotion of such very conservative artists as

---

[1] Hiller, pp. 5, 6.   [2] Dorn, p. 398.
[3] Marx, *Erinnerungen*, ii. 117, confirmed to me by the Duke of Meiningen, Taubert, Schleinitz, Klengel, Davison, and others.
[4] Letter, Nov. 22, 1830.

David, Rietz, and Bennett, to those works, is most probably due to Mendelssohn's influence. Marx [1] challenges his reading of Beethoven; but this is to fly in the face of the judgment of all other critics.

The elder Mendelssohn made at this time [1825] a journey to Paris, for the purpose of fetching his sister Henriette back to Germany, and took Felix with him. They arrived on March 22. One of the first things he mentions is the astonishment of his relatives at finding him no longer a child.[2] He plunged at once into musical society. Hummel, Onslow, Boucher, Herz, Halévy, Kalkbrenner, Moscheles (on his way back from Hamburg to London, with his bride), Pixis, Rode, Baillot, Kreutzer, Rossini, Paer, Meyerbeer, Plantade, and many more, were there, and all glad to make acquaintance with the wonderful boy. At Madame Kiéné's — Madame Bigot's mother — he played his new Quartet (in B minor) with Baillot and others, and with the greatest success.

The French musicians, however, made but a bad impression on him. Partly, no doubt, this is exaggerated in his letters, as in his criticism on Auber's Leocadie; [3] but the ignorance of German music — even Onslow,[4] for example, had never heard a note of Fidelio — and the insults to some of its masterpieces (such as the transformation of Freischütz into ' Robin des Bois,' [5] and the comparison of a passage in Bach to a duet of Monsigny), and the general devotion to effect and outside glitter — these were just the things to enrage the lad at that enthusiastic age. With Cherubini their intercourse was very satisfactory. The old Florentine was more than civil to Felix, and his expressions of satisfaction (so very rare in his mouth) must have given the father the encouragement which he was so slow [6] to take in the great future of his boy. Felix describes him in a few words as ' an extinct volcano, now and then blazing up, but all covered with ashes and stones.' He wrote a Kyrie ' *a* 5 *voci* and *grandissimo* orchestra ' at Cherubini's instance,[7] which he describes as ' bigger than anything he had yet done.' [8] It seems to have been lost. Through all this the

---

[1] *Erinn.* ii. 135.   [2] F.M. i. 146.   [3] G. & M. p. 43.
[4] F.M. i. 149, and MS. letter.   [5] G. & M. 48.
[6] Marx (*Erinn.* ii. 113, 114) says that the father's hesitation as to his son's future was so great that, even to a late date, he constantly urged him to go into business. He believed that his son had no genius for music, and that it was all the happier for him that he had not.
[7] Zelter's Letters, iv. 35; G. & M. 49.   [8] 'An Dickigkeit alles übertrifft.'

letters home are as many as ever, full of music, descriptions, and jokes — often very bad ones. Here, for instance, is a good professional query, ' Ask Ritz if he knows what *Fes moll* is.'

On May 19, 1825, the father and son left Paris with Henriette (' Tante Jette '), who had retired from her post at General Sebastiani's with an ample pension, and thenceforward resided at Berlin. On the road home they paid a short visit (the third) to Goethe, at Weimar. Felix played the B minor Quartet, and delighted the poet by dedicating it to him.[1] It is a marvellous work for a boy of sixteen, and an enormous advance on either of its two predecessors ; but probably no one — not even the composer — suspected that the Scherzo (in F♯ minor, 3-8) was to be the first of a ' family of scherzi which, if he had produced nothing else, would stamp him as an inventor in the most emphatic signification of the word.' It must be admitted that Goethe made him a very poor return for his charming music. Anything more stiff and ungraceful than the verses which he wrote for him, and which are given in ' Goethe and Mendelssohn,' it would be difficult to find, unless it be another stanza, also addressed to Felix, and printed in vol. vi. p. 144 of the poet's works :—

Wenn das Talent verständig waltet,	If Talent reigns with Wisdom great,
Wirksame Tugend nie veraltet.	Virtue is never out of date.
Wer Menschen gründlich konnt' erfreun,	He who can give us pleasure true
Der darf sich vor der Zeit nicht scheun ;	Need never fear what time can do ;
Und möchtet ihr ihm Beifall geben,	And will you Talent your approval give ?
So gebt ihn uns, die wir ihn frisch beleben.	Then give it us who make her newly live.

They were at home before the end of May. The fiery Capriccio for pianoforte in F♯ minor (afterwards published as op. 5), so full of the spirit of Bach, is dated July 23 of this year, and the score of Camacho's Wedding — an opera in two acts by Klingemann, founded on an episode in Don Quixote — August 10. The Capriccio was a great favourite with him, and he called it *un[e] absurdité*.

The Mendelssohn-Bartholdy family was beginning to outgrow the accommodation afforded by the grandmother's roof, and at the end of this summer they removed from No. 7 Neue Promenade to a large house and grounds which had formerly

[1] For the details see G. & M. 50.

belonged to the noble family of Reck, namely to No. 3 of the Leipziger Strasse, the address so familiar to all readers of Felix's subsequent letters. If we were writing the life of an ancient prophet or poet, we should take the name of the ' Leipzig Road ' as a prediction of his ultimate establishment in that town ; but no token of such an event was visible at the time. The new residence lay in a part of Berlin which was then very remote, close to the Potsdam Gate, on the edge of the old Thiergarten, or deer-park, of Frederick the Great, so far from all the accustomed haunts of their friends, that at first the laments were loud. The house was of a dignified, old-fashioned kind, with spacious and lofty rooms ; behind it a large court with offices, and behind that again a beautiful stretch of ground, half park, half garden, with noble trees, lilacs, and other flowering shrubs, turf, alleys, walks, banks, summer-houses, and seats — the whole running far back, covering about ten acres, and being virtually in the country. Its advantages for music were great. The house itself contained a room precisely fitted for large music parties or private theatricals ; and at the back of the court, and dividing it from the garden, there was a separate building called the ' Gartenhaus,' the middle of which formed a hall capable of containing several hundred persons, with glass doors opening right on to the lawns and alleys — in short a perfect place for the Sunday music. Though not without its drawbacks in winter — reminding one of Mr. Hensel's almost pathetic description [1] of the normal condition of too many an English house — it was an ideal summer home, and ' 3, Leipziger Strasse ' is in Mendelssohn's mouth a personality, to which he always turned with longing, and which he loved as much as he hated the rest of Berlin. It was identified with the Mendelssohn-Bartholdys till his death, after which it was sold to the state ; and the Herrenhaus, or House of Lords of the German government, now stands on the site of the former court and Gartenhaus.[2]

Devrient [3] takes the completion of Camacho and the leaving the grandmother's house as the last acts of Felix's musical minority ; and he is hardly wrong, for the next composition

---

[1] F.M. i. 142.
[2] The large yew-tree which stood close outside the Gartenhaus and was endangered by the extension of the new building, was preserved by the special order of the Emperor, and is still (1879) vigorous, and as gloomy as a yew should be.
[3] Dev. 20.

was a wonderful leap into maturity. It was no other than the Octet for strings (afterwards published as op. 20), which was finished towards the end of October 1825, and was dedicated as a birthday gift to Edward Ritz [Rietz]. It is the first of his works which can be said to have fully maintained its ground on its own merits,[1] and is a truly astonishing composition for a boy half-way through his 17th year. There is a radiance, a freedom, and an individuality in the style which are far ahead of the 13th Symphony, or any other of the previous instrumental works, and it is steeped throughout in that inexpressible captivating charm which is so remarkable in all Mendelssohn's best compositions. The Scherzo especially (G minor, 2-4) is a movement of extraordinary lightness and grace, and the Finale, besides being a masterly piece of counterpoint (it is a fugue), contains in the introduction of the subject of the Scherzo a very early instance of the ' transformation of themes,' of which we have lately heard so much. Felix had confided to Fanny [2] that his motto for the Scherzo was the following stanza in the Intermezzo of Faust : —

Orchestra.—*pianissimo.*

Wolkenzug und Nebelflor	Floating cloud and trailing mist
Erhellen sich von oben ;	Bright'ning o'er us hover ;
Luft im Laub, und Wind im Rohr,	Airs stir the brake, the rushes shake —
— Und alles ist zerstoben.	And all their pomp is over.

and never was a motto more perfectly carried out in execution. The whole of the last part, so light and airy — and the end, in particular, where the fiddles run softly up to the high G, accompanied only with staccato chords — is a perfect illustration of ' alles ist zerstoben.' He afterwards instrumented it for the full orchestra, but it is hard to say if it is improved by the process.—The so-called Trumpet Overture, in C (op. 101), was almost certainly composed this autumn, and was first heard at a concert given by Maurer, in Berlin, on November 2,[3] at which Felix played the pianoforte part of Beethoven's Choral Fantasia. This overture was a special favourite of Abraham Mendelssohn, who said that he should like to hear it while

---

[1] It was played 14 times at the Monday Popular Concerts between 1859 and 1878.   [2] F.M. i. 154.
[3] A.M.Z. xxvii. p. 825. The autograph was once in possession of Mr. Schleinitz. From him it went into the omnivorous maw of Julius Rietz, and was probably sold by his executors ; but to whom ? The MS. in our Philharmonic library is a copy with corrections by Mendelssohn.

he died.   It was for long in MS. in the hands of the Philharmonic Society, and was not published till many years after the
death of the composer.   1826 opens with the String Quintet
in A[1] (op. 18), which if not perhaps so great as the Octet, is
certainly on the same side of the line, and the scherzo of which,
in fugue-form, is a worthy companion to its predecessors.   The
Sonata in E (op. 6) is of this date (March 22, 1826).   So is an
interesting looking Andante and Allegro (June 27), written for
the wind-band of a Beer-garden which he used to pass on the
way to bathe ; the MS. is safe in the hands of Dr. Paul Mendelssohn-Bartholdy.

But all these were surpassed by the Overture to ' A Midsummer Night's Dream,' which was composed during the
peculiarly fine summer of 1826, under the charming conditions
of life in the new garden,[2] and the score of which is signed
' Berlin, August 6, 1826.'   It appears to have been the immediate result of a closer acquaintance with Shakespeare, through
the medium of Schlegel and Tieck's version, which he and his
sisters read this year for the first time.   Marx claims to have
been much consulted[3] during its progress, and even to have
suggested essential modifications.   Fanny also no doubt was
in this, as in other instances, her brother's confidante, but the
result must have astonished even the fondest wishes of those
who knew him best.   It is asserted by one[4] who has the best
right to judge, and is not prone to exaggeration, ' that no one
piece of music contains so many points of harmony and orchestration that had never been written before ; and yet none of
them have the air of experiment, but seem all to have been
written with certainty of their success.'   In this wonderful
overture, as in the Octet and Quintet, the airy fairy lightness,
and the peculiar youthful grace, are not less remarkable than
the strength of construction and solidity of workmanship which
underlie and support them.   Not the least singular thing about
it is the exact manner in which it is found to fit into the music
for the whole play when that music was composed 17 years
later.   The *motives* of the overture all turn out to have their
native places in the drama.[5]   After many a performance as a

[1] Zelter, letter of June 6. This MS. too seems to have disappeared.
[2] The first letter that I have found dated from the Leipziger Strasse, ' am
7 July 1826, im Garten,' says, ' to-day or to-morrow I shall begin to dream the
Midsummer night's dream.'
[3] Dev. 35. Marx, *Erinn.* ii. 231—3.
[4] Prof. Macfarren, Philharmonic book, April 30, 1877.   [5] Reissmann, 62.

duet on the piano, the overture was played by an orchestra in the Mendelssohns' garden-house, to a crowded audience, and its first production in public seems to have been at Stettin, in February 1827, whither Felix went in very severe weather to conduct it.[1] With the composition of this work he may be said to have taken his final musical degree, and his lessons with Zelter were discontinued.

Camacho had been submitted to Spontini as General-Music-Director in the preceding year by Felix himself. Spontini was then, by an odd freak of fortune, living in a house which had for some time been occupied by the Mendelssohns in the early part of their residence in Berlin, viz. 28 Markgrafen Strasse, opposite the Catholic church. Taking the young composer by the arm, Spontini led him to the window, and pointing to the dome across the street, said, ' Mon ami, il vous faut des idées grandes comme cette coupole.'[2] This from a man of 52, in the highest position, to a boy of 17, could hardly have been meant for anything but kindly, though pompous, advice. But it was not so taken. The Mendelssohns and Spontini were not only of radically different natures, but they belonged to opposite parties in music, and there was considerable friction in their intercourse. At length, early in 1827, after various obstructions on Spontini's part, the opera was given out for rehearsal and study, and on April 29 was produced. The house — not the Opera, but the smaller theatre — was crowded with friends, and the applause vehement; at the end the composer was loudly called for, but he had left the theatre, and Devrient had to appear in his stead. Owing to the illness of Blum, the tenor, the second performance was postponed, and the piece was never again brought forward. Partly from the many curious obstructions which arose in the course of the rehearsals, and the personal criticisms which followed it, partly perhaps from a just feeling that the libretto was poor and his music somewhat exaggerated, but mainly no doubt from the fact that during two such progressive years as had passed since he wrote the piece he had outgrown his work,[3] Felix seems to have so

[1] F.M. i. 156. Felix's MS. letter from Stettin, Feb. 17, 1827, is the first in which his father is addressed as ' Herr Stadtrath.'

[2] 'My friend, your ideas must be grand—grand as that dome.' Marx, Erinn. i. 247.

[3] ' For God's sake,' says he in 1843 to Mr. Bartholomew, ' do not let my old sin of Camacho's Wedding be stirred up again ! ' (Polko, by Lady Wallace, p. 217.) In the same manner in 1835 he protests to Mrs. Voigt against the performance of his C minor Symphony—at least without the explanation that it was written by a boy of barely 15. (Acht Briefe, etc., p. 20.)

far lost interest in it as not to press for another performance.
The music was published complete in pianoforte score by Laue,
of Berlin, and one of the songs was included in op. 10, as No. 8.
It should not be overlooked that the part of Don Quixote
affords an instance of the use of ' Leit-motif ' — a term which
has very lately come into prominence, but which was here
Mendelssohn's own invention.

A nature so keenly sensitive as his could hardly be expected
to pass with impunity through such worries as attended the
production of the opera. He was so sincere and honest that
the sneers of the press irritated him unduly. A year before
he had vented his feelings in some lines which will be new to
most readers : —

Schreibt der Komponiste ernst
    Schläfert er uns ein ;
Schreibt der Komponiste froh,
    Ist er zu gemein.
	If the artist gravely writes,
	    To sleep it will beguile,
	If the artist gaily writes,
	    It is a vulgar style.

Schreibt der Komponiste lang,
    Ist er zum Erbarmen ;
Schreibt ein Komponiste kurz,
    Kann man nicht erwarmen.
	If the artist writes at length,
	    How sad his hearer's lot!
	If the artist briefly writes,
	    No man will care one jot.

Schreibt ein Komponiste klar,
    Ist's ein armer Tropf ;
Schreibt ein Komponiste tief
    Rappelt's ihn am Kopf.
	If an artist simply writes,
	    A fool he's said to be.
	If an artist deeply writes,
	    He's mad ; 'tis plain to see.

Schreib' er also wie er will,
    Keinem steht es an ;
Darum schreib ein Komponist
    Wie er will und kann. [1]
	In whatsoever way he writes
	    He can't please every man ;
	Therefore let an artist write
	    How he likes and can.

But on the present occasion the annoyance was too deep to
be thrown off by a joke. It did in fact for a time seriously
affect his health and spirits, and probably laid the foundation
for that dislike of the officialism and pretension, the artists
and institutions, the very soil and situation of Berlin, which so
curiously pervades his letters whenever he touches on that city.[2]
His depression was increased by the death of an old friend,
named Hanstein, who was carried off this spring, and by the
side of whose deathbed Felix composed the well-known Fugue
in E minor (op. 35, no. 1). The chorale in the major, which

[1] Written for his mother's birthday, March 15, 1826. See *Ueber Land und
Meer*, 1873, No. 36.
[2] See the two letters to Verkenius, Aug. 14 and 23, 1841 ; also one to Hiller,
March 25, 1843 (H. p. 207), and far more strongly in many an unpublished letter.

forms the climax of the fugue, is intended, as we are told on
good authority, to express his friend's release.[1] But Felix was
too young and healthy, and his nature too eager, to allow him
to remain in despondency. A sonata in B♭, for pianoforte solo
(afterwards published as op. 106) is signed May 31, 1827, and on
Whit-Sunday, June 3, we find him at Sakrow, near Potsdam,
the property of his friend Magnus, composing the charming
Lied, ' Ist es wahr ? ' which within a few months he employed
to advantage in his Quartet in A minor (op. 13). Meantime
— probably in 1826[2] [on May 2, 1826] — he had entered the
university of Berlin, where his tutor Heyse was now a professor.
For his matriculation essay he sent in a translation in verse of
the Andria of Terence, which primarily served as a birthday
present to his mother[3] (March 15). This translation was
published in a volume,[4] with a preface and essay, and a version
of the 9th Satire of Horace, by Heyse. Mendelssohn's translation has been recently examined by an eminent English scholar,
who reports that as a version it is precise and faithful, exceedingly literal, and corresponding closely with the original both
in rhythm and metre, while its language, as far as an Englishman may judge of German, is quite worthy of representing the
limpid Latin of Terence. Professor Munro also points out that
as this was the first attempt in Germany to render Terence in
his own metres, it may be presumed to have set the example to
the scholars who have since that date, as a rule, translated
Plautus and Terence and other kindred Greek and Latin classics
in the original metres. It was by no means his first attempt
at verse ; for a long mock-heroic of the year 1820 has been
preserved, called the Paphleïs, in 3 cantos, occupied with the
adventures of his brother Paul (Paphlos), full of slang and
humour, and in hexameters.

Whether Felix went through the regular university course
or not, does not appear, but no doubt the proceeding was a
systematic one, and he certainly attended several classes,
amongst them those of Hegel,[5] and took especial pleasure in

---

[1] Schubring, 375 *a*.   [2] I cannot obtain the exact date.
[3] Schubring, 374 *b*.
[4] *Das Mädchen von Andros, eine Komödie des Terentius, in den Versmassen des
Originals übersetzt von F. . . . Mit Einleitung und Anmerkungen herausgegeben von
K. W. L. Heyse. Angehängt ist die 9te Satire des Horatius, übersetzt von dem Her-
ausgeber. Berlin 1826. Bei Ferdinand Dümmler.* The preface is dated ' July
1826.'
[5] One course of these was on Music. Zelter, in G. & M. 54.

the lectures of the great Carl Ritter on geography. Of his notes of these, two folio volumes, closely written in a hand like copper-plate, and dated 1827 and 1828, still exist. Italian he was probably familiar with before he went to Italy; and in later years he knew it so thoroughly as to be able to translate into German verse the very crabbed sonnets of Dante, Boccaccio, Cecco Angiolieri, and Cino, for his uncle Joseph in 1840.[1] Landscape drawing, in which he was ultimately to excel so greatly, he had already worked at for several years. For mathematics he had neither taste nor capacity, and Schubring pathetically describes the impossibility of making him comprehend how the polestar could be a guide in travelling.

The change into the new house was a great event in the family life. Felix began gymnastics, and became a very great proficient in them. He also learned to ride, and to swim, and with him learning a thing meant practising it to the utmost, and getting all the enjoyment and advantage that could be extracted from it. He was a great dancer, now and for many years after. Billiards he played brilliantly. Skating was the one outdoor exercise which he did not succeed in — he could not stand the cold. The garden was a vast attraction to their friends, and *Boccia* (a kind of bowls) was the favourite game under the old chestnut-trees which still overshadow the central alley. The large rooms also gave a great impetus to the music, and to the mixed society which now flocked to the house more than ever. We hear of Rahel and Varnhagen, Bettina, Heine, Holtei, Lindblad, Steffens, Gans, Marx, Kugler, Droysen; of Humboldt, W. Müller,[2] Hegel (for whom alone a card-table was provided), and other intellectual and artistic persons, famous, or to be famous afterwards. Young people, too, there were in troops; the life was free, and it must have been a delightful, wholesome, and thoroughly enjoyable time. Among the features of the garden life was a newspaper, which in summer was called ' Gartenzeitung,' ' The Garden Times '; in winter ' Schnee-und-Thee-zeitung,' ' The Snow-and-Tea Times.' It appears to have been edited by Felix and Marx, but all comers were free to contribute, for which purpose pens, ink, and paper lay in one of the summer-houses. Nor was it confined to the

---

[1] They are given in their place in the later editions of the Letters, vol. ii.
[2] Father of Max Müller, and author of Schubert's ' Schöne Müllerin.'

younger part of the society, but grave personages, like Humboldt and Zelter even, did not disdain to add their morsel of fun or satire. In all this brilliant interchange of art, science, and literature, Felix, even at this early date, was the prominent figure. It was now as it was all through his life. When he entered the room every one was anxious to speak to him. Women of double his age made love to him, and men, years afterwards, recollected the evenings they had spent with him, and treasured every word that fell from his lips.[1] One who knew him well at this time, but afterwards broke with him, speaks of the separation as ' a draught of wormwood, the bitter taste of which remained for years.' [2]

The latter half of August and the whole of September were passed in a tour with Magnus and Heydemann [3] through the Harz mountains to Baden-Baden (where his amusing adventures must be read in his letters), and thence by Heidelberg, where he made the acquaintance of Thibaut [4] and his old Italian music, to Frankfort. At Frankfort he saw Schelble and Hiller, and delighted them with his new A minor Quartet (op. 13) — not yet fully written down; and with the ' Midsummer Night's Dream ' overture, which although a year old was still new to the world.

The annoyance about Camacho had vanished with the tour, and Felix could now treat the story as a joke, and take off the principal persons concerned. The A minor Quartet was completed directly after his return home, and is dated ' Berlin, Oct. 27 [26], 1827.' Of further compositions this year we know only of the beautiful fugue in E♭ for strings (on his favourite old ecclesiastical subject), which since his death has been published as the 4th movement of op. 81. It is dated Berlin, November 1. Also a ' Tu es Petrus ' for choir and orchestra, written for Fanny's birthday (November 14), and published as op. 111. A very comic ' Kinder-symphonie ' for the Christmas home party, for the same orchestra as Haydn's, and a motet for 4 voices and small orchestra on the chorale ' Christe du Lamm Gottes,' are named by Fanny in a letter.[5]

---

[1] For instances of this see Dorn, and also Gathy in N.M.Z. 1848.
[2] Marx, *Erinn.* ii. 138.
[3] Louis Heydemann was a very eccentric person. He possessed many MSS. of Mendelssohn's — amongst others the Sonata in E (op. 7) and the Cello variations (op. 17). These — 10 in number, dating from 1824 to 29 — are now all in the possession of Dr. Paul Mendelssohn-Bartholdy.
[4] F.M. i. 161-166.   [5] F.M. i. 180, 181.

Soon after this their circle sustained a loss in the departure of Klingemann, one of the cleverest and most genial of the set, to London as Secretary to the Hans [Hanoverian] Legation. During this winter Felix — incited thereto by a complaint of Schubring's that Bach always seemed to him like an arithmetical exercise — formed a select choir [1] of 16 voices, who met at his house on Saturday evenings, and at once began to practise the Passion. This was the seed which blossomed in the public performance of that great work a year later, and that again in the formation of the Bachgesellschaft, and the publication of the Grand Mass, and all the Church cantatas and other works, which have proved such mines of wealth. Long and complicated as the Passion is, he must have known it by heart even at that early date; for among other anecdotes proving as much, Schubring, who may be implicitly believed, relates that one evening after accompanying one of the choruses at the piano without book, he said, ' at the 23rd bar the sopranos have C and not C sharp.'

March 1828 was occupied by the composition of a long cantata to words by Levezow, for the Tercentenary Festival of Albert Dürer, at the Singakademie at Berlin,[2] on April 18. It was undertaken at the request of the Akademie der [bildenden] Künste, and is written for solo voices, chorus, and orchestra, and contains 15 numbers. The ' Trumpet Overture ' preceded it in performance. Felix was not in love with his task, but as the work grew into shape and the rehearsals progressed, he became reconciled to it; the performance was good, and Fanny's sisterly verdict is that ' she never remembers to have spent a pleasanter hour.' [3] The work remains in MS. at the Singakademie and the Berlin Bibliothek, and has probably the faults of almost all such compositions. Even Beethoven failed when he had to write to order. Fate, however, had a second task of the same kind in store for Felix, with some curious variations. This time the cantata was for a meeting (or, as we should now call it, a ' congress ') of physicians and investigators of natural science, to whom a festival was given by A. von Humboldt as president. Rellstab wrote the words, and Felix was invited to compose the music. It contains 7 numbers for solo and chorus. Owing to a whim of Humboldt the chorus was confined to men's voices, and the orchestra to

---

[1] Schubring, 375 a.   [2] A.M.Z. 1828, p. 364.   [3] F.M. i. 189.

clarinets, horns, trumpets, cellos, and basses. The thing came off in September; but no ladies — not even Fanny — were admitted, no report is given in the musical paper; and as there is no mention of it in the MS. Catalogue the autograph has probably vanished. Chopin was present [1] at the sitting of the congress, and saw Mendelssohn with Spontini and Zelter; but his modesty kept him from introducing himself, and their acquaintance was put off to a later date.

Felix had, however, during the summer been occupied in a more congenial task than such *pièces d'occasion* as these, viz. in the composition of the Overture to Goethe's ' Calm sea and Prosperous voyage,' on which we find him employed in June. Fanny gives us the interesting information [2] that he especially avoided the form of an Overture with Introduction, and wished his work to stand as two companion pictures. She mentions also his having written pianoforte pieces at this time, including some ' Lieder ohne Worte ' (a title not destined to come before the world for some years) and a great Antiphona and Responsorium for 4 choirs, 'Hora est,' etc., which still remains in MS.

For Christmas he wrote a second Kinder-symphonie, which delighted every one so much that it had to be repeated on the spot.[3] He also re-scored Handel's Acis and Galatea, and the Dettingen Te Deum, at Zelter's desire, for the use of the Singakademie.[4] They have since been published, but are not satisfactory specimens of such work. He also wrote the Variations in D for pianoforte and cello (op. 17), dated January 30, 1829, and dedicated to his brother Paul, who was more than a fair cello player. The ' Calm sea and Prosperous voyage ' was finished, or finished as nearly as any score of Mendelssohn's can be said to have been finished before it was publicly performed, and had received those innumerable corrections and alterations and afterthoughts, which he always gave his works, and which in some instances caused the delay of their appearance for years — which in fact prevented the appearance of the Italian Symphony till his removal made any further revision impossible. We have already seen that the basis of the work was furnished by the visit to Dobberan. A MS. letter from that place to Fanny (July 27, 1824) gives her an account

---

[1] Karasowski, chap. iv.   [2] F.M. i. 194.
[3] F.M. i. 199.   [4] F.M. i. 199, compared with Devrient, 161.

of the sea in the two conditions in which it is depicted in the overture.[1]

Felix's little choir had steadily continued their practice of the Passion, and the better they knew the mighty work the more urgent became their desire for a public performance by the Singakademie (300 to 400 voices) under Felix's own care. Apart from the difficulties of the music, with its double choruses and double orchestra, two main obstacles appeared to lie in the way — the opposition of Zelter as head of the Akademie, and the apathy of the public. Felix, for one, 'utterly disbelieved'[2] in the possibility of overcoming either, and with him were his parents and Marx, whose influence in the house was great. Against him were Devrient, Schubring, Bauer, and one or two other enthusiasts. At length Devrient and Felix determined to go and beard Zelter in his den. They encountered a few rough words, but their enthusiasm gained the day. Zelter yielded, and allowed Felix to conduct the rehearsals of the Akademie.[3] The principal solo singers of the Opera at once gave in their adhesion; the rehearsals began; Felix's tact, skill, and intimate knowledge of the music carried everything before them, the public flocked to the rehearsals; and on Wednesday, March 11, 1829, the first performance of the Passion took place since the death of Bach; every ticket was taken, and a thousand people turned away from the doors. Thus in Felix's own words (for once and once only alluding to his descent) 'it was an actor and a Jew who restored this great Christian work to the people.'[4] There was a second performance under Felix on Bach's birthday, March 21. It is probable that these successes did not add to Felix's popularity with the musicians of Berlin. Whether it was his age, his manner, his birth, the position held by his family, or what, certain it is that he was at this time in some way under a cloud. He had so far quarrelled with the Royal Orchestra that they refused to be conducted by him, and concerts at which his works were given were badly attended.[5]

Paganini made his first appearance in Berlin this month, gave four concerts, and bewitched the Berliners[6] as he did

---

[1] 'Sometimes it lies as smooth as a mirror, without waves, breakers, or noise . . . sometimes it is so wild and furious that I dare not go in.'
[2] Dev. 46.   [3] They began about the end of January. F.M. i. 204.
[4] Dev. 57.   [5] See his letter to Ganz, in G. & M. 186.
[6] A.M.Z. 1829, 256.

every one else. He very soon found his way to the Leipziger Strasse.[1] It would be interesting to know if he heard the Passion, and if, like Rossini, some years later, he professed himself a convert to Bach.

Whistling's Handbuch shows that by the end of this year Felix had published his 3 pianoforte Quartets; the Sonata for pianoforte and violin; the Caprice, op. 5; the Sonata for pianoforte solo; the Wedding of Camacho; and the first two books of songs. The dedications of these throw a light on some things. The quartets are inscribed respectively to Prince A. Radzivil (a friend of the family, who was present at the first performance of the ' Beiden Pädagogen ' at the Neue Promenade), Zelter, and Goethe; the Violin Sonata to E. Ritz [Rietz], Felix's favourite violin player; the 7 Characteristic Pieces for piano to Ludwig Berger, his pianoforte teacher. The rest have no dedications.

The engagement of Fanny Mendelssohn to William Hensel the painter of Berlin took place on January 22, 1829, in the middle of the excitement about the Passion; and on April 10 Felix took leave for England. He was now 20. His age, the termination of his liability to military service,[2] the friction just alluded to between himself and the musical world of Berlin — all things invited him to travel, and Zelter was not wrong in saying that it was good for him to leave home for a time.[3] Hitherto also he had worked without fee or reward. He was now to prove that he could make his living by music.[4] But more than this was involved. His visit to England was the first section of a long journey,[5] planned by the care and sagacity of his father, and destined to occupy the next three years of his life. In this journey he was ' closely to examine the various countries, and to fix on one in which to live and work; to make his name and abilities known, so that where he settled he should not be received as a stranger; and lastly to employ his good fortune in life, and the liberality of his father, in preparing the ground for future efforts.' [6] The journey was thus to be to him what the artistic tour of other musicians had been to them; but with the important difference, result-ing from his fortunate position in life, that the establishment

[1] Marx, _Erinn._ ii. 75.　　　　　　　[2] F.M. i. 188.
[3] _Corr. with Goethe_, letter 641.　　　[4] L., April 16, 1835.
[5] ' My great journey ' he calls it, G. & M. 100, 187.
[6] Letter, Feb. 21, 1832.

of his musical reputation was not the exclusive object, but that his journey was to give him a knowledge of the world, and form his character and manners. The answer attributed to a young Scotch student who was afterwards to become a great English archbishop, when asked why he had come to Oxford — 'to improve myself and to make friends' — exactly expresses the special object of Mendelssohn's tour, and is the mark which happily distinguished it from those of so many of his predecessors in the art. Music had not been adopted as a profession for Felix without much hesitation, and resistance on the part of some of his relations, and his father was wisely resolved that in so doing nothing should be sacrificed in the general culture and elevation of his son. 'To improve himself, and to make friends' was Mendelssohn's motto, not only during his grand tour but throughout his career.

It was their first serious parting. His father and Rebecka accompanied him to Hamburg. The boat (the 'Attwood') left on the Saturday evening before Easter Sunday, April 18, and it was not till noon on Tuesday, the 21st, that he reached the Custom House, London. The passage was a very bad one, the engines broke down, and Mendelssohn lay insensible for the whole of Sunday and Monday. He was welcomed on landing by Klingemann and Moscheles, and had a lodging at 103, Great Portland Street,[1] where his landlord was Heincke, a German ironmonger.

It was the middle of the musical season, and Malibran made her first reappearance at the Opera, as Desdemona, on the night of his arrival. His account of her, with other letters describing this period, will be found in Hensel's 'Familie Mendelssohn' (i. 115-294), and in Devrient's 'Recollections.' Other singers in London at that time were Sontag, Pisaroni, Mme. Stockhausen, and Donzelli; also Velluti, the castrato, a strange survival of the ancient world, whom it is difficult to think of in connexion with Felix Mendelssohn-Bartholdy. De Bériot and Madame Dulcken were among the players. Fétis too was in London delivering his lectures on 'La musique à la portée de tout le monde,' in French, to English audiences.

Felix was much with the Moscheleses, and there met Neukomm, with whom, in everything but his music, he sympathised warmly.

[1] The corner of Ridinghouse Street, now, and since 1858, numbered 79.

His first appearance before an English audience was at the Philharmonic Concert (then held in the Argyll Rooms, at the upper end of Regent Street) on Monday evening, May 25, when he conducted his Symphony in C minor. Old John Cramer ' led him to the piano,' at which in those days the conductor sat or stood, ' as if he were a young lady.' [1] The applause was immense, and the Scherzo (scored by him from his Octet for this occasion, in place of the original Minuet and Trio) was obstinately encored against his wish.[2] How deeply he felt the warmth of his reception may be seen from his letter to the Society.[3] He published the Symphony with a dedication to the Philharmonic,[4] and they on their part elected him an honorary member on November 29, 1829. It was thus an English body which gave him his first recognition as a composer.[5] The simple applause of London had wiped out the sneers and misunderstandings of Berlin. This he never forgot ; it recurs throughout his correspondence, and animates his account of his latest visits to us. Near the close of his life he spoke of it as ' having lifted a stone from his heart.' [6] The English had much to learn, and he could laugh heartily at them ; [7] but at least they loved him and his music, and were quite in earnest in their appreciation. Five days afterwards, on the 30th, at 2 p.m., he appeared again in the same room at what is vaguely called in *The Times* of June 1, ' the fourth grand concert.' He played the Concertstück of Weber — as the same journal informs us — ' with no music before him.' A charming letter,[8] equal to any in the whole collection for its gaiety and bright humour, describes his coming to the rooms early to try the piano — a new Clementi — and his losing himself in extemporising till he was recalled by finding that the audience were taking their seats. Two other concerts must be mentioned : — one by Drouet, the flute-player, on Midsummer Eve, at which, most appropriately, the Overture to the Midsummer Night's Dream was given, for the first time in England, and he himself played the E♭ Concerto of Beethoven,

[1] F.M. i. 226.   [2] Ibid.
[3] Hogarth, 51. The letter is in French.
[4] The autograph of the Symphony — in the green cloth boards so familiar to those who know his MS. scores — is now in the society's Library.
[5] See the statement to this effect in the A.M.Z. for 1836, p. 337.
[6] Letter to Mme. Goldschmidt.
[7] See F.M. i. 232, and Dev. 81, 82.
[8] F.M. i. 227, dated June 7.

then an absolute novelty in this country.[1] After the concert
the score of the Overture was left in the hackney coach by Mr.
Attwood, and lost.[2] On Mendelssohn's hearing of it, he said,
' Never mind, I will make another.' He did, and on comparing
it with the parts no variations were found. The other concert
was on July 13, for the benefit of the sufferers from the floods
in Silesia.[3] At this the Overture was repeated, and Felix and
Moscheles played (for the first and only time in England) a
Concerto by the former for two pianofortes and orchestra,
in E.[4] All this was a brilliant beginning as far as compositions
went ; it placed him in the best possible position before the
musical society of London, but it did not do much to solve the
question of livelihood, since the only commission which we
hear of his receiving, and which delighted him hugely, he was
compelled for obvious reasons to decline, viz. a festival hymn
for Ceylon for the anniversary of the emancipation of the
natives ! — an idea so comical that he says it had kept him
laughing inwardly for two days.[5] A MS. letter of this time
(dated June 7) is signed ' Composer to the Island of Ceylon.'

But he found time for other things besides music ; for the
House of Commons, and picture galleries, and balls at Devonshire House and Lansdowne House, and so many other parties,
that the good people at home took fright and thought he was
giving up music for society, and would become a drawing-room
ornament.[6] The charm of his manner and his entire simplicity
took people captive, and he laid a good foundation this year
for the time to come.

An amusing little picture of himself and his friends Rosen
and Mühlenfeld, coming home late from a state dinner at the
Prussian Ambassador's, buying three German sausages, and
then finding a quiet street in which to devour them, with a
three-part song and peals of laughter between the mouthfuls,[7]
shows how gaily life went on outside the concert-room.

At length the musical season was over. Felix and Klingemann left London about July 21, and, stopping at York and

---

[1] First played at the Philharmonic by Mrs. Anderson four years later, June
16, 1834.
[2] On the authority of Mr. W. H. Husk.
[3] This was suggested by Mendelssohn's uncle Nathan, who lived in Silesia,
to his brother Abraham, and by him communicated to Felix. (F.M. i. 236.)
[4] See Felix's letters describing this, July 10, 16, and 17 (F.M. i. 233-240) ;
also Moscheles' Life, i. 227. The autograph of the Concerto is dated Oct. 17, 1823.
[5] F.M. i. 230.   [6] Dev. 78.   [7] F.M. i. 235.

Durham,[1] were in Edinburgh[2] by the 28th. On the 29th they were present at the annual competition of Highland Pipers in the Theatre Royal.[3] On the 30th, before leaving ' the gray metropolis of the north,' they went over Holyrood Palace, saw the traditional scene of the murder of Rizzio, and the chapel, with the altar at which Mary was crowned standing ' open to the sky, and surrounded with grass and ivy, and everything ruined and decayed '; ' and I think,' he continues, ' that I found there the beginning of my Scotch Symphony.'[4] The passage which he then wrote down was the first 16 bars of the Introduction, which recurs at the end of the first movement, and thus forms, as it were, the motto of the work.

From Edinburgh they went to Abbotsford, and thence by Stirling, Perth, and Dunkeld, to Blair-Atholl; then on foot by Fort William to Tobermory, sketching and writing enormous letters at every step. On the way they visited Fingal's Cave, and Felix, writing ' auf einer Hebride ' — ' on one of the Hebrides ' — August 7, gives twenty bars of music, ' to show how extraordinarily the place affected me.' These 20 bars, an actual inspiration, are virtually identical[5] with the opening of the wonderful Overture which bears the name of ' Hebrides ' or ' Fingal's Cave.' Then came Glasgow, and then Liverpool. At Liverpool they went over a new American liner called the Napoleon, and Felix, finding a Broadwood piano in the saloon, sat down to it and played for himself and his friend the first movement of Fanny's ' Easter-Sonata ' — whatever that may have been. Home was always in his thoughts. Then to Holyhead for Ireland, but the weather was dreadful (apparently as bad as in 1879) — ' yesterday was a good day, for I was only wet through three times.' So he turned back to Liverpool, there said good-bye to Klingemann, and went on by Chester to the house of Mr. John Taylor, the mining engineer, at Coed-du near Holywell. Here he remained for some days, seeing a very pleasant side of English country life, and making an indelible impression on his hosts; and here he composed the three pieces which form op. 16, the first of which, in key, tempo,

---

[1] They can be traced by Felix's sketches.
[2] F.M. i. 240.
[3] F.M. i. 240; Hogarth, 77. I owe the date to the kindness of Mr. Glen of Edinburgh.
[4] F.M. i. 244.
[5] 10 of the present score, as he afterwards diminished the notation by one half. A facsimile is given in F.M. i. 257.

and melody, closely resembles the introduction to the Scotch Symphony.[1] The following letter, written after his death by a member of the Taylor family, gives a good idea of the clever, genial, gay, and yet serious nature of the man at this happy time of life : —

It was in the year 1829 that we first became acquainted with Mr. Mendelssohn. He was introduced to us by my aunt, Mrs. Austin, who had well known his cousin Professor Mendelssohn, at Bonn. He visited us early in the season in Bedford Row, but our real friendship began at Coed-du, which was a house near Mold in Flintshire, rented for many years by my father, Mr. John Taylor.

Mr. Mendelssohn came down there to spend a little time with us, in the course of a tour in England and Scotland. My father and mother received him kindly, as they did everybody, but his arrival created no particular sensation, as many strangers came to our house to see the mines under my father's management, and foreigners were often welcomed there. Soon however we began to find that a most accomplished mind had come among us, quick to observe, delicate to distinguish. There was a little shyness about him, great modesty. We knew little about his music, but the wonder of it grew upon us ; and I remember one night when my two sisters and I went to our rooms how we began saying to each other ' Surely this must be a man of genius . . . we can't be mistaken about the music ; never did we hear any one play so before. Yet we know the best London musicians. Surely by and bye we shall hear that Felix Mendelssohn-Bartholdy is a great name in the world.'

My father's birthday happened while Mr. Mendelssohn was with us. There was a grand expedition to a distant mine, up among the hills ; a tent carried up there, a dinner to the miners. We had speeches, and health-drinkings, and Mendelssohn threw himself into the whole thing, as if he had been one of us. He interested himself in hearing about the condition and way of life of the Welsh miners. Nothing was lost upon him. A letter that he wrote to my brother John just after he left Coed-du, charmingly describes the impressions he carried away of that country. Sometimes he would go out sketching with us girls, sitting down very seriously to draw, but making the greatest fun of attempts which he considered to be unsuccessful. One figure of a Welsh girl he imagined to be like a camel, and she was called the camel accordingly. Though he scorned his own drawings, he had the genuine artist-feeling, and great love for pictures. I need not say how deeply he entered into the beauty of the hills and the woods. His way of representing

---

[1] Both Allegros are in 6-8, and the Andante is repeated at the end of each. The piece is dated Coed-du, Sept. 4.

them was not with the pencil; but in the evenings his improvised music would show what he had observed or felt in the past day. The piece called The Rivulet, which he wrote at that time, for my sister Susan, will show what I mean; it was a recollection of a real actual rivulet.[1]

We observed how natural objects seemed to suggest music to him. There was in my sister Honora's garden, a pretty creeping plant,[2] new at that time, covered with little trumpet-like flowers. He was struck with it, and played for her the music which (he said) the fairies might play on those trumpets. When he wrote out the piece (called a Capriccio in E minor) he drew a little branch of that flower all up the margin of the paper.

The piece (an Andante and Allegro) which Mr. Mendelssohn wrote for me, was suggested by the sight of a bunch of carnations and roses.[3] The carnations that year were very fine with us. He liked them best of all the flowers,[4] would have one often in his button-hole. We found he intended the arpeggio passages in that composition as a reminder of the sweet scent of the flower rising up.

Mr. Mendelssohn was not a bit ' sentimental,' though he had so much sentiment. Nobody enjoyed fun more than he, and his laughing was the most joyous that could be. One evening in hot summer we staid in the wood above our house later than usual. We had been building a house of fir branches in Susan's garden up in the wood. We made a fire, a little way off it, in a thicket among the trees, Mendelssohn helping with the utmost zeal, dragging up more and more wood : we tired ourselves with our merry work; we sat down round our fire, the smoke went off, the ashes were glowing, it began to get dark, but we could not like to leave our bonfire. ' If we had but some music,' Mendelssohn said ; ' Could anyone get something to play on?' Then my brother recollected that we were near the gardener's cottage, and that the gardener had a fiddle. Off rushed our boys to get the fiddle. When it came, it was the wretchedest thing in the world, and it had but one string. Mendelssohn took the instrument into his hands, and fell into fits of laughter over it when he heard the sounds it made. His laughter was very catching, he put us all into peals of merriment. But he, somehow, afterwards brought beautiful music out of the poor old fiddle, and we sat listening to one strain after another till the darkness sent us home.

---

[1] This piece was long a favourite of his. A water-colour drawing by Schirmer inspired by Felix's playing of it, is still in the possession of the family (Dev. 175).

[2] *Ecremocarpus.*

[3] The account given above of the origin and intention of these three pieces (op. 16) is confirmed by a letter of his own printed in F.M. i. 279. The autograph of No. 1 is headed ' Nelken und Rosen in menge ' — Carnations and Roses in plenty.

[4] Compare Mos. i. 297.

My cousin John Edward Taylor [1] was staying with us at that time. He had composed an imitation Welsh air, and he was, before breakfast, playing over this, all unconscious that Mr. Mendelssohn (whose bed-room was next the drawing-room) was hearing every note. That night, when we had music as usual, Mr. Mendelssohn sat down to play. After an elegant prelude, and with all possible advantage, John Edward heard his poor little air introduced as the subject of the evening. And having dwelt upon it, and adorned it in every graceful manner, Mendelssohn in his pretty, playful way, bowing to the *composer*, gave all the praise to him.

I suppose some of the charm of his speech might lie in the unusual choice of words which he as a German made in speaking English. He lisped a little. He used an action of nodding his head quickly till the long locks of hair would fall over his high forehead with the vehemence of his assent to anything he liked.

Sometimes he used to talk very seriously with my mother. Seeing that we brothers and sisters lived lovingly together and with our parents, he spoke about this to my mother, told her how he had known families where it was not so; and used the words ' You know not how happy you are.'

He was so far from any sort of pretension, or from making a favour of giving his music to us, that one evening when the family from a neighbouring house came to dinner, and we had dancing afterwards, he took his turn in playing quadrilles and waltzes with the others. He was the first person who taught us gallopades, and he first played us Weber's last waltz. He enjoyed dancing like any other young man of his age. He was then 20 years old. He had written his Midsummer Night's Dream (Overture) before that time. I well remember his playing it. He left Coed-du early in September 1829.

We saw Mr. Mendelssohn whenever he came to England, but the visits he made to us in London have not left so much impression upon me as that one at Coed-du did. I can however call to mind a party at my father's in Bedford Row where he was present. Sir George Smart was there also : when the latter was asked to play he said to my mother, ' No, no, don't call upon the old post-horse, when you have a high-mettled young racer at hand.' The end of it was a duet played by Sir George and Mr. Mendelssohn together. Our dear old master, Mr. Attwood, often met him at our house. Once he went with us to a ball at Mr. Attwood's at Norwood. Returning by daylight I remember how Mr. Mendelssohn admired the view of St. Paul's in the early dawn which we got from Blackfriars bridge. But the happiest visit to us was that one when he

---

[1] Afterwards Gresham Professor.

first brought his sweet young wife to see my mother. Madame
Felix Mendelssohn was a bride then, and we all of us said he could
not have found one more worthy of himself. And with the delightful remembrance of his happiness then, I will end these fragments.

His head was at this time full of music — the E♭ Violin
Quartet[1] (op. 12) ; an organ piece for Fanny's wedding ;[2] the
Reformation Symphony, the Scotch Symphony, the Hebrides
Overture, as well as vocal music, ' of which he will say nothing.'
Other subjects, however, occupied even more of his letters than
music. Such were a private plan for a journey to Italy in
company with the parents and Rebecka, for which he enters
into a little conspiracy with his sister ; and a scheme for the
celebration of his parents' silver wedding (December 26, 1829)
by the performance of three operettas (Liederspiel[e]), his own
' Soldatenliebschaft,' a second to be written by Hensel and
composed by Fanny, and the third an ' Idyll ' by Klingemann
and himself, which, when once it entered his head, rapidly took
shape, and by the end of October appears to have been virtually
complete.[3]

By September 10 he was again in London, this time [4] at 35
Bury Street, St. James's ; on the 14th he finished and signed
the E♭ Quartet, and on the 17th was thrown from a gig and
hurt his knee, which forced him to keep his bed for nearly two
months, and thus to miss not only a tour through Holland and
Belgium with his father, but Fanny's wedding. Confinement
to bed, however, does not prevent his writing home with the
greatest regularity. On September 22 he ends his letter with
the first phrase of the Hebrides Overture — ' aber zum
Wiedersehen,

F.'

On October 23 he informs them that he is beginning again to
compose — and so on. He was nursed by Klingemann, and

---

[1] F.M. 276, 279, 280. The autograph of the Quartet, in the possession of
Mr. Rudorf, is dated ' London, Sept. 14, 1829.' Though published as No. 1 it is
thus really his second string quartet. See above, p. 274.
[2] Fanny herself wrote the piece which was actually played at the wedding,
Oct. 3, 1829 (F.M. 296). Felix's piece, however, was finished and written out
(L. July 25, 1844).
[3] F.M. i. 302-304 ; Dev. 86.   [4] F.M. i. 301.

well cared for by Sir Lewis and Lady Moller, by Attwood and Hawes, the musicians, the Göschens, and others. His first drive was on November 6, when he found London 'indescribably beautiful.' A week later he went to Norwood [1] to the Attwoods, then back to town for 'the fourteen happiest days he had ever known,' and on November 29 was at Hotel Quillacq, Calais, on his road home. He reached Berlin to find the Hensels and the Devrients inhabiting rooms in the garden-house. His lameness still obliged him to walk with a stick; but this did not impede the mounting of his piece for the silver wedding,[2] which came off with the greatest success on December 26, and displayed an amount of dramatic ability which excited the desire of his friends that he should again write for the stage.[3] The Liederspiel however was not enough to occupy him, and during this winter he composed a Symphony [4] for the ter-centenary festival of the Augsburg Confession, which was in preparation for June 25, 1830. This work, in the key of D, is that which we shall often again refer to as the 'Reformation Symphony.' He also wrote the fine Fantasia in F♯ minor (op. 28), which he called his 'Scotch Sonata' [5] — a piece too little played. A Chair of Music was founded in the Berlin university this winter expressly with a view to its being filled by Mendelssohn. But on the offer being made he declined it, and at his instance Marx was appointed in his stead.[6] There can be no doubt that he was right. Nothing probably could have entirely kept down Mendelssohn's ardour for composition; but it is certain that to have exchanged the career of a composer for that of a university teacher would have added a serious burden to the many occupations which already beset him, besides forcing him to exchange a pursuit which he loved and succeeded in, for one for which he had no turn — for teaching was not his *forte*.[7]

[1] Op. 16, No. 2, is dated 'Norwood, Surrey, Nov. 18 [13].' There is a MS. letter from the same address, Nov. 15. The house was on Biggin Hill.
[2] 'Heimkehr aus der Fremde' (the Return from abroad) was translated by Chorley as 'The Son and Stranger,' and produced at the Haymarket Theatre July 7, 1851.
[3] Dev. 94.
[4] For some curious details regarding this see Dev. 96. Schubring (374*b*) tells the same story of the Trumpet Overture.
[5] The MS., in Mr. Schleinitz's possession, is entitled 'Sonate écossaise,' and dated 'Berlin, Jan. 29, 1833'; but he played it at Goethe's, May 24, 1830 (L. i. 7).
[6] Dev. 98.
[7] See a similar remark in Hauptmann's Letters to Hauser (i. 157) in reference to a similar attempt in 1835.

The winter was over, his leg was well, and he was on the point of resuming his ' great journey ' in its southern portion, when, at the end of March, 1830, both Rebecka and he were taken with the measles. This involved a delay of a month, and it was not till May 13 [1] that he was able to start. His father accompanied him as far as Dessau, the original seat of the family, where he remained for a few days with his friend Schubring.

He travelled through Leipzig, Weissenfels, and Naumburg, and reached Weimar on the 20th. There he remained a fortnight in the enjoyment of the closest intercourse with Goethe and his family, playing and leading what he calls a mad life — Heidenleben.[2] There his portrait was taken, which, though like, ' made him look very sulky,' and a copy of the score of the Reformation Symphony was made and sent to Fanny. On June 3 he took leave of Goethe [3] for the last time, and went by Nuremberg to Munich, which he reached on June 6.[4] At Munich he made a long halt, remaining till the end of the month; made the acquaintance of Josephine Lang, Delphine Schauroth, and other interesting persons, and was fêted to an extraordinary extent [5] — ' several parties every evening, and more pianoforte playing than I ever recollect ' — all which must be read in the letter of Marx, and in his own delightful pages.[6] On the 14th, her birthday, he sends Fanny a little Song without Words (Lied) in A, and on the 26th a much longer one in B♭ minor, which he afterwards altered, and published as Op. 30, No. 2.[7] Both here and at Vienna he is disgusted at the ignorance on the part of the best players — Mozart, Haydn, and Beethoven utterly ignored, Hummel, Field, Kalkbrenner, accepted as classics. He himself played the best music, and with the best effect, and his visit must have been an epoch in the taste of both places.[8]

From Munich he went through the Salzkammergut, by Salzburg, Ischl, and the Traunsee, to Linz, and thence to Vienna, August 13. Here he passed more than a month of the

---

[1] F.M. i. 313 (inaccurately August).
[2] Letter, May 25. See letters in G. & M.
[3] G. & M. 70.   [4] L. June 6, 1831.
[5] L. Oct. 16.   [6] F.M. i. 313-327.
[7] In this, as in several other cases, he has altered the notation from quavers to semiquavers.
[8] Letters to Zelter (June 22 and Oct. 16, 1830).

gayest life[1] with Hauser the singer,[2] Merk the cellist, the Pereiras, the Eskeles, and others, but not so gay as to interfere with serious composition — witness a cantata or anthem on ' O Haupt voll Blut und Wunden '[3] (MS.), and an ' Ave Maria ' for tenor solo and 8 voices [8-part chorus] (op. 23, no. 2), both of this date. On September 28 we find him at Pressburg,[4] witnessing the coronation of the Crown Prince Ferdinand as King of Hungary; then at Lilienfeld; and by Graz, Udine, etc., he reached Venice on October 9.

His stay in Italy, and his journey through Switzerland back to Munich, are so fully depicted in the first volume of his Letters, that it is only necessary to allude to the chief points. He went from Venice by Bologna to Florence, reaching it on October 22, and remaining there for a week. He arrived in Rome on November 1 — the same day as Goethe had done, as he is careful to remark — and he lived there till April 10, at No. 5 Piazza di Spagna. The latter half of April and the whole of May were devoted to Naples (Sti. Combi, Sta. Lucia, No. 13, on the 3rd floor) and the Bay — Sorrento, Ischia, Amalfi, etc. Here he met Benedict and renewed the acquaintance which they had begun as boys in Berlin in 1821, when Benedict was Weber's pupil.[5] By June 5 he was back in Rome, and after a fortnight's interval set out on his homeward journey by Florence (June 24), Genoa, Milan (July 7-15), Lago Maggiore and the Islands, the Simplon, Martigny, and the Col de Balme, to Chamounix and Geneva. Thence on foot across the mountains to Interlaken; and thence by Grindelwald and the Furka to Lucerne, August 27, 28. At Interlaken, besides sketching, and writing both letters and songs, he composed the only waltzes[6] of which — strange as it seems in one so madly fond of dancing — any trace survives. At Lucerne he wrote his last letter to Goethe,[7] and no doubt mentioned his being engaged in the composition of the Walpurgisnacht, which must have brought out from the poet the explanation of the aim of his poem which is printed at the beginning of Mendelssohn's music, with the date September 9, 1831. Then, still on foot, he went by Wallenstadt and St. Gall to Augsburg, and returned to Munich early in September.

[1] L. Feb. 18, 1836.
[2] Afterwards Director of the Munich Conservatorium, and Spohr's correspondent.
[3] Dev. 105.   [4] L. i. 21.   [5] B. 7.   [6] L. Aug. 11.   [7] G. & M. 80.

Into both the Nature and the Art of this extended and varied tract he entered with enthusiasm. The engravings with which his father's house was richly furnished, and Hensel's copies of the Italian masters, had prepared him for many of the great pictures; but to see them on the spot was to give them new life, and it is delightful to read his rapturous comments on the Titians of Venice and Rome, the gems in the Tribune of Florence, Guido's Aurora, and other masterpieces. His remarks are instructive and to the point; no vague generalities or raptures, but real criticism into the effect or meaning or treatment of the work; and yet rather from the point of view of an intelligent amateur than with any assumption of technical knowledge, and always with sympathy and kindness.[1] Nor is his eye for nature less keen, or his enthusiasm less abundant. His descriptions of the scenery of Switzerland during the extraordinarily stormy season of his journey there, are worthy of the greatest painters or letter-writers. Some of his expressions rise to grandeur.

'It was a day,' says he, describing his walk over the Wengernalp, 'as if made on purpose. The sky was flecked with white clouds floating far above the highest snow-peaks, no mists below on any of the mountains, and all their summits glittering brightly in the morning air, every undulation and the face of every hill clear and distinct. . . . I remembered the mountains before only as huge peaks. It was their height that formerly took such possession of me. Now it was their boundless extent that I particularly felt, their huge broad masses, the close connexion of all these enormous fortresses, which seemed to be crowding together and stretching out their hands to each other. Then too recollect that every glacier, every snowy plateau, every rocky summit was dazzling with light and glory, and that the more distant summits of the further ranges seemed to stretch over and peer in upon us. I do believe that such are the thoughts of God Himself. Those who do not know Him may here find Him and the nature which He has created, brought strongly before their eyes.'[2] Other expressions are very happy : — 'The mountains are acknowledged to be finest after rain, and to-day looked as fresh as if they had just burst the shell.'[3] Again, in approaching

---

[1] Letters, Oct. 25, 1830, June 25, 1831, Sept. 14, 1839.
[2] L. Aug. 14.   [3] L. Aug. 24.

Naples — 'To me the finest object in nature is and always will be the sea. I love it almost more than the sky. I always feel happy when I see before me the wide expanse of waters.'

In Rome he devoted all the time that he could spare from work to the methodical examination of the place and the people. But his music stood first, and surely no one before or since was ever so self-denying on a first visit to the Eternal City. Not even for the sirocco would he give up work in the prescribed hours.[1] His plan was to compose or practise till noon, and then spend the whole of the rest of the daylight in the open air. He enters into everything with enthusiasm — it is ' a delightful existence.' 'Rome in all its vast dimensions lies before him like an interesting problem, and he goes deliberately to work, daily selecting some different object — the ruins of the ancient city, the Borghese Gallery, the Capitol, St. Peter's, or the Vatican.' ' Each day is thus made memorable, and, as I take my time, each object becomes indelibly impressed upon me. . . . When I have fairly imprinted an object on my mind, and each day a fresh one, twilight has usually arrived, and the day is over.' Into society he enters with keen zest, giving and receiving pleasure wherever he goes, and ' amusing himself thoroughly and divinely.'[2] 'His looking-glass is stuck full of visiting-cards, and he spends every evening with a fresh acquaintance.' His visits to Horace Vernet and Thorwaldsen, Santini's visits to him; the ball at Torlonia's, where he first saw the young English beauty, and that at the Palazzo Albani, where he danced with her; the mad frolics of the Carnival, the monks in the street (on whom he ' will one day write a special treatise '), the peasants in the rain, the very air and sunshine — all delight him in the most simple, healthy, and natural manner. ' Oh! if I could but send you in this letter one quarter of an hour of all this pleasure, or tell you how life actually flies in Rome, every minute bringing its own memorable delights.'[3] On the other hand, he has no mercy on anything like affectation or conceit. He lashes the German painters for their hats, their beards, their dogs, their discontent, and their incompetence, just as he does one or two German musicians for their empty pretension. The few words which he devotes to Berlioz (who although always his good friend is antagonistic to him on every point) and his companion Montfort, are strongly

[1] Berlioz, *Voy. mus.* i. 76.   [2] L. Dec. 10, 1837.   [3] L. Feb. 8.

tinged with the same feeling.[1] On the other hand, nothing can be more genuinely and good-naturedly comic than his account of the attempt to sing Marcello's psalms by a company of dilettanti assisted by a Papal singer.[2]

This sound and healthy habit of mind it is, perhaps, which excludes the sentimental — we might almost say the devotional — feeling which is so markedly absent from his letters. Strange that an artist who so enjoyed the remains of ancient Italy should have had no love of antiquity as such. At sight of Nisida he recalls the fact that it was the refuge of Brutus, and that Cicero visited him there. ' The sea lay between the islands, and the rocks, covered with vegetation, bent over it then just as they do now. These are the antiquities that interest me, and are much more suggestive than crumbling mason-work.' ' The outlines of the Alban hills remain unchanged. There they can scribble no names and compose no inscriptions . . . and to these I cling.' In reference to music the same spirit shows itself still more strongly in his indignation at the ancient Gregorian music to the Passion in the Holy Week services. ' It does irritate me to hear such sacred and touching words sung to such insignificant dull music. They say it is *canto fermo*, Gregorian, etc. No matter. If at that period there was neither the feeling nor the capacity to write in a different style, at all events we have now the power to do so ' ; and he goes on to suggest two alternative plans for altering and reforming the service, suggestions almost reminding one of the proposition in which the Empress Eugénie endeavoured to enlist the other Empresses and Queens of Europe, to pull down the church of the Holy Sepulchre at Jerusalem and rebuild it in conformity with modern taste and requirements. Religious he is, deeply and strongly religious ; every letter shows it. It is the unconscious, healthy, happy confidence of a sound mind in a sound body, of a man to whom the sense of God and Duty are as natural as the air he breathes or the tunes which come into his head, and to whom a wrong action is an impossibility. But of devotional sentiment, of that yearning dependence, which dictated the 130th Psalm, or the feeling which animates Beethoven's passionate prayers and confessions,[3] we find hardly a trace, in his letters or his music.

---

[1] L. Mar. 29. It is curious to compare Berlioz's account (*Voyage mus.* i. 73) of Mendelssohn with the above.

[2] L. March 1.   [3] See p. 84.

He was very fortunate in the time of his visit to Rome.
Pope Pius VIII died while he was there, and he came in for
all the ceremonies of Gregory XVI's installation, in addition
to the services of Holy Week, etc. These latter he has described
in the fullest manner, not only as to their picturesque and
general effect, but down to the smallest details of the music,
in regard to which he rivalled Mozart's famous feat. They
form the subject of two long letters to Zelter, dated December
1, 1830,[1] and June 16, 1831 ; and as all the particulars had
to be caught while he listened, they testify in the strongest
manner to the sharpness of his ear and the retentiveness of his
memory. Indeed it is impossible not to feel that in such letters
as these he is on his own ground, and that, intense as was his
enjoyment of nature, painting, society, and life, he belonged
really to none of these things — was ' neither a politician nor
a dancer, nor an actor, nor a *bel esprit*, but a musician.' [2] And
so it proved in fact. For with all these distractions his Italian
journey was fruitful in work. The ' Walpurgisnight,' the result
of his last visit to Weimar, was finished, in its first form,
at Milan (the MS. is dated ' Mailand, July 15, 1831 ') ; the
' Hebrides,' also in its first form, is signed ' Rome, December 16,
1830.' The Italian and Scotch Symphonies were begun and
far advanced before he left Italy. Several smaller works belong
to this period — the Psalm ' Non Nobis ' (November 16 [15],
1830) ; the three church pieces which form op. 23 ; a Christmas
Cantata, still in MS. (January 28, 1831) ; the hymn ' Verleih'
uns Frieden ' (February 10) ; the 3 Motets for the nuns of the
French Chapel [Trinità de' Monti in Rome] ; and although
few, if any, of these minor pieces can be really said to live, yet
they embody much labour and devotion, and were admirable
stepping-stones to the great vocal works of his later life. In fact
then, as always, he was what Berlioz calls him, ' un producteur
infatigable,' [3] and thus obtained that facility which few composers have possessed in greater degree than Mozart and
himself. He sought the society of musicians. Besides Berlioz,
Montfort, and Benedict, we find frequent mention of Baini,
Donizetti, Coccia, and Madame Fodor. At Milan his encounter with Madame Ertmann, the intimate friend of Beet-

---

[1] This was added to the *Reisebriefe* in a subsequent edition, and is not included
in the English translation.
[2] L. Dec. 28, 1831.   [3] *Voy. mus.* i. 76.

U

hoven, was a happy accident, and turned to the happiest
account. There too he met the son of Mozart, and delighted
him with his father's Overtures to Don Juan and the Magic
Flute, played in his own 'splendid orchestral style' on the
piano. Not the least pleasant portions of his letters from
Switzerland are those describing his organ-playing at the little
remote Swiss churches at Engelberg, Wallenstadt, Sargans, and
Lindau — from which we would gladly quote if space allowed.

Nor was his drawing-book idle. Between May 16 and
August 24, 1831, 35 sketches are in the hands of one of his
daughters alone, implying a corresponding number for the
other portions of the tour. How characteristic of his enormous
enjoyment of life is the following passage (Sargans, September
3) : ' Besides organ playing I have much to finish in my new
drawing-book (I filled another completely at Engelberg) ; then
I must dine, and eat like a whole regiment; then after dinner
the organ again, and so forget my rainy day.'

The great event of his second visit to Munich was the pro-
duction (and no doubt the composition) of his G minor Concerto, ' a thing rapidly thrown off,' [1] which he played on
October 17, 1831, at a concert which also comprised his
Symphony in C minor, his Overture to the Midsummer Night's
Dream, and an extempore performance. Before leaving he
received a commission [2] to compose an opera for the Munich
Theatre. From Munich he travelled by Stuttgart (November
7) and Heidelberg to Frankfort, and thence to Düsseldorf
(November 27), to consult Immermann as to the libretto for
the Munich opera, and arranged with him for one founded on
The Tempest.[3] The artistic life of Düsseldorf pleased him
extremely, and no doubt this visit laid the foundation for his
future connection with that town.

He arrived in Paris about the middle of December, and
found, of his German friends, Hiller and Franck settled there.
He renewed his acquaintance with the Parisian musicians who
had known him as a boy in 1825, especially with Baillot; and
made many new friends, Habeneck, Franchomme, Cuvillon,
and others. Chopin, Meyerbeer, Herz, Liszt, Kalkbrenner,
Ole Bull, were all there, and Mendelssohn seems to have been
very much with them. He went a great deal into society and

---

[1] *Briefe*, ii. 22.   [2] L. Dec. 19, 1831.   [3] L. Dec. 19, 1831; Jan. 11, 1832.

played frequently, was constantly at the theatre, and as constantly at the Louvre, enjoyed life thoroughly, saw everything, according to his wont, including the political scenes which were then more than ever interesting in Paris; knew everybody; and in fact, as he expresses it, 'cast himself thoroughly into the vortex.'[1] His Overture to the Midsummer Night's Dream was performed at the Société des Concerts (Conservatoire) on February 19, 1832, and he himself played the Concerto of Beethoven in G at the concert of March 18. His Reformation Symphony was rehearsed, but the orchestra thought it too learned,[2] and it never reached performance. His Octet was played in church at a mass commemorative of Beethoven, and several times in private; so was his Quintet (with a new Adagio)[3] and his Quartets, both for strings and for piano. The pupils of the Conservatoire, he writes, are working their fingers off to play ' Ist es wahr?'[4] His playing was applauded as much as heart could wish, and his reception in all circles was of the very best.

On the other hand, there were drawbacks. Edward Ritz [Rietz], his great friend, died (January 23) while he was there; the news reached him on his birthday. Goethe too died (March 22). The rejection of his Reformation Symphony, the centre of so many hopes,[5] was a disappointment which must have thrown a deep shadow over everything, and no doubt after so much gaiety there was a reaction, and his old dislike to the French character — traces of which are not wanting in a letter to Immermann dated January 11 — returned. In addition to this his health had not latterly been good, and in March he had an attack of cholera.[6] Though he alludes to it in joke, he probably felt the truth of a remark in the Figaro that 'Paris is the tomb of all reputations.'[7] Brilliantly and cordially as he was received, he left no lasting mark there; his name does not reappear in the programmes of the Conservatoire for 11 years, and it was not till the establishment of the Concerts populaires in 1861 that his music became at all familiar to the

[1] L. Jan. 11, 1832; Dec. 28, 1831.
[2] H. 21.
[3] Written in memory of E. Ritz [Rietz], and replacing a Minuet in F sharp minor, with Trio in double Canon.
[4] The Lied embodied in the A minor Quartet. See above, p. 274.
[5] H. 21.
[6] H. 33. Letter to Bärmann, in Letters of Dist. Musicians, April 16.
[7] Fétis is inaccurate in citing this as Mendelssohn's own expression. See Letter, March 31, 1832.

Parisians.[1] He himself never again set foot in Paris.

On April 23, 1832, he was once more in his beloved London, and at his old quarters, 103 Great Portland Street. 'That smoky nest,' he exclaims, amid the sunshine of the Naples summer, ' is fated to be now and ever my favourite residence; my heart swells when I think of it.' [2] And here he was back in it again! It was warm, the lilacs were in bloom, his old friends were as cordial as if they had never parted, he was warmly welcomed everywhere, and felt his health return in full measure. His letters of this date are full of a genuine heartfelt satisfaction. He plunged at once into musical life. The Hebrides was played in MS. by the Philharmonic on May 14, and he performed his G minor Concerto, on an Erard piano, at the concerts of May 28 and June 18. He gave a MS. score of his overture to the society, and they presented him with a piece of plate. During his stay in London he wrote his Capriccio brillant in B (op. 22), and played it at a concert of Mori's [3] [on May 25]. On Sunday, June 10, he played the organ at St. Paul's.[4] He also published a four-hand arrangement of the M.N.D. Overture with Cramer,[5] and the 1st Book of Songs without Words with Novello,[6] and played at many concerts. A more important thing still was the revision of the Hebrides Overture, to which he appears to have put the final touches on June 20 (five weeks after its performance at the Philharmonic), that being the date on the autograph score in possession of the family of Sterndale Bennett, which agrees in all essentials with the printed copy. On May 15 Zelter died, and he received the news of the loss of his old friend at Mr. Attwood's house, Biggin Hill, Norwood. The vision of a possible offer of Zelter's post at the Singakademie crossed his mind, and is discussed with his father; but it was not destined to be fulfilled. Among the friends whom he made during this visit, never to lose till death, were the Horsleys, a family living in the country at Kensington. Mr. W. Horsley was one of our most eminent glee-writers, his daughters were unusually musi-

[1] This want of sympathy, combined with an astonishing amount of ignorance, is amusingly displayed in the following description from the catalogue of a well-known French autograph collector:—'Mendelssohn Bartholdy (Félix) remarquable intelligence, mais cœur égoïste et froid : qui n'ayant pu gravir d'un pas sur les sommets de l'art, s'est réfugié dans la musique de chambre.' Can ignorance and confidence go further?

[2] L. May 28, 1831.   [3] Rietz's List. Also Mos. i. 271.
[4] Mos. i. 272.   [5] Ibid.
[6] Under the name of *Original Melodies for the P.F.* (Novello).

cal, one of the sons [John Callcott Horsley] is now an R.A., and another [Charles Edward Horsley] was for many years a bright ornament to English music. The circle was not altogether unlike his Berlin home, and in his own words [1] he seldom spent a day without meeting one or other of the family.

In July 1832 he returned to Berlin, to find the charm of the summer life in the garden as great as before. His darling sister Rebecka had been married to Professor Dirichlet in May. Another change was that the Devrients had migrated to another place, and Hensel's studios now occupied all the spare space in the garden-house. Immermann's promised libretto was waiting for him on his return, but from the terms in which he asks for Devrient's opinion on it, it is evident that it disappointed him, and we hear no more of the subject.[2] St. Paul was beginning to occupy his mind (of which more anon), and he had not long been back when the election of the conductor for the Singakademie in Zelter's place came on the *tapis*. The details may be read elsewhere;[3] it is enough to say here that chiefly through the extra zeal and want of tact of his friend Devrient, though with the best intentions, Mendelssohn, for no fault of his own, was dragged before the public as an opponent of Rungenhagen; and at length, on January 22, 1833, was defeated by 60 votes out of 236. The defeat was aggravated by a sad want of judgment on the part of the family, who not only were annoyed, but showed their annoyance by withdrawing from the Akademie, and thus making an open hostility. Felix himself said little, but he felt it deeply. He describes [4] it as a time of uncertainty, anxiety, and suspense, which was as bad as a serious illness; and no doubt it widened the breach in his liking for Berlin, which had been begun by the rejection of Camacho. He doubtless found some consolation in a grand piano which was forwarded to him in August by Mr. Pierre Erard of London.

His musical activity was at all events not impaired. Besides occupying himself with the Sunday music at home, Felix, during this winter, gave three public concerts at the room of the Singakademie [5] in November and December 1832, and January 1833, at which he brought forward his Walpurgisnight, his Reformation Symphony, his Overtures to the Midsummer

[1] G. & M. 97.   [2] Dev. 142.   [3] See especially Dev. 145-156.
[4] L. March 4, 1833.   [5] A.M.Z. 1833, 125. The dates are not given.

Night's Dream, Meeresstille, and Hebrides, his G minor Concerto and his Capriccio in B minor; besides playing two sonatas and the G major Concerto of Beethoven, and a Concerto of Bach in D minor — all, be it remembered, novelties at that time even to many experienced musicians. In addition to this he was working seriously at the Italian Symphony. The Philharmonic Society of London had passed a resolution on November 5, 1832, asking him to compose ' a symphony, an overture, and a vocal piece,' and offering him a hundred guineas for the exclusive right of performance during two years.[1] Of these the Italian Symphony was to be one, and the MS. score of the work accordingly bears the date of March 13, 1833. On April 27 he wrote to the Society offering them the symphony with ' two new overtures, finished since last year ' (doubtless the Meeresstille [Hebrides] and the Trumpet Overture), the extra one being intended ' as a sign of his gratitude for the pleasure and honour they had again conferred upon him.' Graceful and apparently spontaneous as it is, the symphony had not been an easy task. Mendelssohn was not exempt from the lot of most artists who attempt a great poem or a great composition; on the contrary, ' the bitterest moments he ever endured or could have imagined,' were those which he experienced during the autumn when the work was in progress, and up to the last he had his doubts and misgivings as to the result. Now, however, when it was finished, he found that it ' pleased him and showed progress '[2] — a very modest expression for a work so full of original thought, masterly expression, consummate execution, and sunny beauty, as the Italian Symphony, and moreover such a prodigious advance[3] on his last work of the same kind!

On February 6, 1833, a son was born to the Moscheleses, and one of the first letters written was to Mendelssohn, asking him to be godfather to the child. He sent a capital letter in reply, with an elaborate sketch,[4] and he transmitted later a cradle song — published as Op. 47, No. 6 — for his godchild, Felix Moscheles. Early in April he left Berlin for Düsseldorf, to arrange for conducting the Lower Rhine Festival at the end

---

[1] See the Resolution and his answer in Hogarth, 59, 60.
[2] Letter to Bauer, April 6, 1833.
[3] It has been said that the leap from Mendelssohn's C minor to his A major Symphony is as great as that from Beethoven's No. 2 to the Eroica; and relatively this is probably not exaggerated.
[4] Which will be found in Moscheles's Life, i. 283.

of May [26-28]. As soon as the arrangements were completed, he went on to London for the christening of his godchild, and also to conduct the Philharmonic Concert of May 13, when his Italian Symphony was performed for the first time, and he himself played Mozart's D minor Concerto. This was his third visit. He was there by April 26 — again at his old lodgings in Great Portland Street — and on May 1 he played at Moscheles's annual concert a brilliant set of 4-hand variations on the Gipsy March in Preciosa, which the two had composed together.[1] He left shortly after the 13th and returned to Düsseldorf, in ample time for the rehearsal of the Festival, which began on Whit Sunday, May 26, and was an immense success. Israel in Egypt[2] was the *pièce de résistance*, and among the other works were Beethoven's Pastoral Symphony and Overture to Leonora, and his own Trumpet Overture. Abraham Mendelssohn had come from Berlin for the Festival, and an excellent account of it will be found in his letters, printed by Hensel,[3] admirable letters, full of point and wisdom, and showing better than anything else could the deep affection and perfect understanding which existed between father and son. The brilliant success of the Festival and the personal fascination of Mendelssohn led to an offer from the authorities of Düsseldorf that he should undertake the charge of the entire musical arrangements of the town, embracing the direction of the church music and of two associations, for three years, from October 1, 1833, at a yearly salary of 600 thalers[4] (£90). He had been much attracted by the active artistic life of the place when he visited Immermann at the close of his Italian journey, and there appears to have been no hesitation in his acceptance of the offer. This important agreement concluded, Felix returned to London for the fourth time, taking his father with him. They arrived about the 5th, and went into the lodgings in Great Portland Street. It is the father's first visit, and his letters are full of little hits at the fog, the absence of the sun, the Sundays, and other English peculiarities, and at his son's enthusiasm for it all. As far as the elder Mendelssohn was concerned, the

[1] Mos. i. 290.
[2] It had been performed by the Singakademie of Berlin, Dec. 8, 1831, but probably with re-instrumentation. It was now done as Handel wrote it.
[3] F.M. i. 347-364.
[4] I cannot discover his exact *status* or title at Düsseldorf. In his own sketch of his life (see p. 303 n. 10) he styles himself Music-director of the Association for the Promotion of Music in Düsseldorf.

first month was perfectly successful, but in the course of July he was laid up with some complaint in his shin, which confined him to his room for three weeks, and although it gave him an excellent idea of English hospitality, it naturally threw a damp over the latter part of the visit. His blindness, too, seems to have begun to show itself.[1]

His son, however, experienced no such drawbacks. To his father he was everything. ' I cannot express,' says the grateful old man, ' what he has been to me, what a treasure of love, patience, endurance, thoughtfulness, and tender care he has lavished on me; and much as I owe him indirectly for a thousand kindnesses and attentions from others, I owe him far more for what he has done for me himself.'[2]   No letters by Felix of this date have been printed, but enough information can be picked up to show that he fully enjoyed himself. His Trumpet Overture was played at the Philharmonic on June 10. He played the organ at St. Paul's (June 23), Klingemann and other friends at the bellows, and the church empty — Introduction and fugue; extempore; Attwood's Coronation Anthem, 4 hands, with Attwood; and three pieces of Bach's.[3] He also evidently played a great deal in society, and his father's account of a mad evening with Malibran will stand as a type of many such.[4]   The Moscheleses, Attwoods, Horsleys, and Alexanders are among the most prominent English names in the diaries and letters.[5]   Besides Malibran, Schröder-Devrient, Herz, and Hummel were among the foreign artists in London. On August 4 the two left for Berlin,[6] Abraham having announced that he was bringing home ' a young painter named Alphonse Lovie,' who, of course, was no other than Felix himself.[7] They reached Berlin in due course, and by September 27, 1833, Felix was at his new post.

Düsseldorf was the beginning of a new period in his career — of settled life away from the influence of home, which had hitherto formed so important an element in his existence. At Berlin both success and non-success were largely biased by personal considerations; here he was to start afresh, and to be entirely dependent on himself. He began his new career with vigour. He first attacked the church music, and as ' not one

---

[1] F.M. i. 397; ii. 62. Compare ii. 20.
[2] F.M. i. 384.   [3] Ibid. 272.   [4] Ibid. 377.
[5] Mos. i. 298; Abraham M. in F.M. i. 368, 380, 382, etc.
[6] Mos. i. 299.   [7] F.M. i. 386.

tolerable mass ' was to be found, scoured the country as far as
Elberfeld, Cologne, and Bonn, and returned with a carriage-
load of Palestrina, Lasso, and Lotti.   Israel in Egypt, the
Messiah, Alexander's Feast, and Egmont are among the music
which we hear of at the concerts.   At the theatre, after a temporary disturbance, owing to a rise in prices, and a little over-
eagerness, he was well received and successful ; and at first all
was *couleur de rose* — ' a more agreeable position I cannot wish
for.' [1]   But he soon found that the theatre did not suit him ;
he had too little sympathy with theatrical life, and the re-
sponsibility was too irksome.   He therefore, after a few months'
trial, in March 1834,[2] relinquished his salary as far as the
theatre was concerned, and held himself free, as a sort of
' Honorary Intendant.' [3]   His influence, however, made itself
felt.   Don Juan, Figaro, Cherubini's Deux Journées, were
amongst the operas given in the first four months ; and in the
church we hear of masses by Beethoven and Cherubini, motets
of Palestrina's, and cantatas of Bach's, the Dettingen Te Deum,
' and on the whole as much good music as could be expected
during my first winter.' [4]   He lived on the ground floor of
Schadow's house,[5] and was very much in the artistic circle,
and always ready to make an excursion, to have a swim, to
eat, to ride (for he kept a horse),[6] to dance, or to sleep ; was
working hard at water-colour drawing, under Schirmer's
tuition,[7] and was the life and soul of every company he entered.
In May [18-20] was the Lower Rhine Festival at Aix-la-
Chapelle, conducted by Ferdinand Ries ; there he met Hiller,
and also Chopin,[8] whose acquaintance he had already made
in Paris,[9] and who returned with him to Düsseldorf.   During
the spring of 1834 he was made a member of the Berlin Academy
of the Fine Arts.[10]

[1] L. July, 20, 1834.   [2] L. Mar. 28.   [3] L. Aug. 6.
[4] L. Mar. 28.   [5] H. 38.
[6] The acquisition of this horse gives a good idea of his dutiful attitude toward
his father. (L. March 28, 1834.)   [7] Dev. 174.
[8] L. May 23 ; H. 36.   [9] Karasowski, chap. xiv.
[10] L. ii. 15, 34.   On this occasion he sent in the following ' Memorandum of
my biography and art-education.' ' I was born Feb. 3, 1809, at Hamburg ; in
my 8th year began to learn music, and was taught thorough-bass and composition
by Professor Zelter, and the Pianoforte, first by my mother and then by Mr.
Ludwig Berger.   In the year 1829 I left Berlin, travelled through England and
Scotland, South Germany, Italy, Switzerland, and France ; visited England
twice more in the spring of 1832 and 33, was there made Honorary Member of the
Philharmonic Society, and since Oct. 1833, have been Music-director of the
Association for the Promotion of Music in Düsseldorf.' This is preserved in the
archives of the Academy, and I am indebted for it to the kindness of Mr. Joachim.

Meantime, through all these labours and distractions, of
pleasure or business alike, he was composing busily and well.
The overture to Melusina was finished November 14, 1833,
and tried; the E♭ Rondo [brillant] for piano and orchestra
(op. 29) on January 29, 1834; 'Infelice,' for soprano and
orchestra, for the Philharmonic Society[1] (in its first shape),
is dated April 3, 34; the fine Capriccio in A minor (op. 33,
no. 1), April 9, 34. He had also rewritten and greatly improved the Meeresstille Overture[2] for its publication by
Breitkopfs with the M.N.D. and Hebrides. A symphony which
he mentions as on the road appears to have been superseded
by a still more important work. In one of his letters from
Paris (December 19, 1831), complaining of the low morale of
the opera librettos, he says that if that style is indispensable
he 'will forsake opera and *write oratorios*.' The words had
hardly left his pen when he was invited by the Cäcilien-Verein
of Frankfort to compose an oratorio on St. Paul.[3] The general
plan of the work, and such details as the exclusive use of the
Bible and Choral-book, and the introduction of chorales, are
stated by him at the very outset. On his return to Berlin he
and Marx made a compact by which each was to write an
oratorio-book for the other; Mendelssohn was to write
'Moses' for Marx, and Marx 'St. Paul' for Mendelssohn.[4]
Mendelssohn executed his task at once, and the full libretto,
entitled 'Moses, an Oratorio, composed by A. B. M.,' and
signed 'F. M. B., 21 August 1832,' is now in the possession of
the family.[5] Marx, on the other hand, not only rejected
Mendelssohn's book for 'Moses,' but threw up that of 'St.
Paul' on the ground that chorales were an anachronism. In
fact, this singular man's function in life seems to have been to
differ with everybody. For the text of St. Paul, Mendelssohn
was indebted to his own selection and to the aid of his friends
Fürst and Schubring.[6] Like Handel, he knew his Bible well;
in his oratorios he followed it implicitly, and the three books
of St. Paul, Elijah, and the Lobgesang are a proof (if any proof

[1] First sung at the Philharmonic by Mme. Caradori, May 19, 1834.
[2] L. Aug. 6, 1834.
[3] Letter to Devrient, D. 137, 8.
[4] Marx, ii. 139, etc.
[5] It shows how fully Mendelssohn realised the connexion of the Old and
New Testaments that his concluding chorus, after the giving of the Law, is 'This
is the love of God, that we keep His commandments.' — from St. John.
[6] See Sch.; and L. ii. 5, 36, 39, etc.

were needed after the Messiah and Israel in Egypt) that, in his own words, ' the Bible is always the best of all.' [1] He began upon the music in March 1834, not anticipating that it would occupy him long; [2] but it dragged on, and was not completed till the beginning of 1836.

Though only Honorary Intendant at the Düsseldorf theatre, he busied himself with the approaching winter season, and before leaving for his holiday corresponded much with Devrient as to the engagement of singers.[3] September 1834 he spent in Berlin,[4] and was back at Düsseldorf [5] for the first concert on October 23, calling on his way at Cassel, and making the acquaintance of Hauptmann,[6] with whom he was destined in later life to be closely connected. The new theatre opened on November 1. He and Immermann quarrelled as to precedence, or as to the distribution of the duties. The selection of singers and musicians, the bargaining with them, and all the countless worries which beset a manager, and which, by a new agreement, he had to undertake, proved a most uncongenial and moreover a most wasteful task; so uncongenial that at last, the day after the opening of the theatre, he suddenly ' made a *salto mortale* ' and threw up all connection with it,[7] not without considerable irritability and inconsistency.[8] After this he continued to do his other duties, and to conduct occasional operas, Julius Rietz being his assistant. With the spring of 1835 he received an invitation from Leipzig through Mr. Schleinitz, which resulted in his taking the post of Conductor of the Gewandhaus Concerts there. His answers [9] to the invitation show not only how very careful he was not to infringe on the rights of others, but also how clearly and practically he looked at all the bearings of a question before he made up his mind upon it. Before the change, however, several things happened. He conducted the Lower Rhine Festival for 1835 at Cologne (June 7-9). The principal works were Handel's Solomon — for which he had written an organ part in Italy; Beethoven's Symphony No. 8, and Overture Op. 124, a ' religious march ' and hymn of Cherubini's, and the Morning Hymn of his favourite J. F. Reichardt. The

---

[1] L. July 15, 1834.   [2] L. Sept. 6, 1833, etc.
[3] Dev. 177-183.   [4] Dev. 183, 184.   [5] N.M. Zeitung.
[6] Hauptmann's letters to Hauser, i. 139.   [7] L. Nov. 4, 23.
[8] This is brought out in his father's letter, ii. 58. See also Nov. 4.
[9] L. Jan. 26 and April 16, 1835.

Festival was made more than ordinarily delightful to him by
a present of Arnold's edition of Handel in 32 volumes from
the committee. His father, mother, and sisters were all there.
The parents then went back with him to Düsseldorf; there
his mother had a severe attack of illness, which prevented his
taking them home to Berlin till the latter part of July.[1] At
Cassel the father too fell ill, and Felix's energies were fully
taxed on the road.[2] He remained with them at Berlin till the
end of August, and then left for Leipzig to make the necessary
preparations for beginning the subscription concerts in the
Gewandhaus on October 4. His house at Leipzig was in
Reichel's garden, off the Promenade. Chopin visited him
during the interval, and Felix had the pleasure of introducing
him to Clara Wieck, then a girl of 16. Later came his old
Berlin friend David from Russia to lead the orchestra,[3] and
Moscheles from London for a lengthened visit. Mendelssohn's
new engagement began with the best auspices. The relief from
the worries and responsibilities of Düsseldorf was immense,[4] and
years afterwards[5] he refers to it as ' when I first came to
Leipzig and thought I was in Paradise.' He was warmly welcomed on taking his seat, and the first concert led off with his
Meeresstille Overture.

Rebecka passed through Leipzig on October 14, on her
way from Belgium, and Felix and Moscheles accompanied her
to Berlin for a visit of two days, returning to Leipzig for the
next concert. Short as the visit was, it was more than usually
gay. The house was full every evening, and by playing
alternately, by playing four hands, and by the comical extempore tricks of which the two friends were so fond, and which
they carried on to such perfection, the parents, especially the
father, now quite blind, were greatly mystified and amused.[6]
And well that it was so, for it was Felix's last opportunity of
gratifying the father he so tenderly loved and so deeply
reverenced. At half-past 10 a.m. on November 19, 1835,
Abraham Mendelssohn was dead. He died the death of the
just, passing away, as his father had done, without warning,
but also without pain. He turned over in his bed, saying that

---

[1] Letter to Mrs. Voigt, Düsseldorf, July 17, 1835.
[2] Letter to Schadow, in Polko 193.
[3] He joined definitely Feb. 25, 1836, after Matthai's death (A.M.Z. 1836, 133).
[4] Letter to Hildebrandt in P. 191 ; also Hiller 47.
[5] L. June 18, 1839.   [6] F.M. i. 422.

he would sleep a little; and in half an hour he was gone. Hensel started at once for Leipzig, and by Sunday morning, the 22nd, Felix was in the arms of his mother. How deeply he felt under this peculiarly heavy blow the reader must gather from his own letters. It fell on him with special force, because he was not only away from the family circle, but had no home of his own, as Fanny and Rebecka had, to mitigate the loss. He went back to Leipzig stunned, but determined to do his duty with all his might, finish St. Paul, and thus most perfectly fulfil his father's wishes. He had completed the revision of his Melusina Overture on November 17, only three days before the fatal news reached him, and there was nothing to hinder him from finishing the oratorio.

The business of the day, however, had to go on. One of the chief events in this series of concerts was a performance of the 9th Symphony of Beethoven,[1] February 11, 1836. Another was Mendelssohn's performance of Mozart's D minor Concerto ' as written ' (for it seems to have been always hitherto played after some adaptation),[2] on January 29, with cadences which electrified his audience. Leipzig was particularly congenial to Mendelssohn. He was the idol of the town, had an orchestra full of enthusiasm and devotion, a first-rate coadjutor in David, who took much of the mechanical work of the orchestra off his shoulders; and moreover he was relieved of all business arrangements, which were transacted by the committee, especially by Herr Schleinitz. Another point in which he could not but contrast his present position favourably with that at Düsseldorf was the absence of all rivalry or jealousy. The labour of the season, however, was severe, and he confesses[3] that the first two months had taken more out of him than two years composing would do. The University of Leipzig showed its appreciation of his presence by conferring on him the degree of Phil. Doc. in March.[4]

Meantime Schelble's illness had cancelled the arrangement for producing St. Paul at Frankfort, and it had been secured for the Lower Rhine Festival of 1836 at Düsseldorf. The Festival lasted from May 22 to May 24 inclusive, and the programmes included, besides the new oratorio, the two over-tures to Leonore, both in C, ' No. 1 ' (then unknown) and

[1] A.M.Z. 1836, 273.   [2] Ibid. 105.
[3] To Hiller, L. Dec. 10, 1837. [4] A.M.Z. 1836, 216.

'No. 3'; one of Handel's Chandos anthems, the Davidde penitente of Mozart, and the Ninth Symphony. The oratorio was executed with the greatest enthusiasm, and produced a deep sensation. It was performed on the 22nd, not in the present large music hall, but in the long low room which lies outside of that and below it, and is known as the Rittersaal, a too confined space for the purpose. For the details of the performance, including an escapade of one of the false witnesses, in which the coolness and skill of Fanny alone prevented a break-down, we must refer to the contemporary accounts of Klingemann, Hiller, and Polko.[1] To English readers the interest of the occasion is increased by the fact that Sterndale Bennett, then 20 years old, and fresh from the Royal Academy of Music, was present.

Schelble's illness also induced Mendelssohn to take the direction of the famous Cäcilien-Verein at Frankfort. Leipzig had no claims on him after the concerts were over, and he was thus able to spend six weeks at Frankfort practising the choir in Bach's 'Gottes Zeit,' Handel's 'Samson,' and other works, and improved and inspired them greatly. He resided in Schelble's house at the corner of the 'Schöne Aussicht,' with a view up and down the Main. Hiller was then living in Frankfort; Lindblad was there for a time; and Rossini remained for a few days on his passage through, in constant intercourse with Felix.[2]

Mendelssohn's visit to Frankfort was, however, fraught with deeper results than these. It was indeed quite providential, since here he met his future wife, Cécile Charlotte Sophie Jeanrenaud, a young lady of great beauty, nearly ten years younger than himself, the second daughter of a clergyman of the French Reformed Church, who had died many years before, leaving his wife (a Souchay by family) and children amongst the aristocracy of the town. The house was close to the Fahrthor, on the quay of the Main.[3] Madame Jeanrenaud was still young and good-looking, and it was a joke in the

---

[1] See *The Musical World*, June 17, 1836 (and Benedict's *Sketch*, 27, 28); Hiller's *Mendelssohn*, 51; and Polko, 43.

[2] H. 55, etc.

[3] A pencil-drawing of the Main and the Fahrthor, with the 'Schöne Aussicht' in the distance, taken from the Jeanrenauds' windows, has the following inscription:— 'Vendu à Mendelssohn au prix de l'exécution d'un nombre indéterminé de Fugues de J. S. Bach, et de la Copie d'un Rondo du même Maître. LAURENS, à Montpellier.'

family that she herself was at first supposed to be the object of Mendelssohn's frequent visits. But though so reserved, he was not the less furiously in love, and those who were in the secret have told us how entirely absorbed he was by his passion, though without any sentimentality. He had already had many a passing attachment. Indeed, being at once so warm-hearted and so peculiarly attractive to women — and also, it should be said, so much sought by them — it is a strong tribute to his self-control that he was never before seriously or permanently involved. On no former occasion, however, is there a trace of any feeling that was not due entirely, or mainly, to some quality or accomplishment of the lady, and not to her actual personality. In the present case there could be no doubt either of the seriousness of his love or of the fact that it centred in Miss Jeanrenaud herself, and not in any of her tastes or pursuits. And yet, in order to test the reality of his feelings, he left Frankfort, at the very height of his passion, for a month's bathing at Scheveningen near the Hague.[1] His friend F. W. Schadow, the painter, accompanied him, and the restless state of his mind may be gathered from his letters to Hiller.[2] His love stood the test of absence triumphantly. Very shortly after his return, on September 9, the engagement took place,[3] at Kronberg, near Frankfort; three weeks of bliss followed, and on October 2 he was in his seat in the Gewandhaus, at the first concert of the season. The day [five days] after, October 3[7], in the distant town of Liverpool, ' St. Paul ' was performed for the first time in England, under the direction of Sir G. Smart. The season at Leipzig was a good one; Sterndale Bennett, who had come over at Mendelssohn's invitation, made his first public appearance in his own Concerto in C minor, and the series closed with the Choral Symphony.

His engagement soon became known far and wide, and it is characteristic of Germany, and of Mendelssohn's intimate relation to all concerned in the Gewandhaus, that at one of the concerts, the Finale to Fidelio, ' Wer ein holdes Weib errungen,' should have been put into the programme by the directors with special reference to him, and that he should have been forced into extemporising on that suggestive theme, amid the shouts and enthusiasm of his audience. The rehearsals for the

---

[1] H. ch. iv; F.M. ii. 30; Dev. 196.   [2] H. 62-72.
[3] Letter to his mother, F.M. ii. 27; P. 63.

concerts, the concerts themselves, his pupils, friends passing through, visits to his fiancée, an increasing correspondence, kept him more than busy. Bennett was living in Leipzig, and the two friends were much together. In addition to the subscription series and to the regular chamber concerts, there were performances of Israel in Egypt, with new organ part by him, on November 7, and St. Paul, March 16, 1837. The compositions of this winter are few, and all of one kind, namely preludes and fugues for pianoforte.[1] The wedding took place on March 28, 1837, at the Walloon French Reformed Church, Frankfort. For the wedding tour they went to Freiburg, and into the Palatinate, and by the 15th of May[2] returned to Frankfort. A journal which they kept together during the honeymoon is full of sketches and droll things of all kinds. In July they were at Bingen, Horchheim, Coblenz, and Düsseldorf for some weeks. At Bingen, while swimming across to A[s]smannshausen, he had an attack of cramp which nearly cost him his life, and from which he was only saved by the boatman. The musical results of these few months were very important, and include the 42nd Psalm, the String Quartet in E minor, an Andante and Allegro for piano in E (still in MS.), the second Pianoforte Concerto, in D minor, and the 3 Preludes and Fugues for the Organ (op. 37). He was also in earnest correspondence with Schubring[3] as to a second oratorio, on St. Peter.

It must have been hard to tear himself away so soon from his lovely young wife — and indeed he grumbles about it lustily [4] — but he had been engaged to conduct St. Paul, and to play the organ and his new Pianoforte Concerto, at the Birmingham Festival. Accordingly, on August 24, he left Düsseldorf for Rotterdam, crossed to Margate in the 'Attwood,' the same boat which had taken him over in 1829, and on the 27th is in London, on his fifth visit, at Klingemann's house, as cross as a man can well be.[5] But this did not prevent his setting to work with Klingemann at the plan of an oratorio on Elijah,[6] over which they had two mornings' consultation. Before leaving London for Birmingham he played the organ at St. Paul's — on Sunday afternoon, September 10 — and at

[1] Published as Op. 35.   [2] Dev. 200.
[3] L. July 13, 1837.   [4] F.M. ii. 51.   [5] H. 99.
[6] His private journal. He mentioned it to Mr. John C. Horsley (now the R.A.) during this visit.

Christ Church, Newgate Street, on Tuesday morning, the 12th.
It was on the former of these two occasions that the vergers,
finding that the congregation would not leave the Cathedral,
withdrew the organ-blower, and let the wind out of the organ
during Bach's Prelude and Fugue in A minor [1] — 'near the
end of the fugue, before the subject comes in on the Pedals.' [2]
At Christ Church he was evidently in a good vein. He played
'six extempore fantasias,' one on a subject given [by Wesley]
at the moment, and the Bach Fugue just mentioned [and
Bach's Toccata]. Samuel Wesley — our own ancient hero,
though 71 years old — was present and played. It was literally
his Nunc dimittis: he died in a month from that date.[3]
Mendelssohn's organ-playing on these occasions was eagerly
watched. He was the greatest of the few great German organ-
players who had visited this country, and the English organists,
some of them no mean proficients, learned more than one
lesson from him. 'It was not,' wrote Dr. Gauntlett, 'that he
played Bach for the first time here, — several of us had done
that. But he taught us how to play the *slow* fugue, for Adams
and others had played them too fast. His words were, 'Your
organists think that Bach did not write a slow fugue for the
organ.' Also he brought out a number of pedal-fugues which
were not known here. We had played a few, but he was the
first to play the D major, the G minor, the E major, the C
minor, the short E minor,' [4] etc. Even in those that were known
he threw out points unsuspected before, as in the A minor
Fugue, where he took the episode on the swell, returning to the
Great Organ when the pedal re-enters, but transferring the
E in the treble to the Great Organ a bar before the other parts,
with very fine effect.[5] This shows that with all his strictness
he knew how to break a rule. One thing which particularly
struck our organists was the contrast between his massive effects
and the lightness of his touch in rapid passages. The touch of
the Christ Church organ was both deep and heavy, yet he
threw off arpeggios as if he were at a piano. His command of
the pedal clavier was also a subject of much remark.[6] But

[1] For a very interesting account of these two performances by Dr. Gauntlett
see *The Musical World* for Sept. 15, 1837.
[2] His private journal.
[3] Oct. 11, 1837.
[4] He had learned these since his Swiss journey. See Letter, Sept. 3, 1831.
[5] Mr. E. J. Hopkins's recollection.
[6] Mr. Lincoln's recollection.

X

we must hasten on.   On the evening of the Tuesday [September 12] he attended a performance of his oratorio by the Sacred Harmonic Society at Exeter Hall.   He had conducted three rehearsals, but could not conduct the performance itself, owing to the prohibition of the Birmingham committee.   It was the first time he had heard St. Paul as a mere listener, and his private journal says that he found it ' very interesting.' His opinion of English amateurs may be gathered from his letter to the Society,[1] with which his journal fully agrees. ' I can hardly express the gratification I felt in hearing my work performed in so beautiful a manner, — indeed, I shall never wish to hear some parts of it better executed than they were on that night.   The power of the choruses — this large body of good and musical voices — and the style in which they sang the whole of my music, gave me the highest and most heartfelt treat; while I thought on the immense improvement which such a number of *real amateurs* must necessarily produce in the country which may boast of it.'   On the Wednesday he went to Birmingham, and remained there, rehearsing and arranging, till the Festival began, Tuesday, 19th.   At the evening concert of that day he extemporised on the organ, taking the subjects of his fugue from ' Your harps and cymbals ' (Solomon), and the first movement of Mozart's Symphony in D, both of which had been performed earlier in the day ; he also conducted his Midsummer Night's Dream Overture.   On Wednesday he conducted St. Paul, on Thursday evening played his new Concerto in D minor, and on Friday morning, the 22nd, Bach's Prelude and Fugue (' St. Anne's ') in E♭ on the organ.[2]   The applause throughout was prodigious, but it did not turn his head, or prevent indignant reflections on the treatment to which Neukomm had been subjected, reflections which do him honour.   Moreover, the applause was not empty. Mori and Novello were keen competitors for his Concerto, and it became the prize of the former [latter] at what we should now consider a very moderate figure, before its composer left Birmingham.   He travelled up by coach, reaching London at midnight, and was intercepted at the coach-office by the committee of the Sacred Harmonic Society, who presented him

---

[1] I have to thank Mr. Husk and the Committee of the S.H.S. for this and other valuable information.
[2] For these details see *Musical World*, Sept. 1837, pp. 24-40.   He had resolved on the Prelude and Fugue two months before.   See Letter, July 13.

with a large silver snuff-box, adorned with an inscription.[1]
He then went straight through, arrived in Frankfort on the
27th, and was at Leipzig at 2 p.m. of the day of the first concert,
Sunday, October 1. His house was in Lurgenstein's Garden,
off the Promenade, the first house on the left, on the second
floor.[2]

The next few years were given chiefly to Leipzig. He
devoted all his heart and soul to the Gewandhaus Concerts,
and was well repaid by the increasing excellence of the performance and the enthusiasm of the audiences. The principal
feature of the series 1837–8 was the appearance of Clara
Novello for the first time in Germany — a fruit of his English
experiences. She sang first at the concert of November 2, and
remained till the middle of January, creating an extraordinary
excitement. But the programmes had other features to recommend them. In February and March, 1838, there were four
historical concerts (1. Bach, Handel, Gluck, Viotti; 2. Haydn,
Cimarosa, Naumann, Righini; 3. Mozart, Salieri, Méhul,
Romberg; 4. Vogler, Beethoven, Weber); which excited
great interest. Mendelssohn and David played the solo pieces,
and it is easy to imagine what a treat they must have been.
In the programmes of other concerts we find Beethoven's
' Glorreiche Augenblick,' and Mendelssohn's own 42nd Psalm.
His Serenade and Allegro giojoso (op. 43) — like his Ruy Blas
Overture, a veritable impromptu [3] — was produced on April 2,
and his String Quartet in E♭ (op. 44, no. 3) on the following
day.

His domestic life during the spring of 1838 was not without
anxiety. On February 7 his first son was born, afterwards
named Carl Wolfgang Paul, and his wife had a very dangerous
illness.[4] This year he conducted the [Lower Rhine] Festival
at Cologne (June 3-6). He had induced the committee to
include a Cantata of Bach's,[5] then an entire novelty, in the
programme, which also contained a selection from Handel's
Joshua. A silver cup (Pokal) was presented to him at the close.[6]

The summer was spent at Berlin, in the lovely garden of

[1] L. Oct. 4, 1837. The box is with Dr. Paul Mendelssohn-Bartholdy.
[2] H. 149.
[3] Conceived and composed in two days for Mme. Botgorschek's concert. See
Letter, Apr. 2, 1838.
[4] H. 115.
[5] Letter to J. A. Novello, in G. & M. 192. For Ascension Day.
[6] A.M.Z. 1838, 439.

the Leipziger Strasse, and was his wife's first introduction to
her husband's family.[1] To Felix it was a time of great enjoyment and much productiveness. Even in the early part of
the year he had not allowed the work of the concerts to keep
him from composition. The String Quartet in Eb, just mentioned, the Cello Sonata in Bb (op. 45), the 95th Psalm, and
the Serenade and Allegro giojoso are all dated during the hard
work of the first four months of 1838. The actual result of the
summer was another String Quartet (in D; op. 44, no. 1),
dated July 24, 38,[2] and the Andante Cantabile and Presto
Agitato in B (Berlin, June 22, 1838). The intended result is a
symphony in Bb, which occupied him much, which he mentions more than once [3] as complete in his head, but of which
no trace on paper has yet been found. He alludes to it in a
letter to the Philharmonic Society (January 19, 1839) —
answering their request for a symphony — as 'begun last
year,' though it is doubtful if his occupations will allow him
to finish it in time for the 1839 season. So near were we to the
possession of an additional companion to the Italian and
Scotch Symphonies! The Violin Concerto was also begun in
this holiday,[4] and he speaks of a Psalm [5] (probably the noble
one for 8 voices, 'When Israel'), a sonata for piano and violin
(in F,[6] still in MS.), and other things. He was now, too, in
the midst of the tiresome correspondence [7] with Mr. Planché,
on the subject of the opera which that gentleman had agreed
to write, but which, like Mendelssohn's other negotiations on
the subject of operas, came to nothing; and there is the usual
large number of long and carefully written letters. He returned
to Leipzig in September, but was again attacked with measles,[8]
on the eve of a performance of St. Paul, on September 15. The
attack was sufficient to prevent his conducting the first of the
Gewandhaus Concerts (September 30) at which David was his
substitute. On October 7 he was again at his post.[9] The star
of this series was Mrs. Alfred Shaw, whose singing had pleased
him very much when last in England; its one remarkable
novelty was Schubert's great Symphony in C, which had been

[1] F.M. ii. 57, 63.   [2] Autograph in possession of the Sterndale Bennetts.
[3] L. July 30, 1838; June 18, 1839; H. 126.   [4] L. July 30, 1838.
[5] H. 126.   [6] 'Berlin, June 13, 1838.'
[7] For the whole of this, see Mr. Planché's *Recollections and Reflections*, 1872,
chap. xxi. Mr. Planché's caustic deductions may well be pardoned him even
by those who most clearly see their want of force.
[8] A.M.Z. 1838, 642.   [9] Ibid. 696.

brought from Vienna by Schumann, and was first played in
MS. on March 22 [21], 1839, at the last concert of the series.
It was during this autumn that he received from Erard the
grand piano which became so well known to his friends and
pupils, and the prospect of which he celebrates in a remarkable
letter now in possession of that firm.

Elijah is now fairly under way. After discussing with his
friends Bauer and Schubring the subject of St. Peter,[1] in terms
which show how completely the requirements of an oratorio
book were within his grasp, and another subject not very clearly
indicated, but apparently approaching that which he afterwards began to treat as Christus [2] — he was led to the contemplation of that most picturesque and startling of the prophets
of the Old Testament, who, strange to say, does not appear to
have been previously treated by any known composer. Hiller
tells [3] us that the subject was suggested by the passage [4] (1
Kings xix. 11), ' Behold, the Lord passed by.' We may accept
the fact more certainly than the date (1840) at which Hiller
places it. Such a thing could not but fix itself in the memory,
though the date might easily be confused. We have already
seen that he was at work on the subject in the summer of 1837,
and a letter to Schubring, dated November 2, 1838, shows that
much consultation had already taken place upon it between
Mendelssohn and himself, and that considerable progress had
been made in the construction of the book of the oratorio.
Mendelssohn had drawn up a number of passages and scenes
in order, and had given them to Schubring for consideration.
His ideas are dramatic enough for the stage ! A month later
the matter has made further progress,[5] and his judicious
dramatic ideas are even more confirmed ; but the music does
not seem to be yet touched. During the spring of 1839 he
finished the 114th Psalm, and wrote the Overture to Ruy Blas.
This, though one of the most brilliantly effective of his works,
was, with a chorus for female voices, literally conceived and
executed à l'improviste between a Tuesday evening and a Friday
morning — a great part of both Wednesday and Thursday
being otherwise occupied — and in the teeth of an absolute

[1] L. July 14, 1837.   [2] L. Jan. 12, 1835.
[3] H. 171.
[4] He liked a central point for his work. In St. Peter it would have been the
Gift of Tongues ; see L. July 14, 1837.
[5] L. Dec. 6, 1838.

aversion to the play.[1] The performance took place at the
theatre on March 11. A letter to Hiller,[2] written a month
after this, gives a pleasant picture of his care for his friends.
A great part of it is occupied with the arrangements for doing
Hiller's oratorio in the next series of Gewandhaus Concerts, and
with his pleasure at the appearance of a favourable article on
him in Schumann's 'Zeitung' ['Neue Zeitschrift für Musik '],
from which he passes to lament over the news of the suicide
of Nourrit, who had been one of his circle in Paris in 1831.

In May he is at Düsseldorf, conducting the [Lower Rhine]
Festival (May 19–21) — the Messiah, Beethoven's Mass in C,
his own 42nd Psalm, the Eroica, etc. From this he went to
Frankfort, to the wedding of his wife's sister Julie to Mr.
Schunck of Leipzig, and there he wrote the D minor Trio; [3]
then to Horchheim, and then back to Frankfort. On August
21 [4] they were at home again in Leipzig, and were visited by
the Hensels, who remained with them till September 4, and
then departed for Italy. Felix followed them with a long
letter [5] of hints and instructions for their guidance on the
journey, not the least characteristic part of which is the closing
injunction to be sure to eat a salad of broccoli and ham at
Naples, and to write to tell him if it was not good.

The summer of 1839 had been an unusually fine one; the
visit to Frankfort and the Rhine had been perfectly successful;
he had enjoyed it with that peculiar capacity for enjoyment
which he possessed, and he felt 'thoroughly refreshed.' [6] He
went a great deal into society, but found none so charming as
that of his wife. A delightful picture of part of his life at
Frankfort is given in a letter to Klingemann of August 1, and
still more so in one to his mother.[7] Nor was it only delightful.
It urged him to the composition of part-songs for the open air,
a kind of piece which he made his own, and wrote to absolute
perfection. The impulse lasted till the end of the winter, and
many of his best part-songs — including 'Love and Wine,'
'The Hunter's Farewell,' 'The Lark' — date from this time.
In addition to these the summer produced the D minor Trio

---

[1] Letter, Mar. 18, 1839. In fact it was only written at all because the proceeds of the concert were to go to the Widows' fund of the orchestra. He insisted
on calling it 'The Overture to the Dramatic Fund.'

[2] Leipzig, April 15; H. p. 133.

[3] The autograph is dated — 1st Movement, Frankfort, June 6; Finale,
Frankfort, July 18.   [4] F.M. ii. 85.

[5] Sept. 14. 1839.   [6] L. Aug. 1.   [7] L. July 3, Aug. 1.

already mentioned, the completion of the 114th Psalm, and some fugues for the organ, one of which was worked into a sonata, while the others remain in MS.

On October 2 his second child, Marie, was born. Then came the christening, with a visit from his mother and Paul, and then Hiller arrived. He had very recently lost his mother, and nothing would satisfy Mendelssohn but that his friend should come and pay him a long visit,[1] partly to dissipate his thoughts, and partly to superintend the rehearsals of his oratorio of Jeremiah the Prophet, which had been bespoken for the next series of Gewandhaus Concerts.[2] Hiller arrived early in December, and we recommend his description of Mendelssohn's home life to any one who wishes to know how simply and happily a great and busy man can live. Leipzig was proud of him, his wife was very popular, and this was perhaps the happiest period of his life. His love of amusement was as great as ever, and his friends still recollect his childish delight in the Cirque Lajarre and Paul Cousin the clown.

The concert season of 1839–40 was a brilliant one. For novelties there were symphonies by [Lindblad], Kalliwoda, Kittl, Schneider, and Vogler. Schubert's 9th was played no less than three times,[3] and one concert[4] was rendered memorable by a performance of Beethoven's four Overtures to Leonora-Fidelio. Mendelssohn's own 114th Psalm was first performed 'sehr glorios'[5] on New Year's Day, and the new Trio on February 10. The Quartet Concerts were also unusually brilliant. At one of them Mendelssohn's Octet was given, he and Kalliwoda playing the two violas; at another he accompanied David in Bach's Chaconne,[6] then quite unknown. Hiller's oratorio was produced on April 2 with great success. Ernst, and, above all, Liszt, were among the virtuosos of this season; and for the latter of these two great players Mendelssohn arranged a soirée at the Gewandhaus, which he thus epitomises — '350 people, orchestra, chorus, punch, pastry, Meeresstille, Psalm, Bach's Triple Concerto, choruses from St. Paul, Fantasia on Lucia, the Erl King, the

---

[1] H. 147.
[2] H. 134.
[3] Dec. 12, 1839, Mar. 12 and Apr. 3, 1840. The second performance was interfered with by a fire in the town.
[4] Letter, Jan. 4, 1840.
[5] Letter, Jan. 9, 1840.
[6] Probably extempore ; the published one is dated some years later.

devil and his grandmother ' ; [1] and which had the effect of somewhat allaying the annoyance which had been caused by the extra prices charged at Liszt's concerts.

How, in the middle of all this exciting and fatiguing work (of which we have given but a poor idea), he found time for composition, and for his large correspondence, it is impossible to tell, but he neglected nothing. On the contrary, it is precisely during this winter that he translates for his uncle Joseph, his father's elder brother — a man not only of remarkable business power but with considerable literary ability — a number of difficult early Italian poems into German verse. They consist of three sonnets by Boccaccio, one by Dante, one by Cino, one by Cecco Angiolieri, an epigram of Dante's, and another of Alfani's. They are printed in the recent editions of the letters, and are accompanied by a letter [to his uncle Joseph] dated February 20, 1840, describing half-humorously, half-pathetically, the difficulty which the obscurities of the originals had given him amid all his professional labours. With irrepressible energy he embraced the first moment of an approach to leisure, after what he describes as a ' really overpowering turmoil,' [2] to write a long and carefully studied official communication to the Kreis-Director, or Home Minister of Saxony, urging that a legacy recently left by a certain Herr Blümner should be applied to the formation of a solid music academy at Leipzig.[3] This was business ; but, in addition, during all these months there are long letters to Hiller, Chorley, his mother, Fanny, Paul, and Fürst (and remember that only a small part of those which he wrote has been brought within our reach) ; and yet he managed to compose both the Lobgesang and the Festgesang for the Festival in commemoration of the invention of Printing, which was held in Leipzig on June 25, the former of which is as characteristic and important a work as any in the whole series of his compositions. The music for both these was written at the express request of the Town Council, acting through a committee whose chairman was Dr. Raymond Härtel, and the first communication with Mendelssohn on the subject was made about the end of the previous July. We know from Mendelssohn himself [4] that the title ' Symphonie Cantate ' is due to Klingemann, but the words are probably

---

[1] Letter, Mar. 30, 1840.   [2] L. Mar. 30, 1840.
[3] L. April 8, 1840.   [4] L. Nov. 18, 1840.

Mendelssohn's own selection, no trace of any communication with Schubring, Bauer, or Fürst being preserved in the published letters or recollections, and the draft of the words having vanished.

The Festival extended over two days, Wednesday and Thursday, June 24 and 25. On Tuesday evening there was a 'Vorfeier' in the shape of an opera by Lortzing, 'Hans Sachs,' composed for the occasion. At 8 a.m. on Wednesday was a service in the church with a cantata by Richter (of Zittau), followed by the unveiling of the printing press and statue of Gutenberg, and by a performance in the open market-place of Mendelssohn's Festgesang [1] for two choirs and brass instruments, he conducting the one chorus and David the other. On Thursday afternoon a concert was held in St. Thomas's Church, consisting of Weber's Jubilee Overture, Handel's Dettingen Te Deum, and Mendelssohn's Lobgesang.

Hardly was this over when he went to Schwerin with his wife, to conduct St. Paul and other large works, at a Festival there (July 8–10). On the way back they stopped in Berlin for 'three very pleasant days.' [2] Another matter into which at this time he threw all his devotion was the erection of a monument to Sebastian Bach in front of his old habitat at the 'Thomas School.' The scheme was his own,[3] and he urged it with characteristic heartiness. But dear as the name and fame of Bach were to him, he would not consent to move till he had obtained (from the town council) an increase to the pay of the orchestra of the Gewandhaus Concerts. For this latter object he obtained 500 thalers,[4] and on August 10 [6] gave an organ performance *solissimo* in St. Thomas's Church, by which he realised 300 thalers.[5] Even this he would not do without doing his very best, and he describes to his mother how he had practised so hard for a week before ' that he could hardly stand on his feet, and the mere walking down the street was like playing a pedal passage.' [6] After such a six months no wonder that his health was not good, and that his ' physician

[1] The words of this were by Professor Prölss of Freiberg (N.M.Z. 1840, ii, 7). The ' statue ' which is mentioned in the accounts was probably something merely temporary. The second number of the Festgesang, adapted to the words ' Hark, the herald angels sing,' is a very favourite hymn-tune in England.
[2] C. i. 320.   [3] N.M.Z. 1843, i. 144.
[4] L. Feb. 7, 1840.
[5] 13,000 thalers in all were raised (N.M.Z. 1840, ii. 164).
[6] L. Aug. 10, 1840.

wanted to send him to some Brunnen instead of a Musical
Festival.'[1]   To a Festival, however, he went.   The Lobgesang
had not escaped the attention of the energetic Mr. Moore,
who managed the music in Birmingham, and some time before
its first performance he had written to Mendelssohn with the
view of securing it for the autumn meeting.   On July 21
Mendelssohn writes in answer, agreeing to come, and making
his stipulations as to the other works to be performed.[2]   It
was his sixth visit to England.

There was a preliminary rehearsal of the work in London
under Moscheles's care.   Mendelssohn arrived on September
8 [18],[3] visited all his London friends, including the Alexanders,
Horsleys, Moscheles, and Klingemann (with whom he stayed,
at 4 Hobart Place, Pimlico), went down to Birmingham with
Moscheles [on Sunday the 20th], and stayed with Mr. Moore.
On Tuesday he played a fugue on the organ ; on Wednesday,
the 23rd, conducted the Lobgesang, and after it was over, and
the public had left the hall, played for three-quarters of an
hour on the organ.[4]   The same day he played his G minor
Concerto at the evening concert.   On Thursday, after a selection from Handel's Jephthah, he again extemporised on the
organ, this time in public.   The selection had closed with a
chorus, the subjects of which he took for his improvisation,[5]
combining ' Theme sublime ' with ' Ever faithful ' in a masterly
manner.   On his return to town — on September 30 — he
played the organ at St. Peter's, Cornhill — Bach's noble Prelude and Fugue in E minor, his own in C minor (op. 37, no. 1)
and F minor,[6] the latter not yet published —

etc.

and other pieces, concluding with Bach's Passacaglia.   Of this
last he wrote a few bars as a memento, which still ornament
the vestry of the church.   He had intended[7] to give a Charity

[1] Letter in C. i. 314; Polko, 231.   [2] P. 231.
[3] Mos. ii. 67 [where the date is wrongly given].   [4] Mos. ii. 70.
[5] From the recollections of Mr. Turle and the late Mr. Bowley.
[6] I owe this to Miss Mounsey, the organist of the church. The Fugue is
among the MSS. in the Berlin Bibliothek.
[7] See his Letter of July 21 in C. i. 318.

Concert during his stay in London, after the Festival, but it
was too late in the season for this, and he travelled from London
with Chorley and Moscheles [1] in the mail coach to Dover;
then an 8-hours' passage to Ostend, and by Liège and Aix-la-
Chapelle to Leipzig. It was Moscheles's first introduction
to Cécile.

The concerts had already begun, on October 4, but he
took his place at the second. The Lobgesang played a great
part in the musical life of Leipzig this winter. It was performed
at the special command of the King of Saxony at an extra
concert in October.[2] Then Mendelssohn set to work to make
the alterations and additions which the previous performances
had suggested to him, including the scene of the watchman,
preparatory to a benefit performance on December 3; and
lastly it was performed at the 9th Gewandhaus Concert, on
December 17 [16], when both it and the Kreutzer Sonata were
commanded by the King and the Crown Prince of Saxony.
The alterations were so serious and so universal as to compel
the sacrifice of the whole of the plates engraved for the performance at Birmingham. Now, however, they were final,
and the work was published by Breitkopf & Härtel early in the
following year. Before leaving this we may say that the scene
of the watchman was suggested to him during a sleepless night,
in which the words 'Will the night soon pass?' incessantly
recurred to his mind. Next morning he told Mr. Schleinitz
that he had got a new idea for the Lobgesang.

With 1841 we arrive at a period of Mendelssohn's life when,
for the first time, a disturbing antagonistic element beyond his
own control was introduced into it, depriving him of that
freedom of action on which he laid such great stress, reducing
him to do much that he was disinclined to, and to leave undone
much that he loved, and producing by degrees a decidedly
unhappy effect on his life and peace. From 1841 began the
worries and troubles which, when added to the prodigious
amount of his legitimate work, gradually robbed him of the
serene happiness and satisfaction which he had for long enjoyed, and in the end, there can be little doubt, contributed
to his premature death. Frederick William IV, to whom, as
Crown Prince, Mendelssohn dedicated his three Concert-
overtures in 1834, had succeeded to the throne of Prussia on

---

[1] Mos. ii. 74.   [2] Letter, Oct. 27, 1840.

June 7, 1840; and being a man of much taste and cultivation, one of his first desires was to found an Academy of Arts in his capital, to be divided into the four classes of Painting, Sculpture, Architecture, and Music, each class to have its Director, who should in turn be Superintendent of the whole Academy. In music it was proposed to connect the class with the existing establishments for musical education, and with others to be formed in the future, all under the control of the Director, who was also to carry out a certain number of concerts every year, at which large vocal and instrumental works were to be performed by the Royal orchestra and the Opera company. Such was the scheme which was communicated to Mendelssohn by Herr von Massow, on December 11, 1840, with an offer of the post of Director of the musical class, at a salary of 3000 thalers (£450). Though much gratified by the offer, Mendelssohn declined to accept it without detailed information as to the duties involved. That information, however, could only be afforded by the Government Departments of Science, Instruction, and Medicine, within whose regulation the Academy lay, and on account of the necessary changes and adjustments would obviously require much consideration. Many letters on the subject passed between Mendelssohn, his brother Paul, Herr von Massow, Herr Eichhorn the Minister, Klingemann, the President Verkenius, from which it is not difficult to see that his hesitation arose from his distrust of Berlin and of the official world which predominated there, and with whom he would in his directorship be thrown into contact at every turn. He contrasts, somewhat captiously perhaps, his freedom at Leipzig with the trammels at Berlin; the devoted, excellent, vigorous orchestra of the one with the careless perfunctory execution of the other. His radical, *roturier* spirit revolted against the officialism and etiquette of a great and formal Court, and he denounces in distinct terms ' the mongrel doings of the capital — vast projects and poor performances; the keen criticism and the slovenly playing; the liberal ideas and the shoals of subservient courtiers; the Museum and Academy, and the sand.'

To leave a place where his sphere of action was so definite, and the results so unmistakably good, as they were at Leipzig, for one in which the programme was vague and the results at best problematical, was to him more than difficult. His fixed belief was that Leipzig was one of the most influential and Berlin one of the least influential places in Germany in the matter of music; and this being his conviction (rightly or wrongly) we cannot wonder at his hesitation to forsake the one for the other. However, the commands of a king are not easily set aside, and the result was that by the end of May 1841 he was living in Berlin, in the old home of his family — to his great delight.[1]

His life at Leipzig during the winter of 1840–41 had been unusually laborious. The interest of the Concerts was fully maintained; four very interesting programmes, occupied entirely by Bach, Handel, Haydn, Mozart, and Beethoven, and involving a world of consideration and minute trouble, were given. He himself played frequently; several very important new works by contemporaries — including symphonies by Spohr, Maurer, and Kalliwoda, and the Choral Symphony, then nearly as good as new — were produced, after extra careful rehearsals;[2] and the season wound up with Bach's Passion. In a letter to Chorley of March 15[3] he calls his spring campaign ' the most troublesome and vexatious ' he had ever known; ' nineteen concerts since January 1, and seven more to come, with at least three rehearsals a week all through.' The amount of general business and correspondence, due to the constant rise in his fame and position, was also alarmingly on the increase. In a letter to his mother, January 25, he tells of 35 letters written in two days, and of other severe demands on his time, temper, and judgment. And when we remember what his letters often are — the large quarto sheet of ' Bath paper,' covered at least on three sides, often over the flaps of the fourth, the close straight lines, the regular, extraordinarily neat writing, the air of accuracy and precision that pervades the whole down to the careful signature and the tiny seal — we shall not wonder that with all this, added to the Berlin worries, he composed little or nothing. ' I have neither read nor written in the course of this music-mad winter,' says he,[4] and accordingly, with one exception, we find no composition with a date earlier than the latter part of April 1841. The exception

---

[1] F.M. iii. 6.

[2] It was at this performance of the Choral Symphony that Schumann for the first time heard the D in the Bass Trombone which gives so much life to the beginning of the Trio. See his words in N.M.Z. 1841, i. 89.

[3] C. i. 334.   [4] C. i. 334; also L. ii. 24.

was a pianoforte duet in A, which he wrote expressly to play
with his friend Madame Schumann, at her concert on March
31. It is dated Leipzig, March 23, 1841, and was published
after his death as op. 92. As the pressure lessens, however, and
the summer advances, he breaks out with some songs, with and
without words, and then with the ' 17 Serious Variations '
(June 4), going on, as his way was, in the same rut, with the
variations in E♭ (June 25) and in B♭.[1] It was known before
he left Leipzig that it was his intention to accept the Berlin
post for a year only, and therefore it seemed natural that the
' Auf Wiedersehen ' in his Volkslied, ' Es ist bestimmt,' should
be rapturously cheered [2] when sung by Schröder-Devrient to
his own accompaniment, and that when serenaded at his
departure with the same song he should himself join heartily
in its closing words.[3] He took his farewell, as we have said,
with a performance of Bach's Passion, in St. Thomas's Church,
on Palm Sunday, April 4, and the appointment of Kapellmeister to the King of Saxony followed him to Berlin.[4]

For some time after his arrival there matters did not look
promising. But he had bound himself for a year. Many
conferences were held, at which little was done but to irritate
him. He handed in his plan for the Musical Academy,[5] received the title of Kapellmeister to the King of Prussia,[6] the
life in the lovely garden at the Leipziger Strasse reasserted its
old power over him, and his hope and spirits gradually returned. He was back in Leipzig for a few weeks in July, as
we find from his letters, and from an organ prelude in C minor,
a perfectly strict composition of 38 bars, written ' this morning '
(July 9), on purpose for the album of Mr. Dibdin of Edinburgh.
He then began work in Berlin. The King's desire was to revive
some of the ancient Greek tragedies. He communicated his
idea to Tieck, the poet, one of the new Directors; the choice
fell on the Antigone of Sophocles, in Donner's new translation;
and by September 9[7] Mendelssohn was in consultation with
Tieck on the subject. He was greatly interested with the plan,
and with the novel task of setting a Greek drama, and worked
at it with the greatest enthusiasm. By the 28th of the same
month he had made up his mind on the questions of unison,

[1] Letter, July 15, 1841, and MS. Cat.
[2] Schumann in N.M.Z. 1841, i. 118.   [3] Dev. 218.
[4] A.M.Z. 1841, 550.   [5] L. ii. 238; dated Berlin, May 1838.
[6] A.M.Z. 1841, 856.   [7] Dev. 223.

melodrama, etc. The first full stage rehearsal took place on the 22nd, and the performance itself at the Neue Palais at Potsdam on the 28th October, with a repetition on November 6. Meantime he had taken a house of his own opposite the family residence. A temporary arrangement had been made for the Gewandhaus Concerts of this winter to be conducted by David, and they began for the season on that footing. Mendelssohn, however, ran over for a short time, after the second performance of Antigone, and conducted two of the series, and the concert for the benefit of the orchestra, returning to Berlin for Christmas.

On January 10, 1842, he began a series of concerts by command of the king, with a performance of St. Paul in the concert-room of the theatre ; but, if we may believe Devrient, there was no cordial understanding between him and the band ; the Berlin audiences were cold, and he was uncomfortable. ' A prophet hath no honour in his own country.' It must, however, have been satisfactory to see the hold which his Antigone was taking both in Leipzig and Berlin,[1] in each of which it was played over and over again to crowded houses. During the winter he completed the Scotch Symphony, which is dated January 20, 1842. His sister's Sunday concerts were extraordinarily brilliant this season, on account not only of the music performed, but of the very distinguished persons who frequented them ; Cornelius, Thorwaldsen, Ernst (a constant visitor), Pasta, Madame Ungher-Sabatier, Liszt, Böckh, Lepsius, Mrs. Austin, are specimens of the various kinds of people who were attracted, partly no doubt by the music and the pleasant *réunion*, partly by the fact that Mendelssohn was there. He made his escape to his beloved Leipzig for the production of the Scotch Symphony, on March 3,[2] but though it was repeated a week later, he appears to have returned to Berlin. He once more, and for the last time, directed the Düsseldorf Festival [Lower Rhine Festival, held at Düsseldorf] on May 15–17 ; and passing on to London, for his seventh visit, with his wife, conducted his Scotch Symphony at the Philharmonic, amid extraordinary applause and enthusiasm, on June 13, and played his D minor Concerto there on the 27th, and conducted the Hebrides, which was encored. The Philharmonic season wound up with a fish dinner at Greenwich,

[1] First performance in Leipzig, Mar. 5 ; in Berlin, Apr. 13.
[2] N.M.Z. 1842, i. 108.

given him by the directors. On the 12th he revisited St. Peter's, Cornhill. It was Sunday, and as he came in the congregation were singing a hymn to Haydn's well-known tune. This he took for the subject of his voluntary, and varied and treated it for some time extempore in the happiest and most scientific manner. On the 16th he paid a third visit to Christ Church, Newgate Street, and it was possibly on that occasion that he played an extempore fantasia on Israel in Egypt which positively electrified those who heard it. He also again treated Haydn's Hymn, but this time as a fantasia and fugue, entirely distinct from his performance of four days previous.[1] On the 17th, at a concert of the Sacred Harmonic Society at Exeter Hall, mostly consisting of English anthems, he played the organ twice; first, Bach's so-called 'St. Anne's' Fugue, with the great Prelude in E♭, and, secondly, an extempore introduction and variations on the Harmonious Blacksmith, ending with a fugue on the same theme.[2] After this he and his wife paid a visit to their cousins in Manchester, with the intention of going on to Dublin, but were deterred by the prospect of the crossing. During the London portion of this visit they resided with his wife's relations, the Beneckes, on Denmark Hill. He was very much in society, where he always enjoyed himself extremely, and where his wife was much admired; and amongst other incidents described in his letters to his mother[3] are two visits to Buckingham Palace, the first in the evening of June 20, and the second on the afternoon of July 9, which show how thoroughly the Queen and Prince Consort appreciated him. On the latter occasion he obtained Her Majesty's permission to dedicate the Scotch Symphony to her.[4] They left on July 10 [12], and by the middle of the month were safe at Frankfort, in the midst of their relatives, 'well and happy,' and looking back on the past month as a 'delightful journey.'[5] August was devoted to a tour in Switzerland, he and Paul, with their wives. Montreux, Interlaken, the Oberland, the Furka, Meiringen, the Grimsel, are all mentioned. He walked, composed, and 'sketched furiously'; visited the old scenes, found the old landladies and

---

[1] On the authority of Miss Mounsey, Mr. E. J. Hopkins, and the *Athenæum*, June 18, 1842.

[2] *Atlas Newspaper*, June 18; *Musical World*, June 23.

[3] L. June 21, 1842; G. & M. 141.

[4] G. & M. 148.   [5] Ibid. 141.

old guides, always glad to see him; his health was perfect, his mood gay, and all was bright and happy, save when the spectre of a possible prolonged residence in Berlin [1] intruded its unwelcome form. On September 3 they were at Zürich,[2] on the 5th, 6th, and 7th at the Rigi and Lucerne.[3] While at Zürich he visited the Blind Institution, spent two hours in examining the compositions of the pupils, praised and encouraged them, and finished by extemporising on the piano at great length.[4] On his return, he stayed for a gay fortnight at Frankfort. Hiller, Charles Hallé, and their wives were there, and there was much music made, and a great open-air fête [5] at the Sandhof, with part-songs, *tableaux vivants*, etc., etc. A very characteristic and beautiful letter to Simrock, the publisher, urging him to accept some of Hiller's compositions (an appeal promptly responded to by that excellent personage), dates from this time.[6] So well was the secret kept that Hiller never knew of it till the publication of the letter in 1863.

An anecdote of this period may be new to some of our readers. During the summer the King of Prussia had conferred on Mendelssohn, in company with Liszt, Meyerbeer, and Rossini, the great honour of the ' Ordre pour le Mérite,' [7] and the order itself reached him at Frankfort. He set no store by such distinctions, nor perhaps was its Berlin origin likely to increase the value of this particular one. Shortly after it arrived he was taking a walk with a party of friends across the bridge at Offenbach. One of them (Mr. Speyer) stayed behind to pay the toll for the rest. ' Is not that,' said the tollkeeper, ' the Mr. Mendelssohn whose music we sing at our society? ' ' It is.' ' Then, if you please, I should like to pay the toll for him myself.' On rejoining the party, Mr. Speyer told Mendelssohn what had happened. He was enormously pleased. ' Hm,' said he, ' I like that better than the Order.' [8]

He took Leipzig on his way to Berlin, and conducted the opening concert of the Gewandhaus series on October 2, amid the greatest enthusiasm of his old friends. A week later and

---

[1] L. Aug. 18, 1842. [2] L. Sept. 3, 1842.
[3] Diary of Mr. Ella. The above dates preclude the possibility of his having attended the Mozart Festival at Salzburg on Sept. 4 and 5. There is no trace of his having been invited, and the full report in the A.M.Z. (1842, 788, 806), while giving the names of several musicians present, does not allude to him.
[4] A.M.Z. 1842, 907. [5] H. 187.
[6] Sept. 21, 1842; H. 189. [7] A.M.Z. 1842, 534.
[8] Told to the writer by the son of Mr. Speyer.

Y

he was in Berlin, and if anything could show how uncongenial
the place and the prospect were, it is to be found in his letter
to Hiller, and even in the Italian *jeu d'esprit* to Hiller's wife.[1]
It is as if his very teeth were set on edge by everything he
sees and hears there. Nor were matters more promising when
he came to close quarters. A proposition was made to him by
the minister immediately after his arrival that he should act
as superintendent of the music of the Protestant Church of
Prussia, a post at once vague and vast, and unsuited to him.
At the same time it was now evident that the plans for the
organisation of the Academy had failed, and that there was no
present hope of any building being erected for the music school.
Under these circumstances, anxious more on his mother's
account than on his own not to leave Berlin in disgrace, in fact
ready to do anything which should keep him in connection
with the place where she was,[2] he asked and obtained a long
private interview with the King, in which His Majesty expressed his intention of forming a choir of about 30 first-rate
singers, with a small picked orchestra, to be available for
church music on Sundays and Festivals, and to form the
nucleus of a large body for the execution of grand musical
works. Of this, when formed, he desired Mendelssohn to take
the command, and to write the music for it; meantime he
was to be at liberty to live where he chose, and — his own
stipulation — to receive half the salary previously granted.
The King evidently had the matter very closely at heart. He
was, says Mendelssohn, quite flushed with pleasure, could
hardly contain himself, and kept repeating ' You can scarcely
think *now* of going away.' When kings ask in this style it is
not for subjects to refuse them. Moreover Mendelssohn was
as much attracted by the King as he was repelled by the official
etiquette of his ministers, and it is not surprising that he
acceded to the request. The interview was followed up by a
letter from His Majesty dated November 22,[3] containing an
order constituting the Domchor or Cathedral choir, conferring
on Mendelssohn the title of General-Music-Director, with a
salary of 1500 thalers, and giving him the superintendence and
direction of the church and sacred music as his special province.

This involved his giving up acting as Capellmeister to the
King of Saxony, and for that purpose he had an interview

with that monarch at Dresden,[1] in which he obtained the
King's consent to the application of the Blümner legacy to his
darling scheme of a Conservatorium at Leipzig.

Thus then ' this long, tedious, Berlin business ' was at length
apparently brought to an end, and Mendelssohn was back in
his beloved Leipzig, and with a definite sphere of duty before
him in Berlin, for he had learnt in the meantime that he was
at once to supply the King with music to Racine's Athalie,
the Midsummer Night's Dream, The Tempest, and Œdipus
Coloneus.[2] This, with the proofs of the Scotch Symphony
and Antigone to correct, with the Walpurgisnight to complete
for performance, the new Conservatorium to organise, the
concerts, regular and irregular, to rehearse and conduct, and
a vast and increasing correspondence to be kept up, was enough
for even his deft and untiring pair of hands. He is cheerful
enough under it, and although he complains in one letter that
composition is impossible, yet in the next letter Athalie, Œdipus,
the Midsummer Night's Dream, the Walpurgisnight, and the
new Cello Sonata are beginning again to fill his brain, and
he finds time to be pleasant over old Madame Schröder, and
to urge the claims of his old Meiringen guide to a place in
Murray's Handbook.[3] In the midst of all this whirl he lost
his mother, who died in the same rapid and peaceful manner
that his father had done. She was taken ill on the Sunday
evening — her husband's birthday — and died before noon on
Monday December 12 — so quickly that her son's letter [4] of
the 11th cannot have reached her. The loss affected him less
violently than that of his father had done, perhaps because he
was now older and too hard-worked, and also because of the
home-life and ties by which he was surrounded. But it caused
him keen suffering, from which he did not soon recover. It
brings into strong relief his love of the family bond, and his
fear lest the disappearance of the point of union should at all
separate the brothers and sisters ; and he proposes, a touching
offer for one whose pen was already so incessantly occupied,
that he should write to one of the three every week, and the
communication be thus maintained with certainty.[5]

The house now became his, but the hesitation with which

[1] Letter to Klingemann, Nov. 23.   [2] Ibid.
[3] L. Nov. 28 and 23 ; comp. Sept. 23.   [4] L. Dec. 11.
[5] L. Dec. 22.

he accepts his brother's proposal to that effect, lest it should
not be acceptable to his sisters or their husbands, is eminently
characteristic of his delicate and unselfish generosity.[1]   He
admits that his mother's death has been a severe trial, and then
he drops an expression which shows how heavily the turmoil
of so busy a life was beginning to press upon him : — ' in fact
everything that I do and carry on is a burden to me, unless it
be mere passive existence.'   This may have been the mere
complaint of the moment, but it is unlike the former buoyant
Mendelssohn.   He was suffering too from what appears to
have been a serious cough.   But work came to his relief; he
had some scoring and copying to do which, though of the
nature of

> ' The sad mechanic exercise,
> Like dull narcotics numbing pain,' [2]

yet had its own charm — ' the pleasant intercourse with the
old familiar oboes and violas and the rest, who live so much
longer than we do, and are such faithful friends,' [3] and thus
kept him from dwelling on his sorrow.   And there was always
so much in the concerts to interest and absorb him.   The book
of Elijah too was progressing fast, and his remarks on it show
how anxious he was to make it as dramatic as possible.[4]   And
he still clung, though as fastidiously as ever, to the hope of
getting an opera-book.   A long letter [5] in French to M.
Charles Duveyrier, dated January 4, 1843, discusses the merits
of the story of Jeanne d'Arc for the purpose, and decides that
Schiller's play has preoccupied the ground.

At the concert of February 2, 1843, the Walpurgisnight
was produced, in a very different condition from that in which
it was performed at Berlin just 10 years before, in January 1833.
He had rewritten the score ' from A to Z,' amongst other
alterations had added two fresh airs, and had at length brought
it into the condition in which it is now so well known and so
much liked.   On January 12 a Symphony in C minor, by
Gade, of Copenhagen, was rehearsed.   It interested Mendelssohn extremely, and gave him an opportunity to write a
letter [6] full of sympathy and encouragement to the distant

---

[1] L. Dec. 22.   [2] ' In Memoriam,' v.
[3] Letter, Jan. 13, 1843.   [4] To Schubring. L. ii. 295.
[5] I am indebted for this to Mr. J. Rosenthal.
[6] L. Jan. 13, 1843.

and unknown composer, one of those letters which were native to him, but which are too seldom written, and for more of which the world would be all the better. The work was produced on March 2, amid extraordinary applause. Berlioz visited Leipzig at this time, and gave a concert of his compositions. Mendelssohn and he had not met since they were both at Rome, and Berlioz was foolish enough to suppose that some raillery of his might be lurking in Mendelssohn's memory, and prevent his being cordially welcomed. But he was soon undeceived. Mendelssohn wrote at once [1] offering him the room and the orchestra of the Gewandhaus, on the most favourable terms, and asking him to allow one of his works to be played at the approaching concert (February 22) for the Benefit of the orchestra. An account of the whole, with copious *souvenirs* of their Roman acquaintance (not wholly uncoloured), will be found in Berlioz's ' Voyage musical,' in the letter to Heller.[2] It is enough here to say that the two composer-conductors exchanged bâtons, and that if Berlioz did not convert Leipzig, it was not for want of an amiable reception by Mendelssohn and David. On March 9 an interesting extra concert was given [3] under Mendelssohn's direction, to commemorate the first subscription concert, in 1743. The first part of the programme contained compositions by former Cantors, or Directors of the Concerts — Doles, Bach, J. A. Hiller, and Schicht, and by David, Hauptmann, and Mendelssohn (114th Psalm). The second part consisted of the Choral Symphony.

Under the modest title of the Music School the prospectus of the Conservatorium was issued on January 16, 1843, with the names of Mendelssohn, Hauptmann, David, Schumann, Pohlenz, and C. F. Becker as the teachers; the first trial was held on March 27, and on April 3 [4] it was opened in the buildings of the Gewandhaus. Thus one of Mendelssohn's most cherished wishes was at last accomplished. A letter on the subject to Moscheles, dated April 30, is worth notice as showing how practical his ideas were on business matters, and

---

[1] Jan. 25. Letter now in the possession of A. G. Kurtz, Esq., of Liverpool. In printing it Berlioz has shortened it by a half, and sadly garbled it by correcting the French !

[2] And in Berlioz's *Mémoires*.   [3] N.M.Z. 1843, i. 95.

[4] N.M.Z. 1843, i. 102. Hauptmann, letter to Spohr, Feb. 6, 43, says, ' Our music-school is to begin in April, but not on the 1st, Mendelssohn thought that unlucky.'

how sound his judgment. On Sunday, April 23,[1] he had the satisfaction of conducting the concert at the unveiling of the monument to Sebastian Bach, which he had originated and for which he had worked so earnestly. The programme consisted entirely of Bach's music, in which Mendelssohn himself played a concerto. Then the monument was unveiled, and the proceedings ended with Bach's 8-part motet 'Singet dem Herrn ein neues Lied.' Such good services were appropriately acknowledged by the Town Council with the honorary freedom of the city (Ehrenbürgerrecht).[2]

About this time [in the spring of 1843] he made the acquaintance of Joseph Joachim, who came to Leipzig from Vienna as a boy of 12, attracted by the fame of the new music school, and there began a friendship which grew day by day, and only ended with Mendelssohn's death.

On May 1 his fourth child, Felix, was born. On account no doubt partly of his wife's health, partly also of his own — for it is mentioned that he was seriously unwell at the dedication of the Bach monument — but chiefly perhaps for the sake of the Conservatorium, he took no journey this year, and, excepting a visit to Dresden to conduct St. Paul, remained in Leipzig for the whole summer. How much his holiday was interfered with by the tedious, everlasting affair of Berlin — orders and counter-orders, and counter-counter-orders — may be seen from his letters, though it is not necessary to do more than allude to them. By the middle of July[3] he had completed the Midsummer Night's Dream music, had written the choruses to Athalie, and made more than a start with the music to Œdipus, and some progress with a new symphony;[4] had at the last moment, under a pressing order from Court, arranged the chorale 'Herr Gott, dich loben wir' (Te Deum) for the celebration of the 1000th anniversary of the empire, 'the longest chorale and the most tedious job he had ever had,' and had also, a still harder task, answered a long official letter on the matter of his post, which appeared to contradict all that had gone before, and cost him (in his own words) 'four thoroughly nasty, wasted, disagreeable days.'

He therefore went to Berlin early in August, and on the

6th conducted the music of the anniversary; returned to Leipzig in time to join his friend Madame Schumann in her husband's lovely Andante and Variations for 2 Pianofortes at Madame Viardot's concert on August 19,[1] and on August 25 was pursued thither by orders for a performance of Antigone, and the production of the Midsummer Night's Dream and Athalie in the latter half of September. At that time none of the scores of these works had received his final touches; Athalie indeed was not yet scored at all, nor was a note of the overture written. Then the performances are postponed, and then immediately resumed at the former dates; and in the end Antigone was given on September 19,[2] in the Neue Palais at Potsdam, and the Midsummer Night's Dream at the same place — after 11 rehearsals [3] — on October 14,[4] and on the 18th, 19th, 20th, and 21st at the King's Theatre in Berlin. The music met with enthusiastic applause each time; but the play was for long a subject of wonder to the Berliners. Some disputed whether Tieck or Shakespeare were the author; others believed that Shakespeare had translated it from German into English. Some, in that refined atmosphere, were shocked by the scenes with the clowns, and annoyed that the King should have patronised so low a piece; and a very distinguished personage [5] expressed to Mendelssohn himself his regret that such lovely music should have been wasted on so poor a play —a little scene which he was very fond of mimicking.[6]—Antigone procured him the honour of membership of the Philologenversammlung of Cassel.[7]

Mendelssohn's position at Berlin had now apparently become so permanent that it was necessary to make proper provision for filling his place at the Leipzig concerts, and accordingly Ferdinand Hiller was engaged [8] to conduct them during his absence. The first of the series was on October 1. Hiller conducted, and Felix supported his friend by playing his G minor Concerto. Two days afterwards, on October 3, he

---

[1] N.M.Z. 1843, ii. 68; Lampadius. Joachim made his first appearance at this concert. [2] Dev. 245.

[3] H. 213. The band was small — only 6 first and 6 second fiddles; but 'the very pick of the orchestra' (Joachim).

[4] On the 14th Mendelssohn was called for, but did not appear; F.M. iii. 51.

[5] F.M. iii. 73. These court-people were only repeating what the Italian villagers had said to him in 1831. See Letter, July 4, 1831.

[6] Mr. Sartoris's recollection.

[7] A.M.Z. 1843, 804.

[8] H. 212; N.M.Z. 1843, ii. 135.

writes a long communication to the town council of Leipzig,
praying for an increase in the salaries of the town orchestra
for their services at the theatre. On October 30 he joined
Mme. Schumann and Hiller in the triple concerto of Bach;
on November 18 there was a special farewell concert at which
he played [in] his new Cello Sonata (op. 58), and which closed
with his Octet, he and Gade taking the two viola parts; and
by November 25 he had left Leipzig ' with wife and children,
and chairs and tables, and piano and everything,' [1] and was
in Berlin, settled in the old family house, now his own. On
the 30th he conducted the first of the weekly subscription
concerts, which he and Taubert directed alternately, and at
which he often played. With all his aversion to the Berlin
musicians he was obliged to acknowledge that, in some respects
at least, the orchestra was good. ' What pleases me most,' he
says to his old friend and confidant David, ' are the Basses,
because they are what I am not so much accustomed to. The
8 cellos and 4 good double-basses give me sometimes great
satisfaction with their big tone.' [2] Then came performances
of the Midsummer Night's Dream music, of Israel in Egypt,
entertainments and dinners — which amused him notwithstanding all his dislike to aristocrats — and Fanny's Sunday
performances. Once immersed in life and music, and freed
from official correspondence and worries, he was quite himself.
' He is,' says his sister, ' indescribably dear, in the best of
tempers, and quite splendid, as you know he can be in his
best times. Every day he astonishes me, because such quiet
intercourse as we are having is a novelty to me now, and he is
so versatile, and so original and interesting on every subject,
that one can never cease to wonder at it.' [3] His favourite
resort during his later Berlin life was the house of Professor
Wichmann the sculptor, in the Hasenjäger (now Feilner)
Strasse. Wichmann's wife was a peculiarly pleasant artistic
person, and their circle included Magnus the painter, Taubert,
Werder, Count Redern, and other distinguished people, many
of them old friends of Mendelssohn. There, in 1844, he first
met Jenny Lind. The freedom of the life in this truly artistic
set, the many excursions and other pleasures, delighted and
soothed him greatly.

[1] To Macfarren, G. & M. 160.   [2] MS. letter, Dec. 19, 1843.
[3] F.M. iii. 89.

Christmas was kept royally at his house; he was lavish with presents, of which he gives Rebecka (then in Italy) a list.[1] A very characteristic Christmas gift to a distant friend [2] was the testimonial, dated Berlin, December 17, 1843, which he sent to Sterndale Bennett for use in his contest for the professorship at Edinburgh, and which, as it does credit to both these great artists, and has never been published in any permanent form, we take leave to print entire, in his own English.[3]

BERLIN, *Dec.* 17, 1843.

MY DEAR FRIEND,

I hear that you proclaimed yourself a Candidate for the musical Professorship at Edinburgh, and that a testimonial which I might send could possibly be of use to you with the Authorities at the University. Now while I think of writing such a testimonial for you I feel proud and ashamed at the same time — proud, because I think of all the honour you have done to your art, your country, and yourself, and because it is on such a brother-artist that I am to give an opinion — and ashamed, because I have always followed your career, your compositions, your successes, with so true an interest, that I feel as if it was my own cause, and as if I was myself the Candidate for such a place. But there is one point of view from which I might be excused in venturing to give still an opinion, while all good and true musicians are unanimous about the subject : perhaps the Council of the University might like to know what *we German* people think of you, how we consider you. And then, I may tell them, that if the prejudice which formerly prevailed in this country against the musical talent of your Country has now subsided, it is chiefly owing to you, to your compositions, to your personal residence in Germany. Your Overtures, your Concertos, your vocal as well as instrumental Compositions, are reckoned by our best and severest authorities amongst the first standard works of the present musical period. The public feel never tired in listening to, while the musicians feel never tired in performing, your Compositions ; and since they took root in the minds of the true amateurs, my countrymen became aware that music is the same in England as in Germany, as everywhere ; and so by your successes here you destroyed that prejudice which nobody could ever have destroyed but a true Genius. This is a service you have done to English as well as German musicians, and I am sure that your countrymen will not acknowledge it less readily than mine have already done.

Shall I still add, that the Science in your works is as great as

---

[1] Ibid. 91.   [2] It reached him on the 23rd.
[3] I am indebted to Mr. J. R. S. Bennett for an exact copy of this letter.

their thoughts are elegant and fanciful — that we consider your
performance on the Piano as masterly as your Conducting of an
Orchestra? that all this is the general judgement of the best
musicians here, as well as my own personal sincere opinion? Let
me only add that I wish you success from my whole heart, and that
I shall be truly happy to hear that you have met with it.

Always yours, sincerely and truly,

FELIX MENDELSSOHN BARTHOLDY.

To W. STERNDALE BENNETT, Esq.

His exertions for his friend did not stop at this testimonial,
but led him to write several long letters pressing his claims in
the strongest terms, the drafts of which will be found in the
'green books' at Leipzig. The professorship, however, was
not bestowed on Mr. Bennett.

The compositions of the winter were chiefly for the Cathedral, and include the fine setting of the 98th Psalm (op. 91)
for 8-part choir and orchestra, for New Year's Day, 1844; the
2nd Psalm, for Christmas, with chorales and 'Sprüche,' and
pieces 'before the Alleluja'; also the 100th Psalm, the 43rd
ditto, and the 22nd, for Good Friday, for 8 voices, each with
its 'Spruch' or anthem — and 7 psalm-tunes or chorales with
trombones. At these great functions the church was so full[1]
that not even Fanny Hensel could get a place. The lovely
solo and chorus, 'Hear my prayer,' for voices and organ,
belongs to this time. It is dated January 25, 1844, and was
written for Mr. Bartholomew, the careful and laborious trans-
lator of his works into English, and sent to him in a letter[2]
dated January 31. Also the duets 'Maiglöckchen,' 'Volkslied,' and 'Herbstlied' (op. 63, nos. 6, 5, and 4), and many
songs, with and without words. The concerts finished with a
magnificent performance of Beethoven's 9th Symphony on
March 27, and on Palm Sunday (March 31) Israel in Egypt
was sung in St. Peter's church. The rehearsals for these two
difficult works, new to Berlin, had been extremely troublesome
and fatiguing.

At the end of February he received a letter from the Philharmonic Society of London, offering him an engagement as
Conductor of the last six concerts of the season. He looked

[1] F.M. iii. 99.
[2] Polko, 220. It was originally written with an organ accompaniment, but
Mendelssohn afterwards scored it at the instance of Mr. Joseph Robinson of
Dublin. How it came to be dedicated to Taubert is not discoverable.

forward with delight to an artistic position ' of such tremendous distinction,' [1] and which promised him the opportunity of doing a service to a Society to which he felt personally indebted ; [2] and on March 4 he writes ' with a feeling of true gratitude ' accepting for five concerts. [3] Meantime the old annoyances and heartburnings at Berlin had returned. Felix had been requested by the King to compose music to the Eumenides of Æschylus, and had replied that the difficulties were immense, and perhaps insuperable, but that he would try ; and in conversation with Tieck he had arranged that as the work could only be given in the large new opera-house, which would not be opened till December 15, it would be time enough for him to write his music and decide whether it was worthy of performance, after his return from England. Notwithstanding this, he received, as a parting gift, on April 28, a long, solemn, almost scolding, letter from Bunsen, [4] based on the assumption that he had refused to undertake the task, and expressing the great disappointment and annoyance of the King. No wonder that Mendelssohn's reply, though dignified, was more than warm. It appeared to him that some person or persons about the Court disbelieved in the possibility of his writing the music, and had pressed their own views on the King as his, and he was naturally and justifiably angry. A dispute with the subscribers to the Symphony Concerts, where he had made an innovation on ancient custom by introducing solos, [5] did not tend to increase his affection for Berlin.

His presence was necessary on Easter Day (April 7) in the Cathedral, but by the end of the month he had left Berlin with his family. On May 4 they were all at Frankfort, and by the 10th or 11th he himself was settled in London at Klingemann's house, 4 Hobart Place. This was his eighth visit. He conducted the Philharmonic Concert of May 13, and each of the others to the end of the series, introducing, besides works already known, his own Midsummer Night's Dream music, and the Walpurgisnight, as well as Beethoven's Overture to Leonora, No. 1, the Ruins of Athens, Bach's Suite in D. Schubert's Overture to Fierabras, and playing Beethoven's Concerto in G (June 24), then almost a novelty to an English audience. He had brought with him Schubert's Symphony in

---

[1] F.M. iii. 92.   [2] L. July 19, 1844.
[3] Hogarth, 82.   [4] L. April 28, 1844.   [5] Lampadius, 133.

338 MENDELSSOHN

C, and Gade's in C minor, and his own Overture to Ruy Blas. But the reception of the two first at the trial by the band was so cold, not to say insulting,[1] as to incense him beyond measure. With a magnanimity in which he stands alone among composers, he declined to produce his own Overture, and it was not publicly played in England till after his death.[2]

With the directors of the Philharmonic his intercourse was most harmonious. ' He attended their meetings, gave them advice and assistance, and showed the warmest interest in the success of the concerts and the welfare of the Society.'[3] By the band he was received with ' rapture and enthusiasm.'[4] And if during the earlier concerts one or two of the players acted in exception to this, the occurrence only gave Mendelssohn the opportunity of showing how completely free he was from rancour or personal feeling.[5] No wonder that the band liked him. The band always likes a conductor who knows what he is about. His beat, though very quiet, was certain, and his face was always full of feeling, and as expressive as his baton. There are some of the players still remaining who recollect it well. No one perhaps ever possessed so completely as he the nameless magic art of inspiring the band with his own feeling; and this power was only equalled by his tact and good-nature. It is still remembered that he always touched his hat on entering the orchestra for rehearsal. He was sometimes hasty, but he always made up for it afterwards. He would run up and down to a distant desk over and over again till he had made the meaning of a difficult passage clear to a player. If this good nature failed, or he had to deal with obstinacy, as a last resource he would try irony — sometimes very severe. Such pains and tact as this is never thrown away. The band played as if under a new influence. The season was most successful in a pecuniary sense; Hanover Square Rooms had never been so crammed ; as much as 120 guineas were taken on single nights in excess of the usual receipts ; and whereas in 1842 the loss had been £300, in 1844 nearly £400 were added to the reserve fund.[6] Among the events

[1] Few things are more curious than the terms in which Schubert's splendid works were criticised at this date in London, compared with the enthusiasm which they now excite.
[2] At Mrs. Anderson's Concert, 1849.
[3] Hogarth, 83. [4] Mos. ii. 118.
[5] See letter to Moscheles ; June 26, 1846.
[6] Musical World, Aug. 1, 1844.

which combined to render this series of concerts historical were the first appearances of Ernst (April 15), Joachim (May 27),[1] and Piatti (June 24). His playing of the Beethoven G major Concerto on June 24 was memorable, not only for the magnificence of the performance, but for some circumstances attending the rehearsal on the previous Saturday. He had not seen the music of the concerto for two or three years, and ' did not think it respectful to the Philharmonic Society to play it without first looking through it ' — those were his words. He accordingly called at Sterndale Bennett's on the Friday night to obtain a copy, but not succeeding, got one from Miss Horsley after the rehearsal on the Saturday. At the rehearsal itself, owing to some difficulty in the band coming in at the end of his cadence in the first movement, he played it three times over, each time quite extempore, and each time new, and at the performance on the Monday it was again different.[2]

In addition to the Philharmonic, Mendelssohn took part in many other public concerts — conducted St. Paul for the Sacred Harmonic Society on June 28 and July 5, extemporised at the British Musicians, played his own D minor Trio, and his Duet Variations (op. 83), and took part twice in Bach's Triple Concerto — once (June 1) with Moscheles and Thalberg, when he electrified the room with his sudden improvisation in the cadence,[3] and again (July 5) with Moscheles and Döhler. He also finished a scena for bass voice and orchestra, to words from Ossian — ' On Lena's gloomy heath,' which he undertook at the request of Mr. H. Phillips in 1842, and which that gentleman sang at the Philharmonic, March 15, 1847. On June 12 he and Dickens met for the first time. On June 18 he is at Manchester, writing to Mr. Hawes, M.P. to secure a ticket for the House of Commons.[4] Piatti he met for the first time during this visit, at Moscheles's house, and played with him his new Duo in D. No one had a quicker eye for a great artist, and he at once became attached to the noble player who has now made London his winter home, and is so much admired by all frequenters of the Monday Popular Concerts. One of his latest words on leaving England for the

---

[1] The bearer of a letter of introduction from Mendelssohn to Sterndale Bennett, for which see Polko, 157.

[2] I owe this to the recollection of Mr. Kellow Pye and Mr. Davison.

[3] See an account of this (somewhat exaggerated) by C. E. Horsley in the Choir, 1873, p. 81.

[4] Letter in possession of A. G. Kurtz, Esq.

last time was, ' I must write a concerto for Piatti.' In fact, he had already composed the first movement. The enthusiasm for him in London was greater than ever, and all the more welcome after the irritations of Berlin. He was more widely known at each visit, and every acquaintance became a friend. He never enjoyed himself more than when in the midst of society, music, fun, and excitement. ' We have the best news from Felix,' says Fanny during this visit,[1] ' and when I tell you that he has ordered a large *Baum-Kuchen* [a peculiar Berlin cake, looking like a piece of the trunk of a tree] to be sent to London for him, you will know that that is the best possible sign.' ' A mad, most extraordinarily mad time,' says he, ' I never had so severe a time before — never in bed till half past one; for three weeks together not a single hour to myself in any one day,'[2] etc. ' My visit was glorious. I was never received anywhere with such universal kindness, and have made more music in these two months than I do elsewhere in two years.'[3] But even by all this he was not to be kept from work. He laboured at his edition of Israel in Egypt for the Handel Society; and on official pressure from Berlin — which turned out to be mere vexation, as the work was not performed for more than a year — actually, in the midst of all the turmoil, wrote the Overture to Athalie, the autograph of which is dated June 13, 1844. Very trying! and very imprudent, as we now see! but also very difficult to avoid. And his power of recovery after fatigue was as great as his power of enjoyment, so great as often no doubt to tempt him to try himself. Three things were in his favour — his splendid constitution; an extraordinary power of sleep, which he possessed in common with many other great men, and of being lazy when there was nothing to do; and most of all that, though excitable to any amount, he was never dissipated. The only stimulants he indulged in were those of music, society, and boundless good spirits.

On July 10 he left London, and on the 13th was in the arms of his wife and children at Soden, near Frankfort. During his absence they had been seriously ill, but his wife had kept the news from him, and when he returned he found them all well, brown, and hearty. For the life of happy idleness which he passed there in the next two months — ' eating and sleeping,

[1] F.M. iii. 168.   [2] Ibid. 176.   [3] L. July 19, 1844.

without dress coat, *without* piano, *without* visiting cards, *without* carriage and horses, but *with* donkeys, *with* wild flowers, *with* music-paper and sketch-book, *with* Cécile and the children ' [1] — interrupted only by the Festival which he conducted at Zweibrücken on July 31 and August 1, the reader must be referred to his own charming letters.[2] 'Idleness' does not mean ceasing to compose, so much as composing only when he had a mind to it. And that was often; he had no piano, but he completed the Violin Concerto on September 16, after a long and minute correspondence with David, and many of the movements of the six organ sonatas appear in the MS. Catalogue, with dates ranging from July 22 to September 10. Doubtless, too, he was working at the book of 'Christus,' a new oratorio, the first draft of which he had received from Bunsen on Easter Monday of this year. At this time also he arranged [edited] a collection of organ pieces by Bach for the firm of Coventry & Hollier,[3] by whom they were published in London in the summer of 1845. The pleasure in his simple home life which crops out now and then in these Frankfort letters, is very genuine and delightful. Now, Marie is learning the scale of C, and he has actually forgotten how to play it, and has taught her to pass her thumb under the wrong finger! Now, Paul tumbles about so as to crack their skulls as well as his own. Another time he is dragged off from his letter to see a great tower which the children have built, and on which they have ranged all their slices of bread and jam — 'a good idea for an architect.' At ten Carl comes to him for reading and sums, and at five for spelling and geography — and so on. 'And,' to sum up, 'the best part of every pleasure is gone if Cécile is not there.'[4] His wife is always somewhere in the picture.

But the time arrived for resuming his duties at Berlin, and, leaving his family behind him at Frankfort, he arrived there on September 30, alone, and took up his quarters with the Hensels. We are told that before leaving in the spring he had firmly resolved not to return for a permanence; and the extraordinary warmth and brilliancy of his subsequent reception in England, both in public and in social circles, and the delights of freedom in Frankfort, when compared with the

[1] F.M. iii. 177. [2] L. July 17, 19, 25, Aug. 15.
[3] See the letters, P. 245, etc. [4] F.M. iii. 151.

constraint and petty annoyances of Berlin — the difficulty of
steering through those troubled official waters, the constant
collisions with the Singakademie, with the managers of the
theatre, the clergy, the King, and the ministers; the want of
independence, the coldness of the press, the way in which his
best efforts appeared to be misunderstood and misrepresented,
and above all the consciousness that he was at the head of a
public musical institution of which he did not approve [1] — all
these things combined to bring about the crisis. His dislike
to the place and the way in which it haunts him beforehand,
is really quite plaintive in its persistence — ' If I could only
go on living for half a year as I have lived the last fortnight
(Soden, August 15) what might I not get through? But the
constant arrangement and direction of the concerts, and the
exertion of it all, is no pleasure to me, and comes to nothing
after all." [2] So he once more communicated with the King,[3]
praying to be freed from all definite duties, and from all such
commissions as would oblige him to reside in Berlin. To this
the King good-naturedly assented; his salary was fixed at
1000 thalers, and he was free to live where he liked. It is easy
to understand what a blow this was to his sister,[4] but it was
evidently the only possible arrangement for the comfort of the
chief person concerned. ' The first step out of Berlin ' was to
him ' the first step to happiness.' [5] He remained till the end
of November, at the special wish of the King, to conduct a few
concerts and a performance of St. Paul (November 25), and
the time was taken advantage of by Lvoff to commission Hensel
to paint a portrait of him, which has been engraved by Caspar,
but can hardly be called a favourable likeness. On the 30th
he left Berlin amid regret and good wishes, but the coldness
of the ordinary musical circles towards him was but too
evident.[6]

Very early in December he was in Frankfort, where he
found his youngest boy Felix dangerously ill: the child recovered, but only after being in great danger for many weeks.
It was probably a relief in the very midst of his trouble to
write a long letter [7] to Mr. Macfarren (December 8), giving

[1] F.M. iii. 205.   [2] L. Aug. 15, 1844.
[3] Sept. 30; F.M. iii. 191.   [4] F.M. iii. 192.
[5] Dev. 252. His own words.
[6] Recollection of Sig. Piatti, who was there at the time.
[7] G. & M. 165.

him minute directions as to the performance of Antigone at
Covent Garden. His own health began to give him anxiety,
and his resolution was to remain in Frankfort for the whole
year and have a thorough rest. He had always good spirits
at command, and looked well, and would rarely confess to
any uneasiness. But when hard pressed by those with whom
he was really intimate, he confessed that his head had for some
months past been in constant pain and confusion. ' I myself
am what you know me to be; but what you do not know is
that I have for some time felt the necessity for complete rest —
not travelling, *not* conducting, *not* performing — so keenly that
I am compelled to yield to it, and hope to be able to order my
life accordingly for the whole year. It is therefore my wish to
stay here quietly through winter, spring, and summer, *sans*
journeys, *sans* festivals, *sans* everything.' [1] This resolve he was
able to carry out for some months of 1845,[2] even to resisting a
visit to Leipzig when his Violin Concerto was first played by
David, on March 13; and his letters to his sisters show how
thoroughly he enjoyed the rest.

Antigone was brought out at Covent Garden on January 2,
1845, under the management of M. Laurent, the orchestra
conducted by Mr. (now Professor) Macfarren. Musically its
success was not at first great, owing to the inadequate way in
which the chorus was put on the stage. Writing to his sister
at Rome [3] on March 25, Mendelssohn says, ' See if you cannot
find *Punch* for January 18. It contains an account of Antigone
at Covent Garden, with illustrations, especially a view of the
chorus which has made me laugh for three days. The Chorus-
master, with his plaid trowsers shewing underneath, is a
masterpiece, and so is the whole thing, and most amusing.
I hear wonderful things of the performance, particularly of
the chorus. Only fancy, that during the Bacchus chorus there
is a regular ballet with all the ballet-girls! ' A woodcut which
made Mendelssohn laugh for three days has *ipso facto* become
classical, and needs no apology for its reproduction.[4]

The play improved after a short time, and the fact that it
ran for 45 nights (January 2–February 1, February 8–21), and
that the management applied to him for his Oedipus,[5] proves

[1] F.M. iii. 204.   [2] Ibid. 219, 224, 225.   [3] Ibid. 221.
[4] I owe this to the kindness of Mr. Tom Taylor, as Editor of *Punch*.
[5] F.M. iii. 221.

Z

that it was appreciated. His letters show how much work he was doing at this time. By April 20 the six Organ Sonatas (op. 65) were in the hands of the copyist, the C minor Trio was finished — ' a trifle nasty (*eklig*) to play, but not really difficult — seek and ye shall find ' ;[1]   and the splendid String Quintet in B♭ (dated July 8). The sixth book of Songs without Words was shortly to be published, and dedicated to Klingemann's fiancée; a symphony was well in hand (oh that we had got it!), and the book of Elijah progressing steadily, no doubt urged by the invitation (dated September 1, 1844) which he had received to conduct the Birmingham Festival in 1846. Conduct the whole he could not, the labour would be too great, but he replied that he would conduct his own music as before.[2] Nor had the desire to write an opera by any means left him, ' if only the right material could be found.'[3]   He had not forgotten his promise to consider the possibility of setting the choruses of the Eumenides of Æschylus with effect, and a

correspondence had taken place between him and the Geheim-cabinetsrath Müller, in which, in reply to something very like an offensive innuendo, Mendelssohn stated that in spite of strenuous efforts he had utterly failed to see any way of carrying out the commission to his own satisfaction.[4] The Œdipus Coloneus, the Œdipus Rex, and the Athalie, were however finished, and at His Majesty's disposal. The editing of Israel in Egypt had given him considerable trouble, owing apparently to the wish of the council of the Handel Society to print

[1] F.M. iii. 227.   [2] Letters to Moore; P. 233-238.
[3] F.M. iii. 221; Dev. 258, 259, 262.   [4] L. Mar. 12, 1845.

Mendelssohn's marks of expression as if they were Handel's, and also to the incorrect way in which the engraving was executed. These letters [1] are worth looking at, as evidence how strictly accurate and conscientious he was in these matters, and also how gratuitously his precious time was often taken up.

Gade had conducted the Gewandhaus Concerts for 1844–5; but having got rid of the necessity of residing in Berlin, and having enjoyed the long rest which he had proposed, it was natural that Mendelssohn should return to his beloved Leipzig. But in addition to this he had received an intimation from Von Falkenstein as early as June 5, 1845, that the King of Saxony wished him to return to his former position. He accordingly once more took up his residence there early in September (this time at No. 3 Königsstrasse, [2] on the first floor) and his reappearance in the conductor's place at the opening concert in the Gewandhaus on October 5 was the signal for the old applause, and for hearty recognition from the audience and the press. The season was rendered peculiarly brilliant by the presence of Madame Schumann, and of Jenny Lind, who made her first appearance in Leipzig at the subscription concert of December 4. Miss Dolby also made her first appearance October 23, sang frequently, and became a great favourite. Among the more important orchestral items of the season 1845–46 were Schumann's Symphony in B♭, and Mendelssohn's Violin Concerto (David), brought forward together on October 23, 1845.

After the first concert he left for Berlin to produce his Œdipus Coloneus, which was first performed at Potsdam on November 1, and his Athalie at Charlottenburg, both being repeated at Berlin. He returned to Leipzig by December 11 [3] [on December 3], and remained there till the close of the season, taking an active part in all that went on, including Miss Lind's farewell concert on April 12, 1846 — the last occasion of his playing in public in Leipzig. At the end of 1845 a formal offer was made to Moscheles, at that time the fashionable pianoforte teacher in London, to settle in Leipzig as Professor of the Pianoforte in the Conservatorium. He took time to consider so important an offer, and on January 25,

[1] There are seven of them, and they are given in the Appendix to G. & M., ed. 2, p. 169.
[2] The house has since been renumbered, and is now 21. A bronze tablet on the front states that he died there.
[3] Letter to Moore; P. 238.

1846, with a sacrifice of income and position which does his
artistic feeling the highest honour, decided in its favour.
Mendelssohn's connection with the school was no sinecure.
He had at this time two classes [1] — Pianoforte and Composition. The former numbered about half-a-dozen pupils, and
had two lessons a week of 2 hours each. The lessons were given
collectively, and among the works studied during the term
were Hummel's Septuor; 3 of Beethoven's Sonatas; Preludes
and Fugues of Bach; Weber's Concertstück and Sonata in
C; Chopin's Studies. The Composition class had one lesson
a week of the same length. The pupils wrote compositions of
all kinds, which he looked over and heard and criticised in
their presence. He would sometimes play a whole movement
on the same subjects, to show how they might have been better
developed. Occasionally he would make them modulate from
one key to another at the piano, or extemporise on given themes,
and then would himself treat the same themes. He was often
extremely irritable : — ' Toller Kerl, so spielen die Katzen! '
or (in English, to an English pupil) ' Very ungentlemanlike
modulations ! ' etc. But he was always perfectly natural. A
favourite exercise of his was to write a theme on the black-
board, and then make each pupil add a counterpoint; the
task, of course, increasing in difficulty with each addition. On
one occasion the last of the pupils found it impossible to add
a single note, and after long consideration shook his head and
gave in. ' You can't tell where to place the next note? ' said
Mendelssohn. ' No.' ' I am glad of that,' was the reply, ' for
neither can I.' But in addition to the work of his classes, a
great deal of miscellaneous work fell upon him as virtual head
of the School. Minute lists of the attendance and conduct of
the pupils, drawn up by him, still remain to attest the thorough
way in which he did his duty, and we have Moscheles's express
testimony [2] that during the overwhelming work of this summer
he never neglected his pupils.[3] But it was another ounce
added to his load. The fixed labour, the stated hours, when
combined with his composition, his correspondence, his hos-

---

[1] This information I owe to Mr. Otto Goldschmidt and Mr. Rockstro, who
belonged to both of his classes.

[2] Mos. ii. 162.

[3] The English pupils for 1844 and 1845 embrace the names of Ellis, Wells,
Hasker, Ascher, and Rockstro. The English pupils up to 1868 number 109,
heading the list of all countries save Saxony and Prussia. Next comes Russia,
and next North America.

pitality, and all his other pursuits, was too much, and to his intimate friends he complained bitterly of the strain, and expressed his earnest wish to give up all work and worry, and devote himself entirely to his Art — in his own words, to shut himself into his room and write music till he was tired, and then walk out in the fresh air.[1]

Meantime Elijah was fast becoming a realised fact: by May 23, 1846,[2] the first Part was quite finished and six or eight numbers of the second Part written, and a large portion despatched to London to be translated by Mr. Bartholomew and Klingemann.[3] ' I am jumping about my room for joy,' he writes to a very dear friend[4] on the completion of Part I. ' If it only turns out half as good as I fancy it is, how pleased I shall be!' And yet, much as the oratorio engrossed him, he was corresponding with Mme. Birch-Pfeiffer about an opera, and writes to the same friend as if the long-desired libretto were virtually within his grasp. At this date he interrupted his work for three weeks to conduct a succession of performances on the Rhine — at Aix-la-Chapelle, the [Lower Rhine] Festival, May 31 to June 2; at Düsseldorf, a soirée; at Liège, on Corpus Christi day, June 11, his hymn ' Lauda Sion,' composed expressly for that occasion, and dated February 10, 1846; and at Cologne the first festival of the German-Flemish association, for which he had composed a Festgesang on Schiller's poem ' an die Künstler ' (op. 68). His reception throughout this tour was rapturous, and delighted him. The three weeks were one continued scene of excitement. Every moment not taken up in rehearsing or performing made some demand on his strength. He was in the highest spirits all the time, but the strain must have been great, and was sure to be felt sooner or later. It will all be found in a delightful letter to Fanny of June 27, 1846.[5] On June 26 he is again at Leipzig, writing to Moscheles to protest against the exclusion from the band at Birmingham of some musicians who had been impertinent to him at the Philharmonic in 1844.[6] The summer was unusually hot, and his friends well remember how exhausted he often became over his close work. But he kept his time. The remainder of the Oratorio was in Mr. Bartholomew's

---

[1] Letter to Miss Lind.   [2] Letter to Schubring, May 23, 1846.
[3] Letter to Moore; P. 241.   [4] Miss Lind.
[5] F.M. iii. 239-243. See also Chorley's *Modern German Music*, ii. 320-350.
[6] L. June 26, 1846.

hands by the latter part of July; the instrumental parts
were copied in Leipzig and rehearsed by Mendelssohn there
on August 5. One of the last things he did before leaving
was to give his consent to the publication of some of Fanny's
compositions, which, owing to his 'tremendous reverence for
print,' he had always opposed,[1] and now only agreed to
reluctantly.[2] He arrived in London, for the ninth time, on
the evening of August [17 or] 18, had a trial rehearsal with
piano at Moscheles's house, two band-rehearsals at Hanover
Square, went down to Birmingham on Sunday the 23rd, had
full rehearsals on Monday morning and Tuesday evening, and
the Oratorio was performed on the morning of Wednesday the
26th. The Town Hall was densely crowded, and it was observed [3] that the sun burst forth and lit up the scene as
Mendelssohn took his place, amid a deafening roar of applause
from band, chorus, and audience. Staudigl was the Elijah,
and Mr. Lockey sang the air ' Then shall the righteous ' in a
manner which called forth Mendelssohn's warmest praise.[4]
' No work of mine ' — says he in the long letter which he wrote
his brother the same evening — ' no work of mine ever went
so admirably at the first performance, or was received with
such enthusiasm both by musicians and the public, as this.'
' I never in my life heard a better performance — no nor so
good, and almost doubt if I can ever hear one like it again.'[5]
No less than four choruses and four airs were encored.[6] The
applause at the conclusion of both first and second parts was
enormous — almost grotesquely so ; and an old member [7] of
the band well remembers the eagerness with which Mendelssohn
shook hands with all who could get near him in the artists' room,
thanking them warmly for the performance. He returned to
London with Mr. and Mrs. Moscheles, ' on purpose for a fish
dinner at Lovegrove's,' spent four days at Ramsgate [8] with the
Beneckes ' to eat crabs,' and on September 6 recrossed the
Channel with Staudigl. His visit this time had been one of
intense hard work, as any one who knows what it is to achieve
the first performance of a great work for solos, chorus, and
orchestra, will readily understand. And the strain was unre-
mitting, for, owing partly to Moscheles's illness, he had no

---

[1] L. June 2, 1837.   [2] F.M. iii. 234.   [3] B. 51.
[4] L. Aug. 26.   [5] Ibid.
[6] Mrs. Moscheles says 11 pieces; Mos. ii. 157.
[7] Mr. J. T. Willy.   [8] F.M. iii. 244.

relaxation, or next to none. In consequence he was so tired as to be compelled to rest three times [1] between Ostend and Leipzig. It is a sad contrast to the buoyancy of the similar journey ten years before.[2]

But notwithstanding the success of the oratorio the reader will hardly believe that he himself was satisfied with his work. Quite the contrary. His letter to Klingemann of December 6 shows the eagerness with which he went about his corrections; and the alterations were so serious as to justify our enumerating the chief of them: [3] — The chorus 'Help, Lord!' (No. 1), much changed; the end of the double quartet (No. 7), rewritten; the scene with the widow (No. 8) entirely recast and much extended; the chorus 'Blessed are the men' (No. 9), rescored; the words of the quartet 'Cast thy burden' (No. 15), new; the soprano air 'Hear ye' (No. 21), added to and reconstructed; in the Jezebel scene a new chorus, 'Woe to him' (No. 24), in place of a suppressed one, 'Do unto him as he hath done,' and the recitative 'Man of God' added; the trio 'Lift thine eyes' (No. 28) was originally a duet, quite different; Obadiah's recitative and air (No. 25) are new; the chorus 'Go return,' and Elijah's answer (No. 36) are also new. The last chorus (No. 42) is entirely rewritten to fresh words, the text having formerly been 'Unto Him that is able,' etc. The omissions are chiefly a movement of 95 bars, *alla breve*, to the words 'He shall open the eyes of the blind,' which formed the second part of the chorus 'Thus saith the Lord' (No. 41), and a recitative for tenor 'Elijah is come already and they knew him not, but have done unto him whatsoever they listed,' with which Part 2 of the oratorio originally opened. In addition to these more prominent alterations there is hardly a movement throughout the work which has not been more or less worked upon.

The oratorio was then engraved, and published by Simrock of Berlin in July 1847. Meantime Mendelssohn had been again reminded of his duties at Berlin by an urgent command from the King to set the German Liturgy to music. This (still in MS.), and an anthem or motet (published as op. 79, no. 5), both for double choir, are respectively dated October 28

[1] Ibid.   [2] L. Oct. 4, 1837.
[3] For a detailed examination of Nos. 1-8, by Mr. Jos. Bennett, see *Concordia*, pp. 497, 523. A MS. copy of the original score is in the possession of Mr. H. Littleton (Novello's).

and October 5, 1846. A song for the Germans in Lyons [1] —
dear to him as the birthplace of his wife — and a Psalm-tune
for the French Reformed Church in Frankfort, are dated the
8th and 9th of the same month. On October 21 the Moscheleses
arrive at Leipzig, and Moscheles begins his duties as Professor
of Pianoforte-playing and Composition. — Gade again conducted the Gewandhaus Concerts for this season. A trace of
Mendelssohn's interest in them remains in a piano accompaniment to the E major Violin Prelude of Bach,[2] which he evidently
wrote for David's performance at the concert of November 12,
1846. The MS. is dated the day before, and is amongst
David's papers.[3] During October and November he was very
much occupied with the illness of his faithful servant Johann
Krebs, to whom he was deeply attached — ' mein braver guter
Diener ' as he calls him — and whose death, on November 23,
distressed him much. It was another link in the chain of losses
which was ultimately to drag him down. Fortunately he had
again, as at the time of his mother's death, some mechanical
work to which he could turn. This time it was the comparison of the original autograph parts of Bach's grand mass with
his score of the same work.[4] As time went on, however, he was
able to apply himself to more independent tasks, and by
December 6 was again hard at work on the alterations of
Elijah.[5] Since the middle of October he had been in communication with Mr. Lumley,[6] then lessee of Her Majesty's
Theatre, London, as to an opera to be founded by Scribe on
' The Tempest,' already tried by Immermann (see p. 296) ; and
a long correspondence between himself, Scribe, and Lumley
appears to have taken place, no doubt exhaustive on his part.
It came to nothing, from his dissatisfaction with the libretto,[7]
but it was accompanied by extreme and long-continued annoyance, owing to his belief that the opera was announced in
London as if he were under a contract to complete it, and that
for the season of 1847.[8] He was at this moment more or less
committed to the subject of Loreley, on which he had com-

[1] Op. 76, No. 3.
[2] Dörffel's Cat. 634. So well known in London through Joachim's playing.
[3] ' An F. David zur und aus der Erinnerung niedergeschrieben, F.M.B.
Leipzig d. 11ten Nov. 1846.' This (which with many other things in this article
I owe to my friend Mr. Paul David) looks as if the accompaniment had been
originally extemporised.   [4] L. Dec. 6.   [5] Ibid.
[6] Lumley's *Reminiscences*, 167.   [7] Ibid. 168.
[8] Long letters to influential London friends are in existence full of bitter
complaints — most justly founded if his information was correct.

municated with Geibel the poet as early as the preceding April.[1] Geibel, a friend of Mendelssohn and a warm admirer of his wife, was at work on the book, and completed it at the beginning of 1847. Mendelssohn occasionally conducted the later Gewandhaus concerts of this season, and some of the programmes were of special interest, such as two historical concerts on February 18 and 25, 1847. One of these gave him the opportunity to write a charming letter [2] to the daughter of Reichardt, a composer for whom he always had a special fondness, and whose Morning Hymn (from Milton) had been performed at the Festival at Cologne in 1835 at his instance.

This was not on the whole a satisfactory autumn. After the extra hard work of the spring and summer, especially the tremendous struggle against time in finishing Elijah, he ought to have had a long and complete rest, like that which so revived him in 1844; whereas the autumn was spent at Leipzig, a less congenial spot than Frankfort, and, as we have shown, in the midst of grave anxiety and perpetual business, involving a correspondence which those only can appreciate who have seen its extent, and the length of the letters, and the care and neatness with which the whole is registered and arranged by his own hands. Knowing what ultimately happened, it is obvious that this want of rest, coming after so much stress, must have told seriously upon him. He himself appears to have felt the necessity of lessening his labours, for we are told that he had plans for giving up all stated and uncongenial duty, and doing only what he felt disposed to do, for building a house [3] in Frankfort, so as to pass the summer there, and the winter in Berlin with his sisters, and thus in some measure revive the old family life to which he so strongly urges his brother-in-law in a remarkable letter of this time.[4] Nothing, however, could stop the current of his musical power. He was at work on 'Christus,' the new oratorio.[5] As Capellmeister to the King of Saxony he had to arrange and conduct the Court Concerts at Dresden; and he took a large part in the management of the Gewandhaus Concerts this season, though suffering much from his head, and being all the time under the care of his doctor.[6] How minutely, too, he did his duty at this time as chief of the Conservatorium is shown by a MS. memorandum,

[1] Dev. 276.   [2] L. ii. 388.   [3] Dev. 291.
[4] Letter to Dirichlet, Jan. 4, 1847.   [5] Dev. 290.   [6] Lampadius.

dated January 10, 1847, containing a long list of students, with full notes of their faults, and of the recommendations to be made to their professors. His enjoyment of life is still very keen, and his birthday was celebrated with an immense amount of fun. His wife, and her sister, Mrs. Schunck — a special favourite of Mendelssohn — gave a comic scene in the Frankfort dialect; and Joachim (as Paganini), Moscheles (as a cook), and Mrs. Moscheles, acted an impromptu charade on the word 'Gewandhaus.' Happily no presentiment disturbed them; and the master of the house was as uproarious as if he had fifty birthdays before him. On Good Friday (April 2) he conducted St. Paul at Leipzig, and shortly afterwards — for the tenth, and alas! the last time — was once more in England, where he had an engagement [1] with the Sacred Harmonic Society to conduct three performances of Elijah in its revised form. One of those kindnesses which endeared him so peculiarly to his friends belongs to this time. Madame Frege had a son dangerously ill, and was unable to hear the performance of St. Paul. 'Na nun,' said he, ' don't distress yourself; when he gets out of danger I'll come with Cécile and play to you all night.' And he went, began with Beethoven's Moonlight Sonata, and played on for three hours, ending with his own Variations sérieuses. A day or two afterwards, he left, travelled over with Joachim,[2] and reached the Klingemanns' house on Monday evening, April 12. The performances took place at Exeter Hall on the 16th, 23rd, 28th, with a fourth on the 30th. The Queen and Prince Consort were present on the 23rd, and it was on that occasion that the Prince wrote the note in his programme book, addressing Mendelssohn as a second Elijah, faithful to the worship of true Art though encompassed by the idolators of Baal, which has often been printed.[3] In the interval Mendelssohn paid a visit to Manchester for a performance of Elijah on the 20th,[4] and another to Birmingham, where he rehearsed and conducted the oratorio at the Town Hall on the 27th; and also conducted his Midsummer

---

[1] The engagement for one performance had been tendered as early as Sept. 14; see Mendelssohn's reply of Oct. 7 to the letter of Mr. Brewer, the secretary to the society, of that date, in P. 227. The other two were proposed Jan. 26, and arranged for between that date and Mar. 10, 1847; see the letter of that date to Bartholomew, ibid. 229. The fourth was an afterthought.
[2] *Mus. World*, April 17.
[3] Letter, Aug. 26, Martin's Life of Prince Consort, i. 489.
[4] Letter to Moore, Manchester, Apr. 21; P. 244.

Night's Dream music and Scotch Symphony at the Philharmonic on the 26th, and played Beethoven's G major Concerto with even more than his usual brilliancy and delicacy. He probably never played that beautiful concerto — 'my old *cheval de bataille*,' as he called it years before — more splendidly than he did on this occasion. To a friend[1] who told him so after the performance he replied, ' I was desirous to play well, for there were two ladies present whom I particularly wished to please, and they were the Queen and Jenny Lind.' A little trait remembered by more than one who heard the performance, is that during the cadence to the first movement — a long and elaborate one, and, as before (see p. 339), entirely extempore, Mr. Costa, the conductor, raised his baton, thinking that it was coming to an end, on which Mendelssohn looked up, and held up one of his hands, as much as to say ' Not yet.'

On May 1 he lunched at the Prussian embassy and played, and also played for more than two hours at Buckingham Palace in the presence of the Queen and Prince Albert only. On the 4th, at the Beethoven Quartet Society, he played Beethoven's 32 Variations, without book, his own C minor Trio, and a Song without Words; and the same evening was at the opera at Jenny Lind's début. On the evening of the 5th he played a prelude and fugue on the name of Bach on the organ at the Antient Concert. The morning of the 6th he spent at Lord Ellesmere's picture gallery, and in the afternoon played to his friends the Bunsens and a distinguished company [including Mr. and Mrs. Gladstone] at the Prussian embassy. He left the room in great emotion,[2] and without the power of saying farewell. The same day he wrote a Song without Words in the album of Lady Caroline Cavendish, and another in that of the Hon. Miss Cavendish, since published as Op. 102, No. 2, and Op. 85, No. 5, respectively. On the 8th he took leave of the Queen and Prince Consort at Buckingham Palace, and left London the same evening, much exhausted, with the Klingemanns. He had indeed, to use his own words,[3] 'staid too long there already.' It was observed at this time by one[4] who evidently knew him well, that though in the evening and when excited by playing, he looked as he had done on former visits, yet that by daylight his face showed sad traces of wear and a

[1] The late Mr. Bartholomew.   [2] Life of Bunsen, ii. 129, 130.
[3] B. 56.   [4] *Fraser's Mag.* Dec. 1847.

look of premature old age. He crossed on the 9th, Sunday, to Calais, drove to Ostend, and on the 11th was at Cologne.[1] At Herbesthal, through the extra zeal of a police official, who mistook him for a Dr. Mendelssohn of whom the police were in search, he was stopped on his road, seriously annoyed, and compelled to write a long statement which must have cost him as much time and labour as to compose an overture. He had been only a day or two in Frankfort when he received the news of the sudden death of his sister Fanny at Berlin on the 14th. It was broken to him too abruptly, and acting on his enfeebled frame completely overcame him. With a shriek he fell to the ground, and remained insensible for some time.

It was the third blow of the kind that he had received, a blow perhaps harder to bear than either of the others, inasmuch as Fanny was his sister, more of his own age, and he himself was older, more worn, and less able in the then weak state of his nerves to sustain the shock. In his own words, ' a great chapter was ended, and neither title nor beginning of the next were written.' [2]

Early in June, as soon as he had sufficiently recovered to move, the whole family (with Miss Jung as governess, and Dr. Klengel as tutor) went to Baden-Baden, where they were joined by Paul and Hensel ; thence by Schaffhausen to Lucerne, Thun and Interlaken, in and about which they made some stay. To Felix the relief was long in coming. On July 7, though well, and often even cheerful, he was still unable to do any musical work, write a proper letter, or recover a consistent frame of mind. He worked at his drawing with more than usual assiduity at this time. Thirteen large water-colour pictures illustrate the journey, beginning with two views of the Falls of Schaffhausen (June 27 and 29), and ending with one of Interlaken (September 4). Many of them are very highly finished, and all are works which no artist need hesitate to sign. They are on a greater scale than any of his previous sketches, and there is a certainty about the drawing, and a solidity in the perspective, which show how well he understood what he was about. The same love of form that shines so conspicuously in his great symphonies is there, and the details are put in, like the oboe and clarinet phrases in his scores, as if he loved every stroke. They are really beautiful works. In

[1] Mrs. Klingemann.   [2] L. July 7, 1847.

addition to these finished drawings, he sketched a good deal in Indian ink.[1]

In the middle of the month Paul and Hensel returned home, but Felix and his family remained till September.[2] Meantime the world was going on, regardless of private troubles, friends visited him, and plans for music began to crowd round him. Among the former were Professor Graves [3] and his wife, Mr. Grote the historian — old friends, the last of whom had taken a long journey[4] on purpose to see him — and Chorley the musical critic. He had received a request from the Philharmonic Society for a symphony for 1848; an application to write a piece for the opening of the St. George's Hall[5] in Liverpool; had a new cantata in view for Frankfort, and something for the inauguration of Cologne Cathedral. Elijah was to be given under his baton both at Berlin (November 3) and Vienna — at the latter with Jenny Lind — and the long-cherished opera exercised its old charm over him. But his nerves were still too weak to bear any noise, and he suffered much from headache and weariness; his piano was ' not for playing, but for trying a chord,' ' it was the very worst he had ever touched in his life,' [6] and he shrank from the organ at Fribourg when proposed to him.[7] The organ in the village church of Ringgenberg, on the lake of Brienz, was his only resource, and it was there that for the last time in his life he touched the organ keys. He put aside the music for Liverpool, ' for the present,' and declined the request of the Philharmonic,[8] on the ground that a work for the Society ought not to bear the least trace of the hurry and bustle in which he would have to live for the rest of the year. At the same time he was much agitated at the state of home politics, which were very threatening, and looked with apprehension on the future of Germany. For himself he returned strongly to the plans already alluded to at the end of 1846, of giving up playing and concert-giving, and other exciting and exacting business,[9] and taking life more easily, and more entirely as he liked.

At length the power of application came, and he began to

---

[1] L. Aug. 3.
[2] *Mod. Germ. Music*, ii. 384.
[3] Now Bishop of Limerick.
[4] *Personal Life of G. Grote*, p. 176.
[5] Letter to Chorley, July 19.
[6] *Personal Life of G. Grote*, p. 177.
[7] *Mod. Germ. Music*, ii. 394.
[8] Letter to Philharmonic Society, ' Interlaken, Aug. 27, 1847.'
[9] *Mod. Germ. Music*, ii. 392; Dev. 272.

write music. We shall not be far wrong in taking the intensely mournful and agitated String Quartet in F minor (op. 80) as the first distinct utterance of his distress. This over, he arrived by degrees at a happier and more even mental condition, though with paroxysms of intense grief and distress. The contrast between the gaiety and spirit of his former letters, and the sombre, apathetic tone of those which are preserved from this time, is most remarkable, and impossible to be over-looked. It is as if the man were *broken*,[1] and accepted his lot without an idea of resistance. He continually recurred to the idea of retirement from all active life but composition.

Of the music which is due to this time we find, besides the Quartet just mentioned, an Andante and Scherzo in E major and A minor, which form the first movements of op. 81 ; the fragments of Loreley and of Christus ; a Jubilate, Magnificat, and Nunc dimittis for 4 voices (op. 69), which he began before going to London, and finished in Baden-Baden on June 12 ; and a few songs, such as ' Ich wandre fort ' (op. 71, no. 5).

With the close of the summer the party returned home-wards,[2] and on September 17 were again in Leipzig.[3] He found there a new Broadwood grand piano which had been forwarded by the London house during his absence in Switzer-land, and is said to have played upon it for several hours. Those who knew him best found him ' unaltered in mind, and when at the piano or talking about music still all life and fire.' [4] During these days he played to Dr. Schleinitz a new string quartet, complete except the slow movement, which was to be a set of Variations — but not yet put on paper. He took leave of Mr. Buxton [of Ewer & Co.], one of his English publishers, with the words ' You shall have plenty of music from me ; I will give you no cause to complain.' But such moments of vivacity would be followed by great depression, in which he could not bear to speak or to be spoken to even by old friends. He was much changed in look, and he who before was never at rest, and whose hands were always in motion, now often sat dull and listless, without moving a finger. ' He had aged, looked pale and weary, walked less quickly than before, and

---

[1] This expression was used to the writer by Dr. Klengel, the tutor of his boys, who was constantly with him during the last two or three years of his life, and knew him intimately. Dr. Klengel has now gone to join the master he so dearly loved. He died in Nov. 1879.

[2] Mos. ii. 178, 9.   [3] Ibid. 177.   [4] Ibid. 177, 182.

was more intensely affected by every passing thing than he used to be.' Also he complained of the oppressive air of the town.[1] And yet, though more than one person is still alive who remembers this, not even those most near him appear to have realised the radical and alarming change for the worse which had taken place in his strength.

The Gewandhaus concerts began on October 3, but he took no part in them, and left the conducting to his old colleague Rietz. A friend recollects his saying how happy he was — ' as cheerful as a set of organ-passages ' — that he had not to make out the programmes. He dreaded all public music, and complained much, though blaming himself as not deserving the happiness he had in his ' dear Cécile ' and in the recovery of his boy Felix. He had been to Berlin for a week, very shortly after his return, and the sight of his sister's rooms, exactly as she left them, had agitated him extremely,[2] ' and almost neutralized the effects of his Swiss retirement.'[3] He had definitely given up the performance of Elijah at Berlin, but was bent on undertaking that at Vienna on November 14,[4] where he was to hear his friend Jenny Lind in the music which he had written for her voice. On the morning of October 9 he called on the Moscheleses and walked with them to the Rosenthal. He was at first much depressed, but it went off, and he became for the moment almost gay. After this he went to Madame Frege's house, and here his depression returned, and worse than before. His object was to consult her as to the selection and order of the songs in op. 71,[5] which he was about to publish — one of the minute matters in which he was so fastidious and difficult to satisfy. She sang them to him several times, they settled the order, and then he said he must hear them once more, and after that they would study Elijah; she left the room for lights, and on her return found him on the sofa shivering, his hands cold and stiff, his head in violent pain. He then went home, and the attack continued; leeches were applied, and by the 15th he had recovered so far as to listen with interest to

[1] Lamp. 151.   [2] Mme. Frege; Mos. ii. 181.   [3] B. 57.

[4] The last letter stuck into the last (the 29th) of his green volumes is from Fischhoff of Vienna on this subject, dated Oct. 29. It must have been too late to have been read by him.

[5] Of the seven songs which he brought, the ' Altdeutsches Frühlingslied,' though put on paper on Oct. 7, was composed in the summer. The ' Nachtlied ' was composed and written for Schleinitz's birthday, Oct. 1, and is therefore virtually Mendelssohn's last composition. ' An odd birthday present,' said he to Mme. Frege, ' but I like it much, for I feel so dreary.'

the details of the reception of Hiller's new opera at Dresden, and actually to make plans for his Vienna journey. On the 25th he writes to his brother in the old affectionate vein. He is taking tonics, but Paul's face would do him more good than the bitterest medicine. He was not, however, destined to speak to him again. On the 28th he was so much better as to take a walk with his wife, but it was too much, and shortly afterwards he had a second attack, and on November 3 another, which last deprived him of consciousness. He lingered through the next day, fortunately without pain, and expired at 9.24 p.m. on Thursday, November 4, 1847, in the presence of his wife, his brother, Schleinitz, David, and Moscheles. During the illness, the public feeling was intense. Bulletins were issued, and the house was besieged by enquirers. After his death it was as if every one in the town had received a blow and sustained a personal loss. 'It is lovely weather here,' writes a young English student [1] to the York Courant, ' but an awful stillness prevails ; we feel as if the king were dead. Clusters of people are seen speaking together in the streets.' Those who remember what happened in London when Sir Robert Peel died can imagine how a similar loss would affect so small, simple, and concentrated a town as Leipzig. The streets were placarded at the corners with official announcements of his death, as if he had been a great officer of state.

On the Friday and Saturday the public were allowed to see the dead body. On Sunday the 7th it was taken to the Pauliner Church at Leipzig. A band preceded the hearse, playing the Song without Words in E minor (Book 5, no. 3), instrumented by Moscheles ; and after this came a student [2] of the Conservatorium with a cushion, on which lay a silver crown formerly presented to Mendelssohn by his pupils, and his Order ' pour le mérite.' The pall was borne by Moscheles, David, Hauptmann, and Gade ; the professors and pupils of the Conservatorium, the members of the Gewandhaus orchestra, the chief functionaries of the Corporation and the University, and several guilds and societies accompanied the coffin, and Paul Mendelssohn was chief mourner. In the church the chorale ' To thee, O Lord,' and the chorus ' Happy and blest,' from St. Paul, were sung, a sermon or oration was delivered by Herr Howard, the pastor of the Reformed Congregation,

---

[1] Mr. Camidge, son of Dr. Camidge of York.   [2] Mr. de Sentis.

and the service closed with the concluding chorus of Bach's Passion music. At 10 p.m. the coffin was conveyed to the Leipzig station and transported by rail to Berlin. On the road, during the night, it was met at Cöthen by the choir of the place, under Thile their director, and at Dessau, by Friedrich Schneider, who wiped away the recollection of early antagonisms by a farewell part-song, composed for the occasion, and sung by his choir at the station. It arrived at Berlin at 7 a.m., and after more funeral ceremonies was deposited in the enclosed burial-place of the family in the Alte Dreifaltigkeits Kirchhof, close outside the Halle-thor.

His tombstone is a cross. He rests between his boy Felix and his sister Fanny. His father and mother are a short distance behind.

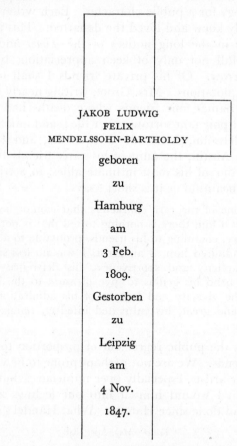

JAKOB LUDWIG
FELIX
MENDELSSOHN-BARTHOLDY

geboren

zu

Hamburg

am

3 Feb.

1809.

Gestorben

zu

Leipzig

am

4 Nov.

1847.

The 5th Gewandhaus concert, which it was piously observed would naturally have ended at the very moment of his
death, was postponed till the 11th, when, excepting the Eroica
Symphony, which formed the second part of the programme,
it was entirely made up of the compositions of the departed
master.   Among them were the Nachtlied of Eichendorf[f]
(op. 71, no. 6), sung by Madame Frege.

In London the feeling, though naturally not so deep or so
universal as in his native place, was yet both deep and wide.
His visits had of late been so frequent, and the last one was so
recent, and there was such a vivid personality about him, such
force and fire, and such a general tone of health and spirits,
that no wonder we were startled by the news of his death.
The tone of the press was more that of regret for a dear relation,
than of eulogy for a public character.   Each writer spoke as if
he intimately knew and loved the departed.   This is especially
conspicuous in the long notices of the *Times* and *Athenæum*,
which are full not only of keen appreciation, but of deep
personal sorrow.   Of his private friends I shall only permit
myself two quotations.   Mrs. Grote, writing nearly thirty years
afterwards, names four friends whose deaths had occasioned
her the most poignant sorrow of her life ; and among these are
Felix Mendelssohn, Alexis de Tocqueville, and John Stuart
Mill.   Mrs. Austin, the aunt of his early friends the Taylors,
and herself one of his most intimate allies, in a tribute to his
memory as beautiful as it is short,[1] says—

' His is one of the rare characters that cannot be known too
intimately.   Of him there is nothing to tell that is not honourable
to his memory, consoling to his friends, profitable to all men. . . .
Much as I admired him as an artist, I was no less struck by his
childlike simplicity and sportiveness, his deference to age, his
readiness to bend his genius to give pleasure to the humble and
ignorant; the vivacity and fervour of his admiration for everything good and great, his cultivated intellect, refined tastes and
noble sentiments.'

Nor was the public regret out of proportion to that of his
intimate friends.   We are not perhaps prone to be very demonstrative over artists, especially over musicians; but this was a
man who had wound himself into our feelings as no other
musician had done since Handel.   What Handel's songs, Har-

---

[1] *Fraser's Mag.* Apr. 1848.

monious Blacksmith, and other harpsichord pieces had done
for the English public in 1740, that Mendelssohn's Songs without
Words, and Part-songs, had done in 1840, and they had already
made his name a beloved household word in many a family
circle both in town and country.   He had been for long looked
upon as half an Englishman.   He spoke English well, he wrote
letters and familiar notes in our tongue freely; he showed
himself in the provinces; his first important work was founded
on Shakespeare, his last was brought out in England, at so
peculiarly English a town as Birmingham; and his ' Scotch
Symphony ' and ' Hebrides Overture ' showed how deeply the
scenery of Britain had influenced him.   And, perhaps more
than this, there were in the singular purity of his life, in his
known devotion to his wife and family, and his general high
and unselfish character, the things most essential to procure
him both the esteem and affection of the English people.

The Sacred Harmonic Society, the only Society in London
having concerts at that period of the year, performed Elijah
on November 17, preceded by the Dead March in Saul, and
with the band and chorus all dressed in black.   At Manchester
and Birmingham similar honours were paid to the departed
composer.   In Germany commemoration concerts (*Todtenfeier*)
were given at Berlin, Vienna, Frankfort, Hamburg, and many
other places.   His bust was set up in the Theatre at Berlin,
and his profile in the Gewandhaus at Leipzig.   The first Concert of the Conservatoire at Paris, on January 9, 1848, was
entitled ' à la mémoire de F. Mendelssohn-Bartholdy,' and
comprised the Scotch Symphony, Hebrides Overture, Violin
Concerto, and fragments from St. Paul.   Among the very
numerous letters of condolence addressed to his widow we will
only mention those from the Queen of England, the King of
Prussia, and the King of Saxony.

Two works were in the printers' hands at the time of
Mendelssohn's death — the Six Songs (op. 71) and the Six
Children's Pieces (op. 72).   These were quickly published.
Then there was a pause, and at length, as he had left no will,
Madame Mendelssohn confided to a kind of committee, com-
posed of her husband's most intimate musical friends, the task
of deciding which pieces out of the immense mass of MS.

music should be published, and of supervising the publication. These gentlemen were Dr. Schleinitz, the acting member of the council of the Conservatorium, David, Moscheles, and Hauptmann, all resident in Leipzig, with Paul Mendelssohn in Berlin, and Julius Rietz in Dresden. The instrumental works still in MS. embraced the Trumpet Overture (1825) and Reformation Symphony (1830), the Italian Symphony (1833), the Overture to Ruy Blas (1839), 2 sets of pianoforte variations (1841), the Quintet in B♭ (1845), the Quartet in F minor (1847), and fragments of another Quartet in E, Songs without Words, and other pianoforte pieces. The vocal works comprised the Liederspiel ' Heimkehr aus der Fremde ' (1829), the Concert-aria ' Infelice ' (1843), the music to Athalie and to Œdipus Coloneus (both 1845), Lauda Sion (1846), fragments of the opera Loreley, and of the oratorio Christus, on which he had been at work not long before his death, Psalms and Sprüche for voices with and without accompaniment, songs and part-songs.

The work of publication began with Lauda Sion, which appeared as op. 73, February 15, 1848. This was followed by Athalie, and by other works down to the four Part-songs which form op. 100 and no. 29 of the posthumous works, which came out in January 1852. Here a pause took place. In the mean-time, borne down by her great loss, and also by the death of her third boy, Felix, in 1851, Madame Mendelssohn herself died on September 25, 1853. The manuscripts then came into the hands of Dr. Carl Mendelssohn, the eldest son, and after some years publication recommenced with the Trumpet Over-ture, which appeared in 1867, and continued at intervals down to the ' Perpetuum mobile ' (op. 119) [Responsorium of Hymnus (op. 121)].

Many of the pieces referred to in the above enumeration are included in the series of MS. volumes already mentioned. Forty-four of these volumes are now deposited in the Imperial Library at Berlin, in pursuance of an arrangement dated December 23, 1877, by which, in exchange for the possession of them, the German government agreed with the Mendelssohn-Bartholdy family to found two perpetual scholarships of 1500 marks (£75) per annum each, tenable for four years, for the education of students of music elected by competition from the music schools of Germany. The Trustees of the Fund are three — the Director of the High School of Music at Berlin, a second nominated by the government, and a third by the family. The first election took place on October 1, 1879, and the successful candidates were Engelbert Humperdinck of Siegburg, and Josef Kotek of Podolia. In addition, Ernst Seyffardt of Crefeld, and Johann Secundus Cruse of Melbourne, Australia, will receive allowances of 750 marks each out of the arrears of the Fund.

Long before the foundation of the Berlin scholarships, however, practical steps in the same direction had been taken in England. In November 1847 a resolution was passed by the Sacred Harmonic Society of London for the erection of a public memorial in honour of Mendelssohn, £50 was subscribed thereto by the Queen and Prince Consort, and like sums by the Sacred Harmonic and Philharmonic Societies. Other subscriptions were raised amounting in the whole to over £600. In April 1859, after many negotiations, a model of a statue by Mr. C. Bacon was approved by the subscribers; it was cast in bronze in the following November, and on May 4, 1860, was set up on the Terrace of the Crystal Palace at Sydenham.

A more appropriate memorial was the Mendelssohn Scholarship, which originated in Madame Lind-Goldschmidt in the year 1850.

In person Mendelssohn was short,[1] not so much as 5 ft. 6 ins. high, and slight of build; in figure lithe, and very light and mercurial. His look was dark and very Jewish; the face unusually mobile, and ever varying in expression, full of brightness and animation, and with a most unmistakable look of genius. His complexion was fresh, and shewed a good deal of colour. His hair was black, thick, and abundant, but very fine, with a natural wave in it, and was kept back from his forehead, which was high and much developed. By the end of his life, however, it showed a good deal of grey and he began to be bald. His mouth was unusually delicate and expressive, and had generally a pleasant smile at the corners. His whiskers were very dark, and his closely shaven chin and upper lip were blue from the strength of his beard. His teeth were beautifully white and regular; but the most striking part of his face were

---

[1] He was shorter than Sterndale Bennett, who was 5 ft. 6.

the large dark brown eyes. When at rest he often lowered
the eyelids as if he were slightly short-sighted — which indeed
he was ; but when animated they gave an extraordinary brightness and fire to his face, and ' were as expressive a pair of eyes
as were ever set in a human being's head.' When he was
playing extempore, or was otherwise much excited, they would
dilate and become nearly twice their ordinary size, the brown
pupil changing to a vivid black. His laugh was hearty, and
frequent ; and when especially amused he would quite double
up with laughter and shake his hand from the wrist to em-
phasize his merriment. He would nod his head violently when
thoroughly agreeing, so that the hair came down over his face.
In fact his body was almost as expressive as his face. His hands
were small, with taper fingers.[1] On the keys they behaved
almost like ' living and intelligent creatures, full of life and
sympathy.' [2] His action at the piano was as free from affectation
as everything else that he did, and very interesting. At times,
especially at the organ, he leant very much over the keys, as if
watching for the strains which came out of his finger tips. He
sometimes swayed from side to side, but usually his whole
performance was quiet and absorbed.[3]

He refused more than once,[4] from motives of modesty, to
have his likeness taken. But a great number of portraits were
painted and drawn at different times of his life. The best of
these, in the opinion of those most capable of judging, is that
painted by his friend Professor Edward Magnus at Berlin in
the year 1844. The original of this is in the possession of
Madame Lind-Goldschmidt, to whom it was presented by
Magnus himself, and although deficient in that lively speaking
expression which all admit to have been so characteristic of
him, it may be accepted as a good representation. It is very
superior to the various replicas and copies in existence, which
are distinguished by a hopeless meek solemnity of look, absolutely impossible in the original, and which therefore convey
an entirely wrong idea of the face. Madame Goldschmidt
with great kindness allowed the portrait to be photographed,
and it was the desire of the writer to give a wood engraving
of it ; but after two attempts to obtain satisfactory representa-

---

[1] A cast of his hand can be bought.   [2] The Bishop of Limerick.
[3] I owe the above description of Mendelssohn's looks chiefly to Mr. John C.
Horsley, R.A. Few knew him better, or are more qualified to describe him.
[4] L. Dec. 20, 1831 ; Apr. 3, May 18, 1835.

tions, he has been reluctantly compelled to abandon the intention.

Other portraits worth notice are (1) a pencil sketch taken in 1820, in possession of Mrs. Victor Benecke, lithographed in ' Goethe and Mendelssohn.' (2) A half-length taken by Begas in 1821, in the possession of the Paul Mendelssohn-Bartholdy family at Berlin. This is very poorly engraved, both as to resemblance and execution, in ' Goethe and Mendelssohn.' The original is probably much idealised, but it is a striking picture. (3) A three-quarter-length, in a cloak, painted by Hildebrand, and engraved as the frontispiece to Elijah ; in possession of Herr Killmann of Bonn. (4) A whole length, sitting, and looking to the side, taken by Hensel in 1844, and now in the possession of the Paul M.-B. family. This, though clever as a picture, can hardly convey the man. The hand is perhaps the most remarkable thing in it, and must be a portrait. (5) A profile taken after death by Hensel, and now in possession of Mrs. V. Benecke. This, which is said by many to be the best representation of him, is fairly engraved as the frontispiece to Lady Wallace's translation of the letters.

A portrait of him in crayons was taken at Weimar for Goethe,[1] which he describes as ' very like, but rather sulky ' ; another was painted at Rome by Horace Vernet,[2] and another by a painter named Schramm.[3] But none of these have been traced by the writer.[4] The sketch by his brother-in-law, taken in 1840, and given as frontispiece to vol. 2 of the ' Familie Mendelssohn,' must surely be too young-looking for that date. Miniatures of the four children were taken in Paris in 1816, and are now in the hands of the Paul M.-B. family.

The bust by Rietschel (engraved as frontispiece to Devrient) and the profiles by Knauer and Kietz are all said to be good.

Not less remarkable than his face was his way and manner. It is described by those who knew him as peculiarly winning and engaging ; to those whom he loved, coaxing. The slight lisp or drawl which remained with him to the end made the endearing words and pet expressions, which he was fond of applying to his own immediate circle, all the more affectionate.

---

[1] L. May 25, 1830.   [2] L. Jan. 17 and Mar. 15, 1831.
[3] Possibly taken in 1840 ; since in Ernst Mendelssohn-Bartholdy's possession is the autograph of three Songs inscribed, ' Dem Maler Schramm zu freundlichem Andenken und mit bestem Dank. F.M.B. Leipzig, d. 4 Nov. 1840.'
[4] I have to thank M. Edouard Detaille, the painter, for his efforts to discover the picture by Vernet.

But outside this immediate circle also he was very fascinating, and it is probable that, devotedly as he was loved at home, few men had fewer enemies abroad. The strong admiration expressed towards him by men of such very different natures as Schumann[1] and Berlioz,[2] both of whom knew him well, shows what a depth of solid goodness there was in his attractiveness. ' His gentleness and softness,' says one of his English friends, ' had none of the bad side so often found with those qualities ; nothing effeminate or morbid. There was a great deal of manliness packed into his little body,' as all readers of the early part of this sketch must be aware. Indeed he had a great capacity for being angry. Anything like meanness or deceit, or unworthy conduct of any kind, roused his wrath at once. ' He had a way,' says a very old friend, ' of suddenly firing up on such occasions, and turning on his heel, in a style which was quite unmistakable,' and astonishing to those who only knew his smoother side. Towards thoughtlessness, negligence, or obstinate stupidity he was very intolerant, and under such provocation said things the sting of which must have remained for long after, and which he himself deeply regretted.[3] But these were rare instances, and as a rule his personal fascination secured him friends and kept them firm to him. And to those to whom he was really attached — outside his own family, of which we are not speaking — there could hardly be a better friend. The published letters to General von Webern, to Verkenius, Klingemann, Schubring, Hiller, Moscheles, are charged with an amount of real affection rarely met with, but which never leads him to sink his own individual opinion on any point which he thought material, as may be seen in many cases. Talent and perseverance he was always ready to encourage, and the cases of Taubert, Eckert, Gade, Joachim, Rietz, Naumann, Sterndale Bennett, Hiller, and the anonymous student whose cause he pleads so earnestly to the king,[4] show how eager he always was to promote the best interests of those whom he believed to be worthy. The present head of the Frankfort Conservatorium owes his advancement in no small degree to the good offices of Mendelssohn. His warm

---

[1] Wassielewsky, 157.
[2] *Correspondance* (1879), 88 ; *Voyage musical*, Letter 4.
[3] He complained bitterly to the Bishop of Limerick in 1847 of his short temper at rehearsals or with his pupils.
[4] Letter, 1844 ; ii. 325.

reception of Berlioz, Liszt, and Thalberg, has been already mentioned, but must be again referred to as an instance of the absence of jealousy or rivalry in his nature, and of his simple wish to give everybody fair play.

The relations of Mendelssohn and Schumann were thoroughly good on both sides. There is a remarkable absence of Schumann's name in Mendelssohn's published letters; but this may have risen from considerations which influenced the editors, and would possibly be reversed if the letters had been fully given, and if others which remain in MS. were printed. The two men were always good friends. They differed much on some matters of music. Mendelssohn had his strong settled principles, which nothing could induce him to give up. He thought that everything should be made as clear as a composer could make it, and that rough or awkward passages were blemishes, which should be modified and made to sound well. On the other hand, Schumann was equally fixed in the necessity of retaining what he had written down as representing his intention. But such differences of opinion never affected their intercourse; they were always friendly, and even affectionate, and loved to be together. More than one person living remembers the strong interest which Mendelssohn took in ' Paradise and the Peri ' on its first appearance, and how anxious he was that his friends should hear it. Of Schumann's string quartets he records that they ' pleased him extremely '; and it is surely allowable to infer that it was the expression of his pleasure that made Schumann dedicate them to him. He had a particular love for some of Schumann's songs, and as this feeling was not shared by all the members of his family he would sometimes ask for the ' forbidden fruit,' as a kind of synonym for something peculiarly pleasant. The fact that he placed Schumann among his colleagues at the starting of the Leipzig Conservatorium of itself shows how much he valued him.

On the other hand, Schumann is never warmer or more in earnest than when he is praising Mendelssohn's compositions, as may be seen by many an article in his *Gesammelte Schriften*. He dedicated his string quartets to him, as we have said. He defended him with ardour when attacked; during his last sad years Mendelssohn's name was constantly in his mouth as that of his best friend, and his last clearly expressed wish was that his youngest boy should be called after him. A

proof of his affectionate feeling is to be found in the no. 28
of his ' Album für die Jugend ' (op. 68), which is inscribed
' Erinnerung (Nov. 4, 1847),' and therefore expresses his feelings at the death of his friend. It is not necessary to discover
that definite direct meaning in this touching little piece which
Mendelssohn found in all music, in order to recognise sadness
tempered by a deep sense of grace and sweetness ; the result
showing how beautiful was the image which Mendelssohn left
in the mind of one so completely able to appreciate him as
Schumann.

Nowhere is Mendelssohn's naturalness and naïveté more
evident than in his constant reference to his own foibles. The
hearty way in which he enjoys idleness, and boasts of it,[1] the
constant references to eating and drinking, are delightful in a
man who got through so much work, who was singularly
temperate, and whose only weakness for the products of the
kitchen was for rice milk and cherry pie. In this, as in everything else, he was perfectly simple and natural. ' I do not in
the least concern myself as to what people wish or praise or
pay for ; but solely as to what I myself consider good.' [2] No
doubt he was very fortunate in being able to disregard ' what
people paid for ' ; but that he did so is a part of his character.

His fun and drollery were more the result of his high spirits
than of any real turn for wit. Unlike Beethoven, he rarely
indulges in plays on words, and his best efforts in that direction
are the elaborately illustrated programmes and *jeux d'esprit*
which are preserved in the albums of some of his friends, and
in which caricatures, verses, puns, and jokes, are mixed up in
a very droll fashion. There is much humour in some of his
scherzos, but especially in the funeral march for Pyramus and
Thisbe in the M.N.D. pieces, one of the most comical things in
all music. It is much to be regretted that he has left no other
specimen of his remarkable power in this direction. Probably
he indulged in a good deal of such fun which has not been
preserved, since both he and his sister[3] refer to that march as
a specimen of a style in which he often extemporised. In
mimicry he was great, not only in music but in taking off
speech and manner. The most humorous passage that I have
met with in his letters is still in MS. — ' Dass jenseits auch

Musik gemacht werden könne, das glauben Sie ja, und haben
mirs oft gesagt.   Dann wirds wohl kein schlechtes Instrument
geben, wie bei Geyer, und keine dumme Flöte pustet da, und
keine Posaune schleppt nach, und nirgends fehlt es, und wankt
es, und eilt es, das glaube ich wohl.' [1]

No musician — unless perhaps it were Leonardo da Vinci,
and he was only a musician in a limited sense — certainly no
great composer, ever had so many pursuits as Mendelssohn.
Mozart drew, and wrote capital letters, Berlioz and Weber
also both wrote good letters, Beethoven was a great walker
and intense lover of nature, Cherubini was a botanist and a
passionate card-player, but none of them approach Mendelssohn in the number and variety of his occupations. Both
billiards and chess he played with ardour to the end of his life,
and in both he excelled. When a lad he was devoted to
gymnastics ; later on he rode much, swam more, and danced
whenever he had the opportunity. Cards and skating were
almost the only diversions he did not care for. But then these
were diversions. There were two pursuits which almost deserve
to rank as work — drawing and letter-writing. Drawing with
him was more like a professional avocation than an amusement.
The quantity of his sketches and drawings preserved is very
large. They begin with the Swiss journey in 1822, on which
he took 27 large ones, all very carefully finished, and all dated,
sometimes two in one day. The Scotch and Italian tours are
both fully illustrated, and so they go on year by year till his
last journey into Switzerland in 1847, of which, as already
said, 14 large highly finished water-colour drawings remain,
besides slighter sketches. At first they are rude and childish,
though with each successive set the improvement is perceptible.
But even with the earliest ones there is no mistaking that the
drawing was a serious business. The subjects are not what
are called ' bits,' but are usually large comprehensive views,
and it is impossible to doubt that the child threw his whole
mind into it, did his very best, and shirked nothing. He already
felt the force of the motto which fronted his conductor's chair
in the Gewandhaus — ' Res severa est verum gaudium.'
Every little cottage or gate is put in with as much care as the

[1] ' That there may be music in the next world I know you believe, for you
have often told me so ; but there will certainly be no bad pianos there like Geyer's,
no stupid puffing flutes, no dragging trombones, no stopping, or wavering, or
hurrying — of that I am quite sure.'   MS. letter.

main features. Every tree has its character. Everything stands well on its legs, and the whole has that architectonic style which is so characteristic of his music.

Next to his drawing should be placed his correspondence, and this is even more remarkable. During the last years of his life there can have been but few eminent men in Europe who wrote more letters than he did. Many even who take no interest in music are familiar with the nature of his letters — the happy mixture of seriousness, fun, and affection, the life-like descriptions, the happy hits, the naïveté which no baldness of translation can extinguish, the wise counsels, the practical views, the delight in the successes of his friends, the self-abnega-tion, the bursts of wrath at anything mean or nasty. We all remember, too, the length to which they run. Taking the printed volumes, and comparing the letters with those of Scott or Arnold, they are on the average very considerably longer than either. But the published letters bear only a small pro-portion to those still in MS.[1] In fact the abundance of material for the biographer of Mendelssohn is quite bewildering. That, however, is not the point. The remarkable fact is that so many letters of such length and such intrinsic excellence should have been written by a man who was all the time engaged in an engrossing occupation, producing great quantities of music, conducting, arranging, and otherwise occupied in a profession which more than any demands the surrender of the entire man. For these letters are no hurried productions, but are distin-guished, like the drawings, for the neatness and finish which pervade them. An autograph letter of Mendelssohn's is a work of art; the lines are all straight and close, the letters perfectly and elegantly formed, with a peculiar luxuriance of tails, and an illegible word can hardly be found. To the fold-ing and the sealing everything is perfect. It seems impossible that this can have been done quickly. It must have absorbed an enormous deal of time. While speaking of his correspond-ence, we may mention the neatness and order with which he registered and kept everything. The 44 volumes of MS. music, in which he did for himself what Mozart's father so carefully did for his son, have been mentioned. But it is not generally known that he preserved all letters that he received, and stuck

---

[1] In the hands of his family, of Schleinitz, Mrs. Moscheles, Schubring, P. David, Mme. Goldschmidt, Mme. Preusser, Mr. Euler of Düsseldorf, the Stern-dale Bennetts, Mr. Sartoris and others.

them with his own hands into books. 27 large thick green volumes exist,[1] containing apparently all the letters and memorandums, business and private, which he received from October 29, 1821, to October 29, 1847, together with the drafts of his oratorio books, and of the long official communications which, during his latter life, cost him so many unprofitable hours. He seems to have found time for everything. Hiller tells us [2] how during a very busy season he revised and copied out the libretto of his oratorio for him. One of his dearest Leipzig friends has a complete copy of the full score of Antigone, *including the whole of the words of the melodrama,* written for her with his own hand; a perfect piece of calligraphy, without spot or erasure! and the family archives contain a long minute list of the contents of all the cupboards in the house, filling several pages of foolscap, in his usual neat writing, and made about the year 1842. We read of Mr. Dickens [3] that ' no matter was considered too trivial to claim his care and attention. He would take as much pains about the hanging of a picture, the choosing of furniture, the superintending of any little improvement in the house, as he would about the more serious business of his life; thus carrying out to the very letter his favourite motto that What is worth doing at all is worth doing well.' No words could better describe the side of Mendelssohn's character to which we are alluding, nor could any motto more emphatically express the principle on which he acted throughout life in all his work.

His taste and efficiency in such minor matters are well shown in the albums which he made for his wife, beautiful specimens of arrangement, the most charming things in which are the drawings and pieces of music from his own hands. His private account-books and diaries are kept with the same quaint neatness. If he had a word to alter in a letter, it was done with a grace which turned the blemish into a beauty. The same care came out in everything — in making out the programmes for the Gewandhaus concerts, where he would arrange and re-arrange the pieces to suit some inner idea of symmetry or order; or in settling his sets of songs for publication as to the succession of keys, connection or contrast of

---

[1] In the hands of Mrs. Wach (Lili M.-B.). Two others seem to be missing.
[2] H. 167.
[3] Preface to his Letters, 1879.

words, etc. In fact he had a passion for neatness, and a
repugnance to anything clumsy. Possibly this may have been
one reason why he appears so rarely to have sketched his
music. He made it in his head, and had settled the minutest
points there before he put it on paper, thus avoiding the litter
and disorder of a sketch. Connected with this neatness is a
certain quaintness in his proceedings which perhaps strikes an
Englishman more forcibly than it would a German. He used
the old-fashioned C clef for the treble voices in his scores to
the last; the long flourish with which he ornaments the double
bar at the end of a piece never varied. A score of Haydn's
Military Symphony which he wrote for his wife bears the
words ' Possessor Cécile.' In writing to Mrs. Moscheles of her
little girls, whose singing had pleased him, he begs to be
remembered to the ' drei kleine Diskantisten.' A note to
David, sent by a child, is inscribed ' Kinderpost,' and so on.
Certain French words occur over and over again, and are
evidently favourites. Such are *plaisir* and *trouble*, *à propos*,
en gros, and others. The word *hübsch*, answering to our ' nice,'
was a special favourite,[1] and *nett* was one of his highest com-
mendations.

But to return for a moment to his engrossing pursuits.
Add to those just mentioned the many concerts, to be arranged,
rehearsed, conducted; the frequent negotiations attending on
Berlin; the long official protocols; the hospitality and genial
intercourse, where he was equally excellent as host or as guest;
the claims of his family; the long holidays, real holidays, spent
in travelling, and not, like Beethoven's, devoted to composition
— and we may almost be pardoned for wondering how he can
have found time to write any music at all. But on the contrary,
with him all this business does not appear to have militated
against composition in the slightest degree. It often drove
him almost to distraction; it probably shortened his life; but
it never seems to have prevented his doing whatever music
came before him, either spontaneously or at the call of his two
posts at Berlin and Dresden. He composed Antigone in a
fortnight, he resisted writing the music to Ruy Blas, he grumbled
over the long chorale for the thousandth anniversary of the
German Empire, and over the overture to Athalie, in the midst
of his London pleasures; but still he did them, and in the

[1] Mos. ii. 165.

cases of Antigone and the two overtures it is difficult to see how he could have done them better. He was never driven into a corner.

The power by which he got through all this labour, so much of it self-imposed, was the power of order and concentration, the practical business habit of doing one thing at a time, and doing it well. This no doubt was the talent which his father recognised in him so strongly as to make him doubt whether business was not his real vocation. It was this which made him sympathise with Schiller [1] in his power of ' supplying ' great tragedies as they were wanted. In one way his will was weak, for he always found it hard to say No; but having accepted the task it became a duty, and towards duty his will was the iron will of a man of business. Such a gift is vouchsafed to very few artists. Handel possessed it in some degree; but with that one exception Mendelssohn seems to stand alone.

Of his method of composing, little or nothing is known. He appears to have made few sketches, and to have arranged his music in his head at first, much as Mozart did. Probably this arose from his early training under Zelter, for the volumes for 1821, 2, 3, of the MS. series now in the Berlin Library appear to contain his first drafts, and rarely show any corrections, and what there are are not so much sketches as erasures and substitutions. Devrient and Schubring tell of their having seen him composing a score bar by bar from top to bottom; but this was probably only an experiment or *tour de force*. The fragment of the first movement of a symphony which is given on p. 392, is a good average example of the shape in which his ideas first came on to the paper.

Alterations in a work after it was completed are quite another thing, and in these he was lavish. He complains of his not discovering the necessity for them till *post festum*.[2] We have seen instances of this in the Walpurgisnight, St. Paul, the Lobgesang, Elijah, and some of the Concert-overtures. Another instance is the Italian Symphony, which he retained in MS. for 14 years, till his death, with the intention of altering and improving the Finale. Another, equally to the point, is the D minor Trio, of which there are two editions in actual circulation, containing several important and extensive differ-

[1] L. Aug. 23, 1831.   [2] L. Dec. 6, 1846.

ences.[1] This is carrying fastidiousness even further than Beethoven, whose alterations were endless, but ceased with publication. The autographs of many of Mendelssohn's pieces are dated years before they were printed, and in most, if not all, cases, they received material alterations before being issued.

Of his pianoforte playing in his earlier days we have already spoken. What it was in his great time, at such displays as his performances in London at the Philharmonic in 1842, 44, and 47; at Ernst's Concert in 1844, in the Bach Concerto with Moscheles and Thalberg; at the British Musicians' matinée in 1844; and the British Quartet Society in 1847; at the Leipzig Concerts on the occasion already mentioned in 1836; at Miss Lind's Concert December 5, 1845, or at many a private reunion at V. Novello's or the Horsleys', or the Moscheleses' in London, or the houses of his favourite friends in Leipzig, Berlin, or Frankfort — there are still many remaining well able to judge, and in whose minds the impression survives as clear as ever. Of the various recollections with which I have been favoured, I cannot do better than give entire those of Madame Schumann, and Dr. Hiller. In reading them it should be remembered that Mendelssohn was fond of speaking of himself as a player *en gros*, who did not claim (however great his right) to be a virtuoso, and that there are instances of his having refused to play to great virtuosi.

1. 'My recollections of Mendelssohn's playing,' says Madame Schumann, 'are among the most delightful things in my artistic life. It was to me a shining ideal, full of genius and life, united with technical perfection. He would sometimes take the *tempi* very quick, but never to the prejudice of the music. It never occurred to me to compare him with virtuosi. Of mere effects of performance he knew nothing — he was always the great musician, and in hearing him one forgot the player, and only revelled in the full enjoyment of the music. He could carry one with him in the most incredible manner, and his playing was always stamped with beauty and nobility. In his early days he had acquired perfection of technique; but latterly, as he often told me, he hardly ever practised, and yet he surpassed every one. I have heard him in Bach, and

[1] The parts of the 'Hebriden' Overture are not in exact accordance with the score of 'Fingals Höhle.' The P.F. arrangement of the M.N.D. Overture published in London is given in notes of half the value of those in the score, published after it in Leipzig.

Beethoven, and in his own compositions, and shall never forget the impression he made upon me.'

2. 'Mendelssohn's playing,' says Dr. Hiller, 'was to him what flying is to a bird. No one wonders why a lark flies, it is inconceivable without that power. In the same way Mendelssohn played the piano because it was his nature. He possessed great skill, certainty, power, and rapidity of execution, a lovely full tone — all in fact that a virtuoso could desire, but these qualities were forgotten while he was playing, and one almost overlooked even those more spiritual gifts which we call fire, invention, soul, apprehension, etc. When he sat down to the instrument music streamed from him with all the fullness of his inborn genius, — he was a centaur, and his horse was the piano. What he played, how he played it, and that he was the player — all were equally riveting, and it was impossible to separate the execution, the music, and the executant. This was absolutely the case in his improvisations, so poetical, artistic, and finished ; and almost as much so in his execution of the music of Bach, Mozart, Beethoven, or himself. Into those three masters he had grown, and they had become his spiritual property. The music of other composers he knew, but could not produce it as he did theirs. I do not think, for instance, that his execution of Chopin was at all to be compared to his execution of the masters just mentioned ; he did not care particularly for it, though when alone he played everything good with interest. In playing at sight his skill and rapidity of comprehension were astonishing, and that not with piano music only, but with the most complicated compositions. He never practised, though he once told me that in his Leipzig time he had played a shake (I think with the 2nd and 3rd fingers) several minutes every day for some months, till he was perfect in it.'

'His staccato,' says Mr. Joachim, 'was the most extraordinary thing possible for life and crispness. In the Frühlingslied (Songs without Words, Bk. v. No. 6) for instance, it was quite electric, and though I have heard that song played by many of the greatest players, I never experienced the same effect. His playing was extraordinarily full of fire, which could hardly be controlled, and yet was controlled, and combined with the greatest delicacy.' 'Though lightness of touch, and a delicious liquid pearliness of tone,' says another of his pupils,[1] ' were prominent characteristics, yet his power in *fortes* was immense. In the passage in his G minor Concerto where the whole orchestra makes a *crescendo* the climax of which is a 6-4 chord on D, played by the piano alone, it seemed as if the band had quite enough to do to work up to the chord he played.' As an instance of the fullness of his tone, the same gentleman mentions the 5 bars of *piano* which begin Beethoven's G major Concerto, and which, though he played them perfectly softly, filled the whole room.

' His mechanism,' says another of his Leipzig pupils,[2] ' was extremely subtle, and developed with the lightest of wrists (never from the arm) ; he therefore never strained the instrument or hammered. His chord-playing was beautiful, and based on a special theory of his own. His use of the pedal was very sparing, clearly defined, and therefore effective ; his phrasing beautifully clear. The performances in which I derived the most lasting impressions from him were the 32 Variations and last Sonata (Op. 111) of Beethoven, in which latter the Variations of the final movement came out more clearly in their structure and beauty than I have ever heard before or since.' Of his playing of the 32 Variations, Professor Macfarren remarks that ' to each one, or each pair, where they go in pairs, he gave a character different from all the others. In playing at sight from a MS. score he characterised every incident by the peculiar tone by which he represented the instrument for which it was written.'[3] In describing his playing of the 9th Symphony, Mr. Schleinitz testified to the same singular power of representing the different instruments. A still stronger testimony is that of Berlioz, who, speaking of the *colour* of the Hebrides Overture, says that Mendelssohn ' succeeded in giving him an accurate idea of it, such is his extraordinary power of rendering the most complicated scores on the piano.'[4]

His adherence to his author's meaning, and to the indications given in the music, was absolute. Strict time was one of his hobbies. He alludes to it, with an eye to the sins of Hiller and Chopin, in a letter of May 23, 1834, and somewhere else speaks of ' nice strict tempo ' as something peculiarly pleasant. After introducing some *ritardandos* in conducting the Intro-

---

[1] Mr. W. S. Rockstro. [2] Mr. Otto Goldschmidt.
[3] See Dorn, p. 398. [4] *Voyage Musical*, Letter 4.

duction to Beethoven's 2nd Symphony, he excused himself by
saying that ' one could not always be good,' and that he had
felt the inclination too strongly to resist it.[1] In playing, however, he never himself interpolated a *ritardando*, or suffered it in
any one else.[2] It especially enraged him when done at the
end of a song or other piece. ' Es steht nicht da ! ' he would
say ; ' if it were intended it would be written in — they think
it expression, but it is sheer affectation.'[3] But though in
playing he never varied the *tempo* when once taken, he did
not always take a movement at the same pace, but changed
it as his mood was at the time. We have seen in the case of
Bach's A minor Fugue (p. 311) that he could on occasion
introduce an individual reading; and his treatment of the
arpeggios in the Chromatic Fantasia [4] shows that, there at
least, he allowed himself great latitude. Still, in imitating
this it should be remembered how thoroughly he knew these
great masters, and how perfect his sympathy with them was.
In conducting, as we have just seen, he was more elastic,
though even there his variations would now be condemned as
moderate by some conductors. Before he conducted at the
Philharmonic it had been the tradition in the Coda of the
Overture to Egmont to return to a *piano* after the *crescendo* ;
but this he would not suffer, and maintained the *fortissimo* to
the end — a practice now always followed.

He very rarely played from book, and his prodigious
memory was also often shown in his sudden recollection of
out-of-the-way pieces. Hiller has given two instances (pp. 28,
29). His power of retaining things casually heard was also
shown in his extempore playing, where he would recollect the
themes of compositions which he heard then and there for the
first time, and would combine them in the happiest manner.
An instance of this is mentioned by his father,[5] in which, after
Malibran had sung five songs of different nations, he was
dragged to the piano, and improvised upon them all. He
himself describes another occasion, a ' field day ' at Baillot's,
when he took three themes from the Bach sonatas and worked
them up to the delight and astonishment of an audience
worth delighting.[6] At the matinée of the Society of British

[1] Mr. Kellow Pye.   [2] Mr. von Bülow.
[3] Mrs. Moscheles and Mr. Rockstro.   [4] Letter to Fanny, Nov. 14, 1840.
[5] F.M. i. 377.   [6] L. i. 305.

Musicians in 1844, he took his themes from two compositions
by C. E. Horsley and Macfarren which he had just heard,
probably for the first time — and other instances could be given.

His extemporising was however marked by other traits
than that of memory. 'It was,' says Professor Macfarren, 'as
fluent and as well planned as a written work,' and the themes,
whether borrowed or invented, were not merely brought together but contrapuntally worked. Instances of this have been
mentioned at Birmingham and elsewhere. His tact in these
things was prodigious. At the concert given by Jenny Lind
and himself on December 5, 1845, he played two Songs without
Words — Bk. vi, No. 1, in E♭, and Bk. v, No. 6, in A major,
and he modulated from the one key to the other by means of
a regularly constructed intermezzo, in which the semiquavers
of the first song merged into the arpeggios of the second with
the most consummate art, and with magical effect.[1] But great
as were his public displays, it would seem that, like Mozart,
it was in the small circle of intimate friends that his improvisation was most splendid and happy. Those only who had the
good fortune to find themselves (as rarely happened) alone [2]
with him at one of his Sunday afternoons are perhaps aware
of what he could really do in this direction, and he 'never
improvised better' or pleased himself more than when *tête
à tête* with the Queen and Prince Albert. A singular fact is
mentioned by Hiller,[3] which is confirmed by another friend
of his : — that in playing his own music he did it with a certain
reticence, as if not desiring that the work would derive any
advantage from his execution. The explanation is very much
in consonance with his modesty, but whether correct or not
there is no reason to doubt the fact.

His immense early practice in counterpoint under Zelter —
like Mozart's under his father — had given him so complete
a command over all the resources of counterpoint, and such
a habit of looking at themes contrapuntally, that the combinations just spoken of came more or less naturally to him. In
some of his youthful compositions he brings his science into
prominence, as in the Fugue in A (op. 7, no. 5) ; the Finale
of the E♭ stringed Quartet (1823) ; the original Minuet and

---

[1] Recollections of Joachim and Rockstro.
[2] Dr. Klengel and Sterndale Bennett once had this good fortune, and it was
a thing never to be forgotten.
[3] H. 18.

Trio of the stringed Quintet in A (op. 18), a double canon of
great ingenuity; the Chorus in St. Paul, 'But our God,'
constructed on the chorale 'Wir glauben all'; but with his
maturity he mostly drops such displays, and Elijah, as is well
known, 'contains no fugues.' In extemporising, however, it
was at his fingers' ends to the last. He was also fond of throwing
off ingenious canons, of which the following, written on the
moment for Joachim, March 11, 1844, is a good example.

Etude for one Violin, or Canon for two Violins

Of his organ-playing we have already spoken. It should
be added that he settled his combinations of stops before
starting, and did not change them in the course of the piece.
He likewise steadily adhered to the plan on which he set out;[1]
if he started in 3 parts he continued in 3, and the same with
4 or 5. He took extraordinary delight in the organ; some
describe him as even more at home there than on the piano,
though this must be taken with caution. But it is certain that
he loved it, and was always greatly excited when playing it.

He was fond of playing the viola, and on more than one
occasion took the first viola part of his own Octet in public.
The violin he learned when young, but neglected it in later
life. He however played occasionally, and it was amusing to
see him bending over the desk, and struggling with his part
just as if he were a boy. His practical knowledge of the instrument is evident from his violin music, in which there are few
difficulties which an ordinarily good player cannot surmount.
But this is characteristic of the care and thoughtfulness of the
man. As a rule, in his scores he gives each instrument the
passages which suit it. He appears to have felt somewhat of
the same natural dislike to brass instruments that Mozart did.
At any rate in his early scores he uses them with great modera-

tion,[1] and somewhere makes the just remark that the trombone is ' too sacred an instrument ' to be used freely.

———

The list of Mendelssohn's works published up to the present time (January 1880) comprises —

5 Symphonies, including the Lobgesang.

6 Concert overtures ; an Overture for military band.

1 Concerto for Violin and Orchestra ; 2 do. for Pianoforte, and 3 shorter works for P.F. and Orchestra.

1 Octet for Strings, 2 Quintets and 7 Quartets for do., with fragments of an 8th ; 3 Quartets for P.F. and strings, 2 Trios for the same, a Sonata for the Violin and P.F. ; 2 Sonatas and a set of Variations for Cello and P.F.

2 pieces for Piano, four hands ; 3 Sonatas for Piano solo, 1 Fantasia for do. (' Scotch Sonata '), 16 Scherzos, Capriccios, etc. ; 8 books of Songs without Words, 6 in each, and 2 separate similar pieces ; 7 Characteristic Pieces ; 6 pieces for children ; 7 Preludes and Fugues ; and 3 sets of Variations.

For the organ, 6 Sonatas, and 3 Preludes and Fugues.

2 Oratorios and fragments of a third.

1 Hymn (Lauda Sion), 2 ditto for Solo, Chorus, and Orchestra.

3 Motets for Female voices and Organ ; 3 Church pieces for Solos, Chorus, and Organ.

5 Motets, Jubilate, Nunc Dimittis, Magnificat, and 2 Kyries for voices only ; 2 ditto Men's voices only ; 2 ditto Chorus and Orchestra.

8 Psalms for Solos, Chorus and Orchestra ; 6 ' Sprüche ' for 8 voices.

1 Opera, and portions of a second ; 1 Operetta ; the Walpurgisnight.

Music to Midsummer Night's Dream, Athalie, Antigone, and Œdipus.

2 Festival Cantatas ; 1 Concert-aria ; 10 Duets and 82 Songs for solo voice, with P.F. ; 28 Part Songs for mixed voices, and 17 for men's voices.

Of these a complete collected edition, edited by Julius Rietz, has been published by Messrs. Breitkopf & Härtel. The

———

[1] Neither of his three Concert overtures, nor the Italian and Scotch symphonies, have trombones. As to St. Paul, see letter to Mr. Horsley, G. & M. 115.

prospectus was issued in July 1876, and the publication began with 1877. The various separate editions are too numerous to be given here, but we may mention that while these sheets are passing through the press, a complete collection of the pianoforte works (solo and with orchestra) has been issued by Messrs. Novello in one volume of 518 pages.

Two editions of the Thematic Catalogue have been published by Messrs. Breitkopf, the 1st in two parts, 1846 and 1853, the 2nd in 1873. A third edition is very desirable, on the model of the admirable catalogues of Beethoven and Schubert, edited by Mr. Nottebohm. The English publishers, and the dates, should in every case be given, since their editions were often published simultaneously with those of the German publishers, and indeed in some cases are the original issues.

The few of Mendelssohn's very early works which he published himself, or which have been issued since his death, show in certain points the traces of his predecessors — of Bach, Mozart, Beethoven, and Weber. But this is only saying what can be said of the early works of all composers, including Beethoven himself. Mendelssohn is not more but less amenable to this law of nature than most of his compeers. The traces of Bach are the most permanent, and they linger on in the vocal works even as late as St. Paul. Indeed, Bach may be tracked still later in the solid construction and architectonic arrangement of the choruses, even of the Lobgesang, the grand Psalms, the Walpurgisnight, and Elijah, works in all respects emphatically Mendelssohn's own, not less than in the religious feeling, the union of noble sentiment with tender expression, and the utter absence of commonness or vulgarity which pervade all his music alike.

In the instrumental works, however, the year 1826 broke the spell of all external influence, and the Octet, the Quintet in A, and above all the M.N.D. Overture, launched him upon the world at 17 as a thoroughly original composer. The Concert-overtures, the 2 great Symphonies, the two piano Concertos, and the Violin Concerto, fully maintain this originality, and in thought, style, phrase, and clearness of expression, no less than in their symmetrical structure and exquisite orchestration, are eminently independent and individual works. The advance between the Symphony in C minor (1824), which we call ' No. I,' though it is really ' No. XIII,' and the Italian

Symphony (Rome, 1831) is immense. The former is laid out
quite on the Mozart plan, and the working throughout recalls
the old world. But the latter has no model. The melodies
and the treatment are Mendelssohn's alone, and while in gaiety
and freshness it is quite unrivalled, it is not too much to say
that the slow movement is as great a novelty as that of Beethoven's Concerto in G major. The Scotch Symphony is as
original as the Italian, and on a much larger and grander
scale. The opening Andante, the Scherzo, and the Finale are
especially splendid and individual. The Concert-overtures are
in all essential respects as original as if Beethoven had not
preceded them by writing Coriolan — as true a representative
of his genius as the Hebrides is of Mendelssohn's. That to
the Midsummer Night's Dream, which brought the fairies into
the orchestra and fixed them there, and which will always
remain a monument of the fresh feeling of youth ; the Hebrides
with its intensely sombre and melancholy sentiment, and the
Melusina with its passionate pathos, have no predecessors in
sentiment, treatment, or orchestration. Ruy Blas is as brilliant
and as full of fire as the others are of sentiment, and does not
fall a step behind them for individuality.

In these works there is little attempt at any modification
of the established forms. Innovation was not Mendelssohn's
habit of mind, and he rarely attempts it. The Scotch Symphony is directed to be played through without pause, and it
has an extra movement in form of a long Coda, which appears
to be a novelty in pieces in this class. There are unimportant
variations in the form of the concertos, chiefly in the direction
of compression. But with Mendelssohn, no more than with
Schubert, do these things force themselves on the attention.
He has so much to say, and says it so well, the music is so good
and so agreeable, that it never occurs to the hearer to enquire
if he has altered the external proportions of his discourse.

His Scherzos are still more peculiarly his own offspring,
and really have no prototypes. That in a movement bearing
the same name as one of Beethoven's most individual creations,
and occupying the same place in the piece, he should have
been able to strike out so entirely different a path as he did, is
a wonderful tribute to his originality. Not less remarkable is
the variety of the many Scherzos he has left. They are written
for orchestra and chamber, concerted and solo alike, in double

and triple time indifferently; they have no fixed rhythm, and
notwithstanding a strong family likeness — the impress of the
gay and delicate mind of their composer — are all independent
of each other. In his orchestral works Mendelssohn's scoring
is remarkable not more for its grace and beautiful effect than
for its clearness and practical efficiency. It gives the conductor
no difficulty. What the composer wishes to express comes out
naturally, and, as already remarked, each instrument has with
rare exceptions the passages most suitable to it.

Mendelssohn's love of ' Programme ' is obvious throughout
the foregoing works. The exquisite imitation of Goethe's
picture in the Scherzo of the Octet (p. 270) is the earliest
instance of it; the Overture founded on his Calm sea and
Prosperous voyage is another; and as we advance each overture and each symphony has its title. He once said,[1] in conversation with F. Schneider on the subject, that since Beethoven
had taken the step he did in the Pastoral Symphony, everyone
was at liberty to follow. But the way in which he resented
Schumann's attempt to discover ' red coral, sea monsters,
magic castles and ocean caves ' in his Melusina Overture [2]
shows that his view of Programme was a broad one, that he
did not intend to depict scenes or events, but held fast by
Beethoven's canon, that such music should be ' more expression
of emotion than painting ' — *mehr Ausdruck der Empfindung als
Malerei*. Thus he quotes the first few bars of the Hebrides
Overture (see p. 284) not as his recollection of the sound of
the winds and the waves, but ' to show how extraordinarily
Fingal's cave had affected him ' — *wie seltsam mir auf den
Hebriden zu Muthe geworden ist*. True, in the M.N.D. Overture
we are said to hear the bray of Bottom in the low G of the
ophicleide; and in the three North Wales caprices (op. 16)
we are told of even more minute touches of imitation (see p.
286); but these, if not imaginary, are at best but *jeux d'esprit*.

Connected with this tendency to programme is a curious
point, namely, his belief in the absolute and obvious ' meaning '
of music. ' Notes,' says he,[3] ' have as definite a meaning as
words, perhaps even a more definite one,' and he devotes a
whole letter to reiterating that music is not too indefinite to

[1] Schubring, 374 *b*, note.
[2] L. Jan. 30, 1836. The reference is to an article in the N.M.Z. When
asked what he meant by this overture he once replied ' Hm, une mésalliance.'
[3] L. Genoa, July 1831.

be put into words, but too definite ; that words are susceptible
of a variety of meanings, while music has only one.[1] This is
not the place to discuss so strange a doctrine, which, though
true to him, is certainly not true to the majority of men, and
which obviously rests on the precise force of the word ' to
mean ' (heissen) ; but it is necessary to call attention to it
en passant.[2]

His great works in chamber music are on a par with those
for the orchestra. The Octet, the Quintets, and the 6 Quartets
are thoroughly individual and interesting, nothing far-fetched,
no striving after effect, no emptiness, no padding, but plenty
of matter given in a manner at once fresh and varied. Every
bar is his own, and every bar is well said. The accusation
which is sometimes brought against them, that they are more
fitted for the orchestra than the chamber is probably to some
extent well-founded. Indeed Mendelssohn virtually antici-
pates the charge in his preface to the parts of the Octet, which
he desires may be played in a symphonic style ; and in that
noble piece, as well as in parts of the Quintet in B♭, and of
the Quartets in D and F minor, many players have felt that
the composer has placed his work in too small a frame, that
the proper balance cannot always be maintained between the
leading violin and the other instruments, and that to produce
all the effect of the composer's ideas they should be heard in
an orchestra of strings rather than in a quartet of solo instruments. On the other hand, the Pianoforte Quartet in B minor
and the two Pianoforte Trios in D minor and C minor have
been criticised, probably with some justice, as not sufficiently
concertante, that is as giving too prominent a part to the piano.
Such criticism may detract from the pieces in a technical
respect, but it leaves the ideas and sentiments of the music,
the nobility of the style, and the clearness of the structure,
untouched.

His additions to the technique of the pianoforte are not
important. Hiller[3] tells a story which shows that Mendelssohn
cared little for the rich passages of the modern school ; his

[1] L. Oct. 15, 1842, to Souchay; and compare that to Frau von Pereira,
Genoa, July 1831.
[2] Mrs. Austin (Fraser's Mag., Apr. 1848) relates that he said to her on one
occasion ' I am going to play something of Beethoven's, but you must tell them
what it is about ; what is the use of music if people do not know what it means ? '
She might surely have replied, ' What then, is the use of the imagination ? '
[3] H. 154, 155.

own were quite sufficient for him. But this is consistent with what we have just said. It was the music of which he thought, and as long as that expressed his feelings it satisfied him, and he was indifferent to the special form into which it was thrown. Of his pianoforte works the most remarkable is the set of 17 Serious Variations; but the Fantasia in F♯ minor (op. 28), the 3 great Capriccios (op. 33), the Preludes and Fugues, and several of the smaller pieces, are splendid works too well known to need further mention. The Songs without Words stand by themselves, and are especially interesting to Englishmen on account of their very great popularity in this country. Mendelssohn's orchestral and chamber works are greatly played and much enjoyed here, but it is to his Oratorios, Songs, Songs without Words, and Part-songs, that he owes his firm hold on the mass of the English people. It was some time before the Songs without Words reached the public ; but when once they became known, the taste for them quickly spread, and probably no pieces ever were so much and so permanently beloved in the country. The piece, like the name, is virtually his own invention. Not a few of Beethoven's movements — such as the Adagio to the Sonate pathétique, or the Minuet to op. 10, no. 3 — might be classed as songs without words, and so might Field's Nocturnes ; but the former of these are portions of larger works, not easily separable, and the latter were little known ; and neither of them possess that grace and finish, that intimate charm, and above all that *domestic* character, which have ensured the success of Mendelssohn's Songs without Words in many an English family. They soon became identified with his name as it grew more and more familiar in England ; some of them were composed here, others had names or stories attached to their origin : [1] there was a piquancy about the very title — and all helped their popularity. His own feeling towards them was by no means so indulgent. It is perhaps impossible for a composer to be quite impartial towards pieces which make him so very popular, but he distinctly says, after the issue of Book 3, ' that he does not mean to write any more at that time, and that if such

[1] Such as the well-known one in A, which, though in Germany known as Frühlingslied, was in England for a long time called ' Camberwell Green,' from the fact of its having been composed on Denmark Hill. The Duet (Bk. iii. no. 6) was for long believed to represent a conversation between the composer and his wife.

animalculæ are multiplied too much no one will care for them,' etc.[1] It is difficult to believe that so stern a critic of his own productions should not have felt the weakness of some of them, and the strong mannerism which, with a few remarkable exceptions, pervades the whole collection. We should not forget, too, that he is not answerable for the last two books, which were published after his death, without the great alterations which he habitually made before publication. One drawback to the excessive popularity of the Songs without Words is, not that they exist — for we might as well quarrel with Goethe for the ' Wandrers Nachtlied ' or the ' Heidenröslein ' — nor yet the number of imitations they produced, but that in the minds of thousands these graceful trifles, many of which were thrown off at a single sitting, are indiscriminately accepted as the most characteristic representatives of the genius of the composer of the Violin Concerto and the Hebrides Overture.

His Songs may be said to have introduced the German *Lied* to England, and to have led the way for the deeper strains of Schumann, Schubert, and Brahms, in English houses and concert-rooms. No doubt the songs of those composers do touch lower depths of the heart than Mendelssohn's do, but the clearness and directness of his music, the spontaneity of his melody, and a certain pure charm pervading the whole, have given a place with the great public to some of his songs, such as ' On song's bright pinions,' which they will probably retain for a long time to come. Others, such as the Nachtlied, the Volkslied (' Es ist bestimmt '), and the Schilflied are deeply pathetic ; others, as the Lieblingsplätzchen, are at the same time extremely original ; others, as ' O Jugend,' the Jagdgesang, and the ' Diese Rosen,' the soul of gaiety. He was very fastidious in his choice of words, and often marks his sense of the climax by varying the last stanza in accompaniment or otherwise, a practice which he was perhaps the first to adopt. One of his last commissions to his friend Professor Graves, before leaving Interlaken in 1847, was to select words from the English poets for him to set.

His Part-songs gave the majority of English amateurs a sudden and delightful introduction to a class of music which had long existed for Germans, but which till about 1840 was

[1] Letter, March 4, 1839.

as much unknown here as our glees still are in Germany.
Many can still recollect the utterly new and strange feeling
which was then awakened in their minds by the new spirit,
the delicacy, the pure style, the delicious harmonies, of these
enchanting little compositions !

Ever since Handel's time, Oratorios have been the favourite
public music here. Mendelssohn's works of this class, St. Paul,
Elijah, the Lobgesang, soon became well known. They did
not come as strangers, but as the younger brothers of the Messiah and Judas Maccabæus, and we liked them at once. Nor
only liked them; we were proud of them, as having been
produced or very early performed in England; they appealed
to our national love for the Bible, and there is no doubt that
to them is largely owing the position next to Handel which
Mendelssohn occupies in England. Elijah at once took its
place, and it is now almost, if not quite, on a level with the
Messiah in public favour. Apart from the intrinsic qualities
of the music of his large vocal works, the melody, clearness,
spirit, and symmetry which they exhibit, in common with his
instrumental compositions; there is one thing which remarkably distinguishes them, and in which they are far in advance
of their predecessors — a simple and direct attempt to set the
subject forth as it was, to think first of the story and next of
the music which depicted it. It is the same thing that we
formerly attempted to bring out in Beethoven's case, ' the
thoughts and emotions are the first things, and the forms of
expression are second and subordinate' (see p. 109). We may
call this ' dramatic,' inasmuch as the books of oratorios are
more or less dramas; and Mendelssohn's letters to Schubring
in reference to Elijah, his demand for more ' questions and
answers, replies and rejoinders, sudden interruptions,' etc.,
show how thin was the line which in his opinion divided the
platform from the stage, and how keenly he wished the personages of his oratorios to be alive and acting, ' not mere musical
images, but inhabitants of a definite active world.' [1] But yet
it was not so much dramatic in any conscious sense as a desire
to set things forth as they were. Hauptmann has stated this
well [2] with regard to the three noble Psalms (op. 78), ' Judge
me, O God,' ' Why rage fiercely the heathen? " and ' My God,
why hast thou forsaken me? ' He says that it is not so much

[1] L. Nov. 2, Dec. 6, 1838.   [2] Haupt. ii. 102.

any musical or technical ability that places them so far above other similar compositions of our time, as the fact that Mendelssohn has 'just put the Psalm itself before him; not Bach, or Handel, or Palestrina, or any other style or composer, but the words of the Psalmist; and the result is not anything that can be classed as new or old, but the Psalm itself in thoroughly fine musical effect; the music not pretending to be scientific, or anything on its own account, but just throwing life and feeling into the dry words.' Any one who knows these psalms will recognise the truth of this description. It is almost more true in reference to the 114th Psalm, 'When Israel out of Egypt came.' The Jewish blood of Mendelssohn must surely for once have beat fiercely over this picture of the great triumph of his forefathers, and it is only the plain truth to say that in directness and force his music is a perfect match for the splendid words of the unknown Psalmist. It is true of his oratorios also, but they have other great qualities as well. St. Paul with all its great beauties is an early work, the book of which, or rather perhaps the nature of the subject, does not wholly lend itself to forcible treatment, and it is an open question whether it can fully vie with either the Lobgesang or Athalie, or still more Elijah. These splendid compositions have that air of distinction which stamps a great work in every art, and which a great master alone can confer. As instances of this, take the scene of the Watchman and the concluding Chorus in the Lob- gesang — 'Ye nations'; or in Elijah the two double Quartets; the Arioso, 'Woe unto them,' which might be the wail of a pitying archangel; the Choruses, 'Thanks be to God,' 'Be not afraid,' 'He watching over,' 'The Lord passed by'; the great piece of declamation for soprano which opens the second part; the unaccompanied trio 'Lift thine eyes,' the tenor air 'Then shall the righteous.' These are not only fine as music, but are animated by that lofty and truly dramatic character which makes one forget the vehicle, and live only in the noble sentiment of the scene as it passes.

'Lauda Sion,' though owing to circumstances less known, has the same great qualities, and is a worthy setting of the truly inspired hymn in which St. Thomas Aquinas was enabled to rise so high above the metaphysical subtleties of his day. This piece of Roman Catholic music — Mendelssohn's only im- portant one — shows what he might have done had he written a Mass, as he once threatened to do.[1] It would have been 'written with a constant recollection of its sacred purpose'; and remembering how solemn a thing religion was to him, and how much he was affected by fine words, we may well regret that he did not accomplish the suggestion.

Antigone and Œdipus, owing to the remoteness of the dramas, both in subject and treatment, necessarily address themselves to a limited audience, though to that audience they will always be profoundly interesting, not only for the lofty character of the music, but for the able and thoroughly natural manner in which Mendelssohn carried out a task full of difficulties and of temptations to absurdity, by simply ' creating music for the choruses in the good and scientific style of the present day, to express and animate their meaning.' [2]

The Midsummer Night's Dream music is a perfect illustration of Shakespeare's romantic play, and will be loved as long as beauty, sentiment, humour, and exquisite workmanship are honoured in the world.

How far Mendelssohn would have succeeded with an opera, had he met with a libretto entirely to his mind — which that of Loreley was not — it is difficult to say. Fastidious he certainly was, though hardly more so than Beethoven (see pp. 90-91), and probably for much the same reasons. Times had changed since the lively intrigues and thinly veiled immoralities of Da Ponte were sufficient to animate the pen of the divine Mozart; and the secret of the fastidiousness of Beethoven and Mendelssohn was that they wanted librettists of their own lofty level in genius and morality, a want in which they were many generations too early. Opera will not take its proper place in the world till subjects shall be found of modern times, with which every one can sympathise, treated by the poet, before they come into the hands of the composer, in a thoroughly pure, lofty, and inspiriting manner.

Camacho is too juvenile a composition, on too poor a libretto, to enable any inference to be drawn from it as to Mendelssohn's competence for the stage. But, judging from the dramatic power present in his other works, from the stage-instinct displayed in the M.N.D. music, and still more from the very successful treatment of the Finale to the first Act of Loreley — the only part of the book which he is said really to

[1] L. Jan. 26, 1835.   [2] Letter, Mar. 12, 1845.

have cared for — we may anticipate that his opera, when he
had found the book he liked, would have been a very fine work.
At any rate we may be certain that of all its critics he would
have been the most severe, and that he would not have suffered
it to be put on the stage till he was quite satisfied with his
treatment.

———

We must now close this long and yet imperfect attempt to
set Mendelssohn forth as he was. Few instances can be found
in history of a man so amply gifted with every good quality of
mind and heart; so carefully brought up amongst good in-
fluences; endowed with every circumstance that would make
him happy; and so thoroughly fulfilling his mission. Never
perhaps could any man be found in whose life there were so few
things to conceal and to regret.

Is there any drawback to this? or, in other words, does
his music suffer at all from what he calls his ' habitual cheerfulness'? It seems as if there was a drawback, and that arising
more or less directly from those very points which we have
named as his best characteristics — his happy healthy heart,
his single mind, his unfailing good spirits, his simple trust in
God, his unaffected directness of purpose. It is not that he
had not genius. The great works enumerated prove that he
had it in large measure. No man could have called up the
new emotions of the M.N.D. Overture, the wonderful pictures
of the Hebrides, or the pathetic distress of the lovely Melusina,
without genius of the highest order. But his genius had not
been subjected to those fiery trials which seem necessary to
ensure its abiding possession of the depths of the human heart.
' My music,' says Schubert, ' is the product of my genius and
my misery; and that which I have written in my greatest
distress is that which the world seems to like best.' Now
Mendelssohn was never more than temporarily unhappy. He
did not know distress as he knew happiness. Perhaps there was
even something in the constitution of his mind which forbade
his harbouring it, or being permanently affected by it. He was
so practical, that as a matter of duty he would have thrown it
off. In this as in most other things he was always under control.
At any rate he was never tried by poverty, or disappointment,
or ill-health, or a morbid temper, or neglect, or the perfidy of

friends, or any of the other great ills which crowded so thickly around Beethoven, Schubert, or Schumann. Who can wish that he had been ? that that bright, pure, aspiring spirit should have been dulled by distress or torn with agony ? It might have lent a deeper undertone to his Songs, or have enabled his Adagios to draw tears where now they only give a saddened pleasure. But let us take the man as we have him. Surely there is enough of conflict and violence in life and in art. When we want to be made unhappy we can turn to others. It is well in these agitated modern days to be able to point to one perfectly balanced nature, in whose life, whose letters, and whose music alike, all is at once manly and refined, clever and pure, brilliant and solid. For the enjoyment of such shining heights of goodness we may well forgo for once the depths of misery and sorrow.

The following opening of the first movement of a symphony was found among the loose papers of Mendelssohn belonging to his daughter, Mrs. Victor Benecke, and is here printed by her kind permission. The MS. is in full score, and has been compressed for this occasion by Mr. Franklin Taylor, so as accurately to represent the scoring of the original. No clue to its date has yet been discovered.

The following is obviously intended for the slow movement:—